State Parks of the South

STATE PARKS *of the* SOUTH

VICI DeHAAN

America's Historic Paradise

A Guide to
Camping, Fishing, Hiking,
& Sightseeing

Johnson Books
Boulder

Published in the United States by Johnson Books, a Division of Johnson Publishing Company, 1880 South 57th Court, Boulder, Colorado 80301.

9 8 7 6 5 4 3 2 1

Front cover photograph: Glade Creek Grist Mill, Babcock State Park (photo by David Fattaleh, courtesy West Virginia Div. of Tourism & Parks)

Back cover photographs (clockwise from left): oxen in Williamsburg, Va. (author photo); Lake Bistineau State Park (photo courtesy Louisiana Dept. of Culture, Recreation and Tourism); author biking in the Smokies (author photo); Kentucky Dam Village State Resort Park, Gilbertsville (photo courtesy Kentucky Dept. of Travel Development); Gamble Plantation Mansion, Florida (author photo)

Maps by Cynthia Young

Library of Congress Cataloging-in-Publication Data
DeHaan, Vici.
    State parks of the South : America's historic paradise / Vici DeHaan
        p.   cm.
    Includes index.
    ISBN 1-55566-167-X (acid-free paper)
    1. Parks—Southern States—Guidebooks.   2. Southern States—
Guidebooks.   3. Outdoor recreation—Southern States—Guidebooks.
I. Title.
F207.3.D43   1996
917.504'43—dc20   96-1303
                                                CIP

Printed in the United States by
Johnson Printing
1880 South 57th Court
Boulder, Colorado 80301

 Printed on recycled paper with soy ink

Contents

Introduction

My long quest to research the state parks across the United States is complete! It began ten years ago, after I'd written two pilots' guides to the national parks. As much as I would like to have had the opportunity, at no point did I ever even attempt to visit all the state parks in any state except for Colorado, my home state. There are simply too many of them.

Instead, I visited all fifty states and my explorations were determined by my mode of arrival. When traveling via commercial airline, Warren and I explored many representative state parks in a rental car or recreational vehicle. Other trips were made in a private plane in which we often carried our porta-bicycles for ground transportation. Still others were done in our travel trailer. For this reason, I've included information on the camping facilities and airports that serve the various parks.

Many of the parks are truly destinations in themselves, with more to do than we had time for. Others were used more as camping and jumping-off points from which we made day trips to visit the many local attractions.

I found the Southern states to be a gold mine for history lovers. The Civil War had a tremendous impact upon the land and its people, and many of the battlefields have been preserved as either national or state parks. Visitors can also tour many historic homes and mansions, and enjoy some magnificent gardens.

One of the best ways to see the South up close is on foot or from the seat of a bicycle. I'll not soon forget the beautiful bike ride we took to Jamestown and Williamsburg, nor the one out of Bryson City near the Smoky Mountains. There's something about breathing in the moistness of a forest or drinking in the salty ocean air that makes me feel so wonderfully alive.

Hiking in the South is very different from what I'm used to at home in the West, where we have more rugged mountains and more pronounced seasonal changes. The South has a much longer growing season than we do in the Rocky Mountains, and it's such a treat for us "Snowbirds" to visit—particularly in the spring, when the azalea, rhododendron, and dogwood are in full bloom. However, I must confess that my favorite time of the year is fall, when the colors are so vibrant and breathtaking. Aspen trees out West are colorful, to be sure, but there's absolutely nothing like the way a hardwood forest takes on a life of its own in the fall.

Water-based activities are abundant in the South. The many lakes and streams provide great fishing and boating. Of course, coastal areas offer ocean-based activities such as deep-sea fishing or scuba diving in the azure waters along the Florida Keys.

If you just happen to have a pilot's license and access to a plane, be sure to take a flight along the coastline on a clear, sunny day. Even better, take a flight in the fall over the mountains when it's "leaf-peeping" time and the woods look like they've been painted by a fairy's wand in a Walt Disney movie.

A note on the phone numbers listed in the text. I've made every attempt at accuracy that I could. I contacted the individual states and they provided phone numbers, and I've also used a CD-ROM national phone listing to double-check the numbers. But with area codes constantly in flux, there will likely be more changes after this book is printed.

Now that I've completed my research, I have a long list of places that I want to explore. Because of the wealth of places from which to select, I probably have enough to last me for a lifetime.

My heartfelt thanks go to my traveling partner, Warren, who has patiently shared in my wanderings. We already have many unforgettable memories stored up, and more to come.

State Parks of the South

ALABAMA

Alabama's 24 state parks run from the Appalachian foothills to the white beaches along the Gulf of Mexico. Many state parks, including Lake Guntersville, Lakepoint, and Joe Wheeler, offer special vacation or weekend packages. Resort state parks include Cheaha, DeSoto, Gulf, Joe Wheeler, Lake Guntersville, and Lakepoint.

For reservations in the state's campsites, cabins, chalets, and resorts, call 334-242-3333 in Montgomery, and 1-800-ALA-PARK or 904-488-9872 nationwide. For general park information, contact the Division of State Parks, Alabama Department of Conservation and Natural Resources, 64 North Union Street, Montgomery, Alabama 36130.

Visitors to the Gulf Coast are treated to long stretches of white beaches, warm Gulf water, deep sea fishing, and year-round mild temperatures. In late winter, come to enjoy the azaleas and dogwood, which are soon followed by magnolia, jasmine, roses, hibiscus, and camellias.

Pilgrimages and home tours are offered annually in the spring in Athens, Huntsville, and Talladega. Contact the Lake Guntersville Chamber of Commerce at 205-582-3612 and Huntsville's Visitors Bureau at 205-533-5723. Tour Bellingrath Home and Gardens in Theodore, and attend the Mardi Gras celebration in Mobile.

BLADON SPRINGS STATE PARK
1

LOCATION   The park is one mile north of Bladon Springs.

ACTIVITIES   The park has four mineral springs, once part of a pre–Civil War spa. Bring along a picnic to enjoy in the shelter.

INFORMATION
Bladon Springs State Park
Bladon Springs, Alabama 36902
334-754-9207

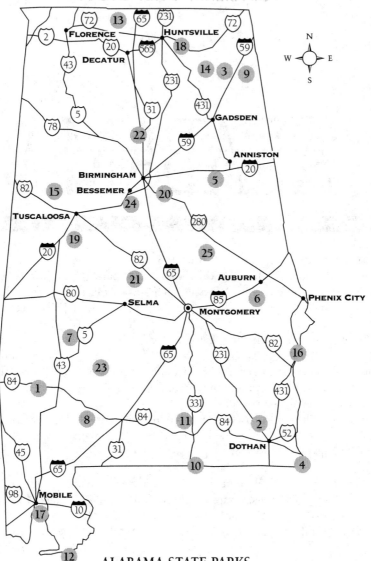

ALABAMA STATE PARKS

1. Bladon Springs State Park
2. Blue Springs State Park
3. Buck's Pocket State Park
4. Chattahoochee State Park
5. Cheaha State Park
6. Chewacla State Park
7. Chickasaw State Park
8. Claude D. Kelley State Park
9. DeSoto State Park
10. Florala State Park
11. Frank Jackson State Park
12. Gulf State Park
13. Joe Wheeler State Park
14. Lake Guntersville State Park
15. Lake Lurleen State Park
16. Lakepoint State Park
17. Meaher State Park
18. Monte Sano State Park
19. Mound State Monument
20. Oak Mountain State Park
21. Paul M. Grist State Park
22. Rickwood Caverns State Park
23. Roland Cooper State Park
24. Tannehill Historical State Park
25. Wind Creek State Park

BLUE SPRINGS STATE PARK
2

LOCATION   The park is six miles east of Clio, off Alabama 10.

ACTIVITIES   Swim in the spring-fed swimming pool. Camp in the 50-site campground, all sites with water and electricity, seven with full hookups, and a dump station. Go pan fishing in the Choctawatchee River, go swimming, and rent a paddleboat to go boating. Play tennis on the tennis court. Refreshments are available.

INFORMATION
Blue Springs State Park
Route 1, Box 132
Clio, Alabama 36017
Park and campground: 334-397-4875
Pool: 334-397-8703

BUCK'S POCKET STATE PARK
3

LOCATION   The park is two miles north of Grove Oak, off Alabama 227, in the Appalachian Mountains.

ACTIVITIES   Camp in the 48-site campground nestled at the bottom of the canyon, 48 sites with water, 30 with electrical hookups, and eight with full hookups. It has a dumping station and laundry facilities. Purchase supplies in the camp store. Go boating, swimming, and bass fishing at Morgan Cove at Lake Guntersville, seven miles from the park. The park has five hiking trails covering 12 miles.

INFORMATION
Buck's Pocket State Park
Route 1, Box 24
Grove Oak, Alabama 35975
205-659-2000

CHATTAHOOCHEE STATE PARK
4

LOCATION   The park is 11 miles southeast of Gordon in the southeast corner of Alabama via Alabama 95. It's also 30 miles southeast of Dothan via U.S. 84 and Alabama 89.

ACTIVITIES   Go swimming, rent a non-motorized boat to go boating or fishing in both the park lake or in the nearby Chattahoochee River. Camp in the 20-site primitive campground. The park has eight trails covering seven miles.

INFORMATION
Chattahoochee State Park
Star Route, Box 108
Gordon, Alabama 36343
334-522-3607

CHEAHA STATE PARK
5

LOCATION   The park is 29 miles south of Anniston. Take Exit 191 from I-20 and go to Alabama 49 south and continue south for 12 miles, following signs. It's also 17 miles north of Lineville, off Alabama 49.

FEATURES   Cheaha is an Indian word for "high." Mt. Cheaha is Alabama's highest point, rising 2,407 feet above sea level. The park covers the crest and upper slopes of the mountain, and it extends 2,719 acres.

ACTIVITIES   Tour the visitor center. Stay in one of 15 rustic stone cabins and chalets, or in one of 31 guest rooms in the resort inn. Bald Rock Lodge also sleeps 50. Camp in the 73-site campground with full hookups and a laundry located near the crest of Cheaha. Purchase supplies in the camp store, or dine in the park restaurant overlooking the valley.

Go boating with rentals available, and fish or swim in the lake. The resort pool is also available for swimming.

Hike 10-mile Odum Scout Trail or go to the top of Cheaha Mountain where you can climb the observation tower for a great view of the surrounding area. If you prefer not to hike to the mountain summit, drive up the park road off Alabama 49, or for a less traveled route, follow Alabama 96 to Alabama 21.

Hikers also have access to an additional 100 miles of trails that are part of the Pinhoti National Recreation Trail System. They pass through the Talladega National Forest and Cheaha Wilderness. The Cheaha Wilderness is 12 miles south of I-20 via Alabama 49. One of the trail entrances is located in the southern part of Cheaha State Park. Here you can go camping, hiking, and backpacking through the southernmost part of the Appalachians. Many of these peaks rise over 2,000 feet.

In Anniston, tour the Anniston Museum of Natural History at 4301 McClellan Boulevard. See over 100 creatures from Africa, Egyptian mummies, and the diorama bird collection featuring many extinct and endangered species. It's closed Mondays. For information, call 205-237-6766.

Ohatchee Creek Ranch is 15 miles north of Anniston on U.S. 431, then 1.5 miles west. Drive through the grounds or walk along the elevated walkway to see over 50 animal species. For information, call 205-442-1453.

The Waldo Covered Bridge, circa 1850, is six miles southeast of Talladega on the east side of Alabama 77 near Waldo. The bridge is Alabama's oldest, and the area contains a pioneer park, grist mill, and log cabin.

INFORMATION
Cheaha State Park
Route 1, Box 77-H
Delta, Alabama 36258
Park: 205-488-5111
Resort Inn: 205-488-5005 or 1-800-846-2654

CHEWACLA STATE PARK
6

LOCATION   The park is four miles south of Auburn, off U.S. 29.

ACTIVITIES   Hike nature trails through the nature preserve or explore five miles of hiking trails. Go swimming in the lake. Play tennis, go bicycling on the bicycle trails, and tour the visitor center. Enjoy fishing and boating, with non-motorized boat rentals available. Camp in the 36-site campground or stay in a vacation cottage. The park offers a getaway package year-round (excluding holidays); you can stay in a rustic cabin for a special price.

In Auburn, tour the historic district on the Auburn University campus. Buildings date from the 1850s to the 1900s. For information, call 205-844-1705.

INFORMATION
Chewacla State Park
P.O. Box 447
Auburn, Alabama 36830-0600
334-887-5621

CHICKASAW STATE PARK
7

LOCATION   The park is four miles north of Linden, on U.S. 43.

ACTIVITIES   Camp in the small, 10-site campground with full hookups. Enjoy a picnic, play on the playground, and hike the half-mile-long trail.

In Demopolis, tour Bluff Hall at 407 North Commissioners Avenue. The plantation home, circa 1832, was built by slaves when cotton was king. It's closed Mondays. For information, call 334-289-1666. Gaineswood at 805 South Cedar is a 20-room Green Revival mansion that required over 40 years to complete. For information, call 334-289-4846. Attend "Christmas on the River" here in December.

INFORMATION
Chickasaw State Park
Route 1, Box 430
Gallion, Alabama 36742
334-295-8230

CLAUDE D. KELLEY STATE PARK
8

LOCATION   The park is 12 miles north of Atmore off I-65, on Alabama 21.

ACTIVITIES   Go bass fishing, swimming, and boating from the ramp in Black Shore Lake. Non-motorized boat rentals are available. Enjoy camping in the 30-site campground, five sites with water and electrical hookups, and a dumping station, or stay in one of the two cottages. The park has two trails covering six miles.

INFORMATION
Claude D. Kelley State Park
Route 2, Box 77
Atmore, Alabama 36502
334-862-2511

DeSOTO STATE PARK
9

LOCATION   The 4,900-acre park is seven miles northeast of Fort Payne. Follow Alabama 35 to the top of Lookout Mountain and then go left on Dekalb City Road 89.

FEATURES   The park stretches for 40 miles along the Little River on the spine of Lookout Mountain. Little River is the only river in the U.S. to form and flow across the top of a mountain range before plunging down the mountain 110 feet to form DeSoto Falls. Little River Canyon is 16 miles long and is the deepest gorge east of the Mississippi River. It has a maximum depth of 600 feet.

At the north end of the canyon, Little River Falls tumble 60 feet. They may be reached by a bridge near the intersection of Alabama 35 and the Rim Parkway.

DeSoto State Park was named for the Spanish conquistador Hernando de Soto, who, in 1540, was the first European to explore the region.

ACTIVITIES   Enjoy a picnic, play tennis, and hike the trails. Go swimming in the pool, boating from the ramp, and go fishing. Stay in the 78-site campground, all sites with water and electricity, 20 with full hookups, and laundry facilities. Purchase groceries in the camp store. Stay in the resort inn with 25 guest rooms, in one of the 11 modern chalets, or in one of 12 rustic cabins. Dine in the restaurant, swim in the Olympic-size pool, and tour the visitor center.

Drive the 22-mile scenic road along the west rim of Little River Canyon. Go bass fishing, boating, and swimming in Little River. Hike 20 miles of trails with views of the deep woods, waterfalls, rocky canyon walls, and into the deep canyon. On one of the hikes, watch for Needle Eye Rock which has been split down its middle.

The park is known for its flowering shrubs and flowers. Be sure to come when the rhododendron and mountain laurel peak from mid to late May, and when the azaleas are in full bloom along the Azalea Cascade Trail.

The Sallie Howard Memorial Chapel is at the north entrance to the park. It was built around a huge boulder that forms part of the roof. It's open 24 hours a day.

In Fort Payne, visit the Opera House, circa 1889, at 510 North Gault Avenue. It's the oldest theater in Alabama still in use. It can be toured by appointment only. Call 205-845-2741. In June, attend the Alabama June Jam's 10-day festival including a parade, bass fishing, tennis, and golf tournaments. For information, call 205-845-3957. Attend September Fest in Childersburg.

INFORMATION
DeSoto State Park
Route 1, Box 210
Fort Payne, Alabama 35967
Campground: 205-845-5075
Park: 205-845-0051.
Resort Inn: 205-845-5380 or 1-800-568-8840
Park Lodge: 205-845-5380
Camp Store: 205-845-5075

FLORALA STATE PARK
10

LOCATION   The park is off U.S. 331 in Florala on Lake Jackson on the Alabama/Florida state line. From Alabama 85, turn left on Lakeside Boulevard.

ACTIVITIES   Go camping in the 33-site campground, 19 sites with water and electricity, four with full hookups. It has a dumping station and laundry. Go bass fishing, swimming, water-skiing, and boating in Lake Jackson. Refreshments are available. Campers can also walk into town for supplies.

INFORMATION
Florala State Park
P.O. Box 322
Florala, Alabama 36442-0322
334-858-6425

*Old Natchez Trace at the Colbert Ferry Site, overlooking the Tennessee River
(photo by John Mohlhenrich, courtesy of the National Park Service)*

FRANK JACKSON STATE PARK
11

LOCATION   The 2,050-acre park is three miles north of Opp, off U.S. 331.

ACTIVITIES   Enjoy boating from the ramp, swimming, and fishing in the stocked lake. Go primitive camping in the campground. Refreshments are available. Hikers have access to two trails covering two miles.

INFORMATION
Frank Jackson State Park
Route 3, Box 73-C
Opp, Alabama 36467
334-493-6988

GULF STATE PARK
12

LOCATION   The park is on the Gulf Beach, 10 miles south of Foley off Alabama 59. It's also 2½ miles east of Gulf Shores, off Gulf Shores Parkway.

FEATURES   The park covers 6,150 acres with 2½ miles of white sand beach.

ACTIVITIES   Play tennis, or golf on the nine- or 18-hole courses. Rental equipment is available at the pro shop. Go saltwater fishing from the 825-foot pier, go swimming and water-skiing in Lake Shelby. Attend a summer beach-side luau. Go bass fishing, swimming, and boating from the ramp in Middle Lake, with rentals available at the marina.

Go bicycling on the bicycle trails, or hike one of the four trails covering four miles. Alligator Trail goes through many pines and ferns. Lakes Trail has blackberries and water lilies. Since this trail follows the lake shore and canal, watch out for alligators.

Stop by the visitor center to check on the daily scheduled activities.

Camp in the 468-site campground, all sites offering water and electrical hookups, and 209 with full hookups. It has laundry facilities. Many campsites are located along the shore of Middle Lake. You can also rent one of 17 modern cabins, one of the four rustic cabins north of Lake Shelby, or stay in the resort inn with 144 rooms. Eat in the restaurant or purchase limited groceries and RV supplies from the camp store. Snack bars are located at the pro shop, pier, and at the beach pavilion.

Two of the best months to visit are April and October. During the summer, the park is crowded.

Festivities in Gulf Shores include Sea Oats Extravaganza the second weekend in May, and the National Shrimp Festival in early October.

Fort Gaines Historic Site and Fort Morgan Historic Site are west of the state park. A ferry provides access to both forts. These twin forts were built in the early 1800s and were used to guard the waters leading into Mobile Bay during the Civil War. However, in 1864, Admiral Farragut was able to take control, and he sealed off Mobile, the last Confederate port then remaining on the Gulf.

Today you can walk along the ramparts and through the rooms underneath to see the fortifications and furnaces where cannonballs were heated hot enough to set fire to any wooden ships entering the port. You'll also see officers' quarters and blacksmith shops.

Tour the museum at Fort Morgan to see a small collection of Civil War artifacts. Bird watchers enjoy coming here to spot some of the 350 species of birds. Go fishing from the pier and hike the nature trail.

INFORMATION
Gulf State Park
Route 2, Box 9
20115 State Highway 135
Gulf Shores, Alabama 36542
Office and Cabins: 334-948-PARK (7275)
Campground: 334-948-6353
Resort Inn: 334-948-GULF or 1-800-544-GULF
Park Lodge: 1-800-544-4853 or 334-948-4853

JOE WHEELER STATE PARK
13

LOCATION   Area A, Joe Wheeler Dam, is nine miles north of Town Creek off Alabama 101. First Creek is two miles west of Rogersville via U.S. 72. Elk River is 15 miles west of Athens off U.S. 72.

FEATURES   The resort park is divided into three separate areas. The main facilities are near Rogersville overlooking Wheeler Lake on the Tennessee River.

ACTIVITIES   At Wheeler Dam, go group camping, or stay in one of 23 rustic vacation cottages. Go boating from the ramp below Wilson Lake, from the cabin area, or in Elk River. Also go fishing and play tennis.

At First Creek, stay in the resort with 74 motel rooms overlooking the Tennessee River, and dine in the restaurant. Go boating from the marina where rentals are available, play tennis, or swim in the pool. The area has six trails covering five miles, and an 18-hole golf course. You can also go bicycling, and tour the visitor center. Camp in the 116-site campground, all sites with water and electricity, 110 with full hookups, and a laundry. Purchase limited camping and RV supplies in the camp store.

At Elk River, go fishing and boating, with rentals available from the bait and tackle store. Stay at the Elk River Lodge with accommodations for 30.

INFORMATION

Joe Wheeler State Park Campground
Route 4, Box 369A
Rogersville, Alabama 35652
205-1-800-544-JOEW (5639) or
   205-247-5461

State Park Lodge: 1-800-544-5639
   or 205-247-5461
P.O. Drawer K
Rogersville, Alabama 35652
Cabins: 205-685-3306

Wheeler Dam
Route 2
Town Creek, Alabama 35672
205-685-3306

First Creek
Route 4, Box 369-A
Rogersville, Alabama 35652
Campground: 205-247-1184
Resort Inn: 205-247-5461
Pro Shop: 205-247-9308

Elk River
Route 5
Athens, Alabama 35611
205-729-8282

LAKE GUNTERSVILLE STATE PARK
14

LOCATION   The park is six miles northeast of Guntersville off Alabama 227, overlooking Guntersville Reservoir.

ACTIVITIES   The park is on top of Little Mountain and has a resort inn with 94 rooms overlooking Guntersville Reservoir. Dine in the dining room or coffee shop. Stay in one of 18 chalets along the ridge top, or in one of 16 lakeview cottages. Camp in the 364-site campground, all sites with water and electricity, 144 with full hookups, and a dump station. Limited groceries, a laundry, and RV supplies are available.

Swim in the lake from the beach complex or in the lodge's pool. Go bass fishing with fishing tackle and fishing supplies available. Enjoy boating from the ramp with rentals of non-motorized boats. Hike one of the 22 trails covering 34½ miles, and go bicycling on the bicycle trails. Play nine or 18 holes of golf, or play tennis on one of the lighted courts.

Tour the visitor center and attend a nature program. January is devoted to special park programs featuring the bald eagles who winter here. Take a guided tour to see eagle habitats, a beaver dam, and visit some old home sites, and the cemetery for pioneers who lived here in the early 1800s.

Attend the Huntsville Depot Springfest in April. The Gerhart Chamber Music Festival is held in June in Guntersville.

INFORMATION
Lake Guntersville State Park
7966 Alabama Highway 227
Guntersville, Alabama 35976
205-582-3666 or 205-571-5444
Campground: 205-571-5455
Park Lodge: 1-800-548-4553 or
   205-571-5440
Pro Shop: 205-571-5458
Camp Store: 205-571-5455

Resort Inn
1155 Lodge Drive
Star Route 63, Box 232
Guntersville, Alabama 35976-9126
205-571-5440 or 1-800-548-4553

LAKE LURLEEN STATE PARK
15

LOCATION   The park is 12 miles northwest of Tuscaloosa, off U.S. 82.

ACTIVITIES   Camp in the 91-site campground, all sites with water and electricity, and 27 with full hookups. The park has four trails covering five miles. Go bass fishing from the piers, swimming, and boating in Lake Lurleen, with non-motorized boat rentals available at the marina. Purchase supplies in the camp store or snacks from the refreshment stand. Tour the visitor center.

In Tuscaloosa, tour the Battle-Friedman House on Greensboro Avenue and Paul W. Bryant Drive. For information, call 205-758-6138. Gulf States Paper Corporation National Headquarters is a half-mile east of U.S. 82. Take the Holt Exit to 1400 River Road. Walk through their collection of paintings, primitive artifacts and sculptures. For tour hours, call 205-553-6200, extension 301.

INFORMATION
Lake Lurleen State Park
Route 1, Box 479
Coker, Alabama 35452
205-339-1558

LAKEPOINT STATE PARK
16

LOCATION   The park is seven miles north of Eufaula, off U.S. 431.

ACTIVITIES   Enjoy great bass fishing in Lake Eufaula or in Walter F. George Reservoir. Stay in the 101-room resort overlooking Lake Eufaula, or in one of 29 fully-equipped cottages. Camp in the 245-site campground, all sites with water and electricity, 80 with full hookups, a dumping station and laundry.

Enjoy swimming in the pool if staying at the motel or cabins, water-skiing, and boating in Lake Eufaula from the marina, with rentals available. Play 18 holes of golf, or tennis on six lighted courts.

Go hiking on three trails covering 4½ miles through the pine woods. Enjoy bicycling and horseback riding with rentals available. Eat in the resort restaurant or purchase supplies from the camp store.

In Eufaula, tour the Shorter Mansion at 340 North Eufaula Avenue. The Greek Revival Mansion, circa 1906, is also used as a state visitor center. For information, call 334-687-3793. The Hart House at 211 North Eufaula Avenue, is a Greek Revival house, circa 1850. It's closed weekends. For information, call 334-687-9755.

Bird watchers can go to Eufaula National Wildlife Refuge on Old Alabama Highway 165. It borders the Walter F. George Reservoir on the Chattahoochee River. Hike the nature trail, climb the observation tower, and stroll through the visitor center.

INFORMATION
Lakepoint State Park
Route 2, Box 94
Eufaula, Alabama 36027-9202
334-687-6676
Resort Inn: 334-687-8011 or 1-800-544-LAKE (5253)
P.O. Box 267
Eufaula, Alabama 36027-9292
Pro Shop: 334-687-6676
Campground: 334-687-6676

MEAHER STATE PARK
17

LOCATION   The park is two miles east of Spanish Fort, on Alabama 90.

ACTIVITIES   The park is in the wetlands of Mobile Bay and is primarily for day-use. Go fishing and boating from the ramp, with non-motorized rentals available. Take a self-guided tour on two nature trails along boardwalks constructed over the Mobile Delta. Future plans call for construction of a campground.

In Mobile, you can attend a Mardi Gras celebration. This celebration begins during Thanksgiving and features a weekly ball until Ash Wednesday. The two weeks before Lent features a different mystic society presents an evening parade. Mardi Gras Day is the first day for the Azalea Trail Festival. For information, call 334-432-2229.

Pick up a self-guided walking or driving tour of Mobile's historic districts. Brochures are available at most downtown hotels or at the Fort Conde Welcome Center. Visit USS Alabama Battleship Memorial Park located 1½ miles east of

Mobile on I-10, Exit Battleship Parkway. Here you can tour the USS *Alabama* and submarine USS *Drum*. For information, call 334-433-2703. Take a cruise from the park dock and learn more about Mobile's Civil War history. For information call 334-433-6101.

Visit Bellingrath Gardens and Home in Theodore. From the intersection of I-10 and U.S. 90W, Theodore Exit 15A, go west three miles on U.S. 90 to Bellingrath Road, and then south for eight miles. Camellias bloom from September through March, and azaleas from February through April. Over 2,000 rose bushes blossom from April through December. Both the home and gardens are listed on the National Register of Historic Places. For information, call 334-973-2217.

INFORMATION
Meaher State Park
P.O. Box 826
Spanish Fort, Alabama 36527
334-626-5529

MONTE SANO STATE PARK
18

LOCATION   The park is four miles east of Huntsville off U.S. 431.

ACTIVITIES   The park has five hiking trails covering 14 miles along the mountaintop. They provide a scenic view of the Tennessee Valley. Camp in the 89-site campground, all with water and electrical hookups, 22 sites with full hookups, or in one of 14 vacation cottages along the cliff overlooking Huntsville. Groceries and limited RV supplies are available in the camp store. Attend a program in the 150-seat amphitheater.

In Huntsville, visit the Space and Rocket Center/NASA Visitor Center. It's at One Tranquillity Base, 15 miles east of I-65, Exit 340, on Alabama 20. Here you can experience the sights and sounds of the Space Shuttle and Apollo flights, and participate in over 60 hands-on exhibits. Tour the Space Camp training center and visit the labs of the NASA-Marshall Space Flight Center. Watch space-flight films at the Spacedome Theater. The area has its own campground. For information, call 205-837-3400 or 1-800-63-SPACE.

Burritt Museum and park are at 3101 Burritt Drive on top of Monte Sano Mountain. The museum is open March through December, Tuesday through Sunday. Several pioneer buildings, containing furnishings from the early Alabama settlers, are located here. For information, call 205-536-2882.

Constitution Hall Village is on 301 Madison Street. Tour the living history museum with costumed guides leading you through the village, circa 1805 through 1819. It's closed Sundays. For information, call 205-532-7551.

Train buffs can tour the Huntsville Depot Transportation Museum at 320 Church Street. Its 1860 passenger depot is one of America's oldest railroad structures. You'll see a working roundhouse, turntable, and steam locomotive. Trolley tours of Huntsville are available from here. For information, call 205-539-1860.

Flower lovers can stop at the Huntsville/Madison County Botanical Gardens at 4747 Bob Wallace Avenue. The gardens boast over 650 varieties of roses and two nature trails with azaleas and wildflowers. The "Constitution Walk" features 56 red maples, each representing a signer of the Constitution. For information, call 205-830-4747.

The Weeden House, circa 1819, is at 300 Gates Avenue Southeast. The house was owned by Maria Howard Weeden, a noted artist and poet. It's open Tuesday through Sunday from 1 to 4, and is closed in January and February. For information, call 205-536-7718.

INFORMATION
Monte Sano State Park
5105 Nolen Avenue
Huntsville, Alabama 35801
205-534-3757

MOUND STATE MONUMENT
19

LOCATION   The monument is 13 miles south of Tuscaloosa on Alabama 69. It's also north of Moundsville.

FEATURES   The monument contains 20 prehistoric platform mounds.

ACTIVITIES   Tour the archeological museum with two preserved excavations and a reconstructed village illustrating the life of the Indians who occupied the site on the Black Warrior River over 700 years ago. Camp in the campground which has hookups. Tour the visitor center. Attend the Easter Pageant offered at sunrise on Easter morning. Confederate Memorial Day is observed the Saturday before April 26 and commemorates the 200 veterans who are buried in the park.

In Tuscaloosa, tour the Battle-Friedman House at 1010 Greensboro Avenue. The Greek Revival Mansion, circa 1835, is restored and serves as a city cultural center. It's closed Mondays. For information, call 205-758-6138.

The Mildred Warner House at 1925 8th Street was built in the 1820s and contains furnishings from 1700 through 1865. It's open weekends. For information, call 205-553-6200, extension 222.

To see one of the most extensive collections of American art, tour the Warner Collection at Gulf States Paper Corporation at 1400 River Road Northeast. Tours leave on the hour. For information, call 205-553-6200.

INFORMATION
Mound State Monument
P.O. Box 5897
Moundsville, Alabama 35474
205-371-2572

OAK MOUNTAIN STATE PARK
20

LOCATION   The park is 15 miles south of Birmingham and is accessible from I-65 at Exit 246. It's also three miles east of U.S. 31 from Pelham.

FEATURES   Oak Mountain is Alabama's largest state park, located in the southernmost part of the Appalachians. It has two fishing lakes and a recreational lake.

ACTIVITIES   The park offers special golf packages on their 18-hole course. Rent a horse to go for a trail ride, or play tennis. Enjoy camping in the 233-site campground, 127 sites with water, 49 with sewer, and 91 with electrical hookups. Stay in one of 131 campsites that are open year-round. Camping supplies are available in the camp store. Ten fully-equipped cottages, also open year-round, are located around a lake.

Go swimming, fishing for catfish, bream, and bass, and boating in Beaver Lake. Bait, tackle, and fishing boats are available at the store. A snack bar is located adjacent to the beach and by the pro shop, and a marina is on Terrace Drive. Go bicycling, and tour the nature center. A BMX track is available, with sanctioned races held throughout the summer.

Hike one of the two nature trails: Treetop nature trail where birds that have been permanently injured are housed, or the Buckeye nature trail. In addition, the park has 13 trails, covering 39½ miles, that wind through the park.

Attend performances in the large Oak Mountain Amphitheater at 1000 Oak Mountain State Park Road, Alabama 119. Take Exit 246 off I-65. Bring the children to the demonstration farm where wagon rides are available. Take a drive to the top of Double Oak Mountain for spectacular views.

Annual events include orientation meets, water-skiing tournaments, triathlons, bicycle moto-cross races, and an annual bowhunters convention.

In Birmingham, tour the Arlington Home and gardens at 331 Cotton Avenue Southwest. For information, call 205-780-5656. Birmingham Botanical Gardens is at 2612 Lane Park Road, and has over 5,000 varieties of rare plants and a Japanese garden. For information, call 205-879-1227.

The Southern Research Institute is at 2000 9th Avenue South, at 20th Street. It offers a 90-minute tour Fridays at 2:30. Reservations are required. Call 205-581-2317.

INFORMATION
Oak Mountain State Park
P.O. Box 278
Pelham, Alabama 35124
Park: 205-620-2522

Campground: 205-620-2527
Golf Packages: 205-663-6771
Pro Shop: 205-620-2522
Cabins: 205-620-2524
Horseback Rides: 205-663-4030

PAUL M. GRIST STATE PARK
21

LOCATION   The park is 15 miles north of Selma, off Alabama 22.

ACTIVITIES   Camp in the six-site campground with hookups, and hike one of the two trails covering three miles. Go boating from the ramp in the 1,000-acre lake, with non-motorized boat rentals available. Enjoy fishing and swimming. Refreshments are available.

In Selma, stroll along five blocks on Water Avenue to see the few remaining antebellum riverfront businesses. The Old Town Historic District encompasses over 500 historic structures. Tour maps and cassette tapes are available at the Chamber of Commerce at 513 Lauderdale Street.

Come in late March to tour several private homes during Spring Historic Pilgrimage. For details, call 334-875-7241. Sturdivant Hall at 713 Mabry Street is a restored 1853 mansion. Guided tours are available Tuesday through Saturday from 9 to 4 and Sundays from 2 to 4. For information, call 334-872-5626.

In April, attend the Battle of Selma Civil War Reenactment that includes Civil War camps. The second weekend in May, attend Old Cahawba Day featuring bluegrass music performances, crafts, and a barbecue. In July, attend the Africana Extravaganza, and in October attend the Alabama "Tale Tellin'" Festival in Old Town.

INFORMATION
Paul M. Grist State Park
1546 Grist Road
Selma, Alabama 36701
334-872-8230

RICKWOOD CAVERNS STATE PARK
22

LOCATION   The park is three miles northwest of Warrior. From I-65 and Alabama 160, take Exit 284, and go west four miles on Alabama 160 to Skyline Drive. Continue west three miles to Rickwood Caverns Road and follow signs. It's also 20 miles north of Birmingham.

FEATURES   The underground caverns feature 260-million-year-old limestone formations. One of the pools is 35 feet wide and 59 feet deep where divers have found salamanders, frogs, and transparent fish that have adapted themselves to being in total darkness.

ACTIVITIES   The caverns are open weekends only, from March through May and in September and October. From June through Labor Day, they're open daily. They're closed November through February. Take a one-hour tour of the underground "miracle mile" with narrow passages and rooms featuring limestone formations, and past spring-fed pools with sightless cave fish.

Go camping in the 13-site campground, with water and electrical hookups. Go hiking on one of the two trails covering three miles, swim in the Olympic-size pool, and play carpet golf.

In Birmingham, visit the Alabama Sports Hall of Fame at 1 Civil Center Plaza in the Birmingham-Jefferson Civic Center. It features displays on football, baseball, archery, and marksmanship. For information, call 205-323-6665.

Arlington's Home and Gardens are at 331 Cotton Avenue Southwest. The Green Revival Mansion, circa 1842, is authentically furnished, with some pieces dating back 200 years. It's closed Mondays. For information, call 205-780-5656.

The Birmingham Botanical Garden is at 2612 Lane Park Road and features thousands of flowers, trees, shrubs, and over 230 bird species. It has the largest conservatory in the Southeast. For information, call 205-879-1227.

Tour the Southern Museum of Flight at 4343 73rd Street North to see eight decades of aviation history. You'll see a World War II link trainer used to train pilots to fly "blind" and hundreds of expertly finished plane models. It's closed Mondays. For information, call 205-833-8226.

INFORMATION
Rickwood Caverns State Park
Route 3, Box 357
Warrior, Alabama 35180
205-647-9692

ROLAND COOPER STATE PARK
23

LOCATION   The park is six miles northeast of Camden, off Alabama 41.

ACTIVITIES   Enjoy water sports on Dannelly Reservoir including bass fishing, water-skiing, swimming, and boating from the ramp, with non-motorized boat rentals available. Camp in the 41-site campground with water and electric hookups, a dumping station, and laundry, or stay in one of the five cottages. Purchase supplies from the camp store. Play golf on the nine-hole course. Tour the visitor center and hike the two trails covering 1½ miles.

INFORMATION
Roland Cooper State Park
49 Deer Run Drive
P.O. Box 301
Camden, Alabama 36726
334-682-4838

TANNEHILL HISTORICAL STATE PARK
24

LOCATION   The park is located midway between Birmingham and Tuscaloosa at 12632 Confederate Parkway. From I-59/20, take Bucksville Exit 100. Off I-459, take Exit 1 and follow signs. It's also 12 miles south of Bessemer via I-459 and Alabama 20.

FEATURES   Remains of the Tannehill Iron Furnaces and cold blast furnaces, which began Birmingham's steel industry, are located in the park. They were destroyed by Union troops near the end of the Civil War. One of the plant's original furnaces has been reconstructed next to a mill creek.

ACTIVITIES   Tour the Iron and Steel Museum of Alabama to learn the history of technology up to 1850. Take a walk or ride the miniature train to see over 27 pioneer homes moved here log by log from their original rural locations, including a farm with outbuildings. Walk through the working blacksmith shop, sorghum mill, grist mill, and cotton gin operation.

Go camping in the 210-site campground, with electrical and water hookups, or tent in the 50-site campground. Dine in the restaurant. Attend craft shows and special park events.

In October, attend Tannehill Heritage Days and Arts and Crafts Fair in Bucksville.

Tour some of the Bessemer pioneer homes spread along Eastern Valley Road, Alabama 20, north of the park. One of these restored Civil War–era homes has upstairs rooms that were divided by sex. For information, call 205-425-3253.

INFORMATION
Tannehill Historical State Park
12632 Confederate Parkway
McCalla, Alabama 35111
205-477-5711

WIND CREEK STATE PARK
25

LOCATION   The park is seven miles southeast of Alexander City, off Alabama 63, on Lake Martin.

ACTIVITIES   Wind Creek has the largest camping facility in the Southeast with 669 campsites, all with water and electrical hookups. Purchase supplies from the camp store. Go fishing for bass, catfish, crappie, and bluegill in Lake Martin from the 210-foot fishing pier, swimming, water-skiing, canoeing, or boating from the ramp or marina with rentals available. Attend naturalist programs from May through September. The nature center is in a converted grain silo, circa 1915.

The park has two hiking trails covering a total of eight miles. You can also go bicycling on the bike trails. An annual Civil War living history presentation is available. Call the park for details.

INFORMATION
Wind Creek State Park
Route 2, Box 145
Alexander City, Alabama 35010
205-329-0845

ARKANSAS

Arkansas is 27th among the states in area, with over 500,000 acres of lakes, and 9,740 miles of streams and rivers. Elevations range from 54 feet above sea level, to 2,753 feet above sea level at Mount Magazine. The state boasts the only public diamond-hunting field in North America: Crater of Diamonds State Park.

Hikers can also hike challenging trails in the Buffalo National River area. A popular three-mile hike, Whitaker Point provides panoramic views of the Ozarks. Lost Valley Trail's 2.3-mile hike takes you to see 170-foot Eden Falls. For a longer hike, follow the 36.5-mile Buffalo River Trail that parallels the waterway. You can also combine hiking with canoeing. The visitor center is at Tyler Bend, off U.S. 65, north of Marshall. For additional information on the river, contact the Buffalo National River Superintendent, P.O. Box 1173, Harrison, Arkansas 72602-1173, or call 501-741-5443.

Hikers have access to the Ouachita Trail that begins near Little Rock, and runs west across the Ouachita Mountains, before continuing into Oklahoma. Other popular trails include the Caney Creek Back Country Trail in southwest Arkansas, and the Ozark Highlands Trail. This 1,000-mile-long trail stretches from St. Louis to Lake Fort Smith State Park. In Arkansas, hikers have access to 165 miles of this trail. For information, call 1-800-334-6946 or 314-751-2479.

Mountain bikers will find miles of trails to ride within the Ouachita National Forest as well as in the Ozark National Forest.

The state's most popular fish is the largemouth bass. Striped bass were introduced into Arkansas waters recently, and each year, a few weighing over 40 pounds are caught. For information on fishing regulations, call the Game and Fish Commission at 501-223-6300.

Arkansas has 44 state parks offering camping opportunities, with 26 of the parks featuring electrical and water hookups. Many provide Rent-a-Camps for visitors without their own camping equipment. For state park information, call 501-682-1191.

Arkansas has many rivers, including the 125-mile-long Buffalo National River, which was the first river in America to be named a national river. The best time to float the Buffalo is during the early spring when rains have provided higher

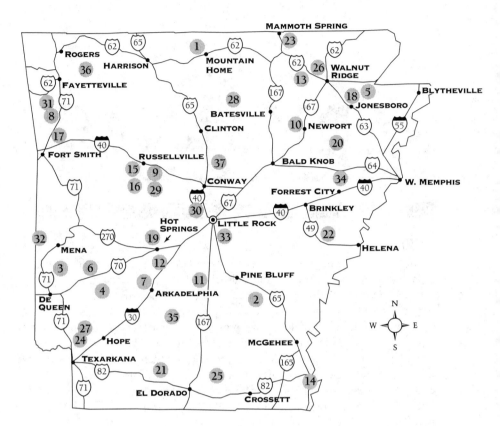

ARKANSAS STATE PARKS

1. Bull Shoals State Park
2. Cane Creek State Park
3. Cossatot River State Park
4. Crater of Diamonds State Park
5. Crowley's Ridge State Park
6. Daisy State Park
7. DeGray Lake Resort State Park
8. Devil's Den State Park
9. Hampson Museum State Park
10. Jacksonport State Park
11. Jenkins' Ferry Battleground State Historical Monument
12. Lake Catherine State Park
13. Lake Charles State Park
14. Lake Chicot State Park
15. Lake Dardanelle State Park
16. Mount Nebo State Park
17. Lake Fort Smith State Paark
18. Lake Frierson State Park
19. Lake Ouachita State Park

20. Lake Poinsett State Park
21. Logoly State Park
22. Louisiana Purchase State Historic Monument
23. Mammoth Spring State Park
24. Millwood State Park
25. Moro Bay State Park
26. Old Davidsonville State Park
27. Old Washington Historic State Park
28. Ozark Folk Center
29. Petit Jean State Park
30. Pinnacle Mountain State Park
31. Prairie Grove Battlefield State Park
32. Queen Wilhelmina State Park
33. Toltec Mounds Archeological State Park
34. Village Creek State Park
35. White Oak Lake State Park
36. Withrow Springs State Park
37. Woolly Hollow State Park

waters. Canoe rentals, shuttle services, hiking trails, camping, fishing, and cabins are also available. For information, call 501-741-5443. Overall, canoers have access to more than 9,700 miles of rivers and streams to explore. The Buffalo National River Canoe Race is held over Easter weekend.

The wildest rivers in the state are the Mulberry and the Cassatot. Only experienced canoeists and kayakers should attempt these rivers when they are at their height. Other canoeing rivers include the Spring, Eleven Point, upper Middle Fork of the Little Red, the Kinds, upper Ouachita, Big Piney and the Caddo. The Ouachita and Caddo Rivers are considered two of the best canoe rivers for families. While floating, bring along your fishing tackle since many have smallmouth bass, and some have rainbow trout.

For general canoeing information, write for the "Arkansas Floater's Kit" from the Arkansas Department of Parks and Tourism, One Capitol Mall, Little Rock, Arkansas 72201; phone 501-682-7777.

Come to Arkansas in the fall when the color changes begin around late September, in the northern Arkansas Ozarks and move slowly south. The state boasts 2.5 million acres of national forests including the Ozark, the Ouachita, and the St. Francis National Forest. For a foliage update beginning in late September, call 1-800-643-8383 (out-of-state) and 1-800-482-8999 (in-state).

BULL SHOALS STATE PARK
1

LOCATION The park is in the Ozark Mountains below Bull Shoals Dam on the White River. Go six miles north of Mountain Home on Arkansas 5, then eight miles west on Arkansas 178.

FEATURES Bull Shoals is the fifth largest lake in the U.S., and is fed by the White River. It has a 1,000-mile-long wooded shoreline. When combined with Norfolk Lake, the two have almost 2,000 miles of shoreline. The lakes are framed by the Ozark Mountains.

ACTIVITIES Enjoy scuba diving with 30- to 60-foot underwater visibility, and excellent rainbow trout fishing in the White River, called "America's best trout river" by *Southern Outdoors* magazine. You can also fish for lunker bass, walleye, crappie, and catfish. Seven state record-size fish have been caught here including a 53-pound striped bass.

Go camping in the 105-site riverside campground, 85 sites with water and electrical hookups. A camp store and laundry are available. Rent-a-Camp tent rentals are available. Dine in the restaurant which is open seasonally. For an alternate camping experience, rent a houseboat from the marina.

Enjoy hiking the trails, playing golf, go boating, water-skiing, sailing, and swimming in the river from the ramp by the campground. Boat rentals are available. Tour the visitor center and attend interpretive programs. Take a scenic Johnboat float trip down the White River, or go for a party-barge scenic tour on the lake.

Free tours are available of the largest dam in mid-America in June and July. You get a great view of Bull Shoals Lake and the White River from the scenic overlook. Rent a canoe and float down the White River, with haul-back service available. Norfolk Dam has a national fish hatchery below the dam with four million trout in various growth stages.

Mountain Village 1890 at the edge of Bull Shoals is a special place to experience living Ozark history. You'll see a collection of authentic 19th-century buildings and artifacts.

For a scenic drive, follow Arkansas 7 as it connects Bull Shoals Lake with the Arkansas River, and continue south. Drive out the causeway from Oakland Recreation Area to Ozark Isle to watch the wildlife. The causeway is closed to driving from November through March.

Tour Bull Shoals Caverns located off Arkansas 178 at Bull Shoals. Follow the trail from the settlement. The caverns contain evidence of prehistoric inhabitants, and you can listen to legends of the Indian tribes who once lived here. You'll also find a crystal altar and a "wishing wall." Visitors come to toss pennies at the wall to make a wish, and the pennies stick to the wall. For information, call 501-445-4302.

Go to "Top O' The Ozarks" on top of Bull Mountain, located one mile west of Bull Shoals on Arkansas 178. Go up the 20-story tower for a great view of Bull Shoals Lake and its dam.

Norfolk Lake also features resort lodging, full service marinas, and a sightseeing tour of the lake aboard the old ferry boat now refitted as a tour boat. Go scuba diving in the crystal-clear water. Fish for trout where a world-record brown trout was caught in 1988. You can also fish for bass, catfish, bluegill, crappie and walleye. Take a guided float trip on the Northfork River where the trout fishing is also excellent. Two ferries cross the lake at U.S. 62 and Arkansas 101. For information on the lake and its activities, call 501-488-5144.

INFORMATION
Bull Shoals State Park
Box 205
Bull Shoals, Arkansas 72619
501-431-5521

CANE CREEK STATE PARK
2

LOCATION   The park is four miles east of Star City on Arkansas 293, adjacent to Cane Creek Lake.

FEATURES   The park is located at the spot where the Mississippi Delta flatlands and rolling hills of the gulf coastal plain come together.

ACTIVITIES   Go camping in the 30-site campground with water and electrical hookups. Enjoy hiking, boating and fishing for bass, bluegill, catfish, and crappie in the 1,675-acre lake, and tour the visitor center.

Come to Star City's Lincoln County Courthouse the first Saturday in May to attend the Springfest celebration. It includes great food, a 5K race, and a bass fishing tournament.

INFORMATION
Cane Creek State Park
P.O. Box 96
Star City, Arkansas 71667
501-628-4714

COSSATOT RIVER
STATE PARK–NATURAL AREA
3

LOCATION   The park is south of Mena in west-central Arkansas. The northern route is via Arkansas 246 between Vandervoort and Athens. The southern route is via Arkansas 4 between Wickes and Umpire. Another access is north of DeQueen via Weyerhaeuser Timber Company roads from Arkansas 146 and 4.

FEATURES   The park and natural area extends for 11 miles along the Cossatot River, one of the state's wildest streams. Its Indian name means "skull crusher." The river forms Cossatot Falls. The Cossatot has been described by the National Park Service as possibly the most challenging white water float in the state.

ACTIVITIES   Go whitewater canoeing or kayaking down the rugged canyon known for its Class IV rapids. It's run by experienced canoeists and kayakers only. River levels generally permit floating in the fall, winter and spring. For river information from the Arkansas 246 access, call 501-387-3141.

Day-use facilities are located in the Brushy Creek Recreation Area adjacent to the Arkansas 246 bridge. Here you'll find a nature trail and a river access point for floating. Further downstream you'll find good fishing for bass. Camping is available at nearby Gillham Lake.

An annual Cossatot Summerfest is held in DeQueen in June.

INFORMATION
Cossatot River State Park–Natural Area
Route 1, Box 170-A
Wickes, Arkansas 71973
501-385-2201

CRATER OF DIAMONDS STATE PARK

4

LOCATION　　The park is two miles southeast of Murfreesboro on Arkansas 301, along the Little Missouri River.

FEATURES　　Imagine visiting a state park where you can dig for diamonds and actually keep what you find. The park is located on the eroded surface of an ancient gem-bearing volcanic pipe. Most specimens found are quite small, but one prospector found a 16.37-carat stone in 1975; a 40.23-carat canary-yellow diamond was discovered in 1980. Over 17,000 diamonds have been discovered here since the site became a state park in 1972.

Other stones found include amethyst, agate, jasper, and quartz. The area containing semiprecious stones is plowed on a regular basis to make your search easier.

ACTIVITIES　　When you come to dig in the park, wear a hat since there is no shade available, and wear boots since the ground is usually muddy. Stop by the park visitor center to rent your digging equipment and learn how to identify the stones you uncover. One of the best times to arrive is during the rainy season from February through June when diamonds are more easily spotted. The park is open year-round, and a fee is charged for the diamond field.

Camp in the 60-site campground with water and electrical hookups, store and laundry, or stay in one of the nearby cabins open year-round. Dine in the short-order restaurant which is open seasonally. Hike the 1.3-mile trail to the Little Missouri River, tour the visitor center, and attend interpretive programs. Go fishing, swimming, and boating, with rentals available at the marina, and play tennis.

Ka-do-ha is an ancient Indian area located on an old channel of the Little Missouri near Murfreesboro. Mound-building Indians lived here a thousand years ago. Some mounds were utilized as homes' foundations and temples, while others were used as tombs. Tour the small museum to see its stone, shell, and pioneer artifacts.

Attend the Diamond Festival in Murfreesboro in early June, and John Huddleston Days in mid-June. Murfreesboro features free Saturday night musicals during the travel season, and a rock and gem show in September.

INFORMATION
Crater of Diamonds State Park
Route 1, Box 364
Murfreesboro, Arkansas 71958
501-285-3113

CROWLEY'S RIDGE STATE PARK
5

LOCATION   The park is 15 miles north of Jonesboro on Arkansas 141 at Walcott. It's also 16 miles east of Walnut Ridge on U.S. 412, then two miles south on Arkansas 141. You can also reach the park by going nine miles west of Paragould on U.S. 412, then two miles south on Arkansas 168.

FEATURES   The ridge features an arc of rolling, forested hills above the Mississippi River delta. It was left over from when the Mississippi and Ohio Rivers retreated to the west around the end of the last Ice Age. This ridge extends from Helena, Arkansas, to Cape Girardeau in Missouri, a distance of 210 miles.

The park was named for Benjamin Crowley, who developed a plantation here after fighting in the War of 1812.

ACTIVITIES   The 270-acre park features swimming in the spring-fed swimming hole, and fishing for bass, catfish and crappie in the 30-acre fishing lake. Hike the trail network and go birding. Dancing Rabbit Trail has two swinging bridges for your enjoyment.

Camp in the 26-site campground, 18 sites with water and electrical hookups. Go boating with rentals available. Enjoy fishing in the 30-acre lake using only electric motors, and swimming with lifeguards on duty. Tour the visitor center, attend interpretive programs, and purchase snacks at the snack bar. Overnight in a fully equipped cabin, or stay in the group lodging facility. A grocery store and cafe are a quarter-mile away.

INFORMATION
Crowley's Ridge State Park
Box 97
Walcott, Arkansas 72474-0097
501-573-6751
1-800-264-2405: cabin reservations

DAISY STATE PARK
6

LOCATION   The park is a quarter-mile south of Daisy off U.S. 70, on the north shore of Greeson Lake. The lake is on the Little Missouri River, in the foothills of the Ouachita Mountains in southwest Arkansas.

ACTIVITIES   Camp in the 118-site campground, 97 sites with water and electrical hookups, or tent in the 21-site tent campground. Hike the trails past bare rock outcroppings, and backpack into 10 backpacking campsites. Go boating from the ramp, and fish for bass, crappie, and bream. One record-sized striper caught here weighed over 27 pounds. Fish for stocked rainbow trout in the Little Missouri River below Narrows Dam. The river joins four popular float streams, and offers challenging spring and early summer trout fishing.

Go water-skiing in protected areas on the lake, swimming, and scuba diving in the crystal-clear water. Tour the visitor center and attend interpretive programs. Bring your mountain bike or motorcycle to ride 10-mile Bear Creek Cycle Trail. A restaurant boat dock and grocery are nearby.

INFORMATION
Daisy State Park
Daisy Route, Box 66
Kirby, Arkansas 71950-8105
501-398-4487

DeGRAY LAKE RESORT STATE PARK
7

LOCATION   The park is off Arkansas 7 north, on the northeastern shores of DeGray Lake. Take Exit 78 off I-30 at Caddo Valley/Arkadelphia.

FEATURES   Lake DeGray was formed by the DeGray Dam on the Caddo River in the Ouachita Mountains in southwest Arkansas. The lake is 22 miles long with 207 miles of shoreline. DeGray and Ouachita Lakes are believed to be the two deepest lakes in mid-continent United States.

ACTIVITIES   Camp in the 113-site campground, 82 sites with water and electrical hookups, a camp store and laundry. Overnight in the 96-room DeGray Lodge located on an island that is connected by a causeway to the mainland. Dine in the Shoreline Restaurant.

Go sailing, scuba diving, water-skiing, and fish for hybrid bass, largemouth bass, catfish, and pan fish. Go boating from the ramp or full-service marina, with rentals available. Enjoy a float trip on the Caddo River below the dam, or a cruise on the 13,800-acre lake.

Swim in the pool, and pick up a snack at the snack bar. Play golf on the 18-hole championship golf course, with a pro shop and rentals available. Go hiking, play tennis, or rent a bicycle to bike the trails. Tour the visitor center and attend an interpretive program.

Participate in the Fall Foliage Tours offered in mid to late October, through the Ouachita Mountains. Play in the DeGray Arthritis Golf Mixed Scramble Tournament in mid-October. In January, come for the Eagles Etc. weekend, to celebrate the migration of bald and golden eagles to DeGray Lake. Attend the Festival of Two Rivers in Arkadelphia in April for their canoe races, music, and arts and crafts.

Tour the DeGray Dam Visitor Center located seven miles north of Arkadelphia on Arkansas 7, then two miles west on the entrance road. You'll see how the dam was constructed, a wildlife exhibit, and Caddo Indian artifacts. For information, call 501-246-5501.

INFORMATION
DeGray State Park
Route 3, Box 490, Department ATG
Bismarck, Arkansas 71929-8194
501-865-4501: park
501-865-2851 or 1-800-737-8355: lodge reservations
501-865-2811: marina
501-865-2801: campground reservations
501-865-2807: golf course

DEVIL'S DEN STATE PARK
8

LOCATION   The park is at the bottom of a steep valley in the Boston Mountains of northwest Arkansas. Go eight miles south of Fayetteville on U.S. 71 to West Fork, then 18 miles south on Arkansas 170. You can also go 13 miles west from Winslow on Arkansas 74. Large trailers should avoid Arkansas 74 from Winslow to the park due to the mountainous road.

FEATURES   The 2,000-acre park adjoins the Ozark National Forest, and boasts some of the state's most spectacular mountain scenery.

ACTIVITIES   Hike 25 miles of trails winding through the park, including the 15-mile Butterfield Backpacking Trail, which features historic sites, scenic vistas, waterfalls, and spectacular natural bridges. Explore Devil's Den Cave and Devil's Icebox, where the temperature never goes over 60 degrees F. One of the hiking trails includes an overnight backpacking trail along the valley, with backpacking rentals available. Equestrians also have a 50-site camping area and riding trails.

Rent one of the 13 mountaintop cabins that are open year-round. Dine in the restaurant overlooking the lake, or grab a snack at the snack bar. Camp in one of the campgrounds totaling 154 campsites with complete hookups. Do your laundry, purchase supplies from the camp store, or take advantage of their Rent-a-Camps.

Go boating, canoeing, fishing, and pedal boating on the lake. Enjoy swimming in the pool, and bike the mountain bike trails. Tour the visitor center, and attend interpretive programs.

INFORMATION
Devil's Den State Park
Route 1, Box 118
11333 West Arkansas Highway 74
West Fork, Arkansas 72774
501-761-3325
1-800-264-2417: cabin reservations

HAMPSON MUSEUM STATE PARK
9

LOCATION   The museum is in Wilson, at the intersection of Arkansas 61 and Lake Drive.

FEATURES   American history buffs enjoy coming here to see an extensive collection of artifacts, including stone tools and weapons from the Nodena, mound-building Indians, who lived here from 1350–1700. These artifacts were excavated from a palisade village where two pyramid mounds were once located.

ACTIVITIES   Tour the museum with over 41,000 artifacts, and bring along a picnic to enjoy. The museum is open Tuesday through Saturday year-round, and on Sunday afternoons from mid-March through mid-November, except for holidays. Admission is charged.

INFORMATION
Hampson Museum State Park
P.O. Box 156
Wilson, Arkansas 72395
501-655-8622

JACKSONPORT STATE PARK
10

LOCATION   The park is on Arkansas 69 at Jacksonport, and three miles north of Newport off U.S. 67. It's located along a sweeping bend of the White River at its confluence with the Black River.

FEATURES   Jacksonport began as a shipping center in early 1800, and later became a busy steamboat port on the Black and White Rivers. However, by the 1870s, the railroad soon ended the area's role as a boating port. The park was established to preserve the steamboat landing.

ACTIVITIES   A restored courthouse, circa 1869, houses a museum with artifacts obtained from the steamboating days. It's listed on the National Register of Historic Places. Take a stroll aboard the *Mary Woods II*, a reconstructed doubledeck sternwheeler, permanently moored at the steamboat landing across the levee from the courthouse. It's open for walking tours Tuesday through Sunday from May through Labor Day, and weekends in April, September, and October. Admission is charged.

Go camping in the 20-site riverside campground, with water and electrical hookups. The 154-acre park provides fishing, swimming from the beach, and boating from the ramp in the White River.

In June, attend "PortFest," one of the area's largest festivals, and on the last weekend in July, the annual Riverboat Festival is held.

INFORMATION
Jacksonport State Park
P.O. Box 8
Jacksonport, Arkansas 72075
501-523-2143

JENKINS' FERRY BATTLEGROUND
STATE HISTORIC MONUMENT
11

LOCATION   The park is 13 miles southwest of Sheridan on Arkansas 46, near Leola.

FEATURES   Three Civil War battles occurred here during the spring of 1864. Jenkins' Ferry was the site of the third battle, where General Frederick Steele's troops fought off a rear attack by the Confederates, and retreated to Little Rock.

ACTIVITIES   Bring along a picnic, and go fishing and swimming. Outdoor exhibits are available.

INFORMATION
Jenkins' Ferry Battleground State Historic Monument
c/o Arkansas State Parks
One Capitol Mall 4A-900
Little Rock, Arkansas 72201
501-371-1191

LAKE CATHERINE STATE PARK
12

LOCATION   The park is 15 miles northwest of Malvern on Arkansas 171 in the Ouachita Mountains, on the shore of Lake Catherine. It's also 15 miles southeast from Hot Springs National Park. From I-30, take Exit 97 at Malvern, and go north 12 miles on Arkansas 171.

FEATURES   The 12-mile-long lake is the first in a chain of three lakes, and is the smallest, with 80 miles of shoreline. It was formed by the 900-foot-long, 75-foot-high Remmel Dam.

ACTIVITIES   Camp in one of 70 lakeside campground sites with water and electrical hookups; a laundry and store are open summers. Rent-a-Camp equipment is available. Overnight in the lodge or in one of 17 housekeeping cabins open year-round. Dine in the restaurant open summers.

*Fordyce Baths at Bath House Row in Hot Springs National Park,
near Lake Catherine State Park (courtesy of the park)*

Hike the trails and go boating from the ramp with rentals available at the marina year-round. Go fishing and swimming. Take a boat tour or party-barge tour. Stop by the visitor center and attend interpretive programs. Attend Wildflower Weekend in mid-April, and "Wonders of Fall" in mid-October.

Hot Springs National Park is southeast of Lake Catherine. Hot Springs was settled in 1808 by pioneers who were attracted to the area's thermal springs. Forty-five of the springs have been capped with the water now piped to the park's bathhouses. Hike the Tufa Trail above the springs. Camp in the Gulpha Gorge campground, tour the visitor center, and attend interpretive programs in the amphitheater.

Go up 1,256 feet above sea level in the Hot Springs Mountain Tower. It's located on top of Hot Springs Mountain. For information, call 501-623-6035 or 1-800-SPA-CITY.

Take a sightseeing or dinner cruise on Lake Hamilton aboard the *Belle of Hot Springs* riverboat. It leaves from Anthony Island, Arkansas 7. For information, call 501-525-4438.

Rockhounds enjoy searching for quartz crystals, novaculite, and other stones in the area. Check with the local rock shops for details.

Visit the National Park Aquarium in Hot Springs at 209 Central Avenue. It features the state's largest fish and reptile exhibit. For information, call 501-624-3474.

For entertainment in Hot Springs, attend Central Country Music Theater at 1008 Central Avenue. For information, call 501-624-2268. Attend The Bath House Show at 701 Central Avenue. For reservations, call 501-623-1415. You can also attend Music Mountain Jamboree in Music Mountain Village, Arkansas 260 West at 2720 Albert Pike. For your reserved seat, call 501-767-3841.

Tour the Mid-America Museum on Arkansas 227, one mile north of U.S. 270 at 400 Mid-America Boulevard. Visitors can enjoy hands-on experiences while learning about light, heat, magnetism, and other forces of nature. For details, call 501-767-3461.

Attend Malvern's Annual Brickfest on the last weekend in June. The festivities celebrate the city's largest industry—brick making, and features a 5K race, car show, parade, talent show, and other events. For information, call the Malvern Chamber of Commerce at 501-333-2721.

INFORMATION
Lake Catherine State Park
1200 Catherine Park Road
Route 19, Box 360
Hot Springs, Arkansas 71913-8605
501-844-4176
1-800-264-2422: cabin reservations

LAKE CHARLES STATE PARK
13

LOCATION   The park is eight miles northwest of Hoxie. Follow U.S. 63 to Black Rock, then go six miles southwest on Arkansas 25. It's in the foothills of the Ozark Mountains, by 645-acre Lake Charles in northern Arkansas.

ACTIVITIES   Go boating in the lake with a 10 horsepower limit; fish for crappie, bream, hybrid and channel catfish, and swim from the sandy beach. Take a springtime floating trip on the area's rivers.

Go camping in the 93-site campground, many with electrical hookups. A snack bar is open summers. Tour the visitor center and attend summer evening interpretive programs. Enjoy a guided hike, or explore the hiking trails on your own.

Historic Powhatan Courthouse is on Arkansas 25, one mile south of Black Rock off Arkansas 63. It's a restored 1888 Victorian structure with exhibits, and an archive vault for old northeast Arkansas records. For information, call 501-878-6794.

Lake Charles is close to the Ozark Folk Center. Additional information is available under that state park.

INFORMATION
Lake Charles State Park
Star Route
Powhatan, Arkansas 72458
501-878-6595

LAKE CHICOT STATE PARK
14

LOCATION   The park is eight miles northeast of Lake Village on Arkansas 144, on Lake Chicot.

FEATURES   Lake Chicot forms the state's largest natural oxbow lake, formed when a 16-mile-long remnant of the Mississippi River was cut off after the river changed its course.

ACTIVITIES   Go camping in the 127-site campground in a large pecan grove, with water and electrical hookups, and a coin laundry. Stay in one of the 14 fully-equipped housekeeping cabins, and purchase supplies from the park store.

Enjoy hiking, boating from the ramp with boat rentals, or go on a party-barge tour from the marina. Go fishing for bass, bream, and crappie, especially at the upper end of the lake, in the spring and fall. Catfish fishing is very good year-round. Go swimming, and get a snack from the snack bar open summers. Tour the visitor center, with interpretive programs offered year-round.

Birdwatchers like to come here since the park is located within the Mississippi Flyway. Each September, you can take swamp tours, levee tours, and attend programs especially established for viewing rare storks, ibis, egrets, ducks and geese.

INFORMATION
Lake Chicot State Park
Route 1, Box 648
Lake Village, Arkansas 71653
501-265-5480
1-800-264-2430: cabin reservations

LAKE DARDANELLE STATE PARK
15

MOUNT NEBO STATE PARK
16

LOCATION   The park has three lakeside locations. Dardanelle's 90 acres are three miles northwest of Dardanelle on Arkansas 155. Ouita's 20 acres are ¾ mile north of Russellville on Arkansas 64, then ¼ mile east on Arkansas 326. Russellville's 184 acres are two miles west of Russellville on Arkansas 326, Dyke Road.

Mount Nebo is seven miles west of Dardanelle on Arkansas 155.

FEATURES   Lake Dardanelle has 315 miles of shoreline and extends 50 miles up the Arkansas River Valley between Russellville and Dardanelle.

Mount Nebo, rising 1,350 feet, overlooks the Arkansas River valley, and features rock formations and spectacular views. Trailers over 15 feet long are not recommended, due to the mountainous road with tight hairpin curves, leading to the park.

ACTIVITIES   At Dardanelle, camp in the campground with 64 sites, all with water and electrical hookups. Hike the trails, go boating from the ramp with rentals available from the marina, and bass fishing. Enjoy scuba diving and water-skiing. Attend interpretive programs.

At Ouita, go scuba diving, water-skiing, camping in the 15-site campground, boating from the ramp, and fishing.

At Russellville, go camping in the 64-site campground, and boating from the ramp, with rentals available at the marina. Enjoy fishing, water-skiing, scuba diving, and swimming. Hike and bike the trails. Enjoy miniature golf, and tour the visitor center.

At Mt. Nebo, play tennis, with racquet rentals available. Camp in the 35-site campground, 25 sites with water and electrical hookups, or overnight in one of 14 housekeeping cabins. Groceries are available at the visitor center. You can also camp in one of 13 hike-in sites.

The park has 14 miles of trails circling Mount Nebo. Go swimming in the Olympic-size pool, tour the visitor center, and rent a bicycle to go cycling on the mountain bike trails. Attend the Mt. Nebo Chicken Fry in mid-May.

INFORMATION

Lake Dardanelle State Park
Route 5, Box 358
Russellville, Arkansas 72801
501-967-5516

Mt. Nebo State Park
Route 3, Box 374
Dardanelle, Arkansas 72834
501-229-3655
1-800-264-2458: cabin reservations

LAKE FORT SMITH STATE PARK
17

LOCATION   The park is off I-40 at Alma, Exit 13, then 12 miles north on U.S. 71 to ¼ mile north of Mountainburg. Watch for the park sign on U.S. 71 for the park entrance turnoff.

FEATURES   Lake Fort Smith covers 125 acres below the dam. The park is surrounded by some of the highest peaks in the Ozarks, and adjoins a 650-acre fishing lake. It's in a wooded valley of the Boston Mountains surrounded by thousands of acres of national forest.

ACTIVITIES   Go camping in one of the 12 tree-shaded sites with water and electrical hookups, or stay in one of the eight housekeeping cabins. Go hiking on a section of the 168-mile-long Ozark Highlands Trail, especially during April and May, when the redbud and dogwood trees are in bloom, and in October when the forests turn to crimson and gold. Although the trail is hikable year-round, the middle of the summer brings temperatures near 100 degrees, humidity, and insects. Winter temperatures, however, can be in the 40s and 60s. The trail is marked with white blazes.

Enjoy fishing, boating from the launch, with rentals available at the visitor center, and swimming in the Olympic-size pool. Bicycle the bike trails, attend summer interpretive programs, and play tennis.

In Van Buren, enjoy strolling down Main Street, restored to its 19th-century appearance. Board a vintage passenger car for a three-hour tour through the rugged mountains on the Ozark Scenic Railway. It leaves from the Old Frisco Depot at 813 Main Street. For information, call 1-800-452-9582. Take a cruise from Riverfront Park on the Arkansas River on the *Frontier Belle* riverboat from April through November. For information, call 501-471-5441.

INFORMATION
Lake Fort Smith State Park
P.O. Box 4
Mountainburg, Arkansas 72946
501-369-2469

LAKE FRIERSON STATE PARK
18

LOCATION   The park is 10 miles north of Jonesboro on Arkansas 141, at the western edge of Crowley's Ridge in northeast Arkansas. It's on the eastern shore of Lake Frierson.

ACTIVITIES   Play tennis, and camp in the seven-site campground without hookups. Hike the trail, go boating from the ramp, with rentals available, water-skiing, and fish year-round for stocked bass, bream, channel catfish, and crappie. Come in the spring when the dogwood is in blossom, and in the fall when the fall foliage hits its peak.

INFORMATION
Lake Frierson State Park
Route 2, Box 319D
Jonesboro, Arkansas 72401
501-932-2615

LAKE OUACHITA STATE PARK
19

LOCATION   The park is on the eastern end of Lake Ouachita. Go three miles west of Hot Springs on Arkansas 270, then 12 miles north on Arkansas 227.

FEATURES   The park contains the largest of the Hot Springs area lakes with 975 miles of shoreline, and extends 52 miles behind Blakely Mountain Dam, circa 1956. The park includes the famous Three Sisters Springs, once believed to have curative powers. This lake, along with DeGray Lake, is believed to be one of the two deepest lakes in mid-continent United States. The area around the lake is known as the quartz capital of the world.

ACTIVITIES   Go camping in the 102-site lakeside campground, 77 sites with electrical and water hookups, and a laundry. Overnight in one of the five fully-equipped A-frame cabins overlooking the lake, and dine in the cafe/restaurant open from Memorial Day through Labor Day. For a unique camping experience, stay in the Camp-A-Float cruiser where campers may secure their travel trailers or other RVs and take off down the lake for a tour.

Purchase supplies in the store, and snacks at the snack bar located in the visitor center. Go boating, sailing, water-skiing, scuba diving, and swimming.

Enjoy excellent fishing for bass, crappie, bream, and walleye along the lake shoreline, and for pike and rainbow trout near the dam or from the river below the dam. The lakes are restocked periodically. The lake is ranked one of the country's top 10 largemouth bass lakes.

Boaters can follow the Geo-Float Trail's self-guided tour to learn about the area's unusual geology, including minicaves. Rent houseboats and boats of all sizes from the full-service marina, or go on a sightseeing boat trip.

Hikers have a couple of hiking trails that go through the woods, including the Caddo Bend Trail's four-mile-long path. Many visitors gather water from the Three Sisters' natural springs. Tour the visitor center and attend interpretive programs, offered year-round.

Attend Wildflower Weekend in late April, and go on a fall foliage tour in mid to late October.

INFORMATION
Lake Ouachita State Park
Star Route 1, Box 1160
Mountain Pine, Arkansas 71956
501-767-9366: visitor center
501-767-9367: marina
1-800-264-2441: cabin reservations

LAKE POINSETT STATE PARK
20

LOCATION   The park is in the forested hills of Crowley's Ridge in northeast Arkansas. Go one mile east of Harrisburg on Arkansas 14, then three miles south on Arkansas 163.

ACTIVITIES   Go camping in the 30-site campground, 27 sites with water and electrical hookups. Go hiking and boating from the ramp, with fishing boat rentals available. Enjoy fishing for crappie, bass, and bream, and tour the visitor center. Groceries are available nearby.

INFORMATION
Lake Poinsett State Park
Route 3, Box 317
Harrisburg, Arkansas 72432
501-578-2064

LOGOLY STATE PARK
21

LOCATION   The park is in the forested hills of the Coastal Plain, ¾ mile east of McNeil on Logoly Road. It's also six miles north of Magnolia.

FEATURES   Logoly is the state's first environmental educational state park. Most of its 345 acres are designated a Natural Area because of its numerous mineral springs and unique plant life.

ACTIVITIES   Camp in the group tenting campground, hike the trails, picnic in the pavilion, and go fishing. Tour the visitor center's exhibits.

INFORMATION
Logoly State Park
P.O. Box 245
McNeil, Arkansas 71752
501-695-3561

LOUISIANA PURCHASE
STATE HISTORIC MONUMENT
22

LOCATION   From I-40, the park is 21 miles south of Brinkley on U.S. 49, then two miles east on Arkansas 362.

FEATURES   In 1815, government surveyors were sent here to find the boundaries of the Louisiana Purchase. Today 37.5 acres of the headwater swamp have been set aside as a state park.

ACTIVITIES   The park is open year-round. Stroll along the 950-foot-long boardwalk across a swamp full of bald cypress and tupelo trees. Watch for the granite monument that marks the spot from which land surveys of Arkansas began in 1815. Bring along plenty of insect repellent.

INFORMATION
Louisiana Purchase State Historic Monument
c/o Arkansas State Parks
One Capitol Mall, 4A-900
Little Rock, Arkansas 72201
501-238-2188 or 501-371-1191

MAMMOTH SPRING STATE PARK
23

LOCATION   Mammoth Spring State Park is in Mammoth Spring on U.S. 63, on the Arkansas/Missouri border.

FEATURES   According to legend, Mammoth Spring suddenly gushed forth, at the time an Indian chief was burying his son, who was killed while hunting for water. The spring has a flow of 150 to 200 million gallons daily, making it Arkansas' largest spring. It then forms a 9.5-acre pond in the park, and the water continues on to join the Spring River.

ACTIVITIES   Tour the visitor center located in the restored depot of the Frisco Railroad, circa 1883. You'll see exhibits of railroad memorabilia and an HO-scale model train. Enjoy a picnic underneath the giant oak trees, and hike the one-mile hiking trail. There's no camping in the park.

The Spring River is one of the state's best for floating, and year-round white-water canoeing. Enjoy fishing for rainbow trout upstream, and for smallmouth bass and walleye near Hardy.

While in Hardy, attend a performance at the Arkansas Traveller Folk and Dinner Theater in the outdoor arena in the Ozark hills. The theater is closed from Labor Day to Memorial Day.

INFORMATION
Mammoth Spring State Park
P.O. Box 36
Mammoth Spring, Arkansas 72554
501-625-7364

MILLWOOD STATE PARK
24

LOCATION   The park is nine miles east of Ashdown on Arkansas 32, next to the dam on Millwood Lake in the lowlands of southwestern Arkansas.

FEATURES   Millwood is one of the South's better-known fishing spots. Its dam is the state's largest earthen dam.

ACTIVITIES   Go camping year-round in the 114-site campground with water and electrical hookups. Hike 1.5-mile Waterfowl Way Trail through the pine and hardwood forest along the lake shore. Groceries are available at the marina.

Go boating from the ramp in 29,500-acre Millwood Lake, with rentals available from the full service marina adjacent to the campground. Go fishing for bass, crappie and catfish, and swimming from the beach. Participate in one of the bass fishing tournaments.

Tour the visitor center. Bird watchers come to observe wintering bald eagles and migrating pelicans in the fall.

In Ashdown, tour Will Reed's pioneer log cabin and the Little River County Courthouse, circa 1907. Both are listed on the National Register of Historic Places.

INFORMATION
Millwood State Park
Route 1, Box 37AB
Ashdown, Arkansas 71822
501-898-2800: park
501-898-5334: boating and information from Millwood Marina

MORO BAY STATE PARK
25

LOCATION   The park is 20 miles northeast of El Dorado on Arkansas 15, and 29 miles southwest of Warren. It's at the junction of the Ouachita River, Moro Bay, and Raymond Lake. One of the highway department's last free ferries crosses the river to connect Arkansas 15 with the park.

ACTIVITIES   Enjoy camping in the 20-site campground with water and electrical hookups, and purchase supplies in the camp store. Hike the trails, including 1/4 mile Deer Run, to get a close-up view of a typical Southern forest. Go boating from the ramp, with rentals available, fishing and swimming. Tour the visitor center, and attend an interpretive program. A restaurant is nearby.

INFORMATION
Moro Bay State Park
6071 Highway 15 South
Star Route
Jersey, Arkansas 71651
501-463-8554

OLD DAVIDSONVILLE STATE PARK
26

LOCATION   The park is on the Black River. Go two miles west of Pocahontas on U.S. 62, then nine miles southwest on Arkansas 166. From Black Rock, follow U.S. 62 to Arkansas 361, then go six more miles to the north.

FEATURES   The park was the site of historic Davidsonville, established by
French settlers in 1815. The town provided a vital link for river traffic on the Black
River and the Old Southwest Trail. It features Arkansas' first post office, land
office, courthouse, and steamboat landing. However, the historic townsite
declined in population when it was bypassed by the Old Military Road.

ACTIVITIES   Tour the visitor center and attend interpretive programs. Camp
in the 25-site campground with water and electrical hookups, or stay in one of the
25 tent campsites. Hike the trails, go swimming and boating from the dock, with
fishing boat rentals available. Enjoy fishing in the 11-acre fishing lake, or in the
Black River. Anglers also have access to nearby Spring and Eleven Point Rivers.

INFORMATION
Old Davidsonville State Park
7953 Highway 166 South
Route 2,
Pocahontas, Arkansas 72455
501-892-4708

OLD WASHINGTON HISTORIC STATE PARK
27

LOCATION   The park is on Arkansas 4, eight miles north of I-30 at the Hope
Exit 30, at Washington.

FEATURES   Early immigrants started their trek from Washington, heading
for Texas and into the Southwest, during the 19th-century. It served as the Confederate Capital for Arkansas during the Civil War. Many of the antebellum homes
have been restored, including the tavern where Houston, Bowie, and Crockett visited. Here the first Bowie knife was made, and Davy Crockett and Sam Houston
planned the battle of the Alamo.

ACTIVITIES   Take a two-hour tour through the village, led by costumed guides who take you back to the era of 1824–1875. The Goodlett cotton gin, now located here, is the last steam-operated gin in the country, and was located along the Old Southwest Trail. The town's historic buildings are open on Monday, Wednesday through Saturday, and on Sunday afternoons except on major holidays.

Tours through the Confederate Capital Tavern Inn, Blacksmith Shop, Gun Museum, and the Sanders, Roysston, and Purdom houses reflect life in early Arkansas. Tour admission is charged. Dine in the Williams Tavern Restaurant.

Jonquils reach their peak in mid-March, when an annual jonquil festival is held. In late October or early November, attend Frontier Days Festival, where 19th-century crafts, music, and food are featured. The park also holds a Candlelight Christmas.

Tour the visitor center, located in the 1874 Courthouse. The Southwest Arkansas regional archives are housed here, where you can do historical and genealogical research.

INFORMATION
Old Washington Historic State Park
P.O. Box 98
Washington, Arkansas 71862
501-983-2684 or 501-983-2733

OZARK FOLK CENTER
28

LOCATION   The Center is one mile north of Mountain View, near the intersection of Arkansas 5, 9, 14, and 66, on Spur 382.

FEATURES   The center is operated by the state parks system. It was set aside to preserve the mountain ways and folk songs of the Ozark pioneers.

ACTIVITIES   The Center is open daily from May through October. Visitors can learn how the state's first residents lived and entertained themselves. Over 25 traditional Ozark crafts are demonstrated by master craftspeople in the Center's huge forum. These include woodcarving, tin-type photography, broom making, and quilting.

Overnight in the 60-room lodge, and dine in the restaurant. Purchase supplies in the store, or snacks at the snack bar which are open seasonally. Go swimming, and attend interpretive programs.

Attend live entertainment in the 1,000-seat music auditorium, where performances of music and dance from the 1800s and early 1900s are presented from April through October.

Blanchard Springs Caverns is on Arkansas 14 south of Yellville, and 15 miles northwest of Mountain View. It features one of the world's largest flowstones, and contains almost every type of calcite formation to be found. The caverns are ranked among the 10 most beautiful caverns in North America. You can either take the ½-mile Dripstone Trail tour, or for those who don't mind climbing many steps, take the 1¼-mile, 1.75-hour-long Discovery Tour. For tour information, call 501-757-2211. Nearby facilities include camping, creek swimming, fishing, and hiking on nature trails.

INFORMATION
Ozark Folk Center
P.O. Box 500
Mountain View, Arkansas 72560
501-269-3851: park
501-269-3871 or 1-800-264-3655: lodge reservations

PETIT JEAN STATE PARK
29

LOCATION   Take Exit 108 off I-40 at Morrilton. The park is nine miles south of I-40 at Morrilton, on Arkansas 9. Then go 12 miles west on Arkansas 154. From Dardanelle, go seven miles south on Arkansas 7, then 16 miles east on Arkansas 154. It's on top of Petit Jean Mountain, 1,100 feet above the Arkansas River valley, between the Ouachitas and Ozarks.

FEATURES   Cedar Creek carved a canyon containing the spectacular 95-foot Cedar Falls, one of the South's highest. Lake Bailey is formed upstream. Other natural features include Indian Cave, Bear Cave, Red House Cave, and the Palisades. In the Seven Hollows area, you'll see the unusual Turtle Rocks, the Grotto, and Petit Jean Natural Bridge.

The park was named for a beautiful French girl who, according to legend, disguised herself as a boy, and secretly accompanied her sweetheart to America.

ACTIVITIES   Camp year-round in the 127-site campground with water and electrical hookups. Rent-a-Camps are available. Overnight in the 24-room Mather Lodge, or in one of the 31 fully-equipped housekeeping cabins, and dine in the restaurant. Purchase snacks at the snack bar open seasonally.

Hike the network of trails past the waterfall. Go into Seven Hollows to get great overlooks of the Arkansas River valley. Play tennis, fish, go boating from the ramp on Lake Bailey, with paddleboat and fishing boat rentals available. Go swimming in the pool, and get a snack at the snack bar. Tour the visitor center, and attend interpretive programs.

Rent a horse to go riding from the stable adjacent to the park. Attend Lumberjack Day in early May.

The Museum of Automobiles, with its 50 antique and classic vehicles, and Winrock Farms, home of the late Governor Winthrop Rockefeller, are also located on the mountain. For museum information, call 501-727-5427. Admission is charged.

Arriving pilots can land at the only state park operated airport capable of handling cabin class aircraft. Shuttle service is available.

INFORMATION
Petit Jean State Park
Route 3, Box 340
Morrilton, Arkansas 72110
501-727-5441: park
501-727-5431 or 1-800-264-2462: cabin and lodge reservations

PINNACLE MOUNTAIN STATE PARK
30

LOCATION   The park is west of Little Rock. Take Exit 9 off I-430 at Little Rock and go seven miles west on Arkansas 10, then north two more miles on Arkansas 300.

FEATURES   Pinnacle Mountain is a dome-shaped mountain surrounded by the state park. Its terrain includes the Big and Little Maumelle Rivers.

ACTIVITIES   The park is open for day use and features 32 miles of trails. Two trails lead through the forest to the summit of Pinnacle Mountain, where you can get a great view of Lake Maumelle. Go up onto the observation platform for a wonderful view of the distant valleys.

The 192-mile-long Ouachita Trail's eastern trailhead begins here. This trail provides access to various side loops, including 23-mile Boardstand, Old Military Road Trail, Fork Mountain Trail, and the Caney Creek Trail in the Caney Creek Wilderness Area. Backpack rental equipment is available. Take guided wild flower walks in late March and April.

Go boating from the ramp, sailing, and fishing in the lake known for its largemouth and striped bass. Enjoy an interpretive canoe trip. Rental canoes, tents, and shuttles are available. Contact the park for its scheduled tours. Participate in one of its regattas.

Tour the visitor center and watch the audiovisual presentation. No camping is available in the park, but is available at Maumelle Park, two miles east of the park on Pinnacle Valley Road.

INFORMATION
Pinnacle Mountain State Park
11901 Pinnacle Valley Road
Route 1, Box 34
Roland, Arkansas 72135
501-868-5806
501-868-5018: Fax

PRAIRIE GROVE BATTLEFIELD STATE PARK
31

LOCATION   The park is 10 miles southwest of Fayetteville in Prairie Grove, on U.S. 62.

FEATURES   Bitter fighting occurred here on December 7, 1862, between Union and Confederate forces. The battle is commemorated with a museum, monuments, and a reconstructed 19th-century village with ante-bellum buildings.

ACTIVITIES   Attend special events in the amphitheater. Take the self-guided driving trail through the battlefield, and hike the one-mile-long Battlefield Trail. The visitor center is located in the Battlefield Museum. Attend interpretive programs, and take a guided tour of the 19th-century buildings available by special request.

Each Labor Day weekend, the park hosts the Clothesline Fair, with three days of arts, crafts, and other activities. Reenactments of the battle are staged the first weekend of December on every even year.

INFORMATION
Prairie Grove Battlefield State Park
Box 306
Prairie Grove, Arkansas 72753
501-846-2990

QUEEN WILHELMINA STATE PARK
32

LOCATION   The park is 13 miles west of Mena, at the summit of 2,681-foot Rich Mountain, on Arkansas 88. It's on the Talimena Scenic Highway that spans Arkansas and Oklahoma. The highway is designated as a National Scenic Byway.

If it's foggy or snowing, from Mena go six miles north on U.S. 71, then nine miles west on U.S. 270, and two miles on Arkansas 272 and follow the steep winding road to reach the mountain summit.

FEATURES   The original Queen Wilhelmina Inn was first built by a Dutch-financed railroad in 1896, and was named for Holland's monarch. Originally the inn was called the "Castle in the Sky." Queen Wilhelmina Peak is the state's second highest.

ACTIVITIES   Go camping in the 40-site campground, 35 sites with water and electrical hookups, with groceries and a coin laundry available. Overnight in the new 38-room Queen Wilhelmina Inn, and dine in the restaurant that features Southern cooking. Hike the trails, including part of the Ouachita Trail. Tour the visitor center, take a miniature train ride, visit the park's animal petting zoo, and play miniature golf.

In Mena, attend the Saturday night Wilhelmina Jamboree, and tour the Ansata Arabian Stud Farm.

Take a drive along the Talimena Scenic Byway, where you top out at almost 3,000 feet to look out over the Holson Valley. The byway spans the highest mountain range between the Appalachians and the Rockies, and is especially beautiful in the fall, around the third week in October, when the sweet gums, maples, sumacs, and red oaks turn the woods into a mosaic of color.

INFORMATION
Queen Wilhelmina State Park
Route 7, Box 53 A
Mena, Arkansas 71953
501-394-2863
1-800-264-2477: lodge reservations

TOLTEC MOUNDS
ARCHEOLOGICAL STATE PARK
33

LOCATION   The state park is five miles south of Scott off U.S. 165. It's also 16 miles southeast of North Little Rock, off U.S. 165, on Arkansas 386. You can also take Exit 7 off I-144 to England, then go 10 miles southeast on U.S. 165.

FEATURES   The park contains the remains of 19 ancient Indian earthworks. The area was a religious and social center of an Arkansas Indian culture called the Plum Bayou, which inhibited this area from 600–950 A.D. The mounds are the state's tallest, and listed on the National Register of Historic Places.

ACTIVITIES   Take a guided tour of the Indian mounds, discovered around 100 years ago. Tour the visitor center to see its exhibits and learn the history of the site's earlier inhabitants. Observe archeologists through a windowed workroom while they are working. Attend the Summer Solstice Celebration held on June 21.

INFORMATION
Toltec Mounds Archeological State Park
#1 Toltec Mounds Road
Scott, Arkansas 72142-8502
501-961-9442

VILLAGE CREEK STATE PARK
34

LOCATION   The park is on Crowley's Ridge in eastern Arkansas. It's east of Forrest City off I-40, Exit 242, then north for 13 miles on Arkansas 284. It's also six miles south of Wynne on Arkansas 284.

FEATURES   Cherokee Indians once lived near Village Creek along Crowley's Ridge, which rises 300 feet above sea level. It was later settled by pioneers during the early 1800s, and includes William Strong's homestead. It has two man-made fishing lakes: Lake Dunn and Lake Austell.

ACTIVITIES   Village Creek is the state's largest state park. Enjoy hiking one of the five trails through the oak, sugar maple, and tulip trees. Numerous hiking trails connect the two lakes. Come especially in the spring, when spring wildflower walks are offered.

Camp in the 104-site campground along Lake Dunn, with water and electrical hookups, groceries, and a laundry. Overnight in one of the fully-equipped cabins. Enjoy boating from the ramp, with rentals available. Enjoy fishing for stocked bass, bream, crappie and catfish, and go swimming in Lake Austell. Play tennis or bike the bicycle trails, with rentals available.

Tour the visitor center to see its interpretive exhibits, and attend programs, concerts and other special events.

INFORMATION
Village Creek State Park
Route 3, Box 49B
Wynne, Arkansas 72396
501-238-9406
1-800-264-2467: cabin reservations

WHITE OAK LAKE STATE PARK
35

LOCATION   The park is two miles southeast of Bluff City on Arkansas 387, and is six miles from Reader on Arkansas 24. From I-30 at Prescott, go east 20 miles on Arkansas 24, then 100 yards south on Arkansas 299, and then two miles southeast on Arkansas 387. It's in the midst of the Poison Springs State Forest in southwest Arkansas, and on the western shore of White Oak Lake.

ACTIVITIES   White Oak Lake State Park has good fishing for bream, bass, and crappie. Fishing supplies are available. Enjoy camping in the 42-site campground, 38 sites with water and electrical hookups. Go swimming, and explore the hiking trails through the park's uplands and unique sandhills. Go boating from the ramp, with boat rentals available at the marina. Tour the visitor center and attend interpretive programs. Birders come to spot heron, egrets, osprey, and green heron. Bald eagles pass through here during the winter.

Reader Railroad is north of the park in Reader. This railroad is the oldest all-steam, narrow-gauge railroad that still operates in the U.S. You can take a 1½-hour ride aboard the "Possom Trot Line." You'll go from the old mill town of Reader, to the site of a logging camp at Camp DeWoody. Once a month from June through October, the train offers a sunset ride, featuring bluegrass and country music to accompany your dinner. Trains generally run on weekends in May, and Thursday through Sunday from June through mid-August. For required reservations, call the office in Malvern at 501-337-9591, or in Reader, call 501-685-2692.

INFORMATION
White Oak Lake State Park
Star Route
Bluff City, Arkansas 71722
501-685-2748 or 685-2132

WITHROW SPRINGS STATE PARK
36

LOCATION   Withrow Springs State Park is on the War Eagle River in the Ozark Mountains, five miles north of Huntsville off Arkansas 68, on Arkansas 23.

ACTIVITIES   Go fishing in the War Eagle River for catfish, perch, bass, and goggle eye. Hike one of three scenic trails including ¾-mile Dogwood Trail that loops along the ridges through the woods. War Eagle Trail starts at the bridge before climbing up the 150-foot bluff for a great overlook of the river, and then passes a large cave with an underground stream. Forest Trail passes through a hardwood forest and makes a 2½-mile loop.

Go canoeing on the river, with rentals and shuttles available, or take an interpretive float trip down the War Eagle, also with shuttle service available. Swim in the pool. Camp in the 25-site campground, 17 sites with water and electrical hookups, which is near a spring that flows from a small cave. Purchase a snack at the snack bar, tour the visitor center, and visit War Eagle Cavern, with its underground stream.

INFORMATION
Withrow Springs State Park
Route 3
Huntsville, Arkansas 72740
501-559-2593

WOOLLY HOLLOW STATE PARK
37

LOCATION   The park is 12 miles north of Conway on U.S. 65, then six miles east on Arkansas 285. Take Exit 125 off I-40 at Conway. It's on Lake Bennett, in the Ozark Mountains in north-central Arkansas.

FEATURES   The park was named for the Woolly family who moved here in the 1850s. Their restored one-room log cabin, circa 1882, is in the park.

ACTIVITIES   Camp year-round in the 32-site campground, 20 sites with water and electric hookups. Hike the 3½-mile-long Huckleberry Nature Trail. Go boating from the ramp in boats with electric motors. Pedal boat, canoes, and fishing-boat rentals are available. Enjoy fishing and swimming from the guarded beach.

Tour the visitor center and Woolly Cabin. Snacks are available at the snack bar.

INFORMATION
Woolly Hollow State Park
Route 1, Box 374
Greenbrier, Arkansas 72058
501-679-2098

FLORIDA STATE PARKS

1. Anastasia State Park
2. Faver-Dykes State Park
3. Guana River State Park
4. Bahia Honda State Park
5. Bill Baggs Cape Florida State Recreation Area
6. Blackwater River State Park
7. Blue Spring State Park
7. Hontoon Island State Park
8. Bulow Plantation Ruins State Historic Park
8. Bulow Creek State Park
9. Caladesi Island State Park
9. Honeymoon Island State Recreation Area
10. Cayo Costa State Park
11. Chekika State Recreation Area
12. Collier-Seminole State Park
13. Fakahatchee Strand State Preserve
14. Crystal River State Archeological Site
15. Dade Battlefield State Historic Site
15. Withlacoochee State Forest
15. Withlacoochee State Trail
16. Dead Lakes State Recreation Area
17. DeLeon Springs State Recreation Area
18. Delnor Wiggins Pass State Recreation Area
19. Devil's Millhopper State Geological Site
20. Edward Ball Wakulla Springs State Park
21. Egmont Key State Park
22. Falling Waters State Recreation Area
23. Florida Caverns State Park
24. Fort Clinch State Park
25. Fort Cooper State Park
26. Fort Gadsden State Park
27. Fort Pierce Inlet State Recreation Area
28. Fort Zachary Taylor State Historic Site
29. Gamble Plantation State Historic Site
30. Gamble Rogers Memorial State Rec. Area
    at Flagler Beach
31. Gasparilla Island State Recreation Area
31. Don Pedro Island State Recreation Area
32. General James A. Van Fleet State Trail
33. Grayton Beach State Recreation Area
34. Henderson Beach State Recreation Area
35. Highlands Hammock State Park
36. Hillsborough River State Park
37. Homosassa Springs State Wildlife Park
37. Yulee Sugar Mill Ruins State Historic Site
38. Hugh Taylor Birch State Recreation Area
38. John U. Lloyd Beach State Recreation Area
39. Ichetucknee Springs State Park
39. Olustee Battlefield State Historic Site
40. John D. MacArthur Beach State Park
41. John Pennekamp Coral Reef State Park
42. Jonathan Dickinson State Park

42. St. Lucie Inlet State Preserve
43. Koreshan State Historic Site
44. Lake Griffin State Recreation Area
45. Lake Kissimmee State Park
46. Lake Louisa State Park
47. Lake Manatee State Recreation Area
48. Lake Talquin State Park
49. Maclay State Gardens
50. Lake Jackson Mounds State Archeological Site
51. Litttle Manatee River State Recreation Area
52. Little Talbot Island State Park
52. Big Talbot Island State Park
52. Amelia Island State Recreation Area
53. Long Key State Recreation Area
54. Manatee Springs State Park
55. Marjorie Kinnan Rawlings State Historic Site
56. Paynes Prairie State Preserve
57. Gainesville-Hawthorne State Trail
58. Mike Roess Gold Head Branch State Park
59. Myakka River State Park
60. New Smyrna Sugar Mills Ruins St. Historic Park
61. North Shore State Recreation Area
62. Ochlockonee River State Park
63. O'Leno State Park
64. Oleta River State Recreation Area
65. Oscar Scherer State Park
66. Pahokee State Recreation Area
67. Paynes Creek State Historic Site
68. Peacock Springs State Recreation Area
69. Perdido Key State Recreation Area
69. Big Lagoon State Recreation Area
70. Rocky Bayou State Park
71. Rainbow Springs State Park
72. Ravine State Gardens
73. St. Andrews State Recreation Area
74. St. George Island State Park
75. St. Joseph Peninsula State Park
76. Sabastian Inlet State Recreation Area
77. Stephen Foster State Folk Culture Center
78. Suwannee River State Park
79. Three Rivers State Recreation Area
80. Tomoka State Park
81. Torreya State Park
82. Tosohatchee State Reserve
83. Waccasassa Bay State Preserve/Cedar Key Scrub
    State Reserve
84. Washington Oaks State Park
85. Wekiwa Springs State Park

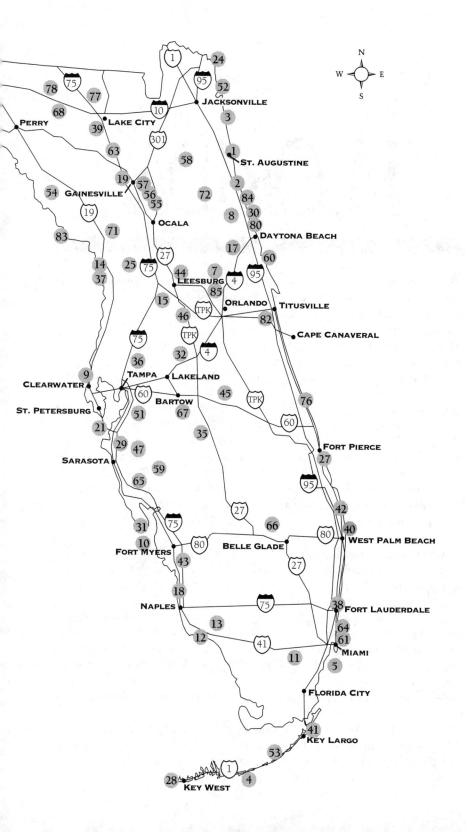

FLORIDA

Florida has over 100 state parks, recreation areas, gardens, and preserves within its state park system. Over two dozen rivers pass through them en route to the Atlantic Ocean or Gulf of Mexico. Many of the state parks offer both saltwater and freshwater fishing.

Many festivals and events are presented in the various state parks. To obtain details, either call the individual park directly, or call 904-488-9872.

Several parks offer living history presentations. These include Dade Battlefield, Fort Cooper, Fort Clinch, Hillsborough River, Lake Kissimmee, Natural Bridge Battlefield and Olustee Battlefield. Annual military reenactments are presented at Dade Battlefield, Olustee Battlefield, and Natural Bridge Battlefield.

The Florida Park Service administers 36 canoe trails within the Florida Recreational Trails System. Boaters can find boat camping at Bahia Honda, Cape Florida, Caladesi Island, Hontoon Island, and John Pennekamp Coral Reef.

The Northwestern Florida panhandle is known as a vacation hideaway because of its sugar-white sandy beaches and blue-green water. In 1994, when a survey of 650 of the nation's beaches was conducted by the University of Maryland's Laboratory for Coastal Research, five Panhandle beaches were ranked in the top dozen, with Grayton Beach voted number one. Beaches along the Panhandle stretch for 200 miles from Pensacola on the west, to Apalachicola on the east. Twelve major rivers flow through the Panhandle's interior's pine forests and bayous, where visitors come to canoe, backpack and hike.

The resort of Fort Walton Beach is the largest city along the Emerald Coast, and home to Eglin Air Force Base, which calls itself "the largest air force base in the Free World." Its Indian Temple Mound Museum is a National Historic Landmark featuring over 10,000 years of Gulf Coast living. Fort Walton Beach features 24 miles of shoreline including John C. Beasley State Park on Okaloosa Island, and Henderson Beach State Park. It's known as having some of the best fishing waters in the world.

The route along A1A from Fernandina Beach to Daytona Beach is called the Buccaneer Trail, where piracy, smuggling, and slave-trading were once rampant. Today the trail is famous for sport fishing and pleasure boating.

The 10,000 islands full of mangrove trees off Marco Island's coast, and the Everglades, were formed by small shells, driftwood, and trapped seaweed. Some estimate there could be as many as 20,000 islands.

The Florida Keys are remnants of a barrier reef that once extended the length of present-day Florida. They were formed nearly 100,000 years ago when sea level was 20 to 30 feet higher than it is today. The Keys are 180 miles long and are accessed by one highway, crossing 42 bridges that connects 32 of the islands, and extends from Biscayne Bay, to within approximately 90 miles of Havana.

Hikers have access to over 1,000 miles of trails established by the Florida Trail Association. When completed, the trail will cover 1,300 miles, extending from the Everglades to the Gulf Islands National Seashore in the northwest peninsula. It's the country's only semitropical trail, and provides hikers a sampling of the state's many diverse ecosystems. It runs through the swamps of Big Cypress National Preserve, along the limestone bluffs of the Suwannee River, to the marshes of St. Mark's Wildlife Refuge.

In southern Florida, hike the Big Cypress Trail, a 60-mile round trip that begins at the Oasis Ranger Station in the heart of the Everglades. For trail descriptions, write P.O. Box 13708, Gainesville, Florida 32604, or call 904-378-8823.

Mosquitoes, sandflies, and other biting insects are abundant in many coastal areas from mid-May through November. Bring along insect repellent and wear loose-fitting, long-sleeved shirts and long pants.

The U.S. has six national marine sanctuaries, and the Florida Keys has two of them. One is off Key Largo on the ocean side of Pennekamp Park, and the other is at Looe Key, five miles offshore from Big Pine Key.

ANASTASIA STATE PARK
1

FAVER-DYKES STATE PARK
2

GUANA RIVER STATE PARK
3

LOCATION   Anastasia is in St. Augustine Beach, off Florida A1A at S.R. 3.
Faver-Dykes' 752 acres are 13 miles south of St. Augustine at the intersection of I-95 and U.S. 1, along Pellicer Creek.
Guana River is off A1A, north of St. Augustine.

ACTIVITIES   At Anastasia, enjoy coastal camping in the 139-site campground, with a laundry and trailer dump site. All sites have water hookups, and 105 have electrical hookups. Enjoy hiking the nature trails, and along four miles of white beaches. Go swimming and surfing in the Atlantic Ocean and boating from the ramp, where boat rentals are available. Go fishing either in the Atlantic Ocean or in the St. Johns River. Anglers can catch trout, snapper, mackerel, and bass.

At Faver-Dykes State Park, enjoy camping in the 30-site campground, all sites with water and electrical hookups. Hike the nature trails, and enjoy water-skiing, saltwater fishing, and boating from the ramp. Canoe rentals are available.

At Guana River State Park's 2,400 acres, visitors can enjoy freshwater and saltwater fishing, boating on the Guana and Tolomato Rivers, plus swimming and surfing in the Atlantic Ocean. Hikers and mountain bikers have access to nine miles of former service roads.

St. Augustine is the nation's oldest city, dating back to 1565 when it was founded by the Spanish. The city was founded 55 years before the Pilgrims landed at Plymouth Rock. Tour the Oldest House at 14 St. Francis. For information, call 904-824-2872.

Take a stroll down the narrow streets, or ride aboard a sightseeing train. For information, call 904-829-6545. You can also take a scenic cruise from City Yacht Pier to see the St. Augustine waterfront and Matanzas Bay. Historical tours of St. Augustine leave from the Historic Old Jail at 167 San Marco Avenue. For information, call 904-829-3800.

Visit the battlements of Fort Castillo de San Marcos. The fort, circa 1672, was built by the Spanish to protect its treasure fleets traveling here.

Tour the Lightner Museum on King Street to see relics from America's Gilded Age. It's located in the former Alcazar Hotel, constructed in 1888. For information, call 904-824-2874.

Zorayda Castle is at 85 King Street on Alternate U.S. 1, across from Flagler College. It was the first poured-concrete structure built in St. Augustine. This Moorish palace was inspired by the Alhambra of Grenada, Spain, and contains a 2,300-year-old sacred cat rug, court of lions, harem quarters, and the zorayda tower. For information, call 904-824-3097.

Arriving pilots can land at St. Augustine Airport, located four miles north of the city. Rental cars are available.

INFORMATION

Anastasia State Park
1340-A A1A South
St. Augustine, Florida 32084
904-461-2000 or 461-2033

Faver-Dykes State Park
1000 Faver Dykes Road
RFD 4, Box 213J-1
St. Augustine, Florida 32086
904-794-0997

Guana River State Park
2690 South Ponte Vedra Boulevard
Ponte Vedra Beach, Florida 32082
904-825-5071

BAHIA HONDA STATE PARK
4

LOCATION   The park is on Bahia Honda Key off U.S. 1 at Mile Marker #37, 12 miles south of Marathon.

FEATURES   Bahia Honda is Spanish for "deep bay." The key was isolated until the railroad spanned the channels linking Key West with the mainland. Bahia Honda has many plants not found on the other islands, including the satinwood tree and dwarf morning glory. Its beach is described by some locals as "the best beach on the Keys."

ACTIVITIES   The park fills fast, and if it's filled, you'll have to wait for a parking place to open up before entering. Attend a campfire program, and go camping year-round in one of three campgrounds with 76 sites, most with water and electrical hookups. You can also stay in one of six furnished duplex cabins, open seasonally. Snacks, limited groceries, and marine supplies are available at the concession building. Boaters can also enjoy boat camping here.

Hike the nature trail located at the far end of Sandspur Beach. It follows the shore of a tidal lagoon and continues through a coastal strand hammock before returning along the beach.

Go boating from the ramp, with boat rentals and charters available. Take a 1.5-hour sunset cruise aboard a 45-foot catamaran available Wednesdays, Fridays and Saturdays, from January through June. Information and reservations are available at the park concession, or by calling 305-872-1127.

Go swimming either in Florida Bay or in the Gulf of Mexico. Fish for tarpon, grouper, red snapper, and grunt.

Go snorkeling and scuba diving. Equipment is available at the dive shop next to the marina. Wind surfing rentals and lessons are also available. An underwater paradise lies five to six miles southwest of Big Pine Key, accessible only by boat.

Looe Key National Marine Sanctuary is offshore from Big Pine. It was named for HMS *Looe*, a British frigate that went aground during a storm in 1744. Go on snorkeling trips into the sanctuary.

Incoming pilots can land at Marathon Airport, located three miles east of town. Rental cars are available.

INFORMATION
Bahia Honda State Park
Route 1, Box 782
Big Pine Key, Florida 33043
305-872-2353

BILL BAGGS CAPE FLORIDA STATE RECREATION AREA

5

LOCATION   The state recreation area is off U.S. 1, at the southern end of Key Biscayne. Go east on the Rickenbacker Causeway off U.S. 1, south of downtown Miami.

ACTIVITIES   Hike the nature trails, go boating from the ramp, saltwater fishing, swimming, scuba diving and snorkeling in the Atlantic Ocean. Tour the visitor center, and get a snack at the concession stand during the summer. Boaters can enjoy boat camping here.

The original Cape Florida lighthouse, circa 1825, was destroyed by the Seminole Indians, and the current tower was constructed in 1846. Climb the 122-steps for a magnificent view of the island. The lighthouse keeper's quarters have been restored to their original 1830s appearance. Tours are offered every day except Tuesday and Wednesday.

Biscayne National Underwater Park is nine miles east of Homestead, and south of Miami. Tour the visitor center. Enjoy a ride aboard a glass-bottomed boat, take a tropical island cruise, or go scuba diving or snorkeling along the reef. Rent a canoe to explore the near-shore bays and creeks, either on your own or under a naturalist's guidance. Boating tours and snorkeling/scuba tours depart from Convoy Point. For reservations, call 305-230-1100. Convoy Point is a good viewing area for occasional manatees, pelicans, wading birds, and shore birds. For park information, call 305-247-2400, or 305-230-1100.

Incoming pilots can land at Kendall-Tamiami Executive Airport, located 13 miles southwest of Miami, or at Miami International, located eight miles northwest of the city. Rental cars are available at both airports.

INFORMATION
Bill Baggs Cape Florida State Recreation Area
1200 South Crandon Boulevard
Key Biscayne, Florida 33149
305-361-5811

BLACKWATER RIVER STATE PARK

6

LOCATION   The state park is 15 miles northeast of Milton off U.S. 90, and three miles north of Holt.

FEATURES   The Blackwater River is one of the few remaining sandy-bottom rivers to be found in the Southeast, averaging a depth of two feet of water.

ACTIVITIES   Go canoeing, kayaking, paddling in a paddleboat, or innertubing along the Blackwater River, with canoe rentals available.

Go swimming in the Blackwater River from the sand beaches. Hike the nature trails, and cross the swamp via a boardwalk to picnic beneath the white cedar trees. Go camping year-round in the 15-site campground, with water and electrical hookups, and a trailer dump station available. Enjoy bass fishing in the Blackwater River.

Incoming pilots can land at Peter Prince Field, located three miles east of Milton. Rental cars are available.

INFORMATION
Blackwater River State Park
Route 1, Box 57-C
Holt, Florida 32564
904-623-2363

BLUE SPRING STATE PARK

HONTOON ISLAND STATE PARK
7

LOCATION   Blue Spring State Park is two miles west of Orange City off I-4 and U.S. 17/92, on West French Avenue.

Hontoon Island State Park's 1,650 acres are six miles west of DeLand off Florida 44, and 25 miles north of Orlando. It is bordered by the St. Johns River and Hontoon Dead River. The island is accessible via passenger ferry or private boat. No vehicles are permitted.

FEATURES   Blue Spring's 518 acres provides a sanctuary for the endangered bald eagle, and its spring water maintains a temperature of 72 degrees Fahrenheit. Florida's endangered manatees gather here from November through March to escape the colder water of the St. Johns River.

At Hontoon Island, a picket encampment was established in 1864 during the Civil War on the St. Johns River, to give the settlers early warning and to delay the Union raid coming out of Jacksonville.

ACTIVITIES   At Blue Springs, enjoy year-round camping in the 51-site campground, or stay overnight in a vacation cabin, open year-round, and hike the nature trails. Go canoeing and boating from the ramp in Blue Spring Run, with boat and canoe rentals available. Enjoy freshwater fishing, swimming, scuba diving and snorkeling in Blue Spring.

Watch for manatees from the manatee-viewing platform. Watch the slide presentation to learn more about these creatures. Snacks are available during the summer. In January, attend the annual Blue Spring Manatee Festival.

On Hontoon Island, go camping year-round in the 24-site campground, five sites with water and electrical hookups, or overnight in one of 6 primitive cabins. Reservations are necessary. Boaters can also go boat camping here.

Hike the nature trails, go boating from the ramp, and enjoy fishing. A great overlook can be enjoyed from the 80-foot observation tower.

Arriving pilots can land at DeLand Municipal–Sidney H. Taylor Field, located three miles northeast of DeLand. Rental cars are available.

INFORMATION

Blue Spring State Park
2100 West French Avenue
Orange City, Florida 32763
904-775-3663

Hontoon Island State Park
2309 River Ridge Road
DeLand, Florida 32720
904-736-5309

BULOW PLANTATION RUINS STATE HISTORIC PARK

BULOW CREEK STATE PARK
8

LOCATION   The Bulow Plantation Ruins' 109 acres are nine miles southeast of Bunnell on Florida 2001, Old Kings Road. It's off Florida S-5A, three miles west of Flagler Beach.

The state park is north of Ormond Beach, at 3351 Old Dixie Highway.

FEATURES   The Bulow Plantation contains the ruins of the coquina foundations, wells, and a spring house. It was destroyed by the Seminoles in 1836 during the Second Seminole War.

ACTIVITIES   At Bulow Plantation, go canoeing on the canoe trail, with rentals available, and hike the trail to see the ruins of the old sugar mill. Tour the interpretive center, and go freshwater and saltwater fishing, or boating from the ramp.

At Bulow Creek State Park, hike the nature trail located adjacent to an 800-year-old Fairchild oak tree.

Arriving pilots can land at Ormond Beach Municipal Airport, located three miles northwest of Ormond Beach. Rental cars are available.

INFORMATION

Bulow Plantation Ruins State
   Historic Park
P. O. Box 655
Bunnell, Florida 32010
904-439-2219

Bulow Creek State Park
3351 Old Dixie Highway
Ormond Beach, Florida 32174
904-677-4645

CALADESI ISLAND STATE PARK

HONEYMOON ISLAND
STATE RECREATION AREA
9

LOCATION   Caladesi Island's 653 acres are off the Gulf of Mexico, west of Dunedin from U.S. 19A. It's only accessible by private boat or public ferry, departing hourly from Honeymoon Island and from Clearwater. For ferry reservations, call 813-734-5263.

Honeymoon Island's 300 acres are three miles north of Dunedin, at the west end of Florida 586, and west of U.S. 19A, via Dunedin Causeway.

FEATURES   Originally called Hog Island, Honeymoon Island was renamed in 1939 when a developer built 50 honeymoon bungalows, which were enjoyed by lucky couples who won a stay here through a department store contest.

ACTIVITIES   At Caladesi Island, one of the last undeveloped barrier islands, hike the island nature trails, and go boating from the ramp. Private boaters have access to a 99-slip bayside marina, or can anchor offshore to boat camp. Enjoy saltwater fishing, shelling, and swimming in the Gulf of Mexico. Concessions are sold during the summer. No camping or cars are allowed on the island. An annual antique and classic boat show is held in mid-March at the park marina.

At Honeymoon Island, go saltwater fishing, boating from the ramp, and swimming in the Gulf of Mexico. Watch for osprey nests along the island's northern loop trail. An annual catch-and-release snook fishing tournament is held in May. Interpretive programs are offered the first and third Saturdays from January through May.

INFORMATION

Caladesi Island State Park
#1 Causeway Boulevard
Dunedin, Florida 34698
813-469-5918 or 813-469-5942

Honeymoon Island State Recreation
  Area
c/o Gulf Island GEOpark
#1 Causeway Boulevard
Dunedin, Florida 34698
813-469-5942

CAYO COSTA STATE PARK
10

LOCATION   The park's 2,506 acres are accessible by private boat or passenger ferry from Boca Grande, or from a marina on Captiva and Pine Island. It's northwest of Fort Myers and west of Pine Island on La Costa Island. It's bordered by the Gulf of Mexico, Pine Island Sound, and Boca Grande Pass.

From I-75, Exit 26, or U.S. 41, go west to Pine Island on Florida 78, Pine Island Road. A 20-mile drive takes you to the Pine Island Center where Florida 78 and 767 intersect. Turn right to go to Bokeelia.

FEATURES   To reach the island from Bokeelia, take the *Tropic Star*, a 59-passenger vessel. The cruise takes one hour and fifteen minutes. For reservations, call 813-283-1125. A tram or pickup truck takes you the other mile required to reach the park campground.

Cayo Costa is one of the largest undeveloped barrier islands in the state, measuring seven miles long, with 90 percent of the land belonging to the park. It includes miles of beaches and dunes facing the Gulf of Mexico, and is known for its bird life. Watch for osprey and bald eagles nesting on the island, and brown pelican rookeries located on the bay side of the island. Loggerhead sea turtles nest on the island beaches during the summer.

ACTIVITIES   Go seasonal tent camping in one of the primitive 30 sites along the park's Gulf side. Stay overnight in one of 12 rustic year-round cabins. For a reservation, call 813-966-3594 or 813-964-0375. There is no electricity, telephone, or store on the island.

Hike the six miles of nature trails that crisscross a mixture of pine flats and oak and palm hammocks. You can also hike for seven miles along the beach. Hiking inland is not advised because there are no developed trails, and you could encounter alligators, wild pigs, and snakes.

Go swimming and fishing in the Gulf of Mexico, or fish in the deep water of Boca Grande for tarpon, snook and snapper. No fishing license is required for saltwater fishing. Peak fishing season is June and July.

Enjoy boating from the dock or ramp. Overnight docking is available for boating campers and cabin occupants on the bayside only. You can also rent a kayak in Matlacha, from the Gulf Coast Kayak Company. They'll arrange an overnight, or three-day two-night camping trip from October to March. Experienced kayakers can paddle the six miles from Pine Island to Cayo Costa.

Shelling is very good during the winter months, where as many as 396 shell species have been discovered.

In Fort Myers, tour the Edison winter home at 2350 McGregor Blvd. Visit his botanical gardens, with over a thousand plant varieties imported from all over the world. His laboratories and museum contain many of his inventions. For information, call 813-334-3614. In February, Fort Myers honors Thomas Edison with a 10-day "Festival of Lights."

Edison's friend, Henry Ford, lived next door, and his house is also open for tours. Here you'll see some vintage Model T's.

Cap your visit here with a jungle cruise up the Caloosahatchee River. It leaves from the Fort Myers yacht basin, a few miles from the Edison estate. For information, call 800-282-5166.

J. N. "Ding" Darling National Wildlife Refuge is 18 miles west, on Sanibel Island Wildlife Drive. Drive or bike the five-mile road through the mangrove swamp, or follow the canoe or walking trails to get a close-up view of the birds. Climb the bird-watching tower.

Go shelling on the beaches along the Gulf, famous for its numerous specimens. However, no shelling is permitted within the refuge, and no live shells should be taken. Be sure to be on the lookout for alligators and give them a wide berth.

Incoming pilots can land at Page Field, located three miles south of Fort Myers. Rental cars are available.

INFORMATION
Cayo Costa State Park
c/o Barrier Islands GEOpark
P.O. Box 1150
Boca Grande, Florida 33921
813-964-0375

CHEKIKA STATE RECREATION AREA
11

LOCATION   The recreation area is north of Everglades National Park, and 16 miles northwest of Homestead on Southwest 177th Avenue.

FEATURES   Three thousand gallons of clear sulfur water flow from an artesian well and cascades down a waterfall into Lake Chekika.

ACTIVITIES   Go swimming, freshwater fishing, walk the nature trail, or enjoy camping in the 20-site campground. Tour the interpretive center.

Everglades National Park offers a multitude of activities for the visitor to enjoy. Stop by the main visitor center, 10.8 miles southwest of Homestead. The park is a wonderful spot for viewing many birds, including the American bald eagle. The best times to go birding are in the early morning or late afternoon.

Some of the best wildlife viewing spots include the Anhinga Trail where you can see alligators, turtles, and birds, along the half-mile-long boardwalk over Taylor Slough. Eco Pond in Flamingo features alligators and birds along the half-mile trail around the pond. Shark Valley Road offers the opportunity to hike, bike, or take a tram on a 15-mile wildlife journey through the heart of the park. For required reservations, call ahead to 305-221-8455. The trams run from November through May.

The E. J. Hamilton observation tower, south of Everglades City on Florida 29, is 80 feet tall with 180 steps, and provides a bird's-eye view of the alligators, turtles, and wading birds.

Hikers have access to many trails, some less than 1/4 mile in length, to more strenuous ones that are 14 miles long. During the warmer, wetter months, be prepared for the many mosquitoes. Bring along insect repellent, and wear a long-sleeved shirt, long pants, and a head cover.

To walk through a mangrove forest along an elevated boardwalk, go to Eden off the Everglades on Florida 29, two miles south of its junction with U.S. 41. You can also take an airboat ride from here. For airboat information, call 813-695-2800.

Anglers come to fish in both the inland and coastal waters of the Everglades. Go largemouth bass fishing in the freshwater ponds. Saltwater fish include snapper, redfish and trout. A license is required for freshwater fishing, but none is required for saltwater fishing.

Boaters have access to many inland and coastal waterways. Marked canoe trails leading into the mangrove wilderness are near Flamingo, and out of Everglades City. These trails include ones to Noble Hammock and Nine Mile Pond. Canoe rentals and shuttle service are available at Nine Mile Pond. Experienced canoers can travel from Flamingo to Everglades City, requiring 7 to 10 days, or the trip can be done overnight in a small motor boat. Scenic boat tours also depart from Everglades City, from the park docks on Chokoloskee Causeway on Florida 29. For information, call 813-695-2591.

Boaters can explore the shallow waters in Florida Bay. As you cruise through the area, watch out for manatees while boating in their habitat. Boat rentals are available. If you prefer, you can take a guided boat tour from Flamingo to explore the mangrove wilderness and Florida Bay. Other sightseeing boats go into the Ten Thousand Islands area, and depart from the Gulf Coast Ranger Station. For information, call 1-800-233-1821 (out-of-state), or 1-800-445-7724 in Florida.

Go camping in one of the campgrounds. No hookups are available. You can also camp in the backcountry, accessible via boat, on foot, and on bicycles, or stay overnight in the Flamingo Lodge Motel. For reservations, call 305-253-2241 or 813-695-3101.

From Flamingo, you can go hiking, or rent a bicycle from November through April, to take a self-guided bicycle tour. For a narrated boat tour or tram tour, call 305-253-2241.

Everglades Park information is available by calling 305-247-6211.

Incoming pilots can land at Homestead General Aviation Airport, located four miles northwest of Homestead. Rental cars are available.

INFORMATION
Chekika State Recreation Area
P.O. Box 1313
Homestead, Florida 33030
305-242-7700

COLLIER-SEMINOLE STATE PARK
12

FAKAHATCHEE STRAND STATE PRESERVE
13

LOCATION   Collier-Seminole State Park's 6,423 acres are 17 miles southeast of Naples, off U.S. 41 on the historic Tamiami Trail. From I-75, take Exit 15, go west on Florida 951 to U.S. 41, and then go south for approximately eight more miles. It's within the Big Cypress Swamp, and borders the Cape Romano/Ten Thousand Islands' aquatic preserve.

Fakahatchee Strand is 16 miles east of Collier-Seminole off Florida 29 at Copeland. Take Florida 29 approximately three miles north of the U.S. 41/Florida 29 intersection. The Strand's headquarters are on Janes Memorial Scenic Drive.

FEATURES   Collier-Seminole was named for an early settler, Barron Collier, and for the Seminole Indians. It contains some of the state's most dense jungle, and extensive mangrove swamps. Some of the final campaigns of the Second Seminole War were conducted near here, and a replica of a U.S. blockhouse has been erected in the park. A "walking dredge," used to build the Tamiami Trail in the 1920s, is also on display.

Collier-Seminole State Park (photo by Vici DeHaan)

The Fakahatchee Strand is the largest of many strands, or long draining channels, found in the Big Cypress Swamp. It's approximately 20 miles long and three to four miles wide, and features 44 species of orchids, plus the only known mix of bald cypress and royal palms to be found anywhere in the world.

ACTIVITIES   If you come to Collier-Seminole State Park during the summer, be prepared with plenty of insect repellent. Take either a self-guided or naturalist conducted walk along the 1,100-foot catwalk through the mangrove swamps. You can also hike a 6.5-mile trail through the pine flatwoods and cypress swamps. Camp year-round in the campground with 130 sites, 67 sites with water and electrical hookups.

The interpretive center is housed in a replica of an 1840s blockhouse. Attend Saturday campfire slide shows and nature walks, interpretive programs presented on Friday, and Sunday canoe trips offered from January through Easter. The park's observation platform provides a good look at the spoonbills, bald eagles, wood storks, and other area birds.

Enjoy a 13.5-mile round trip in a canoe to the northernmost tip of Ten Thousand Islands. Canoe rentals are available. If you're here in January and February, take a conducted canoe trip into the mangrove swamp and estuary bordering the Ten Thousand Islands on the Gulf Coast.

Go boating from the ramp on the Blackwater River that provides access to the Ten Thousand Islands and the Gulf of Mexico. Take a boat tour to see the sawgrass prairies and mangrove wilderness. Go fishing for snook, mangrove snapper, and redfish in the rivers and bays.

At Fakahatchee Strand, enjoy birding, and walk along the 2,000-foot boardwalk located seven miles west of the preserve on U.S. 41. Arrange for a three-hour guided walk through the swamps and cypress trees. Since you'll be wading through the forest and pondapple sloughs, wear long pants, waterproof footwear, and insect repellent. Reservations must be made one week in advance. Call 941-695-4593.

Arriving pilots can land at Naples Municipal Airport, located two miles northeast of the city. Rental cars are available.

INFORMATION

Collier-Seminole State Park
20,200 East Tamiami Trail
Route 4, Box 84B
Naples, Florida 33961
941-394-3397
941-642-8898:
    Boat tour information

Fakahatchee Strand State Preserve
P.O. Box 548
Copeland, Florida 33926
941-695-4593

CRYSTAL RIVER
STATE ARCHEOLOGICAL SITE
14

LOCATION   Crystal River State Archeological Site is 2.5 miles northwest of Crystal River, off U.S. 19/98, on North Museum Point.

FEATURES   The 14-acre park, a National Historic Landmark, contains the most important pre-Columbian Indian mounds in the state, dating from approximately 200 B.C. The area was used as an Indian ceremonial center for 1,600 years. Over 450 burial sites indicate that the local tribes traded with Indian tribes north of the Ohio River.

ACTIVITIES   Tour the park museum, with its glass wall for viewing a temple, burial and refuse mounds. Hike the park trails to get a close-up look at the entire site.

INFORMATION
Crystal River State Archeological Site
3400 North Museum Point
Crystal River, Florida 34428
904-795-3817

DADE BATTLEFIELD STATE HISTORIC SITE

WITHLACOOCHEE STATE FOREST

WITHLACOOCHEE STATE TRAIL
15

LOCATION   Dade Battlefield State Historic Site is 1.5 miles east of Bushnell off I-75, Exit 63 on Florida 48, and west of Florida 301 on Battlefield Drive.

Withlacoochee State Forest's 113,000 acres are in central Florida, west and south of Bushnell.

Withlacoochee State Trail is on Croom Rital Road, starting north of Florida 50, one mile east of I-75 in Ridge Manor.

FEATURES   Dade's 80-acre park was set aside as a memorial to Major Francis L. Dade and his troops, ambushed here by the Seminole Indians and runaway slaves on December 28, 1835. This ambush led to the seven-year Seminole War, when the Indians were forced to leave their lands for relocation in the West.

ACTIVITIES   At Dade Battlefield State Historic Site, bring along a picnic to enjoy, and play tennis. Hike the interpretive trail, marking the military road where you can see a reproduction of the log breastworks utilized in the battle. Tour the interpretive center to see artifacts and exhibits. An annual commemorative battle reenactment is held the end of December.

At Withlacoochee State Forest, go horseback riding, with rentals available. Enjoy camping in the campground. Go boating from the ramp, with rentals available. Enjoy fishing and swimming.

Withlacoochee State Trail extends for over 40 miles, and is enjoyed by hikers, bikers with mountain bikes, and equestrians. It passes through the state forest, over hardwood hammocks, near the Withlacoochee River, and continues on through Floral City, Inverness, Citrus Springs, and ends south of Dunnellon at Gulf Junction.

Dade City, south of Bushnell on U.S. 301, has many azaleas which bloom in the spring. Stop by St. Leo Abbey, located on the grounds of St. Leo College. This Benedictine abbey has a Pilgrim Center patterned after the Lourdes Grotto.

INFORMATION

Dade Battlefield State Historic Site
Withlacoochee State Forest
P.O. Box 938
Bushnell, Florida 33513
904-793-4781

Withlacoochee State Trail
12549 State Park Drive
Clermont, Florida 34711
904-394-2280

DEAD LAKES STATE RECREATION AREA
16

LOCATION   The state recreation area's 83 acres are one mile north of Wewahitchka, on Florida 71.

FEATURES   The area was named for the thousands of dead cypress, oak, and pine trees that drowned when the Apalachicola River blocked the Chipola River, creating a floodplain.

ACTIVITIES   Enjoy year-round camping in the 29-site campground, 10 sites with electrical hookups. Hike the nature trails, and go boating from ramp. Go fishing for bream, bass, and other freshwater fish.

INFORMATION

Dead Lakes State Recreation Area
P.O. Box 989
Wewahitchka, Florida 32465
904-639-2702

DeLEON SPRINGS STATE RECREATION AREA
17

LOCATION The park's 441 acres are one mile south of Ponce DeLeon Springs on Florida 181, and off U.S. 17 at the corner of Ponce DeLeon and Burt Parks Road. It's five miles north of DeLand.

FEATURES The park's main spring has two flows coming out of a limestone cavity, producing 14 million gallons of crystal clear water on a daily basis. This water then runs into the Choctawatchee River and on to the Gulf of Mexico.

ACTIVITIES Hike the nature trails, and go boating from ramp, with boat and canoe rentals available. Enjoy freshwater fishing, swimming, scuba diving, and snorkeling, in the year-round 68 degree water of DeLeon Springs. Concessions are available. You can also dine in the Old Spanish Sugar Mill Restaurant.

In DeLand, attend presentations offered in the Cultural Arts Center, located ½ mile north of the intersection of U.S. 17/92 and Florida 44, at 600 North Woodland Boulevard. For information, call 904-736-7232.

Arriving pilots can land at DeLand Municipal–Sidney H. Taylor Field, located three miles northeast of DeLand. Rental cars are available.

INFORMATION
DeLeon Springs State Recreation Area
P.O. Box 1338
DeLeon Springs, Florida 32130
904-985-4212

DELNOR-WIGGINS PASS
STATE RECREATION AREA
18

LOCATION The state park's 166 acres are 11 miles northwest of Naples off Florida 846, and six miles south of Bonita Springs, off U.S. 41 on County Road 901.

FEATURES The recreation area is a narrow barrier island located on the state's southwest coast. A pass on the north end of the island serves as a natural outlet for the Cocohatchee River.

ACTIVITIES Enjoy shell gathering and turtle watching during nesting season. Climb the observation tower. Hike the nature trails and boardwalks, and go boating from the ramp. Go saltwater fishing and swimming in the Gulf of Mexico. Attend an interpretive program, presented on Friday mornings from December through March. These programs include guided beach walks, cast netting, salt-water fishing, and since group sizes are limited, reservations are required.

Arriving pilots can land at Naples Municipal Airport, located two miles north-east of the city. Rental cars are available.

INFORMATION
Delnor-Wiggins Pass State Recreation Area
11100 Gulf Shore Drive North
Naples, Florida 33963
941-597-6196

DEVIL'S MILLHOPPER
STATE GEOLOGICAL SITE

SAN FELASCO HAMMOCK STATE PRESERVE
19

LOCATION   The site is two miles northwest of Gainesville on Millhopper Road, Florida 232.

FEATURES   Devil's Millhopper is registered as a National Natural Land-mark because of the fossil shark teeth, marine shells, and fossilized remains of the land animals found in the sink. The site features a sinkhole 120 feet deep and 500 feet across, that formed 10,000 years ago when an underground cavern collapsed.

ACTIVITIES   Walk the 1/2-mile path that circles the sinkhole, and descend the 232 winding stairs to reach its bottom. A geological formation is on display. Take a guided tour on Saturdays at 10:00 A.M. Tour the interpretive center, and watch the audiovisual program to learn more about sinkholes.

Tour the Fred Bear Museum located 1/4 mile west of the site, on Archer Road. Here you'll see many of the big game animals he bagged as he traveled all over the world. It's closed Monday and Tuesday. For information, call 904-376-2411.

San Felasco Hammock State Preserve is four miles northwest of Gainesville on Florida 232. Hike the nature trail into the preserve, or explore the three- to 10-mile loops along the hard-packed dirt. Participate in naturalist-guided hikes and horseback rides, offered weekends from October through April, upon request. To make required reservations, call 904-336-2008 or 904-462-7905.

Tour the Kanapaha Botanical Gardens at 4625 Southwest 63rd Boulevard, and stroll through its various plant and flower gardens. For information, call 904-372-4981.

Arriving pilots can land at Gainesville Regional Airport, located three miles northeast of the city. Rental cars are available.

INFORMATION
Devil's Millhopper State Geological Site
San Felasco Hammock State Preserve
4732 Millhopper Road
Gainesville, Florida 32609
904-336-2008

EDWARD BALL WAKULLA SPRINGS STATE PARK
20

LOCATION   The park is 14 miles south of Tallahassee, and ½ mile east of Wakulla Springs, at the intersection of Florida 61 and 267.

FEATURES   Wakulla is Indian meaning "mysterious waters." It's one of the world's largest and deepest natural springs, pumping out 400,000 gallons of water every minute at a constant temperature of 70 degrees. The sandy bottom of the spring area is 185 feet deep, and clearly visible from a glass-bottomed boat.

Its 4½-acre lagoon has been used as a setting in motion pictures including several early *Tarzan* films, *Creature from the Black Lagoon,* and *Airport 77.*

ACTIVITIES   The park covers 2,860 acres. Enjoy hiking the nature trails, and go bicycling along the bicycle trails. Stay overnight in the 27-room Wakulla Springs Lodge, and dine in the dining room. Take a ranger-guided, glass-bottomed boat tour over the spring to see many fish, marine plants, and mastodon bones. Watch a sight-and-sound film tour of the underwater world. Swimming and snorkeling are enjoyed in a designated area near the head spring.

Enjoy a 30-minute jungle boat tour down the wild and scenic Wakulla River. Twilight cruises with dinner are offered when the moon is full. Enjoy great bird watching, with 2,000 waterfowl arriving during the winter. Follow the "Walk of the Champions" to see one of the park's champion magnolia trees.

In March, attend the Battle of Natural Bridge reenactment at the Natural Bridge State Historic Site, six miles east of Woodville off Florida 363. The battle was fought in 1865 to prevent Union troops from capturing the state's capitol at Tallahassee. While there, you can also enjoy fishing and picnicking. For information, call 904-922-6007.

Attend the Stephen C. Smith Memorial Regatta the last weekend in April in Wakulla.

Arriving pilots can land at Tallahassee Regional Airport, located four miles southwest of the city. Rental cars are available.

INFORMATION
Edward Ball Wakulla Springs State Park
1 Wakulla Springs Road
Wakulla Springs, Florida 32305
904-224-5950: lodge reservations
904-922-3633: park

EGMONT KEY STATE PARK
21

LOCATION   The park is at the mouth of Tampa Bay, southwest of Fort DeSoto Beach. Access is via private boat only.

FEATURES   Egmont Key is the site of the only manned U.S. lighthouse, and is now a wildlife refuge. It once served as a camp for captured Seminoles during the Third Seminole War, and served as a Union Navy base during the Civil War.

ACTIVITIES   At Egmont, enjoy swimming, boating and fishing in Tampa Bay.

Fort DeSoto Park is located eight miles from I-275, Exit 4 at Pinellas Bayway. Fort DeSoto is located on the southern end of Mullet Key. In the park, you can enjoy camping in the 235-site campground, all sites providing electrical and water hookups. Groceries are available. Enjoy picnicking, boating from the ramp, fishing and swimming. For information, call 813-866-2484.

In St. Petersburg, attend the Festival of States in late March or early April, with waterfront fireworks, a car rally, and parade. Triathletes come in late April for the St. Anthony's Tampa Bay Triathlon. Attend Shakespeare's plays in early May. A sandcastle contest is featured in June, and a lighted boat parade occurs on the waterfront in mid-December.

For a cruise aboard a sidewheeler, the rivership *Grand Romance,* is located four miles east of I-4, Exit 51, at the Monroe Harbor Marina. For required reservations, call 407-321-5091. Other cruises are available along the St. Johns River located three miles east of St. Petersburg on Florida 415. For reservations, call 407-330-1612.

Arriving pilots can land at St. Petersburg–Clearwater International Airport, located eight miles north of the city, or at Albert Whitted Municipal Airport, located east of the city. Rental cars are available at both airports.

INFORMATION
Egmont Key State Park
Slip 656, 4275 34th Street South
St. Petersburg, Florida 35711
813-893-2627

FALLING WATERS STATE RECREATION AREA
22

LOCATION   The area's 155 acres are three miles south of Chipley, off Florida 77A.

FEATURES   The park is named for its 67-foot waterfall that drops from Falling Waters Sink, a 100-foot deep, 20-foot wide, pit.

ACTIVITIES   Enjoy camping in the 24-site campground, all sites with water hookups and 16 with electrical hookups. Hike the nature trails through unique plant and geological park formations, and go swimming, and freshwater fishing in the lake.

From March through May, come to see the beautiful flowering dogwood trees and wild azaleas. Also in May, attend the Historic Day celebration where you can experience early Florida folklife through demonstrations of traditional trades and crafts. Observe encampments of the Creek and Seminole Indians, and Civil War soldiers.

INFORMATION
Falling Waters State Recreation Area
Route 5, Box 660
Chipley, Florida 32428
904-638-6130

FLORIDA CAVERNS STATE PARK
23

LOCATION   The park's 1,280 acres are three miles north of Marianna, off Florida 166.

FEATURES   Seawater once covered the state, and after withdrawing millions of years ago, the peninsula was left exposed. Rain then seeped through the limestone and filled the cavities beneath the surface. When the groundwater level dropped below the level of the cavities, they dried out to become a labyrinth of caves. Approximately 23 underground caves have been mapped, with more than 30 surface holes remaining to be explored. Indians are thought to have used the mouths of the caves for shelter over 1,000 years ago.

ACTIVITIES   Take a tour of the caverns located 65 feet below the surface of the earth. Spelunkers are permitted to explore other park caves on their own, and the park service sponsors several spelunking tours for experienced explorers each year.

The park also features a natural bridge with a disappearing river, and a beach of white sand surrounding the 70-degree water in Blue Hole Springs. Enjoy playing golf, and go seasonal camping in the 32-site campground, with water and electrical hookups, and a dump station.

Hike the nature trails, go boating from the ramp, with rentals available, and enjoy pan fishing and swimming in the Chipola River. Tour the interpretive center.

You can also go horseback riding from the stables along equestrian trails, with overnight facilities available. Go canoeing on a section of the 50-mile Cipola River Canoe Trail, which is part of the larger Florida Canoe Trail System.

INFORMATION
Florida Caverns State Park
3345 Caverns Road
Marianna, Florida 32446
904-482-9598

FORT CLINCH STATE PARK
24

LOCATION   The park is on the northern end of Amelia Island at 2601 Atlantic Avenue, two miles east of Fernandina Beach on Florida A1A.

FEATURES   The brick and masonry fort was begun in 1847, but was abandoned by the Confederates and used by Union forces during the Civil War. The fort is one of the best preserved relics from the war. It was abandoned following the development of more powerful armament.

ACTIVITIES   The park covers 1,153 acres. Hike the nature trails, and go fishing for bass in St. Mary's River. Enjoy boating from the ramp, swimming, and surf and pier fishing in the Atlantic Ocean. Go seasonal camping in the 62-site campground, with water and electrical hookups, and a trailer dump station.

Tour the interpretive center, and take a guided tour of the restored fort, where you can observe rangers garbed in Union uniforms perform the daily chores once performed by soldiers stationed here during the Civil War in 1864. A reenactment of its Civil War–era operation is presented from January through April, and again in June. In May, a Union garrison reenactment is presented.

Candlelight tours are offered after sundown on Saturdays in March and April, and on Fridays and Saturdays in May and June. Reservations are required. Call 904-277-7274. From April through June at 10:00 A.M., take a guided walk on the Willow Pond nature trail.

Fernandina Beach's downtown section, Centre Street, has restored buildings from the 1850s, featuring many Tiffany windows, gables, and turrets.

Arriving pilots can land at Fernandina Beach Municipal Airport, located three miles south of the city. Rental cars are available.

INFORMATION
Fort Clinch State Park
2601 Atlantic Avenue
Fernandina Beach Florida 32034
904-261-4212

FORT COOPER STATE PARK
25

LOCATION   The state park's 707 acres are off U.S. 41 southeast of Inverness, off Old Floral City Road. Take Florida 44 off I-75.

FEATURES   The park was named for Major Mark Anthony Cooper, who commanded five companies of the First Georgia Battalion of Volunteers fighting in the Second Seminole War.

ACTIVITIES   Tour the fort, where a reenactment of the war is presented the first weekend in March. Hike 10 miles of self-guided nature trails, and go horseback riding along the equestrian trails. Go freshwater fishing, and swimming in Lake Holathilikaha. Enjoy canoeing, with canoe and paddleboat rentals available. No boats with motors are permitted.

Arriving pilots can land at Inverness Airport, located two miles southeast of the city. Rental cars are available.

INFORMATION
Fort Cooper State Park
3100 Old Floral City Road
Inverness, Florida 32650
904-726-0315

FORT GADSDEN STATE PARK
26

LOCATION   The park's 78 acres are six miles southwest of Sumatra on Florida 65.

ACTIVITIES   Hike the nature trails, go freshwater fishing, and tour the museum.

INFORMATION
Fort Gadsden State Park
Sumatra, Florida
904-670-8988

FORT PIERCE INLET
STATE RECREATION AREA
27

LOCATION   The park's 1,014 acres are on a barrier island in the Atlantic Ocean, four miles east of Fort Pierce on Florida A1A via North Causeway.

FEATURES   The island consists of an Atlantic beach, sand dunes, and a coastal hammock.

ACTIVITIES   Hike the nature trails, and go boating from ramp, with rentals available. Enjoy saltwater fishing, swimming, scuba diving, snorkeling, and tour the visitor center. Watch for shorebirds at low tide along Dynamite Point. Along the south beach, the fishing jetty is the state's longest, where anglers catch snook, sea trout, and bass. Bike the bicycle trail.

Jack Island on the Intracoastal Waterway is a bird watcher's mecca.

Arriving pilots can land at St. Lucie County International Airport, located three miles northwest of Fort Pierce. Rental cars are available.

INFORMATION
Fort Pierce Inlet State Recreation Area
905 Shorewinds Drive
Fort Pierce, Florida 34949
305-468-3985

FORT ZACHARY TAYLOR
STATE HISTORIC SITE
28

LOCATION   The state historic site's 78 acres are at the southwest end of Key West, via Southard Street in the Truman Annex.

FEATURES   The three-story-high fort was constructed in 1845 to fortify the entrance to the island's natural harbor. When the Civil War broke out in 1861, the action of Captain John Brannan put the fort and Key West into Union hands, where they remained throughout the Civil War. The fort was reactivated during the Spanish-American War and updated in the 20th century. It's now listed on the National Registry of Historic Places, designated as a National Historic Landmark because it contains the largest collection of Civil War cannons in the U.S.

ACTIVITIES   Key West is the only frost-free place in the U.S. Its lowest temperature was recorded in 1886, when it was 40 degrees F.

Enjoy saltwater fishing along the deep water channel, and snorkeling and swimming in the ocean. Tour the interpretive center to see its artifacts. Take a guided tour of the site offered daily at 12 noon and 2 P.M. Its beach is one of the largest in Key West. Concessions are available at the end of Southard Street.

Living-history weekends are held the last weekend of the month from January through June. Observe Civil War garrison life with period drills, work details, mortar, and cannon firing. An annual reenactment of the outbreak of the war is held in late January.

In Key West, tour the Curry Mansion at 511 Caroline Street. Registered as a National Register Landmark, the mansion has Tiffany glass and beautiful woodwork. Tour the 22 rooms filled with antiques. For information, call 305-294-5349.

Ernest Hemingway's home and museum are at 907 Whitehead Street. Now a Registered National Landmark, Hemingway lived here from 1931 to 1961 where he wrote 75 percent of his works. He built Key West's first swimming pool. The home is open daily from 9 to 5. Many cats and kittens still live here, a living memorial to the author who was known as a cat lover. For information, call 305-294-1575.

Tour Wrecker's Museum at 322 Duval Street. It's housed in the oldest house in Key West, circa 1829, and features wrecking history, ship models, and miniature conch houses. For information, call 305-294-9502.

Take a 1.5-hour narrated trolley ride aboard the Old Town Trolley in Key West, starting from 1910 North Roosevelt Boulevard. For information, call 305-296-6688. Tour the Audubon house and gardens built in the early 1800s. Its museum has period antiques, Audubon's original engravings and a video tape presentation. For information, call 305-294-2116.

Watch the wharf dolphin show in the natural ocean lagoon. For information, call 305-294-8882.

Hemingway Days Festival is held in July, and the Fantasy Fest and Marlin Tournament are in October.

Fly aboard a seaplane to the Fort Jefferson National Monument, located 70 miles off Key West in the Gulf of Mexico. The Civil War–era military fort is the largest brick fortification in the Western world. The fort is open daily during daylight hours. Enjoy swimming, snorkeling, scuba diving, picnicking, and bird watching. Camping is permitted in the grassy picnic area, but no drinking water is available. Thousands of sooty terns and brown noddy terns nest on Bush Key, and many migrating birds rest inside the fort. For reservations, call 305-294-6978.

Arriving pilots can land at Key West International Airport, located two miles east of the city. Rental cars are available.

INFORMATION
Fort Zachary Taylor State Historic Site
P.O. Box 289
Key West, Florida 33041
305-292-6713

GAMBLE PLANTATION
STATE HISTORIC SITE
29

LOCATION   The mansion is at 3708 Patten Avenue in Ellenton, five miles northeast of Bradenton on U.S. 301.

FEATURES   The Gamble Plantation's mansion was home to Major Robert Gamble, and served as headquarters for his extensive sugar plantation, which stretched 3,500 acres along the Manatee River. It's the only antebellum plantation house still surviving in southern Florida.

ACTIVITIES   Take a guided tour of the house, furnished in the style of the mid 19th century. See the bed with supporting ropes that could be loosened or tightened by the occupant, leading to the expression, "sleep tight." Guests originally stayed here for a month since the boat only came that often. The site is open Thursday through Monday, from 9 to 5. Bring along a picnic to enjoy.

Arriving pilots can land at Sarasota/Bradenton Airport, located three miles north of the city. Rental cars are available.

INFORMATION
Gamble Plantation State Historic Site
3708 Patten Avenue
Ellenton, Florida 34222
813-723-4536

GAMBLE ROGERS MEMORIAL STATE RECREATION AREA AT FLAGLER BEACH
30

LOCATION   Flagler Beach is bordered by the Atlantic Ocean and the Intracoastal Waterway. The beach is ½ mile south of Flagler Beach on Florida A1A, and north of Daytona Beach.

ACTIVITIES   Go camping year-round in the 34-site campground, with water and electrical hookups, and a dumping station. Hike the nature trails, and enjoy boating from the ramp. Go saltwater fishing, swimming, scuba diving, and snorkeling in the Atlantic Ocean. Enjoy birding where shore birds come to feed in the area's tidal ponds, and observe the sea turtles who come to lay their eggs during the summer.

INFORMATION
Gamble Rogers Memorial State Recreation Area at Flagler Beach
3100 South A1A
Flagler Beach, Florida 32036
904-439-2474

GASPARILLA ISLAND STATE RECREATION AREA

DON PEDRO ISLAND STATE RECREATION AREA

31

LOCATION   Gasparilla Island State Park's 144 acres are three miles south of Placida on Florida 775. It's approximately nine miles south of Englewood, on the south end of Gasparilla Island. Access is via the Boca Grande Causeway, at Florida 775 and Placida.

Don Pedro Island State Recreation Area's 115 acres are accessible by private boat or ferry from Placida. This barrier island is between Knight Island and Little Gasparilla Island.

FEATURES   The Boca Grande Lighthouse is listed as a National Historic Landmark, and was instrumental in guiding boats through Boca Grande Pass almost a century ago, after the Lighthouse Act was signed by George Washington on August 7, 1789.

Gasparilla Island is reportedly named for the infamous pirate, Jose Gaspar, who hid here during the 1700s while making his forays. The island, like Don Pedro's Island, is a barrier island.

ACTIVITIES   At Gasparilla, tour the interpretive center. Go fishing, swimming, and shelling along the Gulf of Mexico, especially during the winter months. Take a beach walk through the mangroves. Call for the dates of the lighthouse open houses.

At Don Pedro, hike the nature trails, and go shelling, boating, saltwater fishing, and swimming in the Gulf of Mexico.

INFORMATION
Don Pedro Island State Recreation Area
Gasparilla Island State Recreation Area
c/o Barrier Islands GEOpark
P.O. Box 1150
Boca Grande, Florida 33921
813-964-0375

GENERAL JAMES A. VAN FLEET
STATE TRAIL
32

LOCATION   The trail is located off I-4, on Florida 33 and 655, in Polk City.

FEATURES   The 29-mile Van Fleet Trail that passes through the Green Swamp, was originally a railroad track.

ACTIVITIES   Hikers, bicyclists, and equestrians can begin from the Mabel, Bay Lake, Green Pond, and Polk City trailheads.

INFORMATION
General James A. Van Fleet State Trail
12549 State Park Drive
Clermont, Florida 34711
904-394-2280

GRAYTON BEACH STATE RECREATION AREA
33

LOCATION   Grayton Beach is next to the village of Grayton Beach on Florida 30-A, south of U.S. 98 on the Gulf of Mexico.

FEATURES   The area has 356 acres of sea oats and white quartz sand, towering barrier dunes, and Gulf waters that border inland salt marshes, freshwater lakes, and pine forests. Grayton Beach is one of the Panhandle's oldest communities, dating back to the mid-1880s.

In 1995, when the University of Maryland conducted a survey of 650 of the nation's beaches, Grayton Beach was ranked number one.

ACTIVITIES   Go seasonal camping in the 37-site campground, all sites with water and electrical hookups, a dumping station, and groceries available during the summer. Attend summer campfire interpretive programs.

Hike the nature trail winding through the 35-foot-high sea oat-covered sand dunes, pine flatwoods, and salt marshes, where you can see the effects of hundreds of years of wind sculpting.

Go fishing for bass, redfish, trout, bream, and bluegill in Western Lake. Enjoy saltwater fishing, swimming, water-skiing, scuba diving, and snorkeling in the Gulf of Mexico.

Tour the Eden State Ornamental Gardens located in Point Washington, five miles from Grayton on Choctawhatchee Bay, and one mile north of U.S. 98 on Florida 395. You can see 11 acres of landscaped grounds, and tour the restored Greek Revival Mansion, circa 1898. Tours are offered Thursday through Monday. For information, call 904-231-4214.

INFORMATION
Grayton Beach State Recreation Area
Route 2, Box 6600
Santa Rosa Beach, Florida 32459
904-231-4210

HENDERSON BEACH
STATE RECREATION AREA
34

LOCATION   The area is east of Destin on U.S. 98.
ACTIVITIES   Walk along boardwalks providing beach access. Enjoy swimming and surf fishing. The beaches provide a habitat for black skimmers, brown pelicans, and the protected sea turtle.

Arriving pilots can land at Destin–Fort Walton Beach Airport, located one mile east of Destin. Rental cars are available.
INFORMATION
Henderson Beach State Recreation Area
17000 Emerald Coast Parkway
Destin, Florida 32541
904-837-7550

HIGHLANDS HAMMOCK STATE PARK
35

LOCATION   The park is 3.5 miles west of U.S. 27/98 on Florida 634, and six miles west of Sebring.
FEATURES   The 4,694-acre park features steamy jungles, cypress swamps, and a tropical wilderness. It was established to preserve the virgin hardwood forest, called a hammock. Trees range in age from over 400 years to almost 1,000 years old.
ACTIVITIES   The park covers 3,800 acres. Go seasonal camping in the 138-site campground, 70 sites with water hookups, and 113 with electrical hookups. It has a laundry, limited groceries, and a trailer dump station. You can also stay in the primitive campground.

Hike 11 miles of marked nature trails and catwalks, past rare orchids and wild alligators.

One of the park trails passes through a fern garden, another through an orange grove, and still another through an ancient hammock. One of the most popular trails follows a catwalk through a cypress swamp.

Rent a bicycle to ride the paved loop drive through the hammock. Equestrians have access to horse trails. Tour the interpretive center, and pick up a snack at the concession stand, which is open summers. Take a wildlife tour offered daily on the park's "trackless tram." Park rangers offer guided nature walks and campfire slide programs from November through April.

Arriving pilots can land at Sebring Regional Airport, located six miles southeast of the city. Rental cars are available.

INFORMATION
Highlands Hammock State Park
5931 Hammock Road
Route 1, Box 310
Sebring, Florida 33872
941-386-6094

HILLSBOROUGH RIVER STATE PARK
36

LOCATION   The park's 2,990 acres are six miles southwest of Zephyrhills off U.S. 301, and 20 miles northeast of Tampa.

ACTIVITIES   Attend the living history program. Enjoy year-round camping in the 118-site campground, 76 sites with water and electrical hookups, and a trailer dump station. Campfire programs are presented December through April.

Enjoy hiking eight miles of nature trails through the hammocks which border the Hillsborough River. Go boating from the ramp, with canoe and boat rentals available. Go swimming in the pool, and bass fishing in the Hillsborough River. Ride the bicycle trails. Concessions are sold during the summer.

Tour reconstructed Fort Foster, which was utilized during the Second Seminole War and watch its living history programs of life from 1837, presented by costumed interpreters. Tours are provided Saturdays, Sundays, and holidays.

Visit Ybor City State Museum in Tampa, at 9th and 19th Street. From 1886 to the 1930s, Ybor City was known as the "Cigar Capital of the World." Today you can tour La Casita, the restored cigar worker's house, Tuesday through Saturday. For information, call 813-247-6323.

Arriving pilots can land at Zephryhills Municipal Airport, located one mile southeast of the city. Rental cars are available.

INFORMATION
Hillsborough River State Park
15402 U.S. 301 North
Thonotasassa, Florida 33592
813-987-6771

HOMOSASSA SPRINGS STATE WILDLIFE PARK

YULEE SUGAR MILL RUINS STATE HISTORIC SITE

37

LOCATION   Homosassa Springs State Wildlife Park is in Homosassa Springs. Its entrance is in town, ¾ mile west of U.S. 19. Turn west at the traffic light onto Hall's River Road, then go left at the fork in the road to Fishbowl Drive.

Yulee Sugar Mill Ruins is on Florida 490, 2.5 miles west of U.S. 19/98, via Florida 490A and Fish Bowl Drive in Homosassa.

FEATURES   Homosassa Spring is the source of the Homosassa River, and it produces millions of gallons of water hourly, at a temperature of 75 degrees Fahrenheit. Both saltwater and freshwater fish live in the spring, and may be observed through a floating glass observatory.

Yulee Sugar Mill was once run by 1,000 slaves, and operated for 13 years. It supplied sugar for the southern troops during the Civil War.

ACTIVITIES   Homosassa Springs focuses on its wildlife, particularly the manatee, American alligator, and American crocodiles. Programs on these animals are presented three times daily.

You can take a scenic boat tour of Pepper Creek, offered daily between 10:00 and 4:00. A snack bar is located near the park entrance. Hike the park's nature trails, where you can see animals, both in wetlands and hammock environments. Many animals are brought here to be restored to health.

Yulee Sugar Mill Ruins State Historic Site, constructed in 1851, was part of a 5,100-acre plantation, but now it's only a ruin. Come to enjoy a picnic.

INFORMATION

Homosassa Springs
   State Wildlife Park
9225 West Fishbowl Drive
Homosassa, Florida 34448
904-628-5343 or 628-2311

Yulee Sugar Mill Ruins
   State Historic Site
c/o Crystal River State
   Archeological Site
3400 North Museum Point
Crystal River, Florida 34428
904-795-3817

HUGH TAYLOR BIRCH
STATE RECREATION AREA

JOHN U. LLOYD BEACH
STATE RECREATION AREA
38

LOCATION   Hugh Taylor Birch State Recreation Area is in Fort Lauderdale, at Sunrise Boulevard and Florida A1A. It lies between the Atlantic Ocean and the Intracoastal Waterway.

John U. Lloyd Beach State Recreation Area is three miles south of Fort Lauderdale, and northeast of Dania on Florida A1A.

ACTIVITIES   At Hugh Taylor Birch State Park, hike the nature trails, go boating from the ramp, with canoe rentals available, saltwater fishing, and swimming in the Atlantic Ocean. Concessions are available during the summer. Keep in shape on the 1.7-mile exercise course.

At John U. Lloyd State Park, hike the nature trails, go boating from the ramp on the Intracoastal Waterway, with rentals available. Enjoy fishing from rock jetties, surf casting, swimming, scuba diving, and snorkeling. Purchase a snack. Nearby Dania Beach features a 2-mile strip of public beach.

In Fort Lauderdale you can take a cruise from the Bahia Mar Marina through the Everglades, or along the Intracoastal Waterway. The Voyager Sightseeing Train completes four, 18-mile daily tours through the city.

Flamingo Gardens is west of the city via Florida 84 and 823. Take a tram ride through its natural jungle hammock.

Arriving pilots can land at Fort Lauderdale Executive Airport, located five miles north of the city, or at Fort Lauderdale Hollywood International Airport, three miles southwest of the city. Rental cars are available at both airports.

INFORMATION

Hugh Taylor Birch State Recreation Area	John U. Lloyd Beach State Recreation Area
3109 East Sunrise Boulevard	6503 North Ocean Drive
Fort Lauderdale, Florida 33304	Dania, Florida 33004
305-564-4521	305-923-2833

ICHETUCKNEE SPRINGS STATE PARK

OLUSTEE BATTLEFIELD

STATE HISTORIC SITE

39

LOCATION   Ichetucknee Springs is 20 miles southwest of Lake City off Florida 27, four miles northwest of Fort White. It's off Florida 47 and 238, and ½ mile east of Hildreth.

Olustee Battlefield is on U.S. 90, 15 miles east of Lake City.

FEATURES   Ichetucknee Park's springs produce 233 million gallons of water daily, which empties into the Ichetucknee River. Its head spring is a National Natural Landmark.

Olustee Battlefield commemorates Florida's only major Civil War battle. Union troops arrived on February 6, 1864. A battle ensued 2½ miles east of Olustee, forcing the Union forces to retreat from the area to Jacksonville.

ACTIVITIES   Ichetucknee Springs State Park covers 2,241 acres. Hike the nature trails, rent a canoe to go canoeing, or an inner tube to float downstream. A free shuttle operates from May 1 through Labor Day. Enjoy swimming, exploring an underwater cave in Ichetucknee Springs, tour the visitor center, and purchase a snack.

From October through March, take a moonlight canoe trip to see the animals of the night. Reservations are required. On the second Saturday of each month, from October through March, take a sunrise canoe trip, for which reservations are also required.

At Olustee Battlefield, tour the interpretive center (closed Tuesday and Wednesday). A reenactment of the battle is held every February. Observe colors ceremonies, medical unit demonstrations, artillery demonstrations, and infantry drilling.

In Lake City, visit the Florida Sports Hall of Fame, located ¼ mile west of town on U.S. 90 from I-75, and then another ¼ mile north on the Hall of Fame Drive. For information, call 904-758-1312.

Arriving pilots can land at Lake City Municipal Airport, located three miles east of the city. Rental cars are available.

INFORMATION

Ichetucknee Springs State Park
Route 2, Box 108
Fort White, Florida 32038
904-497-2511 and 497-4690

Olustee Battlefield State Historic Site
P.O. Box 2
Olustee, Florida 32072
904-752-3866 or 904-397-4331

JOHN D. MacARTHUR BEACH STATE PARK
40

LOCATION   The beach is north of Palm Beach on Singer Island on Florida A1A, 2.8 miles south of the intersection of U.S. 1 and PGA Boulevard. The park, a barrier island, covers 760 acres, located between the Atlantic Ocean and Lake Worth.

ACTIVITIES   Hike the nature trails, and cross the 1,600-foot-long bridge over a cove to reach the sand dunes, located along the ocean. You can take a free tram to reach the beach front. Go saltwater fishing, snorkeling, and swimming, in the ocean. Guided snorkel tours are offered for experienced snorkelers along the park's limestone rock reef, the first and third Saturday in May and June. Tour the William T. Kirby Nature Center.

For a 90-minute motorized tour of the park, come on Wednesdays and Fridays, from January through June.

Go for a riverboat cruise down Lake Worth aboard a Mississippi paddlewheeler replica, leaving from Star Landing in Phil Foster Park. It's located at the east end of Blue Heron Bridge on Florida A1A. For required reservations, call 407-848-7827.

INFORMATION
John D. MacArthur Beach State Park
10900 S.R. 703 (A1A)
North Palm Beach, Florida 33408
407-624-6950 or 407-624-6952

JOHN PENNEKAMP CORAL REEF
STATE PARK
41

LOCATION   The reef is on U.S. 1, north of Key Largo at Mile Marker 102.5.

FEATURES   The 78,000-acre "dive-in aquarium" has over 300 species of fish, and 50 species of coral. It's the first undersea park to be established in the continental U.S., and was set aside to honor the memory of John Pennekamp, a Florida conservationist who worked to protect the reef.

This reef is the most extensive and luxuriant living coral reef on the North American coast. It extends for approximately eight miles from the shoreline out to the continental shelf, and covers approximately 70 nautical miles of coral reefs, seagrass beds, and mangrove swamps. At least 40 species of coral, and hundreds of different tropical fish and plants, are found in the park.

The park's small upland limestone area has a tropical hammock, where you can see some of the park's numerous tropical trees.

Key Largo Marine Sanctuary is adjacent to the state park. The combined territory of Pennekamp and Key Largo Sanctuary encompasses 178 nautical miles, and contains many favorite dive sites, extending from Carysfort Reef on the north, to the Molasses Reef at the southern perimeter. Besides the underwater sea life, the area includes many shipwrecks lying on the floor of the straits of Florida.

ACTIVITIES   Come to snorkel or go scuba diving down to depths of 40 feet. Padi divers' certification is available. Boats provide transportation for both snorkelers and scuba divers. Rental equipment for both snorkeling and scuba diving is available at the dive shop.

Divers can swim among the colorful reef fish, and can dive the Benwood Wreck, a 285-foot-long steel freighter located 1.5 miles northeast of French Reef. Divers can also visit Christ of the Abyss, a nine-foot-high bronze statue located 20 feet below the water's surface along the Inner Bank Reefs. In addition, you can explore the Patch Reefs located in the shallow waters of the Sanctuary. Tour the Outer Bank reefs, featuring a series of long limestone ridges with colorful coral formations.

Take a 2.5 hour cruise on the glass-bottomed boat *Discovery* to view sea fans, parrot fish, and colorful coral. One of the best times for underwater viewing is around noon when the sun is most direct. Allow approximately one hour to reach the coral reef. For boating schedules, call 305-451-1621.

Go saltwater fishing and boating from the ramp in Largo Sound. Rent a boat, including a Hobie Cat, windsurfer, sailboat, motorboat, or canoe, to explore the reef. Sailing and windsurfing instruction is available. Pick up a snack at the snack bar.

Camp year-round in the 47-site campground at Key Largo, with water and electrical hookups located near the park headquarters. Boaters can also enjoy boat camping.

Go swimming from the beach at Largo Sound, or at the other two designated areas. Tour the visitor center. Maps of the coral reef and marine sanctuary are available at the park headquarters.

Two short nature hikes are available, one through the hammock, and the other along a boardwalk through the mangroves.

Go snorkeling or scuba diving in Key Largo's Undersea Park. Explore the Museum of Science and Technology to see the Marinelab undersea classroom, shipwrecks, canons, anchors, and schools of tropical fish. For details, call 305-451-2353.

For a unique overnight, stay in the Jules' Undersea Lodge in Key Largo. Scuba divers enjoy diving from the hotel by using a hookah rig, a 100-foot-long hose with a scuba regulator at one end. For information, call 305-451-2353.

INFORMATION
John Pennekamp Coral Reef State Park
P.O. Box 487
Key Largo, Florida 33037
305-451-1202: campground reservations
1-800-432-2871 or 1-800-451-1621: tour information
305-248-4300 or 305-451-1621: park

JONATHAN DICKINSON STATE PARK

ST. LUCIE INLET STATE PRESERVE
42

LOCATION   Jonathan Dickinson State Park is six miles north of Jupiter on U.S. 1 near Hobe Sound. It's also 13 miles south of Stuart.

St. Lucie Inlet is in Port Salerno on the Intracoastal Waterway, ⅔ of a mile south of the inlet.

FEATURES   Jonathan Dickinson was shipwrecked here in 1696, and managed to survive until he was driven off by the Indians. Fortunately, he escaped to St. Augustine.

ACTIVITIES   Jonathan Dickinson State Park encompasses 12,000 acres, including the Loxahatchee River, Florida's only designated national wild and scenic river, and one of the last wild and scenic rivers in the southeast U.S. Rent a boat or canoe to paddle up the river. Go freshwater fishing. Take a guided tour to the Trapper Nelson Interpretive Center, located 3½ miles up the Loxahatchee River, and only accessible by boat.

Rent a bicycle to cycle the bike trails. Hike the nature trail, go backpacking, or horseback ride along the equestrian trails, with overnight facilities available. Enjoy seasonal camping in the 135-site campground, 107 sites with water and electrical hookups, and a trailer dump station. Overnight in a vacation cabin available year-round. Groceries are available.

Take a guided nature walk on Sunday, or attend a campfire program presented in the Pine Grove campfire circle, on Saturdays from January through June.

Purchase a snack at the concession stand. Take a 1.5 hour jungle cruise of the river aboard the *Loxahatchee Queen*. For required reservations, call 407-746-1466.

Hobe Sound National Wildlife Refuge is a site for nesting turtles who come up the beach to lay their eggs. Hike the nature trails.

The Jupiter Beach Resort is the only resort honored by the Florida Audubon Society for its Turtle Watch Program. From June through September, giant loggerheads and greenbacks come up on its beach to lay their eggs.

The Jupiter Lighthouse, circa 1860, still guides ships coming up the Florida coast. Its beam is visible for 18 miles from the sea. Climb up the 105-foot lighthouse to get a great view of the Gulf Stream. Come during SeaFare Festival Days in early June.

At St. Lucie Inlet State Preserve, walk the 3,300-foot boardwalk through mangrove forests and coastal hammocks. Enjoy picnicking, swimming, and fishing in the Atlantic Ocean.

Arriving pilots can land at Witham Field Airport, located one mile southeast of Stuart. Rental cars are available.

INFORMATION

Jonathan Dickinson State Park
16450 Southeast Federal Highway
Hobe Sound, Florida 33455
407-546-2771

St. Lucie Inlet State Preserve
c/o Jonathan Dickinson State Park
16450 Southeast Federal Highway
Hobe Sound, Florida 33455
407-744-7603

KORESHAN STATE HISTORIC SITE
43

LOCATION   The park's 139 acres are on Corkscrew Road, ½ mile south of Estero on U.S. 41, on the banks of the Estero River. It's also 15 miles south of Ft. Myers.

FEATURES   Cyrus Reed Teed brought his followers here in 1894 to live in a commune, where they shared property and practiced celibacy. Today the Koreshan magazine, *The Flaming Sword,* and the newspaper, *The American Eagle,* are still published by descendants of his followers.

ACTIVITIES   Take a self-guided tour of the tropical gardens and restored village, with ranger-guided tours offered on weekends, from January through April. Go seasonal camping in the 60-site campground, all sites with water, 45 with electrical hookups, and a trailer dumping station.

Go boating from the ramp, with canoe rentals available. Enjoy fishing in the Estero River, and tour the interpretive center. From January through April, attend interpretive programs offered on Fridays. Hike the nature trails. Bring along plenty of insect repellent.

Arriving pilots can land at Southwest Florida International Airport, located 10 miles southeast of the city. Rental cars are available.

INFORMATION

Koreshan State Historic Site
P.O. Box 7
Estero, Florida 33928
813-992-0311

LAKE GRIFFIN STATE RECREATION AREA
44

LOCATION   The park's 423 acres are one mile east of Fruitland Park. It's also two miles north of Leesburg at the intersection of U.S. 27 and U.S. 441.

ACTIVITIES   Camp year-round in the 40-site campground, all sites with water and electrical hookups. It has a trailer dump station and laundry. Hike the nature trails, enjoy bass fishing, and go boating from the ramp in Lake Griffin. Rental canoes are available.

Arriving pilots can land at Leesburg Municipal Airport, located three miles northeast of the city. Rental cars are available.

INFORMATION
Lake Griffin State Recreation Area
103 Highway 441/27
Fruitland Park, Florida 32731
904-787-7402

LAKE KISSIMMEE STATE PARK
45

LOCATION   The park's 5,027 acres are 15 miles northeast of Lake Wales. Go east on Florida 60, four miles north on Boy Scout Road, and then five miles north on Camp Mack Road.

FEATURES   The park is bordered by three lakes: Kissimmee, Tiger, and Rosalie.

ACTIVITIES   Go seasonal camping in the 60-site campground, located in a pristine oak hammock. Thirty sites have water and electrical hookups. Enjoy boating from the ramp, and freshwater fishing. Watch the sandhill cranes and bald eagles from the observation tower by the picnic area, where you also get a spectacular view of Lake Kissimmee.

Kissimmee River Trail is 33.6 miles long, and follows the west bank of the Kissimmee River, through one of the state's most remote back country areas. You can camp along the trail at designated areas. The Florida Trail has 13½ miles of trails within the park, beginning at the junction of the North Loop Trail and Bridge Trail. For a map, contact the Florida Trail Association, P.O. Box 13708, Gainesville, Florida, 32604.

Attend living-history programs at the reconstructed Cow Camp, circa 1876, an authentic old-time Florida cattle cowboy camp. Watch ranch hands ride horses and rope cattle. Pick up a leaflet describing the camp, and take a tour, offered Saturdays, Sundays and holidays.

Three miles north of Lake Wales near US. 27, stroll through Bok Tower Gardens, located on the peninsula's highest point at 295 feet. The gardens cover 128 acres, and feature thousands of azaleas, camellias, and magnolias. Camellias bloom from November through March, and the azaleas from December through April. Stop by the Garden Cafe for a light meal.

Bok's 225-foot bell tower is located on top of Iron Mountain, and contains one of the world's great carillons. Come listen to the 45-minute concerts presented daily at 3 P.M. Clock music is also presented each half hour beginning at 10 A.M. Other special events include moonlight recitals, Easter Sunrise Service, Christmas programs, festivals, and Pinewood concerts. Stop by the visitor center to learn more about the tower. For information, call 813-676-1408.

Go two miles south of Lake Wales on Florida 27A to see the Black Hills Passion Play, depicting the last seven days in the life of Christ. It's presented several times a week from mid-February through mid-April. For a schedule and reservations, call 813-676-1495.

Rent an airboat to tour the cypress swamp back waters. For information, call 407-847-3672.

Special events include the Silver Spurs Rodeo each February and July, at the Silver Spurs Rodeo Arena on East Irlo Benson Memorial Highway in Kissimmee. The Kissimmee Bluegrass Festival is held the first weekend in March. The third week in June, take a nine-day cruise through Florida's waterways. In late October participate in the boating jamboree.

Also in October attend the Florida State Air Fare, featuring an air show held at the Kissimmee Municipal Airport.

The St. Cloud Spring Fling's day-long celebration, featuring a bass fishing tournament, 10K race and Olympic sports, is held at the lakefront in St. Cloud.

For information on other special events in Kissimmee or in St. Cloud, call the tourist information center at 407-847-5000.

Arriving pilots can land at Lake Wales Municipal Airport, located two miles west of the city. Rental cars are available.

INFORMATION
Lake Kissimmee State Park
14248 Camp Mack Road
Lake Wales, Florida 33853
813-696-1112

LAKE LOUISA STATE PARK
46

LOCATION   The park's 1,790 acres are seven miles southeast of Clermont on Lake Nellie Road, and 10 miles south of Florida 50 off Florida 561.

FEATURES   Lake Louisa is in the northeast corner of the Green Swamp, and is one of 13 lakes forming a chain of lakes connected by the Palatlakaha River. The river is designated an Outstanding Florida Water Area.

ACTIVITIES   Bring along a picnic to enjoy. Go freshwater fishing, canoeing, and swimming in the lake.

In Clermont, take an elevator up the Florida Citrus Tower to see the surrounding lakes and hills. It's located one mile north of Florida 50. Take a tram ride through the citrus trees, and purchase a snack. For information, call 904-394-8585.

Visit Lakeridge winery and vineyards, located three miles south off the Florida Turnpike, Exit 285 onto U.S. 27. For information, call 904-394-8627.

INFORMATION
Lake Louisa State Park
12549 State Park Drive
Clermont, Florida 34711
904-394-3969

LAKE MANATEE STATE RECREATION AREA
47

LOCATION   The park's 558 acres are 14 miles east of Bradenton on Florida 64, along the south shore of Lake Manatee.

ACTIVITIES   Go camping year-round, hike the nature trails, and go boating from the ramp, with boat rentals available. Boat motors are limited to 20 horsepower, and no water-skiing is permitted. Enjoy freshwater fishing and swimming in Lake Manatee, and cycling the bicycle trails.

In Bradenton, visit the Manatee Village Historical Park at 604 15th Street East, to see its group of late 19th-century buildings. For information, call 813-749-7165.

The DeSoto National Memorial is seven miles from Bradenton. Go west on Florida 64 and north on 75th Street Northwest. Conquistador Hernando de Soto and his men started a cross-country search for gold from here, after landing on the Manatee River in 1539. Exhibits at the memorial tell the story of his doomed quest. Hike the trail through the mangrove swamp to learn more about what the explorers experienced. For information, call 813-792-0458.

Arriving pilots can land at Sarasota/Bradenton International Airport, located three miles north of Sarasota. Rental cars are available.

INFORMATION
Lake Manatee State Recreation Area
20007 S.R. 64
Bradenton, Florida 34202
813-741-3028

LAKE TALQUIN STATE PARK
48

MACLAY STATE GARDENS
49

LAKE JACKSON MOUNDS
STATE ARCHEOLOGICAL SITE
50

LOCATION   Lake Talquin State Park's 30,000 acres are 20 miles west of Tallahassee off Florida 20 on Vause Road.

Maclay State Gardens are five miles northeast of Tallahassee and ½ mile north of I-10 on U.S. 319.

Lake Jackson Mounds are two miles north of I-10 at the southern tip of Lake Jackson.

FEATURES   Lake Talquin was formed when the Jackson Bluff Dam was constructed in 1927 for the production of hydroelectric power.

ACTIVITIES   At Lake Talquin, go hiking through thick forests of pines and hardwoods, bring along a picnic, and go freshwater fishing for largemouth bass, shellcracker, and perch.

At Maclay State Gardens, open year-round, stroll through the grounds featuring azaleas, camellias, and magnolias. Blooming season is from January 1 to April 10, with its peak in mid to late March. Stop by the Maclay house to learn more about the park's camellias. Go boating from the ramp, freshwater fishing, and swimming in Lake Hall. Bike the bicycle trails, and enjoy scuba diving or snorkeling. Purchase a snack.

At the Lake Jackson Mounds State Archeological Site, you'll discover six earth temple mounds left from a ceremonial center which was located here from 1200 through 1500 A.D. Guided tours are given, with two weeks notice, by calling 904-562-0042.

If you're in town in late March, attend "Springtime Tallahassee," a month-long festival with concerts, hot air balloon rallies, plus house and garden tours. In April, attend the Flying High Circus performances at Florida State University, the Stephen C. Smith Memorial Regatta, and the LPGA Golf Classic. In September, attend the Native American Heritage Festival.

Maps of Tallahassee's historic homes are available at the visitor center in the Capitol Building on North Duval. For information, call 904-681-9200.

Tour Natural Bridge Battlefield on Natural Bridge Road in Woodville. Civil War buffs can learn about the crucial role this area played in March, 1865. As the result of this battle, Tallahassee was the only Confederate capital east of the Mississippi that was never occupied by Union armies. The 1865 battle is reenacted each year in early March.

Walk through the battlefield, marked with stone markers and a monument commemorating the participating regiments and Confederate officers. Bring along a picnic to enjoy. It's open year-round. For information, call 904-922-6007.

Tallahassee–St. Marks Historic Railroad State Trail begins on Florida 363, south of Tallahassee. The railroad was Florida's oldest, operating from 1837 until 1984. The 16-mile section of the trail now used by bikers, skaters, hikers, and equestrians, follows the historic route to St. Marks. Bike rentals are available at the northern end of the trail. A paved parking lot is on Florida 363 south of Tallahassee. For information, call 904-922-6007.

Arriving pilots can land at Tallahassee Regional Airport, located four miles southwest of the city, or at Tallahassee Commercial Airport, eight miles northwest of the city. Both airports have rental cars.

INFORMATION
Lake Talquin State Park
1022 DeSoto Park Drive
Tallahassee, Florida 32301
904-922-6007

Maclay State Gardens
35340 Thomasville Road
Tallahassee, Florida 32308
904-487-4556

Lake Jackson Mounds State Archeological Site
1022 DeSoto Park Drive
Tallahassee, Florida 32301
904-922-6007

LITTLE MANATEE RIVER
STATE RECREATION AREA
51

LOCATION   The park's 1,638 acres are four miles south of Sun City, off U.S. 301 on Lightfoot Road.

FEATURES   The recreation area was named for the river flowing through it. The river has been designated as an Outstanding Florida Water Area, and is included in the Cockroach Bay Aquatic Preserve.

ACTIVITIES Go horseback riding along Mustang or Dude Lake horse trails. You'll need to provide your own horse. Overnight facilities are available.

Camp year-round in the 30-site campground, with water and electrical hookups, and a trailer dump station. A primitive campground is located along the hiking trail, and is available by reservation only.

Hike the nature trails, or walk the 10K volksmarch trail through the woods. Go canoeing from the canoe launch. However, no rentals are available. Enjoy swimming, and fishing for bass, bream and catfish.

INFORMATION
Little Manatee River State Recreation Area
215 Lightfood Road
Wimauma, Florida 33598
813-671-5005

LITTLE TALBOT ISLAND STATE PARK

BIG TALBOT ISLAND STATE PARK

AMELIA ISLAND STATE RECREATION AREA
52

LOCATION Little Talbot Island State Park is 17 miles northeast of Jacksonville on Florida A1A. The area is accessible via the Mayport Ferry and State Road 10.

Big Talbot Island is 20 miles northeast of Jacksonville on Florida A1A North, north of Little Talbot Island State Park.

Amelia Island is seven miles north of Little Talbot Island on Florida A1A, and eight miles south of Fernandina Beach.

FEATURES Little Talbot Island has five miles of beach, white vegetated dunes on the front side of the ocean, and a thick forest on its north side. Originally established in 1564, the fort was the site of the first U.S. Protestant colony begun by the French Huguenots. The state park is part of the Talbot Islands GEOpark.

ACTIVITIES At Little Talbot Island, camp in the 40-site campground, 32 sites with water and electrical hookups, and a trailer dump station. Go swimming, boating from the ramp in the ocean, and bass fishing from the fishing pier in Myrtle Creek. Hike the nature trails.

Big Talbot Island provides canoe routes through the salt marshes. Enjoy saltwater fishing along Nassau Sound's shoreline, hike along historic hiking trails, go for a swim in the Atlantic Ocean, and enjoy birdwatching.

At Amelia Island, take a guided horseback ride along the Atlantic Ocean. For ride reservations, call 904-261-4878. Enjoy fishing, hiking, swimming, and bird watching.

Ten miles east of Jacksonville and eight miles west of Mayport at 12713 Fort Carolina Road, tour the Fort Carolina National Memorial. Take Florida 10 and turn on St. Johns Bluff Road, and continue east to Fort Caroline Road.

Tour the visitor center and museum, and walk the short hiking trails. The fort walls have been reconstructed. If you come during the summer, bring along plenty of mosquito repellent. For information, call 904-641-7155.

In downtown Jacksonville, stop at the Friendship Park fountain, one of the world's tallest, with water spraying up to 120 feet. The fountains are lighted at night.

Tour Anheuser-Busch Brewery at 111 Busch Drive at I-95, and visit its Hospitality Room to sample their beers. For tour information, call 904-751-0700. Spend the day at the Jacksonville Zoo with over 225 animal species.

Kingsley Plantation National Historic Site is on the north bank of Fort George Island, three miles north of the St. Johns River Ferry. The plantation is believed to be the oldest in Florida. Take a guided tour of the site's 23 slave cabins and main house ruins, and tour the interpretive center. For information, call 904-251-3537.

Timucuan Ecological and Historic Preserve in Jacksonville has three nature areas and seven miles of trails through the woods and wetlands. For information, call 904-641-7155.

Arriving pilots can land at Craig Municipal Airport, located eight miles east of Jacksonville, at Herlong Airport, eight miles southwest of the city, or at Jacksonville International Airport, nine miles north of the city. All three airports have rental cars available.

INFORMATION
Big Talbot Island State Park
Little Talbot Island State Park
Amelia Island State Recreation Area
c/o Talbot Islands GEOpark
11435 Fort George Road East
Fort George, Florida 32226
904-251-2320

LONG KEY STATE RECREATION AREA
53

LOCATION   The park's 845 acres are at 67400 Overseas Highway on Long Key at Layton, on U.S. 1 at Mile Marker 67.5.

ACTIVITIES Go year-round camping in the 60-site campground located on a long sandy beach overlooking the ocean, and shaded by Australian pines. All campsites have water and 30 have electrical hookups, and a dump station is available.

Hike the two marked nature trails leading to tropical hammocks like those found in the wilderness a century ago. Go boating from the ramp, saltwater fishing, swimming, scuba diving, and snorkeling in the Atlantic Ocean. Rangers teach snorkeling and marine ecology in the shallows. Take a ranger-guided canoe trip on Long Key Lake, or enjoy a guided walk on Layton Trail and Golden Orb Trail. You'll also find excellent fishing in the deep waters of the Gulf Stream.

Go boating or snorkeling at San Pedro Underwater Archeological Preserve. The site is located in 18 feet of water, approximately 1¼ miles south of Indian Key. The *San Pedro* was a 287-ton Dutch-built ship that sailed in 1733. Major salvaging efforts occurred in 1960, and today all you can see is a large pile of ballast stones.

INFORMATION
Long Key State Recreation Area
P.O. Box 776
Long Key, Florida 33001
305-664-4815

MANATEE SPRINGS STATE PARK
54

LOCATION The park is six miles west of Chiefland off U.S. 19 and 98, at the end of Florida 320.

FEATURES Manatee Springs produce 116 million gallons of clear water daily, which flows into the Suwannee River.

ACTIVITIES Enjoy year-round picnicking, swimming in Manatee Springs, scuba diving, snorkeling, and fishing for bass in the Suwannee River. Keep an eye out for the endangered manatee.

Go hiking and bicycling on the 8½ miles on the north end of the trail system. Enjoy camping year-round in the 100-site campground, all sites with water, and 45 with electrical hookups; a disposal station and groceries are available. The park has a boat dock and boardwalk leading to the Suwannee River. Boats, canoes and bicycles may be rented. A concession stand is open summers.

INFORMATION
Manatee Springs State Park
Route 2, Box 671
Chiefland, Florida 32626
904-493-6072

MARJORIE KINNAN RAWLINGS
STATE HISTORIC SITE
55

PAYNES PRAIRIE STATE PRESERVE
56

GAINESVILLE-HAWTHORNE STATE TRAIL
57

LOCATION   Marjorie Rawlings State Historic Site is 13 miles north of Cross Creek. Go east on Florida 234, and follow signs to Florida 325.

Paynes Prairie State Preserve's 2,000 acres are one mile east of Gainesville on Florida 234, then two miles north on U.S. 441, and two miles east of Olustee on U.S. 90. It's also one mile north of Micanopy. Access to the park is along the southern rim.

Gainesville-Hawthorne State Trail begins on Southeast 15th Street in Gainesville, and goes to Hawthorne near U.S. 301.

FEATURES   The preserve contains Indian artifacts dating back to 7,000 B.C. A herd of buffalo once roamed around a large lake. Today the lake is gone, disappearing into a sinkhole that was located in one corner of the lake. As late as 1892, a small steamer plying the lake became stranded when the water disappeared. Since then, the basin has been a treeless prairie.

Today you can still see a few buffalo, and herds of Spanish horses galloping across the 20,000-acre preserve. Sandhill cranes come here to nest during the winter.

ACTIVITIES   Marjorie Rawlings lived in this one-story, cracker-style farmhouse, from 1928 until her death in 1953. Here she wrote *The Yearling* for which she won a Pulitzer Prize. Tours leave hourly for the farmhouse, Thursday through Sunday, from October through July. The grounds are open year-round. For information, call 904-466-3672.

At Paynes Prairie, go camping in the 57-site campground, all sites with water and electrical hookups, and a dump station. Hike the preserve trails. Ranger-led hikes are provided weekends from October through March. For information, call 904-466-4100. A list of the 213 bird species that have been spotted in the area is available at the visitor center. Watch the audiovisual program to learn more about the early activity in the area, dating back to as early as 10,000 B.C.

Water activities are available on Lake Wauberg (ramp available) and on Sawgrass Pond, with canoes, sailboats, and boats using electric motors only. Go horseback riding along the several miles of riding trails.

On Saturdays from November through April, take a half-day prairie rim ramble covering approximately 3½ miles. Go to Persimmon Point for a panoramic view of the freshwater wetland. The first weekend of the month in November through April, accompany a ranger on an overnight backpacking trip of 6½ miles to camp at a primitive campsite on Persimmon Point. Rangers also lead mountain-bike tours of approximately 10 miles through the pine trees west of Hawthorne. Reservations are required for both of these trips.

Gainesville-Hawthorne State Trail is 17 miles long, and leaves from Gainesville's Boulware Springs Park, and passes through Paynes Prairie State Preserve and Lockloosa Wildlife Management. It's enjoyed by walkers, bicyclists with mountain bicycles, and equestrians. Parking is available in Boulware Springs Park and in Hawthorne.

Arriving pilots can land at Gainesville Regional Airport, located three miles northeast of the city. Rental cars are available.

INFORMATION

Marjorie Kinnan Rawlings
  State Historic Site
Route 3, Box 92
Hawthorne, Florida 32640
904-466-3672

Paynes Prairie State Preserve
Route 2, Box 41
Micanopy, Florida 32667
904-466-3397 or 904-466-4100

Gainesville-Hawthorne State Trail
4801 Southeast 17th Street
Gainesville, Florida 32601
904-336-2135

MIKE ROESS GOLD HEAD BRANCH
STATE PARK
58

LOCATION   The park's 1,414 acres are six miles northeast of Keystone Heights, on Florida 21.

FEATURES   Gold Head Branch is in a deep ravine containing several springs.

ACTIVITIES   Rent a canoe, paddleboat, or a bicycle to go cycling. Go swimming, water-skiing, bass fishing, scuba diving, or snorkeling in Johnson Lake.

Camp in the 74-site campground, all sites containing water hookups, and 37 sites with electrical hookups, with a dump station available. Overnight (seasonally) in a vacation cabin along the lakefront. Hike the nature trails. Snacks are available. Visit the remains of the old mill site.

INFORMATION
Mike Roess Gold Head Branch State Park
6239 S.R. 21
Keystone Heights, Florida 32656
904-473-4701

MYAKKA RIVER STATE PARK
59

LOCATION   The park's 28,825 acres are nine miles east of Sarasota, on Florida 72.

FEATURES   The park, one of the state's largest, encompasses wetlands, prairies, and dense woodlands, along the Myakka River as it spills into Upper Myakka Lake. It's considered one of the most outstanding wildlife sanctuaries and breeding grounds in the U.S., and is home to many species of plants, alligators, and over 200 bird species.

ACTIVITIES   The park is open from 8 A.M. until sunset year-round. The north entrance is only open on weekends and holidays. Guided walks and campfire programs are presented seasonally.

Tour the interpretive center, attend a campfire program, or participate in a guided nature walk, on Saturdays only from Thanksgiving through Easter.

Take an airboat ride aboard the 70-passenger *Gator Gal* on Myakka Lake. Go for a safari tram tour on the 50-passenger tour train that runs daily, and on Sundays at 1:00 and 2:30 P.M. A sundown train takes you on a 1½-hour ride to the bird observation tower. For information, call 305-365-0100.

Rent a bicycle to go cycling on the paved seven-mile drive that winds through the wildlife refuge. If you encounter an alligator, don't approach it, or attempt to feed it.

Hike the self-guided nature trail or on one of the other park trails, and watch for the many bird species. Register at the entrance station to go backpacking through the hammocks, dry prairies, and pine flatwoods. Bring your own horse and go horseback riding along 15 miles of equestrian trails. Proof of a current Coggins Test is required.

Go seasonal camping in one of two campgrounds, with a total of 76 sites, 48 sites with water and electrical hookups, and a trailer dump station, or stay overnight in one of 5 rustic cabins that are open year-round. Groceries are available.

Purchase a snack at the Upper Myakka Lake concession, which also has boat, canoe, and bicycle rentals. Go boating from the ramp.

Myakka River State Park is considered one of the best fishing parks in the state. Try your luck at landing bass weighing anywhere from two to 12 pounds. Fish for bream and catfish in both the Upper Myakka Lake and in the Myakka River. A fishing license is required for anyone over 16 years of age.

Go scuba diving in the area reefs, both natural and artificial. Also enjoy canoeing, water-skiing, sailing, wind surfing, and deep-sea sport fishing.

A limited number of visitors are allowed in the 7,500 acre section of the park designated as a wilderness preserve.

Visit the Marie Selby Botanical Gardens with its orchid center and 20,000 tropical plants. Tour the Museum of Botany and the Arts, located in the Christy Payne House. It's on the downtown waterfront at 811 South Palm Avenue in Sarasota, at U.S. 41. For information, call 941-366-5730.

Also in Sarasota, visit the Mote Marine Aquarium at 1600 City Island Park, south of Longboat Key, at the south end of New Pass Bridge on Florida 789. It features an outdoor shark tank. Guided tours are available. For information, call 941-388-2451.

Stroll the beaches at Venice and Englewood, and watch for fossilized sharks' teeth.

Visit the John and Mable Ringling Museum of Art, three miles north of downtown Sarasota on U.S. 41. It features Circus Galleries with a miniature circus. The Ringling's residence is located on the 68-acre estate of John Ringling, who made his fortune from the "Greatest Show on Earth." Come in early March to attend the 4-day Medieval Fair. For information, call 941-355-5101.

Ca'd'Zan, Venetian for "John's house," is located on Sarasota Bay, 1/2 mile from the entrance to the museum. The 30-room mansion was inspired by the Doge's in Venice, and was built in 1926.

Across the highway, at 33500 North Tamaimi Trail, is Bellum's Cars and Music of Yesterday. It features over 2,000 mechanical music machines including player pianos, cylinder phonographs, and crank-up hurdy-gurdies. For information, call 941-355-6228.

The Asolo Center for the Performing Arts is at 5555 North Tamiami Trail, where you can take a tour and attend a performance. For information, call 941-351-8000.

From January through March, the Royal Lipizzan Stallions from Austria are in town, at Colonel Herrman's Ranch on Singletary Road. Attend the 1 1/2-hour training sessions on Thursday and Friday at 3:00 P.M., and Saturdays at 10:00 A.M.

Arriving pilots can land at Sarasota/Bradenton International Airport, located three miles north of the city. Rental cars are available.

INFORMATION

Myakka River State Park
13207 State Road 72
Sarasota, Florida 34241-9542
941-361-6511

NEW SMYRNA SUGAR MILLS RUINS
STATE HISTORIC PARK
60

LOCATION   The ruins are off U.S. 1 in New Smyrna Beach, and off Florida 44 on Old Mission Road.

ACTIVITIES   The ruins of the large plantation's sugar mill are west of town. Constructed in the 1830s, it was destroyed during the Second Seminole War.

Cars may be driven along the firm white sand on the beach. Often called the "world's safest bathing beach," it extends for 13.2 miles from Ponce Inlet to the Canaveral National Seashore. Enjoy surf and pier fishing, boating with rentals available, and deep sea fishing.

You can see the coquina foundations of the Turnbull home, circa 1565, on North Riverside Drive, between Washington and Julia Streets in Old Fort Park.

Ponce DeLeon Inlet Lighthouse is at 4931 South Peninsula Drive in Ponce Inlet. The lighthouse originally guided mariners past the shoals from 1887 to 1970, and was reactivated in 1982. Climb to the top of the lighthouse for a great view of Daytona Beach. The lighthouse keepers' cottages have been converted to museums. For information, call 904-761-1821.

In April, attend the New Smyrna Beach Jazz Festival at Riverside Park. For information, call 904-428-5741, extension 351. An aviation festival is held in November, featuring vintage airplanes and sky diving exhibitions. For information, call 904-423-5057.

Arriving pilots can land at Masey Ranch Airpark, located three miles south of New Smyrna Beach. Taxis are available for transportation. You can also land at New Smyrna Beach Municipal Airport. Rental cars are available.

INFORMATION
New Smyrna Sugar Mills Ruins State Historic Site
New Smyrna, Florida 32169
904-427-5450

NORTH SHORE STATE RECREATION AREA
61

LOCATION   The park's 30 acres are in Surfside, east of Collins Avenue between 79th and 87th Streets. It's surrounded on three sides by Miami Beach.

FEATURES   Despite its location so close to an urban area, the park provides an escape to the residents of this busy city.

ACTIVITIES   Go fishing and swimming in the Atlantic Ocean, or ride the bicycle trail.

Arriving pilots can land at Miami International Airport, located eight miles northwest of the city; at Kendall-Tamiami Executive Airport, located 13 miles southwest of the city; or at Opa Locka Airport, located 10 miles north of the city. All airports have rental cars available.

INFORMATION
North Shore State Recreation Area
c/o Oleta/North Shore GEOpark
3400 Northeast 163rd Street
North Miami Beach, Florida 33160
305-940-7439

OCHLOCKONEE RIVER STATE PARK
62

LOCATION   The park is four miles south of Sopchoppy on U.S. 319, and is bordered by the Sopchoppy and Ochlockonee Rivers.

ACTIVITIES   Go seasonal camping in the 30-site riverside campground, 24 sites with water and electrical hookups, and a trailer dump station. Hike the nature trails; go boating from the ramp, with rentals available; bass fish in one of the small ponds or in the Ochlockonee River, and enjoy swimming in the Dead River.

INFORMATION
Ochlockonee River State Park
P.O. Box 5
Sopchoppy, Florida 32358
904-962-2771

O'LENO STATE PARK
63

LOCATION   The park's 5,938 acres are six miles north of High Springs on U.S. 441, along the banks of the Santa Fe River. It's also 20 miles south of Lake City.

FEATURES   Visitors will find many sinkholes, hardwood hammocks, river swamps, and a sandhill community.

ACTIVITIES   Camp year-round in the 64-site campground, all sites with water, 62 with electrical hookups, and with a trailer dump site located in the Dogwood and Magnolia camping loops. The group campground can accommodate 140 campers, and includes 17 cabins. You can also go backpacking.

Hike the nature trails. The Santa Fe River Trail goes along the river to the "river sink," where the river disappears underground for over three miles before resurfacing again. The Limestone Trail passes through a hardwood hammock and along a limestone outcrop.

Go swimming, canoeing with rentals available, and fishing for bass, bream, and catfish in the Santa Fe River. You can also go horseback riding along the equestrian trails, and cycle the bike trails with bike rentals available.

In March, attend Leno Heritage Days to learn about life in the pioneer town of Leno during the 1800s.

Arriving pilots can land at Lake City Municipal Airport, located three miles east of the city. Rental cars are available.

INFORMATION
O'Leno State Park
Route 2, Box 1010
High Springs, Florida 32643
904-454-1853

OLETA RIVER STATE RECREATION AREA
64

LOCATION   The park's 90 acres are in North Miami Beach at 3400 Northeast 163rd Street off U.S. 1, on the bank of the Oleta River and Intracoastal Waterway.

ACTIVITIES   A primitive camping area for young people is available by reservation. Go canoeing and boating from the ramp, saltwater fishing and swimming from the 1,200-foot beach in Biscayne Bay. Watch for porpoises and manatees that often visit the area. Bike the 1.5-mile bicycle trail, and hike the nature trail.

INFORMATION
Oleta River State Recreation Area
c/o Oleta/North Shore GEOpark
3400 Northeast 163rd Street
North Miami Beach, Florida 33160
305-947-6357

OSCAR SCHERER STATE PARK
65

LOCATION   The park's 463 acres are two miles south of Osprey on U.S. 41. It's also six miles south of Sarasota and 1.6 miles north of Florida 681, between Osprey and Venice on U.S. 41.

ACTIVITIES   Go seasonal camping in the 104-site campground, all sites with water and electrical hookups, and a trailer dump station. Attend campfire programs presented Saturdays from December through Easter. Hike the nature trails, and go bicycling on the bike path.

Go boating from the ramp, canoeing in the streams, with canoe rentals available, and enjoy bass fishing and swimming in Lake Osprey. Take a ranger-guided canoe trip on South Creek, offered on Wednesdays year-round. Take a safari tour aboard *Gator Gal*, the world's largest airboat, to see alligators, wading birds, and other wildlife. For information, call 813-365-0100.

Historic Spanish Point is 9½ miles from Osprey. Here you'll see evidence of centuries of human settlement, dating from prehistoric Indians to northern home-steaders. Visitors can see restored buildings, and hike the trails. A footbridge pro-vides a view of ospreys and other wildlife. For information, call 813-966-5214.

Arriving pilots can land at Sarasota/Bradenton International Airport, located three miles north of Sarasota. Rental cars are available.

INFORMATION
Oscar Scherer State Park
1843 South Tamiami Trail
P.O. Box 398
Osprey, Florida 34229
813-483-5956

PAHOKEE STATE RECREATION AREA
66

LOCATION   The park is on Lake Okeechobee, one mile north of Pahokee on U.S. 441.

FEATURES   Lake Okeechobee is the second largest lake in the U.S. (exclud-ing the Great Lakes), and means "big water" in Seminole.

ACTIVITIES   Go camping in the campground, and boating from the ramp, with rentals available. The park has an enclosed harbor. Enjoy swimming, and fishing for large-mouth bass. Climb to the top of the Pahokee Observation Tower on top of Hoover Dike, to get a great overlook of the lake.

Lake Okeechobee has a 110-mile trail that circles the entire perimeter of the 488,000-acre lake. Following two disastrous hurricanes in the 1920s, the Army Corps of Engineers built a 34-foot-high wall around the lake. Most of the trail is on top of the massive Herbert Hoover Dike. Be prepared for hiking that is high and dry, with no shade available. Camping is permitted along the dike at desig-nated areas. For information, contact the Army Corps office at 813-983-8101.

For a shorter hike, explore the Highlands-Okeechobee Trail north of the lake. This section of the trail follows the levees built along the heavily channeled Kissimmee River. You can take a cooling dip in the river by the Florida 70 bridge.

Arriving pilots can land at Palm Beach County Glades Airport, located three miles southwest of Pahokee. Taxi transportation is available.

INFORMATION
Pahokee State Recreation Area
Pahokee, Florida 33476
407-924-7832

PAYNES CREEK STATE HISTORIC SITE
67

LOCATION   The park is ½ mile east of Bowling Green on Florida 664A.

FEATURES   A fort was built ½ mile from a trading post to protect the early settlers from the Seminole Indians' attacks.

ACTIVITIES   Tour the interpretive center where slide programs are offered on Saturday, Sunday and holidays, from January through June. Go canoeing, fishing, and hike the interpretive trail.

INFORMATION
Paynes Creek State Park
P.O. Box 547
Bowling Green, Florida 33834
813-375-4717

PEACOCK SPRINGS
STATE RECREATION AREA
68

LOCATION   The area is 16 miles southwest of Live Oak on Florida 51, and two miles north of Luraville on Peacock Springs Road.

FEATURES   Peacock Springs has two major springs, many sinks, and one of the longest underwater cave systems found in the continental U.S. Approximately 28,000 feet of its passages have been explored.

ACTIVITIES   Visitors come to enjoy picnicking, swimming in Peacock Orange Grove Springs, and diving—available to certified divers only.

Arriving pilots can land at Suwannee County Airport, located two miles west of Live Oak. Rental cars are available.

INFORMATION
Peacock Springs State Recreation Area
Route 4, Box 370
Live Oak, Florida 32060
904-497-2511

PERDIDO KEY STATE RECREATION AREA

BIG LAGOON STATE RECREATION AREA
69

LOCATION   Perdido Key State Park's 247 acres are 15 miles southwest of Pensacola off Florida 292, on a finger of land extending out from the Gulf Islands National Seashore.

Big Lagoon State Recreation Area is 10 miles southwest of Pensacola on Florida 292A.

ACTIVITIES   At Perdido Key, bring along a picnic to enjoy, go fishing for pompano and spotted sea trout, and enjoy swimming in the Gulf of Mexico. The water temperature averages 75 degrees. Go snorkeling and watch for star fish, sand dollars, and porpoises playing around in the water just beyond the sandbar.

Go camping on the beach beside the Gulf of Mexico, making sure to pitch your tent above the high-tide line. Watch for jellyfish, and be prepared for the biting blackflies that arrive in August.

On Saturdays in June, join the naturalists for a slide show, and beach walk to learn about the endangered sea turtles. Advance reservations are required.

In January, participate in the Annual Polar Bear Dip. In April, the Interstate Mullett Toss and Great Gulf Coast beach party are held. For details, contact the Chamber of Commerce at 904-492-4660.

Big Lagoon has 698 acres, featuring year-round camping in 104 campsites, all sites providing water and electrical hookups, and a disposal station. Enjoy hiking the nature trails, boating from the ramp, saltwater fishing, and swimming in the Intracoastal Waterway.

Spot pelicans and herons, and enjoy a panoramic view of Big Lagoon and the Gulf Islands National Seashore from the park's observation tower. Its open air auditorium features concerts by local musicians, and is a popular site for weddings.

Tour downtown Pensacola's historic district, now designated as a National Historic Landmark. Tours are available through restored homes and museums. Pensacola is well known to anglers who fish for grouper, red snapper, and triggerfish. Try your luck at one of the many freshwater and saltwater fishing tournaments. Fish from the pier at Pensacola Bay Bridge and from the Pensacola Beach pier at Casino Beach.

Visitors can also go snorkeling and scuba diving among the natural reefs, featuring playful dolphins and loggerhead turtles. Artificial reefs include the battleship USS *Massachusetts,* resting in 30 feet of water, which attracts a large variety of fish life.

Pensacola has several historical districts which include Seville, Palafox, and the North Hill Preservation District. To learn more about the city's history, visit the historic Pensacola Village Museum at 405 South Adams Street. It features 19th-century houses, costumed guides, and guided tours.

The National Museum of Naval Aviation is one of the largest air and space museums in the world, and has over 100 aircraft, including the F6F Hellcat Fighter and the NC-4, the first plane to fly across the Atlantic.

In June, celebrate the Fiesta of Five Flags, featuring parties, parades, contests and seafood festivals.

The Gulf Islands National Seashore is a 150-mile-long strip of barrier islands and natural harbors. The visitor center is on Florida 98, east of Gulf Breeze. For park information, call 904-934-2600. The seashore has historic forts, and sparkling white sand beaches. Stop by to see their interpretive exhibits, and go hiking, fishing, and scuba diving.

Take guided tours of Fort Barrancas and Fort Pickens. Bring along a flashlight when exploring the forts, since their passageways are dimly lighted.

Enjoy swimming from the beaches, which have lifeguards on duty. The beaches are closed from September through May. Be aware of strong currents that occur in heavy surf, and watch for stinging jellyfish and Portuguese man-of-war.

Go boating from the boat ramp, and purchase supplies in the campground store. Enjoy hiking the trails and cycling the bicycle trails. If camping, bring long tent stakes because of the sand, and mosquito netting. Snacks are available in the Santa Rosa area and at Ship Island.

At Bay Bluffs Park, enjoy the picturesque elevated boardwalk that descends the state's only scenic bluffs, formed over 20,000 years ago. Stop at the vista overlooking Pensacola Bay.

Arriving pilots can land at Ferguson Airport, located seven miles southwest of Pensacola, or at Pensacola Regional Airport, three miles northeast of the city. Rental cars are available at both airports.

INFORMATION
Big Lagoon State Recreation Area
Perdido Key State Recreation Area
12301 Gulf Beach Highway
Pensacola, Florida 32507
904-492-1595

ROCKY BAYOU STATE PARK
70

LOCATION   The park's 632 acres are six miles southeast of Niceville on Florida 20.

ACTIVITIES   Enjoy year-round camping in the 42-site campground, 31 sites with water and electrical hookups, and a dump station. Hike the nature trails, both in the park and in the nearby wetlands. Go boating from ramp, with boat rentals available, bass fishing, and swimming, in Choctawhatchee Bayou.

INFORMATION
Rocky Bayou State Park
4281 Highway 20
Route 1, Box 597
Niceville, Florida 32578
904-833-9144

RAINBOW SPRINGS STATE PARK
71

LOCATION   The park is three miles east of Dunnellon on the east side of U.S. 41. The campground is reached via Florida 484 and Florida Southwest 180.

FEATURES   Rainbow Springs is the state's third largest spring, and forms the headwaters for the Rainbow River. Early Native Americans lived here almost 10,000 years ago.

ACTIVITIES   Camp year-round in the 105-site campground, all sites with water and electrical hookups, and 40 sites with sewer hookups. Groceries, limited RV supplies, and a laundry, are available.

Explore the historic spring and garden. Go bass fishing in Rainbow River, and swimming and boating from the ramp, with canoe and inner-tube rentals available at the campground.

Come in February and March when the azaleas are in full bloom. Attend the Will McLean Festival and Dunnellon "Boomtown Days."

Arriving pilots can land at Dunnellon's Marion County Airport, located four miles east of the city. Rental cars are available.

INFORMATION
Rainbow Springs State Park
19158 Southwest 81st Place Road
Dunnellon, Florida 34432
904-489-5201

RAVINE STATE GARDENS
72

LOCATION   The gardens are in Palatka, off Twigg Street.

FEATURES   The ravine was cut by the St. Johns River, and the gardens were created in 1933 by the WPA, the federal Works Progress Administration.

ACTIVITIES   Go hiking or bicycling, particularly in March and April when the Palatka Azalea Festival is held. Take a hayride through the gardens.

Arriving pilots can land at Kay Larkin Airport, located two miles northwest of Palatka. Rental cars are available.

INFORMATION
Ravine State Gardens
P.O. Box 1096
Palatka, Florida 32178
904-329-3721

ST. ANDREWS STATE RECREATION AREA
73

LOCATION   The park's 1,260 acres are three miles east of Panama City Beach via Florida 392, Thomas Drive, and south of U.S. 98.

ACTIVITIES   St. Andrews is one of Florida's most visited state parks. Go seasonal camping along the waterfront on the Gulf of Mexico in the 176-site campground, with water and electrical hookups. It has a laundry, limited groceries, and RV supplies.

Hike the nature trails through the various plant communities, watching for wading birds and alligators. Go boating, saltwater fishing from the fishing piers, water-skiing, swimming, scuba diving, and snorkeling in the Gulf. Tour the interpretive center, and the park's restored turpentine still.

While in Panama City, visit Gulf World's underwater extravaganza and tropical garden, and the Snake-A-Torium which features guided tours and exhibitions of venom extractions.

Arriving pilots can land at Panama City–Bay County International Airport, located three miles northwest of Panama City. Rental cars are available.

INFORMATION
St. Andrews State Recreation Area
4415 Thomas Drive
Panama City, Florida 32408
904-233-5140

ST. GEORGE ISLAND STATE PARK
74

LOCATION   The park's 1,833 acres are 10 miles southeast of Eastpoint, off U.S. 98 on St. George Island, via Florida G1A and 300, and offshore from Apalachicola on the eastern end of the Florida Panhandle.

FEATURES   The park has nearly 2,000 acres of undeveloped barrier island. It features nine miles of secluded beaches, sand dunes, and marshland along the Gulf of Mexico and Apalachicola Bay.

ACTIVITIES St. George is best known for its beaches. as well as a bird watching sanctuary. Go backpacking or camping year-round in the 60-site campground, all sites with water and electrical hookups. Hike the nature trails along nine miles of sandy shoreline, or along a series of boardwalks.

Go boating from the ramp, with rentals available, saltwater fishing, and swimming in the Gulf of Mexico.

Walk through the Chestnut Street Cemetery where the graves are surrounded by iron fences, and watched over by oak trees dripping with Spanish moss. You'll see the graves of young men who died fighting for the Confederacy's Florida Brigade, and of veterans who died in Pickett's Charge at Gettysburg.

In Apalachicola, tour the John Gorrie State Museum, on Sixth Street off U.S. 98. John Gorrie invented an ice-making machine that laid the groundwork for modern refrigeration and air conditioning. For information, call 904-653-9347.

Arriving pilots can land at Apalachicola Municipal Airport, located two miles west of Apalachicola. Rental cars are available.

INFORMATION
St. George Island State Park
P.O. Box 62
Eastpoint, Florida 32328
904-927-2111

ST. JOSEPH PENINSULA STATE PARK
75

LOCATION The park is 12 miles southwest of Port St. Joe, off Florida 30 and west of U.S. 98.

FEATURES The 2,516-acre park is on a barrier reef extending north between St. Joseph Bay and the Gulf of Mexico. Its beach extends for 20 miles. The park was named for the first postmaster of Port St. Joe.

ACTIVITIES The park is open year-round. Go swimming and saltwater fishing from its long beach. In the fall, catch large redfish, shark, bluefish, and flounder. Spring brings good fishing for pompano, whiting, and speckled trout. Birders enjoy searching for herons and pelicans from the three overlooks on the dunes. The fall brings migrating hawks and peregrine falcons. Over 209 bird species have been recorded.

Camp seasonally near the Gulf in the 119-site campground, all sites with water, and 79 with electrical hookups, and an available trailer dump station. Primitive camping is available in the 1,650-acre wilderness preserve at the northern end of the park. Vacation cottages are also available.

The bay side of the park features a marina and launching ramp. Go scuba diving, water-skiing, and snorkeling. Explore the salt marshes to find crabs, horse conch, sea turtles, and watch for alligators.

Enjoy a picnic, go backpacking, hike two nature trails, or stroll along miles of beach. Rent a bicycle to go cycling. Purchase a snack at the concession stand, which is open during the summer.

One mile south of Port St. Joe off U.S. 98, is the Constitution Convention State Museum, dedicated to the constitution convention held in 1838–39, when the first of Florida's five constitutions were drafted. Guided tours are available. For information, call 904-229-8029.

Arriving pilots can land at Costin Airport, located two miles south of Port St. Joe. However, no rental cars are available. The airport is 15 miles from the park.

INFORMATION
St. Joseph Peninsula State Park
Star Route 1, Box 200
Port St. Joe, Florida 32456
904-227-1327

SEBASTIAN INLET
STATE RECREATION AREA
76

LOCATION   The Inlet is north of Wabasso along the Sebastian Inlet on the Atlantic Ocean. It's eight miles south of Melbourne Beach on Florida A1A.

FEATURES   The inlet is known as the largest sea turtle nesting area in the U.S. Loggerheads, greenbacks, and leatherbacks come ashore from May until August. Hatchlings can be seen struggling back to the ocean until late October.

ACTIVITIES   Tour the McLarty Treasure Museum at the southern end of the recreation area and watch its presentation on modern shipwreck salvaging. Enjoy seasonal camping in the 51-site campground, all sites with water and electrical hookups, a laundry, and trailer dump station. You can also purchase groceries and snacks, or eat in the restaurant.

Go boating from the ramp, and saltwater fishing from an Atlantic jetty for snook, redfish, bluefish, and Spanish mackerel. You can also go pan fishing in the Indian River. Enjoy swimming, scuba diving, and snorkeling in the Atlantic Ocean.

Pelican Island Bird Sanctuary, maintained by the Audubon Society, is south of Sebastian.

Arriving pilots can land at Sebastian Municipal Airport, located one mile west of Sebastian. Taxi transportation is available.

INFORMATION
Sebastian Inlet State Recreation Area
9700 South A1A
Melbourne Beach, Florida 32951
407-984-4852: recreation site
407-589-9659: campground reservations

STEPHEN FOSTER
STATE FOLK CULTURE CENTER
77

LOCATION   The center is three miles east of I-75, off U.S. 41 North in White Springs, along the banks of the Suwannee River. From I-75, exit SR 136, go east to U.S. 41, and then turn left. From I-10, exit onto U.S. 41 and go north to White Springs.

FEATURES   Stephen Foster's song, *Old Folks at Home,* was immortalized here, even though he never saw the river itself.

ACTIVITIES   Tour the visitor center to see several dioramas and period exhibits. Listen to a carillon recital, offered four times daily. Visit the craft shop which has five studios. Take a guided tour of the Stephen Foster Museum and Memorial Carillon.

Special events held at the center include the National Stephen Foster Day Celebration in January, Antique Tractor and Engine Show the end of March, and a Folk Festival held Memorial Day weekend. If you come in early February, you can enjoy the camellia garden show.

INFORMATION
Stephen Foster State Folk Culture Center
Post Office Drawer G
White Springs, Florida 32096
904-397-2733 or 904-397-4331

SUWANNEE RIVER STATE PARK
78

LOCATION   The park's 1,831 acres are 13 miles west of Live Oak on U.S. 90, at the confluence of the Suwannee and Withlacoochee Rivers.

FEATURES   "Suwannee" is believed to come from an American Indian word meaning "black muddy water." Stephen Foster made its name well known in his song, "Old Folks at Home." At one time, steamboats were a familiar sight along the Suwannee and Withlacoochee Rivers.

South of the two rivers' intersection is an earthworks constructed by the Confederates during the Civil War. One of the state's oldest cemeteries is located off Old Stage Road.

ACTIVITIES   Go seasonal camping in the 31-site campground which has a laundry, dump station, and 22 of the sites have water and electrical hookups. Go boating from the ramp on the Suwannee River. The Suwannee River canoe trail and Withlacooche River canoe trails begin in Georgia and end here in the park. The lower Suwannee River canoe trail also begins here, ending at the Gulf of Mexico.

Anglers enjoy fishing for catfish, bass, and panfish. Hikers can wander along Lime Sink Run's interpretive trail. Sandhills Trail goes to the old Columbus Cemetery. Part of this trail follows the route of the old stage road, which went from Pensacola to Jacksonville.

INFORMATION
Suwannee River State Park
Route 8, Box 297
Live Oak, Florida 32060
904-362-2746

THREE RIVERS STATE RECREATION AREA
79

LOCATION   The area is two miles north of Sneads, off Florida 271.

FEATURES   The recreation area is located by Lake Seminole, and the Chattahoochee, Fling, and Apalachicola Rivers.

ACTIVITIES   Go camping year-round in the 65-site campground, 44 sites with water and electrical hookups, and a trailer dump station. Enjoy boating from the ramp and bass fishing in Lake Seminole. Hike through the hardwood hammock and pine forest.

INFORMATION
Three Rivers State Recreation Area
7908 Three Rivers Road
Box 15A
Sneads, Florida 32460
904-482-9006

TOMOKA STATE PARK
80

LOCATION   The park is three miles north of Ormond Beach on North Beach Street.

FEATURES   Tomoka State Park is on the site of an Indian village located at the fork of the Halifax and Tomoka Rivers. Some believe the park was the site of the first Christian marriage, performed in 1567.

ACTIVITIES   Go seasonal camping in the 100-site campground, all sites with water, and 63 with electrical hookups. Hike the nature trail, and go trout fishing and boating in the Halifax River from the ramp. Canoe rentals are available. No fishing is permitted in the park rivers.

Rent a bicycle to ride the bicycle trails. Tour the visitor center and museum, and purchase a snack and limited camping supplies.

In February, attend Tomokafest to enjoy folk and bluegrass music, and living-history representations with Timucuan and Seminole Indians, traders, trappers, and Civil War soldiers.

Arriving pilots can land at Ormond Beach Municipal Airport, located three miles northwest of the city. Rental cars are available.

INFORMATION
Tomoka State Park
2099 North Beach Street
Ormond Beach, Florida 32174
904-676-4050

TORREYA STATE PARK
81

LOCATION   The park's 1,063 acres are 13 miles north of Bristol off Florida 12, on Florida 271. It's also approximately 45 miles west of Tallahassee between Bristol and Greensboro.

FEATURES   The park features rugged bluffs that overlook the Apalachicola River. Local legend holds that the Torreya evergreens were used to build Noah's ark. These Torreya trees only grow along the Apalachicola River bluffs.

ACTIVITIES   Take a naturalist-guided tour of the restored historic Gregory mansion. Hike the 7-mile loop hiking trail, or go backpacking. Rent a horse to go horseback riding. Camp year-round in the 35-site campground, 31 sites with water, and 15 with electricity. Go freshwater fishing, and tour the interpretive center.

INFORMATION
Torreya State Park
Route 2, Box 70
Bristol, Florida 32321
904-643-2674

TOSOHATCHEE STATE RESERVE
82

LOCATION   The preserve's 28,000 acres are four miles south of Christmas on Taylor Creek Road, off Florida 50. It's east of Orlando.

ACTIVITIES   Go hiking, mountain bicycling on the bike trail, and horseback riding on 27 miles of loops by the reserve trails that run along a 19-mile stretch of the St. Johns River. Camp in the primitive campground and go freshwater fishing.

In Christmas, tour the Fort Christmas Museum, located two miles north of Florida 50 on Florida 420, Fort Christmas Road. Explore two blockhouses' continuing exhibits on the Seminole Indian Wars, and the area's pioneers. For information, call 407-568-4149.

Arriving pilots can land at Kissimmee Municipal Airport, located 16 miles southwest of Orlando, or at Orlando Executive Airport, located three miles east of the city. Rental cars are available at both airports.

INFORMATION
Tosohatchee State Reserve
3365 Taylor Creek Road
Christmas, Florida 32708
305-568-5893

WACCASASSA BAY STATE PRESERVE/ CEDAR KEY SCRUB STATE RESERVE
83

LOCATION   The area is located six miles east of Cedar Key, on Florida 24.

FEATURES   Waccasassa Bay covers 30,784 acres of salt marsh, and many wooded islands. Visitors can see many endangered animal species, including the manatee, bald eagle, and black bear. Cedar Key covers 4,000 acres.

ACTIVITIES   In Cedar Key, hike service roads now utilized as trails. Hunting is permitted from September through December. Also go fishing and canoeing.

Tour Cedar Key State Museum located off Florida 24 on Museum Drive. It's closed Tuesday and Wednesday, and has exhibits depicting the area's history, and a shell collection. For information, call 904-543-5350.

Arriving pilots can land at George T. Lewis Airport, located one mile west of Cedar Key. Transportation is provided by a van or taxi.

INFORMATION
Waccasassa Bay State Preserve/Cedar Key Scrub State Reserve
P.O. Box 187
Cedar Key, Florida 32625
904-543-5567

WASHINGTON OAKS STATE PARK
84

LOCATION   The park is three miles south of Marineland off Florida A1A, within the boundaries of the Atlantic Ocean and Matanzas River.

FEATURES   The park features an oceanfront area with many exotic flowers and plants.

ACTIVITIES   Tour the interpretive center and attend the programs, presented at 1:30 P.M. on Saturdays and Sundays. Hike the nature trail that goes through the ornamental gardens, and along the river. Go swimming and saltwater fishing.

INFORMATION
Washington Oaks State Park
6400 North Ocean Boulevard
Palm Coast, Florida 32137
904-445-3161

WEKIWA SPRINGS STATE PARK
85

LOCATION   The park's 6,396 acres are four miles northwest of I-4, off U.S. 441 near Apopka. Take the Longwood exit to Wekiwa Springs Road.

FEATURES   The springs are the headwaters for the Wekiva River, which continues for 15 miles to flow into the St. Johns River. It's the southern range for Southern black bear.

ACTIVITIES   The park's open forest and jungle attract many hikers. Go backpacking and camping year-round in the 60-site campground, with water and electrical hookups available. Go boating and canoeing, with rentals available, and freshwater stream fishing in Rock Springs Run and the Wekiva River.

Enjoy hiking the nature trails, or walk three loops of easy to moderate trails totaling 13.5 miles, and watch for whitetail deer, bobcats, and Florida black bears. Enjoy swimming, and purchase a snack at the concession stand. Equestrians have access to an 8-mile horseback riding trail. Overnight facilities are available.

Lake Apopka is southwest of town, and is the second largest lake in Florida. Anglers enjoy fishing for bass here.

Lower Wekiva River State Preserve is nine miles west of Sanford on Florida 46. It borders two miles of St. Johns River, and four miles of the Wekiva River and Blackwater Creek. Visitors come to experience its blackwater streams and wetlands, with black bears, alligators, and sandhill cranes. You can also go canoeing, hiking, and primitive backpack camping.

Rock Springs Run State Reserve is in Sorrento, off Florida 46 via Florida 433. The reserve contains over 12 miles of frontage along Rock Springs Run and the

Wekiva River. Visitors can go hiking, primitive backpacking, canoeing, and horse-back riding. Camping permits are required. Contact Wekiwa Springs State Park.

INFORMATION
Wekiwa Springs State Park
1800 Wekiwa Circle
Apopka, Florida 32712
407-884-2009

GEORGIA

Georgia is the largest state east of the Mississippi River, encompassing the Appalachian Mountains and continuing east to the Atlantic Ocean. Part of the Blue Ridge Mountains are located in Georgia's north-central and northeastern section, where you'll also find the state's highest elevations.

Georgia has a large network of trails, each with a theme reflecting the character of the area. In the northwest corner of the state is the 150-mile-long Chieftains Trail that features the history of the Native Americans who inhabited this region including the prehistoric Mississippian Culture, the Creek Nation, and the Cherokee Nation. The route involves U.S. 27, 76, and 411, and Georgia 2, 52, 53, and 515.

The Blue and Gray Trail follows I-75 and U.S. 41 from Chattanooga to Atlanta, and centers on the events leading to the Battle of Atlanta and General Sherman's march through Georgia.

The 100-mile-long Antebellum Trail, Georgia 22/U.S. 441 and east of I-75, passes through Athens, Madison, and Macon. It features the beauty of the Old South with its many grand antebellum mansions and plantation homes. Along the trail you pass through Watkinsville, site of the still-used Elder Mill Covered Bridge, and a popular stop for fans of the novel, *The Bridges of Madison County*.

The 100-mile-long Peach Blossom Trail, U.S. 341/41 west of I-75, goes from Perry north to Jonesboro, to take visitors through the peach capital of the world. The Andersonville Trail in the southwest region of the state highlights events during the Civil War.

Hikers begin their over 2,000-mile-long trek along the Appalachian Trail in Georgia from Amicalola Falls State Park.

The 435,000-acre Okefenokee Swamp is in the southeastern part of Georgia, and is the source of the Suwannee and St. Marys Rivers.

Georgia has 58 state parks which are located in the mountains, along big lakes, and includes several historic and conservation parks. Over 20 of the state parks have housekeeping cabins, which may be reserved up to 11 months in advance. Most park facilities are kept open during the winter months, except during freezing weather when their water systems must be protected. For park information, call 404-656-3530.

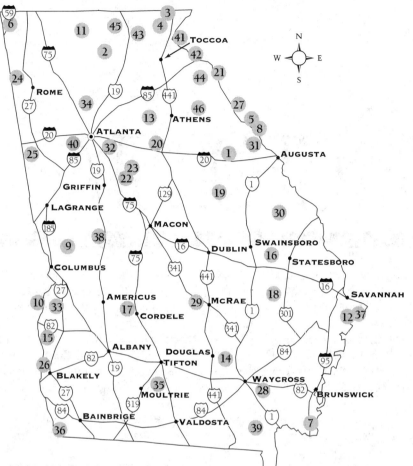

GEORGIA STATE PARKS

1. Alexander H. Stephens State Historic Park
2. Amicalola Falls State Park
3. Black Rock Mountain State Park
4. Moccasin Creek State Park
5. Bobby Brown State Park
6. Cloudland Canyon State Park
7. Crooked River State Park
8. Elijah Clark State Park
9. F. D. Roosevelt State Park
10. Florence Marina State Park
11. Fort Mountain State Park
12. McAllister State Historic Park
12. Richmond Hill State Park
13. Fort Yargo State Park
13. Will-A-Way State Recreation Area
14. General Coffee State Park
15. George T. Bagby State Park
16. George L. Smith State Park
17. Georgia Veterans State Park
18. Gordonia-Altamaha State Park
19. Hamburg State Park
20. Hard Labor Creek State Park
21. Hart State Park
22. High Falls State Park
23. Indian Springs State Park

24. James H. "Sloppy" Floyd State Park
25. John Tanner State Park
26. Kolomoki Mounds State Park
27. Lake Richard B. Russell State Park
28. Laura S. Walker State Park
29. Little Ocmulgee State Park
30. Magnolia Springs State Park
30. Millen National Fish Hatchery and Aquarium
31. Mistletoe State Park
32. Panola Mountina State Conservation Park
33. Providence Canyon State Conservation Park
34. Red Top Mountain State Park
35. Reed Bingham State Park
36. Seminole State Park
37. Skidaway Island State Park
38. Sprewell Bluff State Park
39. Stephen C. Foster State Park
40. Sweetwater Creek State Conservation Park
41. Tallulah Gorge State Park
42. Tugaloo State Park
43. Unicoi State Park
44. Victoria Bryant State Park
45. Vogel State Park
46. Watson Mill Bridge State Park

Georgia's coastline is 112 miles long, and its tidal marshes and barrier islands have been preserved as pockets of wilderness. Begin in Savannah and travel by canoe and sea kayak, or begin from Wassaw Island National Wildlife Refuge, accessible from Skidaway Island State Park.

Savannah is Georgia's oldest city, first settled in 1733 by General James Edward Oglethorpe and his band of English colonists, who established Georgia as one of the 13 original colonies. Today the city boasts the largest historic landmark district in the U.S., with over 1,000 homes and buildings located within a 2⅕-mile square area.

ALEXANDER H. STEPHENS STATE HISTORIC PARK
1

LOCATION   The park is two miles north of I-20 in Crawfordville, on Georgia 22.

ACTIVITIES   Alexander Stephens was a U.S. congressman who became vice president of the Confederacy, even though he loved the Union. His antebellum home, circa 1875, is off I-20, Exit 55, and contains many of his possessions. The museum contains a collection of weapons, uniforms, and civilian artifacts from the Civil War. For museum information, call 706-456-2221.

Enjoy camping in the 36-site campground, 22 sites with water and electrical hookups, a coin laundry, and trailer dumping station. Go swimming in the pool or from the beach, and hike the trails. Enjoy fishing and boating from the ramp or dock, with paddleboat and fishing boat rentals available.

The city of Crawfordville becomes a fairyland of 120,000 lights that are set up for its annual "Christmas in Dixie" celebration. Its Confederate Museum is considered to have the best collection of its kind in Georgia.

INFORMATION
Alexander H. Stephens State Historic Park
P.O. Box 235
Crawfordville, Georgia 30631
706-456-2602: park
706-456-2221: museum

AMICALOLA FALLS STATE PARK
2

LOCATION   The park's 1,020 acres are 15 miles northwest of Dahlonega on Georgia 52, near its intersection with Georgia 183. It's also 16 miles northwest of Dawsonville.

FEATURES   The park features the state's highest water falls, which drop 729 feet.

ACTIVITIES   Enjoy camping in the 17-site campground, all sites with electrical and water hookups, a coin laundry, groceries, and a dump station. Overnight in one of the 15 cabins, or stay in the 58-room lodge with an all-you-can-eat buffet restaurant. Tour the visitor center, and pick up a snack at the snack bar.

Go fishing, white water boating, rafting, and hiking. The eight-mile approach to Springer Mountain is the start of the 78-mile Georgia portion of the well known Appalachian Trail.

In Dahlonega, tour the Dahlonega Gold Museum State Historic Site located in the Public Square. Dahlonega is Cherokee for "precious yellow metal." The phrase, "thar's gold in them thar hills" was coined here. The city was the site of America's first gold rush in 1828, and site of a U.S. mint. Try your luck at panning for gold. For information, call 706-864-2257.

Visit the Consolidated Gold Mines, the largest mining operation east of the Mississippi. You can tour the tunnel systems that go back 250 feet, which were dug prior to the turn of the century. For information, call 706-864-8473. Go gold panning both here and at Crisson's Gold Mine, open year-round. For information on Crisson, call 706-864-6363.

Arriving pilots can land at Lumpkin County–Wimpys Airport, three miles northwest of Dahlonega. However, no rental cars are available.

INFORMATION
Amicalola Falls State Park
Star Route, Box 215
Dawsonville, Georgia 30534
706-265-8888

BLACK ROCK MOUNTAIN STATE PARK
3

MOCCASIN CREEK STATE PARK
4

LOCATION   Black Rock Mountain State Park is three miles north of Clayton via U.S. 441 and U.S. 23, situated within the boundaries of the Chattahoochee National Forest.

Moccasin Creek State Park is 20 miles north of Clarkesville, and 16 miles southwest of Clayton on Georgia 197, on Lake Burton.

ACTIVITIES   At Black Rock, camp in the 64-site campground, 52 sites with water and electrical hookups, and a dump station, or overnight in one of the 10 cabins. Purchase your supplies in the camp store. Go fishing, tour the visitor center, and hike the nature trails. Once on top of the mountain, you can see four states.

In Moccasin Creek, camp in the 53-site campground; no hookups are available, but it does have a dump station and coin laundry. Go boating from the ramp or dock, and fishing, and water-skiing on Lake Burton. The lake is 1,866 feet above sea level, encompasses 2,775 acres, and has 62 miles of shoreline. Hike the mountain trails. Visit the Lake Burton Trout Hatchery on Georgia 197 North. Its raceways are filled with trout, and kids under 11 can go fishing. For information, call 706-947-3112.

The 40-mile-long Bartram Trail's mid-point is three miles east of Clayton in Warwoman Dell on Warwoman Road. Originally laid out 200 years ago by Quaker naturalist, William Bartram, it's marked with yellow and black signs. The second highest mountain in Georgia is located within the Warwoman Wildlife Management Area.

Chattooga Wild and Scenic River is seven miles east of Clayton on U.S. 76. Section IV has seven miles of water, with 30 rapids rated Class III, IV and V. Guided raft trips are available. For river information, call 706-782-3320. For rafting information, call 1-800-778-RAFT (7238).

Hike up 4,633-foot-high Rabun Bald Mountain from Clayton, via the Rabun Bald Trail, to access the Chattahoochee National Forest.

INFORMATION

Black Rock Mountain State Park
P.O. Drawer A
Mountain City, Georgia 30562
706-746-2141

Moccasin Creek State Park
Route 1, Box 1634
Lake Burton, Georgia 30523
706-947-3194

BOBBY BROWN STATE PARK

5

LOCATION   The park is 21 miles southeast of Elberton off Georgia 72, on Clark Hill Lake.

ACTIVITIES   Enjoy camping in the 61-site campground, all sites with water and electrical hookups, a coin laundry and dumping station. Go swimming in the pool, and boating from the ramp or dock. Fish for hybrid and striped bass, water ski, and hike the nature trails.

Tour the Granite Museum at #1 Granite Plaza at Georgia 17 and 72, to see exhibits on how Elberton became the "Granite Capital of the World." For information, call 706-283-251. Then go 7.2 miles north of Elberton on Georgia 77 to see the Guidestones, also known as "America's Stonehenge." It has a 10-part message to mankind written in 12 languages. For information, call 706-283-5651.

Arriving pilots can land at Elbert County Patz Field, two miles east of Elberton. Rental cars are available.

INFORMATION
Bobby Brown State Park
2509 Bobby Brown State Park Road
Route 4, Box 232
Elberton, Georgia 30635
706-213-2046

CLOUDLAND CANYON STATE PARK
6

LOCATION   The park is east of Trenton on Georgia 136. It's also 25 miles northwest of Lafayette, on the western edge of Lookout Mountain.

FEATURES   Sitton Gulch Creek has carved a large gorge, dropping 800 feet down the western side of Lookout Mountain, leaving behind ridges, valleys, rock faces, and waterfalls, one which drops almost 100 feet.

The top of Lookout Mountain was the Civil War site of the "Battle Above the Clouds," the final clash in the fight for control at Chickamauga-Chattanooga.

ACTIVITIES   The 2,000-acre park has a 4.7-mile West Rim Loop Trail through thick woods of hemlock, dogwood, mountain laurel, and rhododendron. You can also hike along the 6⅕-mile Backcountry Trail that descends into the canyon to cross Bear Creek several times, before ascending into the maple, poplar, and oak forest.

Visitors can enjoy a picnic, and stay in one of the 16 rustic cabins, or in five fully-equipped cabins. Camp in the 105-site family campground, or hike into the more-remote sites, 30 of them available April through October. Supplies are available in the camp store. Go swimming in the pool, and play tennis. The visitor center has concessions.

Launch your hang glider from Lookout Mountain's Flight Park at McCarty's Bluff, eight miles south of Rock City, off Georgia 189. For directions and information, call 404-398-3549.

Rock City Garden, with 400 varieties of wildflowers, is on top of Lookout Mountain where you get great views of the ageless rock formations, and can visit Fairyland Caverns and Mother Goose Village. Attend Rock City's Fairy Tale Festival held in August, when storytellers, puppeteers, magicians, and performers arrive. Stroll along the flagstone path, through the gardens where warring Creek Indians once sought refuge in its many rock pockets. For information, call 706-820-2531.

In Rising Fawn, attend the New Salem Mountain Festival in late May and mid-October. It's held on top of Lookout Mountain on Georgia 136 between Trenton and Lafayette. For information, call the Chamber of Commerce at 706-398-1988.

Arriving pilots can land at Barwick-LaFayette Airport, one mile south of Lafayette. Rental cars are available.

INFORMATION
Cloudland Canyon State Park
Route 2, Box 150
Rising Fawn, Georgia 30738
706-657-4050

CROOKED RIVER STATE PARK

7

LOCATION   The park is eight miles east on Georgia Spur 40, along the south bank of Crooked River. It's also 12 miles east of Kingsland, and six miles north of St. Marys.

ACTIVITIES   Go camping in the 60-site campground, 30 sites with water and electrical hookups, a coin laundry, and dump station, or stay in one of the 11 cabins. Enjoy water-skiing, fishing, and boating from the ramp or dock, with fishing boat and paddleboat rentals available. Go swimming in the pool, attend nature programs, play miniature golf, and tour the visitor center. Rent a bicycle to go cycling, and hike the nature trails.

Nearby Cumberland Island National Seashore is accessible from Georgia 40 in St. Marys. Ferries leave twice daily from St. Marys for the island. Reservations are advisable. Call 912-882-4335. At the seashore, turn right at the waterfront to reach the visitor center.

Wildlife abounds here where horses wander freely, and loggerhead turtles deposit their eggs along the beach by the white dunes. Overnight camping is permitted, but reservations must be made through the park service. For island information, call 912-882-4336.

Tour one of the homes built by Andrew Carnegie's descendants. Enjoy saltwater fishing, and swimming from the pristine beach, with its many shells and shorebirds. Hike the island's walking trails, including the self-guided Dungeness Trail. Walk through the museum to see Indian artifacts, and to learn the island's history.

While in St. Marys, take a guided tour of Orange Hall, a Green Revival antebellum mansion listed on the National Register of Historic Places.

Arriving pilots can land at St. Marys Airport, two miles north of the city. Rental cars are available.

INFORMATION
Crooked River State Park
3092 Spur 40
St. Marys, Georgia 31558
912-882-5256

ELIJAH CLARK STATE PARK
8

LOCATION   The state park is seven miles northeast of Lincolnton off U.S. 378. Go 28.5 miles northeast via U.S. 78, Georgia 43, and U.S. 378.

FEATURES   The 447-acre park memorializes a Revolutionary War hero. His reconstructed log home is now a museum of local colonial life, circa 1780.

ACTIVITIES   Go camping in the 165-site campground, all sites with water and electrical hookups, and a dumping station, or overnight in one of the 20 cabins. Enjoy picnicking and swimming from the beach. Go boating from the ramp, fishing, water-skiing, play miniature golf, and hike the trails. Tour the museum where tours are available from 9–5.

In Lincolnton, tour the Lincoln County Historical Park/May House at 147 Lumber Street. The home was lived in by an early town doctor and has been restored with period furniture. For information, call 706-359-4697. Price's Store at 5021 Double Branches Road, is one of Georgia's oldest rural stores still in existence. For information, call 706-359-4401.

In addition to these places, the town features over 200 homes and buildings listed on the National Register. For information, call 706-359-1737.

Tour the Clarks Hill Lake Dam and Powerhouse to learn how water is converted into electricity.

INFORMATION
Elijah Clark State Park
Route 4, Box 293
Lincolnton, Georgia 30817
706-359-3458

F. D. ROOSEVELT STATE PARK
9

LOCATION   The park is five miles southeast of the city of Pine Mountain, on top of Pine Mountain on Georgia 190.

FEATURES   The state park incorporates the President's favorite driving route and picnic site.

ACTIVITIES   Enjoy camping in the 140-site campground, all sites with water and electrical hookups, a coin laundry, and dumping station, or overnight in one of the 21 cabins. Camping supplies are available. Go fishing and boating in one of the lakes from the dock. Fishing boat rentals are available. Hike the nature and other hiking trails, and go swimming in the pool. Go horseback riding, with rentals available. No private horses are allowed in the park. The park is open year-round.

Tour the Little White House Historic Site located ½ mile south of Warm Springs on Georgia 85W. It was built in 1932 so President Roosevelt could be near

Warm Springs for his polio therapy. Tours are offered daily from 9–5, except on Thanksgiving and Christmas. The last tour begins at 4:15 P.M. For information, call 706-655-5870.

The Warm Springs Regional Fisheries Center is on U.S. 27 Alternate, east of town. Tour the visitor center and see its aquarium displays. For information, call 706-655-3382.

Pine Mountain's 23-mile-long blazed trail begins at the Callaway Country Store on U.S. 27, and goes to the WJSP-TV tower on Georgia 85. Pick up a trail map in the state park office.

At Pine Mountain, tour the Callaway Gardens on U.S. 27. Stroll along the 1.5-mile-long Azalea Trail in May, when the azaleas are in bloom. Other trails to explore include three-mile-long Meadowlark Arboretum Area trail, the 1.5-mile-long Mountain Creek Lake Trail, and the ⅖-mile Laurel Springs Trail through the Appalachian hardwood forest and mountain laurel. Callaway's Cecil B. Day Butterfield Center has the nation's largest glass-enclosed butterfly conservatory, with 1,000 butterflies from three continents.

While at Callaway Gardens, play on one of the four golf courses, three with 18 holes. Two pro shops provide your golfing needs, with instruction available. Play tennis on either 11 paved or 8 Rubico courts, with instruction available. Go horseback riding along the woodland trails. Enjoy fishing in the 175-acre Mountain Creek Lake for bream and bass. Take a ride on the riverboat *Robert E. Lee,* and watch the summer "Water Ski Spectacular." Attend Florida State University's Flying High Circus. For information, call 404-663-2281.

Enjoy sun bathing on the longest man-made beach in the world. Take a 7.5-mile-long bicycle ride on the paved bicycle trail.

The Pine Mountain Heritage Festival is held the end of October, featuring the region's fall colors, arts and crafts, and entertainment. For information, call 706-663-4000.

Arriving pilots can land at the Callaway Gardens/Harris County Airport, located five minutes from the gardens, and two miles southwest of Pine Mountain. A courtesy car is available.

INFORMATION
F. D. Roosevelt State Park
Box 749
Pine Mountain, Georgia 31822
706-663-4858

FLORENCE MARINA STATE PARK
10

LOCATION   The park is four miles south of Omaha on Georgia 39C, at the northern end of Lake Walter F. George, on the Chattahoochee River.

FEATURES   The three-mile-long Walter George Dam has a lock that is believed to be one of the highest lifts in the world.

ACTIVITIES   Enjoy camping in the 44-site campground, all sites with water and electrical hookups, and dumping station, or overnight in one of the 11 cottages. Go swimming in the pool, and boating from the ramp and dock, with rental boats available. Go fishing from the lighted fishing pier; water-ski, play tennis, or miniature golf. Tour the Kirbo Interpretive Center to see artifact displays from as long ago as the Paleo-Indian period. For information, call 912-838-4706.

INFORMATION
Florence Marina State Park
Route 1, Box 36
Omaha, Georgia 38121
912-838-6570

FORT MOUNTAIN STATE PARK
11

LOCATION   The park is seven miles southeast of Chatsworth via Georgia 52.

FEATURES   The park has a prehistoric, man-made fortification located on the point of the mountain, believed to be the work of Indians over a thousand years ago. It's located along the Chieftains Trail.

ACTIVITIES   Camp in the 70-site campground, all sites with water and electrical hookups, and a dump station, or overnight in one of the 15 cabins. Go swimming from the beach, and boating from the dock, with boat, canoe, and paddleboat rentals available. Enjoy fishing, and hiking the trails. Tour the visitor center, and play miniature golf.

The Cohutta Wilderness is on U.S. 411, in the Chattahoochee National Forest. It includes the southern end of the Appalachian Mountains, and two of the state's best wild trout streams: Conasauga and Jacks Rivers. Besides fishing, you can go hiking and backpacking.

Tour the Chief Vann House State Historic Site on U.S. 76, three miles west of Chatsworth. The house, circa 1804, is an example of Cherokee Indian wealth and culture. It's called the "Showplace of the Cherokee Nation." The Cohutta Lodge, also on U.S. 76, is a 60-room, historical landmark Old English lodge, located on top of Fort Mountain. For information, call 404-695-2598.

INFORMATION
Fort Mountain State Park
Route 7, Box 7008
Chatsworth, Georgia 30705
706-695-2621

FORT McALLISTER STATE HISTORIC PARK

RICHMOND HILL STATE PARK
12

LOCATION   The fort is off I-95 on Georgia 144, 10 miles east of Richmond Hill on the bank of the Great Ogeechee River.

Richmond Hill State Park is nine miles east of Richmond Hill on Georgia 144 spur, adjacent to the Ft. McAllister Historic Site.

FEATURES   Fort McAllister's earthen fortifications were constructed at the mouth of river in 1861, to protect Savannah from sea warfare during the Civil War. It was able to withstand 9 battles with Union gunboats from 1862–1863, but was finally overpowered by General William T. Sherman in 1864, during his march to the sea.

ACTIVITIES   The historic park encompasses 1,690 acres. Take a walking tour of the fort's central parade ground, plus 21 other locations described in the tour guide. Walk through the small museum to see depictions of the final battle at the fort, and artifacts from the wreck of a Confederate blockade runner. Attend Civil War lectures and watch small arms demonstrations on summer weekends. Bring along a picnic to enjoy under the tall pines along the riverfront.

Cross over the causeway to Savage Island to go camping in the 65-site campground at Richmond Hill State Park, all sites with water and electrical hookups, a coin laundry, and dumping station. Hike the nature trail, but use caution when hiking in the woods where poisonous snakes may be encountered. Go water-skiing and boating from the ramp, and fishing for whiting, flounder, mullet, shrimp, and crab.

INFORMATION
Fort McAllister State Historic Park
Route 2, Box 394-A Fort McAllister Road
Richmond Hill, Georgia 31324
912-727-2339

FORT YARGO STATE PARK

WILL-A-WAY STATE RECREATION AREA
13

LOCATION   The state park and state recreation area are 10 miles south on Georgia 211. When you reach Winder, turn right after passing the courthouse, and continue one mile south on Georgia 81.

FEATURES   The log blockhouse, circa 1792, was constructed by settlers as protection against the Indians. Its hand-hewn logs of virgin pine still contain the marks of heavy caliber gun bullets.

Will-A-Way has been especially designed for the handicapped, and includes a group camp, handicap-accessible cottages, food service, and a swimming beach.

ACTIVITIES   At the state recreation area, enjoy camping in the 47-site campground, 40 sites with water and electrical hookups, a coin laundry, and dumping station, or overnight in one of the three cabins. Go swimming in the pool or from the beach. Go boating from the ramp or dock; power limits are established for motorboats. Boat, canoe, and paddleboat rentals are available. Go fishing, play tennis and miniature golf, and tour the museum. Hike the trails. The park is open year-round.

Arriving pilots can land at Winder Airport, three miles east of the city. Rental cars are available.

INFORMATION
Fort Yargo State Park
P.O. Box 764
Winder, Georgia 30780
770-867-3489

Will-A-Way State Recreation Area
Winder, Georgia 30780
770-867-5313

GENERAL COFFEE STATE PARK
14

LOCATION   The park is six miles east of Douglas, on Georgia 32.

ACTIVITIES   Enjoy camping in the 50-site campground, 25 sites with water and electrical hookups, a coin laundry, and dumping station. Go fishing and swimming in the pool. Enjoy boating, with fishing and paddleboat rentals available. Play nine holes of golf, and test your skill at archery on the archery range.

Tour the unique Pioneer Village to watch living history. Hike nature trails from the village to a 19th-century bed and breakfast inn.

Arriving pilots can land at Douglas Municipal Airport, two miles south of Douglas. Rental cars are available.

INFORMATION
General Coffee State Park
Route 2, Box 83
Nichols, Georgia 31554
912-384-7082

GEORGE T. BAGBY STATE PARK
15

LOCATION   The park is 15 miles north of Fort Gaines, off Georgia 39.

ACTIVITIES   Enjoy camping in the 50-site campground, with some hookups, and dumping station, or overnight in one of the five cabins. You can also stay in the 30-room lodge, with a restaurant available. Go boating from the ramp or dock, with rentals available from the full service marina. Go water-skiing, fishing, and hike the trails. Rent a cassette tape at the lodge for a narrated tour of the historic sites around the lake and Fort Gaines.

Lake Walter F. George, with its 640-mile-long shoreline, is two miles north of Fort Gaines, on the Chattahoochee River. Here you can also go camping, swimming, boating, and fishing from the pier. Its lock is the second highest east of the Mississippi River. Tour the interpretive center. For information, call 912-768-2516.

Outpost Replica is on South Georgia 39. Turn right on Commerce Street and go three blocks further. The replica is on the left. The reconstructed fort, circa 1816–1830, was used to protect the early settlers from Creek and Seminole Indian attacks.

Frontier Village, located on a bluff overlooking the Chattanooga River, features authentic log cabins, and an 18-foot tall oak statue memorial to the Creek Indians.

INFORMATION
George T. Bagby State Park
Box 661
Fort Gaines, Georgia 31751
912-768-2660: park
912-768-2571: lodge

GEORGE L. SMITH STATE PARK
16

LOCATION   The park is four miles southeast of Twin City off Georgia 23. It's also near Meter and I-16.

ACTIVITIES   The park is open year-round. Enjoy camping in the 21-site campground, all sites with water and electrical hookups, and a dump station. Go boating from the ramp or dock, with boating limits established. Fishing-boat and canoe rentals are available. Visit the scenic 1880s covered bridge, old mill, and dam, located on the cypress pond.

Arriving pilots can land at Metter Municipal Airport, two miles south of Metter. Rental cars are available.

INFORMATION
George L. Smith State Park
P.O. Box 57
Twin City, Georgia 30471
912-763-2759

GEORGIA VETERANS STATE PARK
17

LOCATION   The park is on Lake Blackshear, nine miles west of Cordele via U.S. 280, off I-75.

ACTIVITIES   Enjoy camping in the 85-site campground, all sites with water and electrical hookups, and dumping station, or overnight in one of the 10 cottages. Go swimming in the pool, or from the beach in Lake Blackshear. Go boating from the ramp or dock. Play golf on the 18-hole championship course. For a tee-time, call 912-276-2377.

Enjoy fishing and water-skiing, and tour the visitor center. The museum has photos, maps, vintage aircraft, military equipment, weapons, and outdoor exhibits, memorializing Georgia's veterans. The park is also a haven for model airplane enthusiasts.

Cordele is the southern starting point for a 75-mile historic driving tour. The tour includes Camellia Gardens, Americus Historic District, Robins AFB Museum of Aviation, and the Andersonville National Historic Site. At Andersonville, tour the Confederate prison, built in 1864, and used for 14 months. Here, over 12,900 Union prisoners died of disease and starvation. The Confederate Village is across from the prison, and features a log church, prison officials' quarters, a living pioneer farm, the Civil War Drummer Boy Museum, and an open air theater. The first weekend in October, attend the Andersonville Historic Fair. For information, call 912-924-2558.

Attend Cordele's Watermelon Days Festival in July, with watermelon eating, and seed-spitting contests. Take a walking tour of historic downtown Cordele, the state's capital during the Civil War's latter days. Maps are available at the Chamber of Commerce, 302 16th Street, on U.S. 280.

In Andersonville, attend the Anderson Historic Fair which is held in late May and early October. It features Civil War reenactments, old-time craftsmen, Civil War collectibles, and antique dealers. For information, call the Anderson Guild at 912-924-2558.

Arriving pilots can land at Crisp County–Cordele Airport, two miles northeast of Cordele. Rental cars are available.

INFORMATION
Georgia Veterans State Park
Route 3
Cordele, Georgia 31015
912-276-2371

GORDONIA-ALTAMAHA STATE PARK
18

LOCATION   The park is located at the city limits of Reidsville, off U.S. 280.

ACTIVITIES   Enjoy camping in the 25-site campground, all sites with water and electrical hookups, a coin laundry, and a dumping station. Go swimming in the pool, and play miniature golf or 9 holes of regulation golf, with a pro shop available. For a tee-time, call 912-557-5445.

Go boating from the dock with fishing-boat, canoe, and paddleboat rentals available. Go fishing in one of the premier largemouth bass fishing rivers in Southeast Georgia.

Take a canoe float-trip from the Ohoopee River Plantation. The plantation also offers camping with hookups, fishing, and hunting trips for deer, turkey, and wild hogs. For information, call 912-557-6464.

Arriving pilots can land at Reidsville Airport, three miles southwest of the city. However, no rental cars are available.

INFORMATION
Gordonia-Altamaha State Park
P.O. Box 1047
Reidsville, Georgia 30453
912-557-4763

HAMBURG STATE PARK
19

LOCATION   The park is 16 miles north of Sandersville, on Georgia 248.

ACTIVITIES   The park is open year-round. Enjoy camping in one of the 30 campsites, all sites with water and electrical hookups, a coin laundry, and dumping station. Go boating from the dock or ramp, with boating limits set for motorboats. Go fishing and hiking. Rental fishing boats, canoes, and paddleboats are available. The park has a working grist mill that still grinds corn daily. Tour the museum.

INFORMATION
Hamburg State Park
Route 2, Box 233
Mitchell, Georgia 30820
912-552-2393

HARD LABOR CREEK STATE PARK
20

LOCATION   The park is two miles north of Rutledge, off U.S. 278.

ACTIVITIES   The park is open year-round. Enjoy camping in the 49-site campground, all sites with water and electrical hookups, and dumping station, or overnight in one of the 20 cabins. Groceries are available. Go swimming from the beach, and boating from the ramp or dock, with limits set for motor boats. Fishing-boat, canoe, and paddleboat rentals are available. Hike the trails, and play golf on the 18-hole golf course. For a tee-time, call 706-557-3006.

Bring your own horse to go horseback riding along 15 miles of equestrian trails. No rentals are available. Horses must have a current negative Coggins test.

INFORMATION
Hard Labor Creek State Park
Rutledge, Georgia 30663
404-557-3001

HART STATE PARK
21

LOCATION   The park is three miles north of Hartwell, off U.S. 29, on Lake Hartwell.

FEATURES   Lake Hartwell, located on the Savannah River, is one of the Southeast's largest and most popular lakes, with a 962-mile-long shoreline.

ACTIVITIES   Enjoy camping along the lakefront of Lake Hartwell in the 83-site campground, 55 sites with water and electrical hookups, a coin laundry, and dumping station, or overnight in one of the five mobile homes. Supplies are available in the camp store. Go boating from the ramp or dock, with boat rentals available. Go fishing and water-skiing.

Hartwell Dam is seven miles east of Hartwell on U.S. 29, where you can go fishing, boating, swimming, water-skiing, and camping. Tours of the dam's power-house are available from June 1st through Labor Day. Tour the museum, and take the paved walkway across the dam. Bluegrass music is played Saturday nights. For information, call 706-376-8590.

Go for a one-hour excursion aboard the Hart County Scenic Railway, on an authentic passenger train. The station is on Georgia 77 South, then 1.5 miles to Liberty Hill Road. Go to the end of the pavement at Cedar Creek. For train information, call 404-376-2627.

INFORMATION
Hart State Park
330 Hart Park Road
Hartwell, Georgia 30643
706-376-8756

HIGH FALLS STATE PARK
22

LOCATION   The park is 13 miles north of Forsyth, two miles east of I-75.

ACTIVITIES   Enjoy camping in the 142-site campground, 140 sites with water and electrical hookups, a coin laundry, and dumping station. Go swimming in the pool or from the beach. Enjoy boating from the dock or ramp. You can rent fishing boats, canoes, and paddleboats. Go fishing, hike the nature trails, and play miniature golf. Bring along a picnic to enjoy by the scenic cascading waterfall. The park is open year-round.

In Forsyth, visit the commercial historic district, where Courthouse Square and eight surrounding blocks contain 40 structures from the 1800s, listed on the National Register. Attend the Forsythia Festival in late April. For information, call the Chamber of Commerce at 912-994-9239.

INFORMATION
High Falls State Park
Route 5, Box 202-A
Jackson, Georgia 30233
912-993-3053 or 912-994-0914

INDIAN SPRINGS STATE PARK
23

LOCATION   The park is four miles southeast of Jackson on Georgia 42. From I-75, take Exit 67.

FEATURES   Indian Springs is the oldest state park in the U.S. The site was used by the Creek Indians, who believed that the water was able to heal their sick and bring additional strength to the healthy.

ACTIVITIES   Enjoy camping in the 90-site campground, all sites with water and electrical hookups, a coin laundry, and dumping station, or overnight in one of the 10 cottages. Go swimming from the beach, and boating from the ramp or dock (with boating limits). Fishing-boat and paddleboat rentals are available.

Go fishing, and hike the nature trails. Collect some of the medicinal spring water. Tour the visitor center and attend interpretive programs.

INFORMATION
Indian Springs State Park
Indian Springs, Georgia 30231
770-504-2277

JAMES H. "SLOPPY" FLOYD STATE PARK
24

LOCATION   The park is three miles southeast of Summerville, off U.S. 27.

ACTIVITIES   Camp in the 25-site campground, all sites with water and electrical hookups, a coin laundry, and dumping station. Go boating from the dock or ramp, with limits imposed upon motor boats. Go fishing in one of the two fishing lakes, with fishing-boat or paddleboat rentals available. The park is adjacent to the Chattahoochee National Forest.

INFORMATION
James H. "Sloppy" Floyd State Park
Route 1, Box 201
Summerville, Georgia 30747
706-857-0828

JOHN TANNER STATE PARK
25

LOCATION   The park is six miles west of Carrollton, off Georgia 16.

ACTIVITIES   Enjoy camping in the 78-site campground, 36 sites with electrical and water hookups, a coin laundry, and dumping station, or overnight in one of the 13 beach cabins. Purchase your camping supplies from the camp store. Go swimming from the longest sand swimming beach found within the state parks. Canoe and paddleboat rentals are available. Go boating (speed limits are set), fishing, play miniature golf, rent a bicycle to go cycling, and hike the trails.

Arriving pilots can land at West Georgia Regional Airport, five miles northwest of Carrollton. Rental cars are available.

INFORMATION
John Tanner State Park
354 Tanner's Beach Road
Carrollton, Georgia 30117
770-830-2222

KOLOMOKI MOUNDS STATE PARK
26

LOCATION   The park is six miles north of Blakely, off U.S. 27.

FEATURES   Seven 12th- and 13th-century mounds have been preserved. Besides the mounds, a plaza and outlying villages indicate that approximately 2,000 people once lived here. The Great Mound sits on a base 325 feet by 200 feet, and is 56 feet high. One of the excavated mounds is now utilized as a museum, where you can look down into the archeological dig.

ACTIVITIES   Go fishing in one of the two lakes or in Kolomoki Creek for bass, crappies, bream, catfish, and trout. Rent a rowboat or fishing boat, with launch ramp available. Note that motors are limited to 10 horsepower.

Hike the two short nature trails, watching for bluebirds, cardinals, and maybe an alligator. Go swimming in the pool, or camp in the 35-site campground, with a dumping station, and all sites with water and electrical hookups.

Tour the museum which is open Tuesday through Saturday, and on Sunday afternoon. Admission is charged. Play miniature golf and attend interpretive programs in the visitor center. Refreshments are available.

The Coheelee Creek Covered Bridge, circa 1891, is nine miles west of Blakely, off Georgia 62 and Old River Road. The bridge is 96 feet long, two spans wide, and is the Southern-most "kissing bridge" still standing.

Arriving pilots can land at Early County Airport, three miles east of Blakely. However, no rental cars are available.

INFORMATION
Kolomoki Mounds State Historic Park
Route 1, Box 114
Blakely, Georgia 31723
912-723-5296: park
912-723-3398: museum

LAKE RICHARD B. RUSSELL STATE PARK
27

LOCATION   The park is on Lake Richard B. Russell, northeast of Elberton.

ACTIVITIES   Go boating from the beach, take a guided tour of the powerhouse (advance reservations required), and tour the visitor center. For information, call 706-283-5121 or 706-283-8731.

Arriving pilots can land at Elbert County–Patz Field, two miles east of Elberton. Rental cars are available.

INFORMATION
Lake Richard B. Russell State Park
2650 Russell State Park Road
Elberton, Georgia 30635
706-213-2045

LAURA S. WALKER STATE PARK
28

LOCATION   The park is 10 miles southeast of Waycross, off U.S. 84, near the Okefenokee Swamp.

ACTIVITIES   Enjoy camping in the 44-site campground, all sites with water and electrical hookups, a coin laundry, and dumping station. Go swimming in the pool, and boating from the ramp and dock, with canoe rentals available. Boating limits are enforced. Go fishing and water-skiing. Attend interpretive programs. Food service is also available. Play golf and call for a tee-time at 912-284-2882.

Okefenokee Swamp Park is eight miles south of Waycross on U.S. 1/23, and then 4.75 miles south on Georgia 177. Okefenokee is Indian, and means "land of the trembling earth." The 438,000-acre National Wildlife Refuge can also be reached from U.S. 82 via Georgia 177. Take a two-mile guided boat tour to see wildlife in its natural habitat.

There are two accesses to the refuge: Fargo's Stephen C. Foster State Park, and the Folkston Suwannee Canal Recreation Area. Stroll along the swamp boardwalk, and climb the 50-foot observation tower to get great views of the nearby prairies, lakes, and cypress domes.

The swamp is the largest national wildlife refuge in the eastern U.S. It features interpretive exhibits, elevated wilderness walkways, an observation tower, canoe rentals, and guided boat tours. Pioneer Island is an original swamp homestead, where tours are available. For information, call 912-283-0583.

Okefenokee Heritage Center/Southern Forest World is on North Augusta Avenue, between U.S. 1 and U.S. 82. You'll see exhibits of local history, including a 1912 steam locomotive, restored depot, late 1800s print shop, and antique vehicles. Hike the nature trails. For information, call 912-285-4260 or 4056.

Obediah's Okefenok is on Barber Island, on the southwest edge of the Swamp. Homesteader Obediah Barber, called the "King of the Okefenokee," built his cabin here in the 1800s. It has a smokehouse, grist mill, print shop, and blacksmith shop. Stroll along the boardwalk or nature trail. For information, call 912-287-0090.

Arriving pilots can land at Waycross-Ware County Airport, three miles northwest of Waycross. Rental cars are available.

INFORMATION
Laura S. Walker State Park
5653 Laura Walker Road
Route 6, Box 205
Waycross, Georgia 31503
912-287-4900

LITTLE OCMULGEE STATE PARK
29

LOCATION   The park is two miles north of McRae, via U.S. 319 and U.S. 441.
FEATURES   Little Ocmulgee State Park encompasses 14,000 acres and a
265-acre lake.
ACTIVITIES   The park is open year-round. Go hiking along the two hiking
trails: one approximately two miles long, and the other, a shorter one, winding
through the dogwood, oak, and hickory trees. Come in April when the wild azalea is in full bloom. Birders can spot many birds including wood ducks, cardinals,
egrets, and four species of woodpeckers.

Fishing-boat and canoe rentals are available. Fish in the 265-acre lake for largemouth bass, crappies, shellcrackers, and large bluegill. Go canoeing along the 1/4-
mile-long canoe trail.

Stay overnight in one of the 10 lakeside cottages that are fully equipped and air
conditioned, or in the 30-room Little Ocmulgee Lodge. Camp in the 58-site campground, all sites with water and electrical hookups, TV cable hookups, a coin
laundry, and dumping station. Dine in the restaurant, or pick up a snack at the
snack bar. Swim in the two pools, and play tennis on one of the four courts.

Play golf on the Wallace Adams 18-hole championship course, with a pro shop,
cart rentals, driving range, and a putting green. For a tee-time, call 912-868-8851.
You can also play miniature golf.

In McRae, see the replica of the Statue of Liberty and Liberty Bell, located in
Liberty Square.

A world record largemouth bass was caught in 1932 in Montgomery Lake, off
the Ocmulgee River. It weighed 22 pounds, 4 ounces, and the record still stands.

Arriving pilots can land at Telfair-Wheeler Airport, three miles northeast of
McRae. However, no rental cars are available.

INFORMATION
Little Ocmulgee State Park
Box 97
McRae, Georgia 31055
912-868-7474: lodge
912-868-5949: park

MAGNOLIA SPRINGS STATE PARK

MILLEN NATIONAL FISH HATCHERY AND AQUARIUM
30

LOCATION   Magnolia Springs State Park is five miles north of Millen, via U.S. 25.

Millen National Fish Hatchery is adjacent to the state park.

FEATURES   Camp Lawton was constructed here in the 1860s, and over 10,000 Union troops were held in the POW camp in 1864. Part of the fortifications are still on the hill next to the main entrance to the state park. The park was named for a crystal-clear spring that feeds a 15-foot deep pool. It's near the Bo Ginn National Fish Hatchery.

ACTIVITIES   Bring along a picnic to enjoy at the crystal-clear spring. Anglers come to fish in two lakes, Upper and Lower, or in two small ponds for bass, crappies, catfish, and bream. Launch your boat from the ramp or boat dock at Upper Lake, where you can also go water-skiing. Boating limits are posted. Rental fishing boats are available, and so are concessions.

Go swimming in the pool, or rent a bicycle to go for a ride. Stay overnight in one of the 5 cabins, or in one of the 50 campsites, 25 sites with water and electrical hookups, and a coin laundry.

Hike the Woodpecker Woods Nature Trail to get a look at the seven species of resident woodpeckers. The trail goes through dogwood and magnolias, making this a great place to visit in the spring. The park is open year-round.

The Millen National Fish Hatchery has ponds covered with plankton used to feed the fingerlings. Striped bass are grown here for future stocking of Chesapeake Bay and Albemarle Sound. Stroll through the aquarium to see many fish, turtles, and an alligator. It's open year-round. For information, call 912-982-1700.

Arriving pilots can land at Millen Airport, five miles north of Millen. However, no rental cars are available.

INFORMATION
Magnolia Springs State Park
Route 5, Box 488
Millen, Georgia 30442
912-982-1600

MISTLETOE STATE PARK
31

LOCATION   The park is 12 miles north of I-20, Exit 60, northwest of Appling.
ACTIVITIES   Enjoy camping in the 107-site campground (with dumping station), or overnight in one of the 10 cabins. Purchase your camping supplies from the camp store. Go swimming from the beach; go fishing, water-skiing, and boating from the ramp or dock. Hike the trails.

Group tours of Heggie Rock on Old Louisville Road are available by appointment only. The rock is one of the state's 12 natural landmarks. For information, call 706-873-6946.

INFORMATION
Mistletoe State Park
3723 Mistletoe Road
Route 1
Appling, Georgia 30502
706-541-0321

PANOLA MOUNTAIN
STATE CONSERVATION PARK
32

LOCATION   The mountain is 18 miles southeast of Atlanta, on Georgia 155.
FEATURES   Panola Mountain was made a state park to preserve the granite formation in its natural state.
ACTIVITIES   Tour the nature center. Take a guided hike up the mountain, offered Saturday and Sunday at 10:00, from Memorial Day through Labor Day, and at 2:30 the rest of the year. Hikes going up the mountain are always guided for conservation reasons. You can also hike the three park trails along the granite monadnock. The park has no camping facilities. Parking is free on Wednesdays.

INFORMATION
Panola Mountain State Conservation Park
2600 Highway 155 S.W.
Stockbridge, Georgia 30281
770-389-7801

PROVIDENCE CANYON
STATE CONSERVATION PARK
33

LOCATION   The park is 35 miles south of Columbus and seven miles west of Lumpkin, on Georgia 39C.

FEATURES   A scenic 200-acre canyon known as "Georgia's Little Grand Canyon" dominates the 1,108-acre park. The park preserves this area which contains 16 canyons eroded to a depth of 150 feet. It was named for its deposit of sandy soil, called the Providence Formation, which created some unusual colored sand formations. This soil was highly subject to erosion, as a result of the early farmers' plowing techniques. The park has extensive growths of the rare Plumleaf Azalea.

ACTIVITIES   Hike the two-mile Canyon Rim Trail with its 20 overlooks, or follow one of the two short trails through the multi-color sand walls, going down to the canyon floor. Backpackers have access to an eight-mile backpacking trail.

Stop by the interpretive center to see soil samples, iron chunks, and primitive seashells. Watch the bees in the enclosed working beehive. The park has no camping facilities.

Westville is ½ mile south of Lumpkin. The recreated village, circa 1850, has authentic buildings that were moved here, and is a living history village depicting life in the early 19th century. Observe blacksmithing, pottery making, weaving, and brick masonry. For information, call 912-838-6310.

In Lumpkin, you can see old houses that survived the Civil War, and the Bedingford Inn, once a stopping place for stagecoach passengers.

INFORMATION
Providence Canyon State Park
Route 1, Box 158
Lumpkin, Georgia 31815
912-838-6202

RED TOP MOUNTAIN STATE PARK
34

LOCATION   The park is 55 miles north of Atlanta, east of Cartersville, and 1.5 miles east of I-75 at the Red Top Exit.

FEATURES   Red Top Mountain was named for its red, iron-rich soil, and is one of Georgia's most visited state parks. It's on the 1,950-acre peninsula of Lake Allatoona.

ACTIVITIES   The park is surrounded by scenic Lake Allatoona, and has five hiking trails, ranging in length from one mile to 5.5 miles. Enjoy camping in the

286-site campground, 80 sites with water and electrical hookups, and a dump station. Overnight in one of the 18 cabins, or stay in the 33-room lodge. Purchase your camping supplies from the camp store, or dine in the lodge's restaurant.

Go swimming from the beach, and boating from the ramp or dock, with boat rentals available. Enjoy fishing and water-skiing. Hike the trails, and play tennis.

Tour the visitor center on top of the dam to learn about the natural and cultural history of the area.

Take a walking tour of Carrollton's main street to see the historic courthouse, depot, theater, and the first outdoor Coca-Cola advertisement. For information, call 770-386-6458.

In Kingston, visit the Kingston Confederate Memorial Museum at 13 East Main Street, which features the "Great Locomotive Chase." This was the starting point of the "March to the Sea," and was the last Confederate place located east of the Mississippi to surrender. For information, call 770-336-5269.

Visit the Etowah Mounds, three miles southwest of Cartersville. They're also accessible 5.5 miles southwest of I-75 off Georgia 61. Hike the trails, climb the mounds that were built by the corn farmers from the Mississippean Culture, circa 1000–1500 A.D. Visit the museum. For information, call 770-382-2704.

The Lowery Covered Bridge, also known as Euharlee Creek Bridge, is six miles from Carrollton via Georgia 113, and then two miles further north. It's the state's oldest covered bridge, and the numbers are still legible on the timbers, indicating the bridge was assembled elsewhere and then rebuilt here over the stream.

Tour the Weinman mineral center and museum off I-75, Exit 126 and Georgia 411 at Culver Road. The simulated limestone cave has many gemstones, including a rare amethyst collection, Indian artifacts, and mining history displays. For information, call 770-386-0576.

Arriving pilots can land at Cartersville Airport, three miles southwest of Cartersville. Rental cars are available.

INFORMATION
Red Top Mountain State Park
Route 7
Cartersville, Georgia 30120
770-975-0055: park and restaurant
770-975-4200: cabins

REED BINGHAM STATE PARK
35

LOCATION   The park is six miles west of Adel, on Georgia 37.

ACTIVITIES   Enjoy camping in the 118-site campground, 47 sites with water and electrical hookups, with dumping station, camper supplies, and a coin laundry available. Go swimming from the beach, and boating from the ramp or dock, with canoe rentals available. Enjoy fishing, water-skiing and miniature golf. Hike the 3.5-mile-long Coastal Plains Nature Trail. Stroll through the butterfly and hummingbird gardens.

Watch for the many buzzards on the Little River. Because of the numerous buzzards, the park hosts an annual Buzzard Days Festival the first Saturday in September.

Incoming pilots can land at Cook County Airport, located one mile west of Adel. A courtesy car and taxis are available for ground transportation.

INFORMATION
Reed Bingham State Park
Route 2, Box 394 B-1
Adel, Georgia 31620
912-896-3551

SEMINOLE STATE PARK
36

LOCATION   The park is on the north shore of Lake Seminole, 16 miles south of Donalsonville via Georgia 39.

FEATURES   Seminole was named after the Indians who lived here prior to the arrival of the white settlers.

ACTIVITIES   The 300-acre park is known for its water sports, including boating from the ramp or dock, water-skiing, canoeing, and swimming from the beach. Enjoy some of the best largemouth bass fishing in the U.S., and also try your luck at landing crappie, jack, bream, catfish, and yellow perch.

Enjoy a picnic along the lakefront. Rent a cottage, stay in the 50-site shaded campground, 25 sites with water and electrical hookups, and dumping station, or overnight in one of the 10 fully-equipped cottages. Come in the spring when the dogwood are in bloom. The park is open year-round. Concessions are available.

Lake Seminole Wildlife Management Area is near the state park, and is one of the state's largest game reserves, where hunters can hunt for duck, deer, rabbit, quail, and turkey.

Arriving pilots can land at Donalsonville Municipal Airport, one mile south of the city. However, no rental cars are available.

INFORMATION
Seminole State Park
Route 2
Donalsonville, Georgia 31745
912-861-3137

SKIDAWAY ISLAND STATE PARK
37

LOCATION   The park is six miles southeast of Savannah to Georgia 21. Take I-16 to Georgia 21. It's on the Diamond Causeway.

ACTIVITIES   Camp in the 100-site campground, 88 sites with water and electrical hookups, and dumping station. Concessions are available. Enjoy swimming in the pool, fishing, and hiking the trails through the coastal marsh.

Launch your boat into the Intracoastal Waterway and paddle 12 miles to the Wassaw Island National Wildlife Refuge, one of the state's six undeveloped barrier islands. The island is open for day-use only.

Stop by the Skidaway Marine Science Complex on Skidaway Island Drive at the Modena Plantation. Exhibits include the 12,000-gallon aquarium, and coastal archeological finds. For information, call 912-356-2453.

Ten miles southeast of Savannah, at 7601 Skidaway Road on the Isle of Hope, visit the Wormsloe Plantation Historic Site. The site contains the remains of the fortified home and farm constructed by Noble Jones, circa 1756. He was one of the original 114 colonists who arrived in Georgia with General James E. Oglethorpe. Tour the visitor center, and watch the slide show on the early settlement. For information, call 912-353-3023.

In Savannah, tour the nation's largest urban-registered National Historic Landmark District, covering 2.5 square miles. It features statues, fountains, 21 squares and parks, plus 1,400 restored 19th-century mansions, row houses, and cottages. Davenport House, circa 1820, is at 119 Habersham Street. The birthplace of Juliette Gordon Low, who founded the Girl Scouts in Savannah in 1912, is at 142 Bull Street.

Other historic houses to tour include the King-Tisdell Cottage at 514 East Huntington Street. It preserves Savannah's African-American history and culture. Owens-Thomas House, circa 1816, is at 124 Abercorn Street, and the William Scarborough House, circa 1819, is at 41 West Broad Street.

Antique car lovers can tour the Evans Antique Car Museum at 313 West River Street to see one of the finest private collections of rare automobiles. To learn more about Savannah's history, watch "The Great Savannah Exposition" at 303 West Broad Street, or "The Savannah Experience, shown in an old cotton warehouse at 1 East River Street.

Old Fort Jackson at 1 Fort Jackson Road, three miles from downtown on President Street, is the oldest standing fort in Georgia. It houses the largest cannon fired in the U.S. Weapons demonstrations are presented from 1-5 daily. For information, call 912-232-3945.

Factor's Walk, on Bay Street, was the center of commerce during the years when cotton was king. It was where world cotton prices were set. Ornate iron bridgeways connect buildings used as the merchants' offices.

Fort Pulaski National Monument is on U.S. 80 E. It was partly engineered by Robert E. Lee, and was named for Revolutionary War hero Casimir Pulaski. Tour the visitor center's exhibits, and walk the trails. For information, call 912-786-5787.

Savannah is known for one of America's largest St. Patrick's Day celebrations, held the last weekend in March. Attend the "Night in Old Savannah" in mid-May, celebrating the city's diversity with a multi-ethnic food fest. The first Saturday of the month, Riverfront Plaza features First Saturday Festivals, with changing themes.

Ride aboard the *Savannah River Queen* at 9 East River Street. For reservations, call 912-232-6404.

Arriving pilots can land at Savannah International Airport, seven miles northwest of the city. Rental cars are available.

INFORMATION
Skidaway Island State Park
Savannah, Georgia 31411
912-598-2300

SPREWELL BLUFF STATE PARK
38

LOCATION   The park is eight miles west of Thomaston on Old Alabama Road, off Georgia 74.

ACTIVITIES   The river park has hiking trails along the Flint River, with boating allowed in the river.

Stop by the Flint River Outdoor Center seven miles west of town to go canoeing, rafting, and tubing on the river's Class I, II and III rapids. Shuttle service, rentals, and concessions are available. For information, call 706-647-2633.

In Thomaston, tour the Pettigrew-White-Stamps House on Andrews Drive. Built circa 1834, the home has many period furnishings and local artifacts. Check with the Chamber of Commerce for directions to the Auchumpkee Creek Covered Bridge, and for the date of the Potato Creek Heritage Festival. Call 706-647-9686.

Arriving pilots can land at Reginald Grant Memorial Airport, three miles northwest of Thomaston. Rental cars are available.

INFORMATION
Sprewell Bluff State Park
Thomaston, Georgia 30286
706-848-8028

STEPHEN C. FOSTER STATE PARK
39

LOCATION   The park is 18 miles northeast of Fargo on Georgia 177, in the heart of the Okefenokee Swamp.

ACTIVITIES   Go camping in the 68-site campground, all sites with water and electrical hookups, a coin laundry, and dumping station, or stay overnight in one of the nine cabins. Purchase your supplies in the camp store. Enjoy fishing and boating from the ramp or dock (boating limits of 10 mph), with rentals available. Boat tours of Okefenokee Swamp are available. Go water-skiing, swimming, hike the swamp trails, go fishing, tour the visitor center, and attend nature programs. Take a guided tour of the park.

The Suwannee Canal Recreation Area and Okefenokee National Wildlife Refuge are on the east side of Okefenokee Swamp. Over 40 kinds of fish and 230 species of birds are native to the area. The swamp is home to alligators, black bears, muskrat, and otter. Fish for bass, bluegill, catfish, and pickerel.

Walk along the 4,000-foot boardwalk, constructed over the bogs, that leads to a 50-foot observation tower. Ride aboard the interpretive tram, and take a guided after-dark tour. Walk through the restored homestead.

Rent a motorboat to explore the 11-mile Suwannee Canal. Take a wilderness canoe trip. Reservations are necessary. Call 912-496-7156. If you arrive from April through October, be sure to bring along plenty of insect repellent. Walk through the interpretive center, and bring along a picnic. Bicycle rentals, food service, and fishing supplies, are available. For information, call 912-496-7836.

INFORMATION
Stephen C. Foster State Park
Route 1, Box 131
Fargo, Georgia 31631
912-637-5274

SWEETWATER CREEK
STATE CONSERVATION PARK
40

LOCATION   The park is 15 miles west of Atlanta. Take I-20 west to Thornton Road/Camp Creek Parkway.

FEATURES   A textile mill ruin used during the Civil War is still visible. After the war, Lithia Springs became known as a health spa, with its lithium-fortified mineral water that many believed held curative powers. Today a bottle company still operates here, and visitors can tour the Family Doctor Museum and medicinal garden.

ACTIVITIES   Go boating (boating limits enforced) from the ramp or dock. Canoe and fishing-boat rentals are available. Enjoy fishing and hiking. The park has over 10 miles of scenic, marked trails, climbing past old homesteads and through Cherokee Indian settlements located along the historic Sweetwater Creek. Several miles of the trail are beside the broad cascades and whitewater rapids of the creek. No camping facilities are available.

INFORMATION
Sweetwater Creek Conservation State Park
P.O. Box 816
Lithia Springs, Georgia 30057
770-732-5871

TALLULAH GORGE STATE PARK
41

LOCATION   The park is in the center of the town of Tallulah Falls, on U.S. 441.

FEATURES   The park, at 1,500 feet above sea level, and is the state's newest state park, located along one of the most spectacular and oldest natural gorges in the eastern U.S. The gorge has a vast chasm two miles long, and almost 1,000 feet deep. It's second in depth to the Grand Canyon. Tightrope walker, Karl Wallenda, once walked across this gorge. The tallest falls drop 700 feet to the canyon floor.

"Tallulah" is an Indian word meaning "terrible" or "awesome." Legend holds that actress Tallulah Bankhead was named with the second meaning of the word in mind.

ACTIVITIES   The park has an interpretive center where you can see exhibits on the Tallulah Gorge, and watch an interactive video on the Northeast Georgia Mountains. Go trout fishing, swimming, and boating. Play tennis on the lighted courts.

Enjoy mountain biking trails, hiking the 500-foot trail along the gorge rim or down into the gorge, and stopping at scenic overlooks. You can also hike along the wildflower trail. Camp in the campground which is open seasonally.

INFORMATION
Tallulah Gorge State Park
Box 248
Tallulah Falls, Georgia 30573
706-754-7970

TUGALOO STATE PARK
42

LOCATION   The park is six miles north of Lavonia off Georgia 328. It's near I-85.

ACTIVITIES   Go camping in the 120-site campground, all sites with water and electrical hookups, a coin laundry, and dump station, or overnight in one of the 20 cottages. In Lake Hartwell, go swimming from the beach, or boating from the ramp or dock. Enjoy fishing, water-skiing, and hike the nature trails. Play tennis or miniature golf. Tour the visitor center.

INFORMATION
Tugaloo State Park
Route 1, Box 1766
Lavonia, Georgia 30553
706-356-4363

UNICOI STATE PARK
43

LOCATION   The park is one mile northeast of Helen via Georgia 356, below Anna Ruby Falls in the Blue Ridge Mountains, on the Chattahoochee River.

ACTIVITIES   Camp in the 96-site campground, 50 sites with water and electrical hookups, groceries, coin laundry, and dumping station, or overnight in one of the 30 modern, furnished cabins. You can also stay in the 100-room lodge, and eat at the buffet-style restaurant. Purchase your camping supplies from the camp store.

Go swimming in the lake from the beach, trout fishing, tubing, and boating in the river, with canoes and paddleboats available for rent. Hike the trails, play tennis, tour the visitor center, and attend interpretive programs.

Follow the .4-mile interpretive trail to see Anna Ruby's twin waterfalls, located ½ mile north of the park. There you can go fishing, hiking, or picnicking.

In Helen, attend Oktoberfest in September, featured as the South's longest Oktoberfest, lasting for almost three weeks. Also come for the hot air balloon races in the spring, and the Facshing Karnival in the winter. Helen's International Fest is held in late June, with international performers presenting dances from all over the world, and a Fourth of July celebration is also held. For information, call 706-878-2181 or 1-800-858-8027.

Tour the Gold Mines of Helen on Edelweiss Drive, where you can pan for gold and other gems, and observe a gem cutter at work. Walk the nature trail. For information, call 706-878-3052.

The Stovall Covered Bridge, circa 1895, is three miles north of the Old Sautee Store on Georgia 255. It's the state's smallest covered bridge. It was featured in the movie, *I'd Climb the Highest Mountain.*

North of Helen, drive the 38-mile loop on the Russell-Brasstown Scenic Byway, Georgia 348, with elevations ranging between 2,040 to 3,644 feet. Nearby is the state's highest mountain, Brasstown Bald, rising 4,884 feet. Stop by the interpretive center, and walk out on the observation deck to get a panoramic view of four states.

INFORMATION
Unicoi State Park
P.O. Box 849
Helen, Georgia 30545
706-878-2201

VICTORIA BRYANT STATE PARK
44

LOCATION   The park is four miles northwest of Royston off U.S. 29, on Georgia 327.

ACTIVITIES   Enjoy camping in the 25-site campground, 19 sites with water and electrical hookups, a coin laundry, and dumping station. Go swimming in the pool, fishing, hike the nature trails, and play golf on the nine-hole course. Concessions are available.

Royston is the hometown of baseball legend, Ty Cobb, where you can tour the Ty Cobb Museum.

INFORMATION
Victoria Bryant State Park
Route 1, Box 1767
Royston, Georgia 30662
706-245-6270

VOGEL STATE PARK
45

LOCATION   The park is 11 miles south of Blairsville off U.S. 19 and U.S. 129, within the boundaries of the Chattahoochee National Forest.

ACTIVITIES   The park is on Lake Trahlyta. Go swimming from the white sand beach. Hike along 17 miles of park trails. Other trails, including the Appalachian Trail, are located outside the park. Camp in the 100-site campground, all sites with water and electrical hookups, dumping station, groceries, and a coin laundry. You can also overnight in one of the 36 cottages. Go fishing and boating, with canoes and paddleboats available for rent. During the summer, guided walks, campfire programs, and square dancing are available.

INFORMATION
Vogel State Park
7484 Vogel Park Road
Route 1, Box 1230
Blairsville, Georgia 30512
706-745-2628

WATSON MILL BRIDGE STATE PARK
46

LOCATION   The bridge is three miles south of Comer, on Georgia 22.
FEATURES   The bridge is the longest covered bridge remaining in Georgia.
ACTIVITIES   Enjoy camping in the 21-site campground, all sites with water and electrical hookups, a coin laundry, and dumping station. Go hiking, fishing, and boating, with canoe and paddleboat rentals available.
INFORMATION
Watson Mill Bridge State Park
Watson Mill Park Road
Route 1, Box 190
Comer, Georgia 30629
706-783-5349

The Watson Mill covered bridge at the Watson Mill Bridge State Park, overlooking the Broad River (courtesy of the Tourist Division, Georgia Dept. of Industry and Trade)

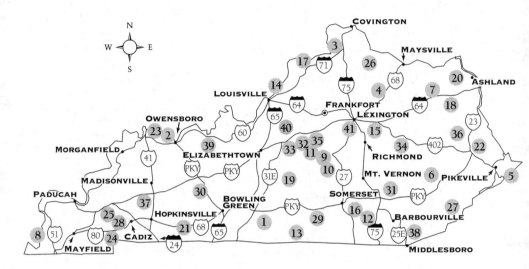

KENTUCKY STATE PARKS

1. Barren River State Park
2. Ben Hawes State Park
3. Big Bone Lick State Park
4. Blue Licks Battlefield State Park
5. Breaks Interstate Park
6. Buckhorn Lake State Resort Park
7. Carter Caves State Resort Park
8. Columbus-Belmont Battlefield State Park
9. Constitution Square State Historic Site
10. Isaac Shelby Cemetery State Historic Site
11. Perryville Battlefield State Historic Site
12. Cumberland Falls State Resort Park
13. Dale Hollow Lake State Park
14. E. P. "Tom" Sawyer State Park
15. Fort Boonesborough State Park
16. General Burnside State Park
17. General Butler Resort State Park
18. Grayson Lake State Park
19. Green River Lake State Park
20. Greenbo Lake State Resort Park
21. Jefferson Davis Monument State Historic Site

22. Jenny Wiley Resort State Park
23. John James Audubon State Park
24. Kenlake State Resort Park
25. Kentucky Dam Village State Resort Park
26. Kincaid Lake State Park
27. Kingdom Come State Park
28. Lake Barkley State Resort Park
29. Lake Cumberland Resort State Park
30. Lake Malone State Park
31. Levi Jackson Wilderness Road State Park
32. Lincoln Homestead State Park
33. My Old Kentucky Home State Park
34. Natural Bridge Resort State Park
35. Old Fort Harrod State Park
36. Paintsville Lake State Park
37. Pennyrile State Resort Park
38. Pine Mountain State Resort Park
39. Rough River Dam State Resort Park
40. Taylorsville Lake State Park
41. Waveland State Historic Site

KENTUCKY

Kentucky has been a leading nursery for thoroughbred champion horses for over 150 years. Horses were brought from Virginia to Lexington to run in the streets until 1780. After that, a race track was established, and now raising and racing horses has become a multi-billion-dollar industry. The Kentucky Derby held each May is the country's premier horse racing event.

Fifteen of Kentucky's 44 state park resorts, recreational parks, and historic sites, are located on lakes. They are classified as resort parks, featuring reasonably-priced rooms, tennis courts, swimming pools, riding stables, and golf courses. Fifteen of the parks have lodges. Twenty-six parks have campsites with electrical/water hookups. For state park information, call 1-800-255-PARK. Kentucky's state parks contain 135 miles of marked trails, with seven parks found in the state nature preserves.

Anglers and hunters can get information from the Kentucky Department of Fish and Wildlife Resources, by calling 502-564-4336.

Kentucky has 14 major river systems where visitors can go canoeing, kayaking, and rafting. Some of the whitewater in the mountain streams is rated Class V. Nine of the state's most scenic river sections are designated as Kentucky Wild Rivers.

Hikers in the state parks have access to 1,400 miles of marked and maintained routes. Two major trails, the Sheltowee Trace National Recreation Trail, and the Jenny Wiley National Recreation Trail, pass through the forested highlands of eastern Kentucky. The Sheltowee Trace goes through the Daniel Boone National Forest, from north of Morehead to Pickett State Park in Tennessee. The Jenny Wiley Trail runs 185 miles from the state's northeastern tip to Jenny Wiley State Resort Park. Two connector trails off Jenny Wiley include the 25-mile Tygart Trail to Greenbo Lake, and the 9-mile Simon Kenton Trail to Carter Caves State Park.

Bicyclists have access to over 600 miles of the national TransAmerica Trail, which extends from Crittenden County in the west, to Pike County in the east. For maps and information, contact Bike Centennial, P.O. Box 80308, Missoula, Montana 59807, or call 406-721-1776.

The state has the fourth largest number of National Historic Register sites found in the U.S. Visitors can tour the birthplace of Abraham Lincoln and Jefferson

Davis, the fort founded by Daniel Boone, and the homes of Henry Clay and George Rogers Clark. You also have access to the mansion that inspired Stephen Foster to write *My Old Kentucky Home,* and you can visit the Shaker Village of Pleasant Hill.

Mammoth Cave in south-central Kentucky is often called one of the seven wonders of the modern world. It winds for 300 miles under the 52,000-acre national park. Take one of the nine tours offered daily, or go hiking on some of its 165 miles of hiking trails. Enjoy a boat ride on the *Miss Green River II* cruise boat, and go canoeing on some of the state's best canoe runs.

Cumberland Gap National Historical Park is in the eastern highlands of the state, straddling the crest of the Cumberland Mountains, where Kentucky, Virginia, and Tennessee meet.

Fall is a particularly beautiful time to visit the state. Some of the best color is along U.S. 42 beside the Ohio River, between Cincinnati and Louisville, or on U.S. 68 from Lexington to Bowling Green. Another great spot is the mountainous area around Cumberland Gap National Historic Park in the extreme southeastern part of the state. Color usually begins the last week of September, and runs through the end of October, with the peak usually occurring in the third week in October. For weekly updates on the color changes, call 1-800-225-TRIP.

BARREN RIVER STATE RESORT PARK
1

LOCATION   The resort by the 20,000-acre lake is 12 miles southwest of Glasgow, on U.S. 31E.

ACTIVITIES   Stay overnight in the 51-room lodge, or in one of the 12 cottages that are open year-round. Eat in the dining room of the lodge. Camp in the 99-site campground, open from April through November, with water and electrical hookups, groceries, and a laundry.

Go swimming in the lake or in the lodge's heated pool, and boating from the marina or boat launch. Houseboats, fishing boats, and pontoon boat rentals are available.

Enjoy fishing for bass, catfish, and crappie. Play golf on the nine-hole course, with a pro shop and rental clubs available. Go horseback riding from the riding stable, or explore 1.8 miles of hiking trails. Bicycle on the 2.5-mile paved bike trail, with bike rentals available, or play tennis.

Tour Mammoth Cave National Park, northeast of Bowling Green, west of Cave City, and northwest of Park City. The cave itself features over 300 miles of underground passages, and is one of the longest cave systems known. Cave tours are conducted year-round, or you can take a self-guided tour. Hikers have access to 70 miles of woodland trails. Anglers can fish in the Green and Nolin Rivers, which boast 30 miles of fishing and boating waters. Camp in the campground; take a cruise aboard the *Miss Green River.* For further information, call 502-758-2328.

Arriving pilots can land at Glasgow Municipal Airport, two miles northwest of the city. Rental cars are available.

INFORMATION
Barren River State Resort Park
1149 State Park Road
Route 1, Box 191
Lucas, Kentucky 42156-9709
502-646-2151: lodge
800-325-0057: reservations out of state
800-862-0261: in-state reservations
502-646-2357: marina

BEN HAWES STATE PARK

2

LOCATION　　The park is four miles west of Owensboro off U.S. 60, on West Roost Road.

ACTIVITIES　　Enjoy the archery range, golf on either the nine-hole, par-three course, or on the 18-hole course, with a pro shop and rental clubs available. Play tennis, and go hiking on the 1.5-mile-long trail.

Take Kentucky 56 west for 10 miles to Diamond Lake to attend the Diamond Lake Jubilee's country music show on Saturdays at 8:00 P.M. from Memorial Day through Labor Day. For information, call 502-229-4961. For additional country music, go to Goldie's Best Little Opryhouse at 418 Frederica, where shows are presented each Friday and Saturday at 8 P.M. For information, call 502-926-0254.

In Owensboro, attend one of the annual riverfront music festivals, and the famous Bar-B-Q Festival held in May. Tour the International Bluegrass Music Museum in the downtown River Park Center. Take a walking tour of the city. Brochures are available at the information center, 326 Saint Elizabeth. For information, call 502-926-1100.

Come in the spring when the dogwood and azalea are in bloom, and enjoy the display for 25 blocks along Griffith Avenue. The largest sassafras of its kind is at 2100 Frederica Street. It's estimated to be between 250 to 300 years old, and is over 100 feet tall.

Arriving pilots can land at Owensboro–Davless County Airport, three miles southwest of Owensboro. Rental cars are available. You can camp on the field.

INFORMATION
Ben Hawes State Park
Box 761
Owensboro, Kentucky 42302-0761
502-684-9808
502-685-2011 or 502-683-9420: pro shop

BIG BONE LICK STATE PARK
3

LOCATION   The park is six miles southwest of Union on the Ohio River Inlet. From I-75, Exit 171, go south on Kentucky 338. It's also 26 miles southwest of Covington via I-75 and U.S. 42.

FEATURES   Giant mammoths, ground slots, tapirs, arctic bears, and mastodons roamed here after the last Ice Age. Many became stuck in the bogs, and died while attempting to lick the salt from the sulphur springs. Plaques and a small museum interpret the area's geology and history.

ACTIVITIES   Tour the museum, with both indoor and outdoor exhibits, and watch their slide show on the giant animals. Hike the mile-long, self-guided nature trail through the Ice Age swamp, or go around the lake. The museum is open daily from April through October, and weekends only from November through March. Admission is charged.

Camp in the 62-site campground, open year-round, with electrical and water hookups, a grocery store, and laundry. Swim in the swimming pool. Hike 2½ miles of hiking trails, and play miniature golf or tennis. Fish in the manmade lake, stocked with bluegill, bass, and catfish.

In Covington, tour Cathedral Basilica of the Assumption at 1140 Madison. Built circa 1901, it was modeled after Notre Dame in Paris, and features 80 stained glass windows, including the largest stained glass church window in the world. Guided tours are offered from June through August on Sundays at 2:00. For information, call 606-431-2060.

While in Covington, stroll through Main Strasse Village and see the 100-foot Carroll Chimes Bell Tower, located in the updated German neighborhood. Seven minutes past each hour, watch the mechanical figures come out to perform the "Pied Piper of Hamelin" story.

Take a ride along the river in a riverboat docked at Covington Landing, available from Memorial Day through Labor Day. For information, call 606-261-8500.

Walk along the 13-block Riverside Drive Licking River Area, at the junction of the Ohio and Licking Rivers. Here you'll see 38 Civil War homes, and you can tour the Mimosa House at 412 East 2nd, circa 1853, the area's largest single-family dwelling. Tours are offered weekend afternoons. For information, call 606-216-9000.

Arriving pilots can land at Covington/Erlanger Airport, eight miles southwest of Covington. However, no rental cars are available.

INFORMATION
Big Bone Lick State Park
3380 Beaver Road
Union, Kentucky 41091-9627
606-384-3522

BLUE LICKS BATTLEFIELD STATE PARK
4

LOCATION The state park is eight miles north of Carlisle in Mount Olivet, off U.S. 68.

FEATURES The salt licks and salt springs once attracted prehistoric mammoths, and later became a center for Indian life. Frontiersmen, including Daniel Boone, arrived later to make salt. The last battle of the Revolutionary War was fought here in 1782.

ACTIVITIES Camp in the 51-site campground from April through October, with water and electrical hookups, grocery, and laundry. You can also stay in a cottage available year-round. Swim in the Olympic-size pool, purchase concessions, and go fishing for channel catfish, bass, bluegill, and walleye. Explore 1.3 miles of hiking trails.

Play miniature golf, and participate in planned recreation programs. Tour the museum and watch the audiovisual program to see bones of prehistoric animals, and Indian and pioneer artifacts. It's open from April through October.

Pick up a brochure of Carlisle at Eddie's Restaurant, 106 West Main, and take a walking and driving tour of the historic town, with 350 of its buildings listed on the National Register. It includes the only Daniel Boone cabin still standing in the state.

Arriving pilots can land at Fleming-Mason Airport, seven miles north of Flemingsburg. Rental cars are available.

INFORMATION
Blue Licks Battlefield State Park
P.O. Box 66
Mt. Olivet, Kentucky 41064-0066
606-289-5507

BREAKS INTERSTATE PARK
5

LOCATION The park is 30 miles southeast of Pikeville on Kentucky/Virginia 80. It's also seven miles east of Elkhorn City.

FEATURES The park is on the Kentucky/Virginia border, and covers 4,600 acres along the eastern edge of the Cumberland Mountain Plateau. It features the largest canyon east of the Mississippi. Cut by the Russell Fork of the Big Sandy River, the gorge, called the "Grand Canyon of the South," is five miles long and 1,600 feet deep.

ACTIVITIES Overnight in one of the 34 rooms in the Rhododendron Lodge, with a dining room available seasonally, or stay in a cottage available year-round.

The campground, open seasonally, has 122 campsites with utilities. Tour the visitor center with natural, historical, and coal exhibits, and go swimming in the pool. Go boating from the ramp, and rent a pedal boat. Go fishing and white-water rafting.

Laurel Lake features caves, hidden springs, horseback riding, hiking, and outstanding wildflowers.

Drive up the paved road from the entrance to the canyon rim for some fantastic gorge overlooks. Places to visit include Duty's Knob, Initial Rock, and Lover's Leap. Come in the spring when the rhododendron are in full bloom. Attend an Autumn Gospel Song Festival held on Labor Day weekend.

Incoming pilots can land at Pike County–Hatcher Field, six miles northwest of Pikeville. Rental cars are available.

INFORMATION
Breaks Interstate Park
P.O. Box 100
Breaks, Virginia 24607
703-865-4413: information and cottage reservations
703-865-4414: lodge reservations

BUCKHORN LAKE STATE RESORT PARK
6

LOCATION   The park is on Buckhorn Lake, 25 miles northwest of Hazard, in the Daniel Boone National Forest. Take Kentucky 15 south to Kentucky 28 west, and then Kentucky 1833 to reach the park.

ACTIVITIES   The mountain park has a lake created by a 162-foot dam, built on the middle fork of the Kentucky River. Go swimming from the sandy beach, and boating from the ramp or marina, with fishing-boat and pontoon boat rentals available. Anglers can fish for largemouth and smallmouth bass, crappies, bluegill, channel catfish, and muskie, from the fishing pier or from a fishing boat.

Play tennis on the courts, or hike 1½ miles of hiking trails through the woods. One trail heads down to Moonshiner Hollow, or you can follow a path from the lodge to the 1,200-acre mountain lake below. Rent a bicycle to cycle the park roads.

The park operates a 36-room lodge with a dining room, and three vacation cottages that are open year-round. The lodge offers musical shows, square dancing, and other entertainment. For camping, go to one of the privately-operated campgrounds located nearby.

Take a free tour of the Buckhorn Log Church, circa 1927, located 12 miles from the park, featuring a Hook and Hasting pipe organ. For information, call 606-398-7245.

In the Daniel Boone National Forest, go fishing in Big Double Creek, and hike along the Redbird Crest Trail. To get to the fishing area, take Kentucky 66 south from the Peabody interchange of the D.B. Parkway for three miles. Turn at the first right after the Redbird Ranger Station, follow signs for two miles up Big Double Creek.

Arriving pilots can land at Wendell H. Ford Airport, 11 miles northwest of Hazard. Rental cars are available.

INFORMATION
Buckhorn Lake State Resort Park
HC 36, Box 1000
Buckhorn, Kentucky 41721-9602
606-398-7245
606-398-7510: marina
1-800-325-0058: toll free reservations

CARTER CAVES STATE RESORT PARK

7

LOCATION   The park is eight miles northeast of Olive Hill, and 30 miles west of Ashland. From Olive Hill, follow U.S. 60 for 5½ miles east, then go four miles north on Kentucky 182.

FEATURES   Approximately 29 caves are located in this area, some explored and some yet uncharted. They were once utilized by the Cherokee Indians for shelter and storage of fur pelts.

ACTIVITIES   Take a guided cave tour offered daily from April through October, or by request at the lodge the rest of the year. If you don't have a lot of time, tour X Cave with its luminous stone fans and spirals. If you can, visit Cascade Cave known for its 30-foot underground waterfall. Bats Cave, the largest in the park, is the protected winter home to thousands of the rare social bats, and is only toured during the summer.

Overnight in the 28-room Caveland Lodge with a dining room, or in one of 15 cottages, open year-round. Stay in the 89-site campground, open year-round, with water and electrical hookups, and groceries available. Swim in the pool, play tennis, or golf on the nine-hole course, with a pro shop. Go horseback riding and hiking the six miles of trails through the state nature reserve. The ½-mile Natural Bridge Trail follows a stream.

Tour the visitor center and participate in planned recreational activities, including interpretive programs presented in the wooded amphitheater. Go fishing and boating from the dock. Rental fishing boats, pedal boats, and rowboats are available. No motorboats are permitted. Float down Tygart's Creek on a guided canoe trip. Anglers come to fish for bass, bluegill, catfish, and crappie. Rent a horse from the stable to go horseback riding.

Tour the Northeastern Kentucky Museum. Take U.S. 60 to Kentucky 182 north. You'll find artifacts including fossils, and items from the Civil War through the Vietnam War. For information, call 606-286-6012.

Special events include Strange Music weekend in June, and Pioneer Life week in July, and the Fraley Family Mountain Music Festival in September.

Arriving pilots can land at Olive Hill–Sellers' Field, three miles southeast of Olive Hill. However, no rental cars are available.

INFORMATION
Carter Caves State Resort Park
R.R. #5, Box 1120
Olive Hill, Kentucky 41164-9032
606-286-4411
800-325-0059: reservations

COLUMBUS-BELMONT BATTLEFIELD STATE PARK
8

LOCATION   The park is 36 miles southwest of Paducah on Kentucky 80. It's on a bluff above the Mississippi River in Columbus, at the intersection of Kentucky 58 and 123/80.

FEATURES   The park, called the Confederacy's "Gibraltar of the West," features a massive chain and anchor used to block the passage of Union gunboats on the Mississippi River during the Civil War, and recalls the 1861 Battle of Belmont. You can also see a Confederate cannon, and the network of earthen trenches.

Paducah is where over 42,000 Union soldiers boarded 173 steamboats and 12 gunboats, to form a military convoy going up the Tennessee River to Shiloh.

ACTIVITIES   Hike the 2.5-mile-long Anchor Trek Trail through earthworks that were constructed to protect Confederate artillery. You can also take a longer hike on the Chalk-Bluff Indian Trail. Stroll through the museum, originally used as an infirmary, to see Civil War and Indian artifacts. It's open daily from May through Labor Day, and on weekends in April and October.

Enjoy a picnic at one of the stone shelters, and camp in the 38-site campground, with water and electrical hookups, a laundry, and a grocery store. Go boating from the boat launch, play miniature golf, and enjoy fishing. Concessions are available.

North of the intersection of U.S. 51/60/62, at the confluence of the Ohio and Mississippi Rivers, is the site of the ancient Wickliffe Mounds. This ceremonial site and trade center was lived in for 300 years by the people from the Mississippian period, circa 800–1350 A.D. It's open daily from March through November. For information, call 502-335-3681.

INFORMATION
Columbus-Belmont Battlefield State Park
P.O. Box 8
Columbus, Kentucky 42032-0008
502-677-2327

CONSTITUTION SQUARE
STATE HISTORIC SITE
9

ISAAC SHELBY CEMETERY
STATE HISTORIC SITE
10

PERRYVILLE BATTLEFIELD
STATE HISTORIC SITE
11

LOCATION   Constitution Square is at 105 East Walnut Street in Danville. Isaac Shelby Cemetery is five miles south of Danville, off U.S. 127. Perryville Battlefield is two miles north of Perryville, off U.S. 150 and U.S. 68.

FEATURES   Constitution Square is the site where ten constitutional conventions were held, that eventually led to statehood. Kentucky became the fifteenth state in the union on June 1, 1792.

Isaac Shelby was a Revolutionary War hero who was named the first and fifth governor of the Commonwealth. He was revered for his military, political, and educational accomplishments, and served as chair of the conventions on Constitution Square when the state was formed.

Perryville was the site of the most destructive Civil War battle in Kentucky, fought on October 8, 1862. Over 6,000 men were killed, wounded, or missing, when 40,000 troops stopped the Confederate advance in Kentucky.

ACTIVITIES   Visit many of the original buildings in Constitution Square including Grayson's Tavern, the old courthouse, and the first jail and first post office located west of the Alleghenies.

At Perryville, walk through the park museum and learn of the battle that was the South's last serious attempt to gain possession of Kentucky. Hike the trails and bring along a picnic to enjoy. Attend the mock battle presented the weekend closest to October 8.

Attend outdoor dramas presented at the Pioneer Playhouse Outdoor Theater, at 80 Stanford Road in Danville, from mid-June through August. It's located in a recreated 18th-century pioneer village. For information, call 606-236-2747.

Arriving pilots can land at Stuart Powell Field, three miles south of Danville. Rental cars are available. It's three miles to Constitution Square, and 15 miles to Perryville Battlefield.

INFORMATION

Constitution Square State Historic
  Site
105 East Walnut Street
Danville, Kentucky, 40422-1817
606-236-5089

Perryville Battlefield State Historic
  Site
P.O. Box 296
Perryville, Kentucky 40468-9999
606-332-8631

Isaac Shelby Cemetery State
  Historic Site
Danville, Kentucky 4022-1880
606-236-5089

CUMBERLAND FALLS STATE RESORT PARK
12

LOCATION   Cumberland Falls is 20 miles southwest of Corbin, in the Daniel Boone National Forest. From I-75, take the Corbin Exit to U.S. 25W to Kentucky 90.

FEATURES   Cumberland Falls' 1,794-acre resort is one of the state's showplaces. The park is famous for its waterfall, which forms a 125-foot wide curtain and drops 68 feet into the Cumberland River gorge. It's often called the "Niagara of the South." Mist rising from the waterfall creates the only known moonbow in the Western Hemisphere, and is visible on a clear, moon-lit night.

Little Eagle Falls are formed by a small mountain creek that tumbles 125 feet into the Cumberland River, which was once considered to be sacred by the Indians. The Cumberland River is designated a Kentucky Wild and Scenic River.

ACTIVITIES   Cumberland Falls State Park offers hiking on 17 miles of hiking trails. Go camping in two campgrounds with 50 sites, electrical and water hookups, grocery store, and laundry. It's open from April through October. Overnight in the 52-room DuPont Lodge, in one of the 20 Woodland rooms, or in one of the 26 cabins open year-round. Eat in the dining room or coffee shop, and tour the Bob Blair Museum.

Swim in the Olympic-size pool, play tennis, go backpacking, and fishing in the Cumberland River for bass, catfish, and panfish. Go whitewater-river rafting on

Cumberland Falls State Resort Park
(courtesy of the Kentucky Dept. of Travel Development)

the Cumberland River below the falls. Guided rafting trips are available daily from May through October, depending upon the water levels.

Take a scenic train excursion through nearby Big South Fork National River and Recreation Area. Go horseback riding from the stables, or hike the trails that wind through the park to waterfalls and firetowers in the forest. The Moonbow Trail connects with many other trails in the Daniel Boone National Forest. Observation points provide views of Cumberland Falls and its boulder-strewn gorge.

Get a close-up view of the falls aboard the *Cumberland Falls Rainbow Mist.* Rafts depart hourly from the state park from Memorial Day through Labor Day on Wednesday, Friday through Sunday, and on holidays from noon to 5 P.M. Sheltowee Trace Outfitters offer 6-hour river rafting trips from mid-May through October. For information call 800-541-RAFT.

Tombstone Junction is a mile west of the park on Kentucky 90, where you can watch country entertainers perform Sundays at 1:00 and 5:00 P.M. Take a ride in the steam locomotive, enjoy amusement rides, and watch gunfights at the recreated frontier town. It's open from Memorial Day through Labor Day, Tuesday through Sunday, from 10 to 6, and weekends in May. For information, call 606-376-5087.

Attend the Lake Laurel horse show on the last Saturday in June. Participate in the Nibroc Festival's parades, dances, and nightly entertainment in downtown Corbin. For information, call 800-528-7123.

Kentucky Fried Chicken fans can tour Colonel Harland Sanders Cafe and Museum, where the colonel created his recipe for fried chicken. It's located one mile south of Corbin on U.S. 25 off I-75, Exit 29. For information, call 606-528-21163.

Dr. Thomas Walker State Historic Site is five miles southwest of Barbourville, on Kentucky 459. Walker was the first frontiersman to arrive in Kentucky, and led the first expedition through the Cumberland Gap in 1750. A replica of his one-room cabin is located on its original cabin site. For information, call 606-546-4400.

Attend the Daniel Boone Festival in Barbourville held the first weekend in October.

Arriving pilots can land at Williamsburg-Cumberland Falls Airport, located six miles north of Williamsburg. Contact the resort for transportation to the park.

INFORMATION
Cumberland Falls State Resort Park
7351 Highway 90
Corbin, Kentucky 40701-8814
606-528-4121
1-800-325-0063: toll free reservations

DALE HOLLOW LAKE STATE PARK
13

LOCATION   The park is 12 miles southeast of Burkesville. From Kentucky 90 go to Kentucky 449.

FEATURES Dale Hollow Lake is on the border between Kentucky and Tennessee, and covers 48 square miles, with 620 miles of shoreline. It's famous as a stopover for migratory fowl.

ACTIVITIES Go camping in the campground with 144 sites, open year-round, with water and electrical hookups. Groceries are available, or eat in the restaurant. Go swimming in the pool, and water-skiing, and boating from the marina, with fishing and pontoon boat rentals available. Fish for bass, rainbow trout, catfish, walleye, and bluegill. The lake holds the world record for a 12-pound smallmouth bass, caught at the northern tip of the lake.

Hike the hiking trails, or bring your own horse to go horseback riding along the equestrian trails.

Tour the Old Mulkey Meetinghouse State Historic Site, circa 1804. Go west for 35 miles to Tompkinsville on Kentucky 1446 south; or from Bowling Green off I-65, take U.S. 231 south to Kentucky 100 east, to 1819 Old Mulkey Road. Daniel Boone's sister and Revolutionary War soldiers are buried in the churchyard. The church, circa 1773, is Kentucky's oldest log church. For information, call 502-487-8481.

INFORMATION
Dale Hollow Lake State Park
6371 State Park Road
Box 145, HC 61
Bow, Kentucky 42714-9728
502-433-7431

E. P. "TOM" SAWYER STATE PARK
14

LOCATION The park is eight miles northeast of Louisville at 3000 Freys Hill Road. From Louisville, take I-71 north to the Jefferson Freeway, then go south to the Westport Road Exit.

ACTIVITIES Come fly your model airplanes and ride the BMX moto-cross track. Swim in the Olympic-size pool, play tennis, and stop by the archery range to test your skill. The park offers team sports, scheduled year-round in the gym.

Take a cruise aboard the *Belle of Louisville,* circa 1914. The steamboat is the oldest operating steamboat on the Mississippi River. It operates from Memorial Day through Labor Day, and departs from 4th and River Road in Louisville. For reservations, call 502-625-BELL. Go camping, and attend nature programs.

Go to Churchill Downs at 700 Central Avenue, where the Kentucky Derby has been run since 1875. The Derby is held in early May. Take a tour from late April through July. Call 502-636-4400 for information. To learn more about the Derby, visit the Kentucky Derby Museum at 704 Central Avenue, at the entrance of Churchill Downs. For special event schedules and information, call 502-637-1111.

Tour Conrad House, circa 1895, at 1402 St. James Court in Old Louisville. It's open Sunday through Wednesday from 1–5. For information, call 502-636-5023. Farmington Mansion, circa 1810, is at 3033 Bardstown Road. For information, call 502-452-9920.

Attend the Kentucky Shakespeare Festival in the Park, performed in Central Park's Douglas Ramey Amphitheater at 4th and Magnolia, from mid-June through mid-August. For information, call 502-634-8237.

Pick up a map of West Main Street's historic district at the Preservation Alliance, 716 West Main. The 100–900 blocks between 6th and 10th feature the largest collection of 19th-century cast-iron storefronts found outside of New York City. For information, call 502-583-8622.

Arriving pilots can land at Bowman Field, five miles southeast of Louisville, or at Standiford Field, located four miles south of the city. Both have rental cars available.

INFORMATION
E. P. "Tom" Sawyer State Park
300 Freys Hill Road
Louisville, Kentucky 40241-2172
502-426-8950

FORT BOONESBOROUGH STATE PARK
15

LOCATION   The park is six miles northeast of Richmond on the Kentucky River, on Kentucky 388. From I-75, take Exit 95 onto Kentucky 627. From I-64, exit at Winchester.

FEATURES   The park has a replica of Fort Boone which was originally built here by Daniel Boone, on the banks of the Kentucky River in 1775. The fort, which included 26 log cabins and four blockhouses, came under a series of Indian attacks. The most famous attack was known as the "Great Siege of Boonesborough." The fort cabins are furnished as they might have been during Boone's day. A Civil War battle was fought south of town in 1862, resulting in a Confederate victory.

ACTIVITIES   The park is open April through October, and is closed Mondays and Tuesdays after Labor Day. Tour the reconstructed fort, whose costumed craftsmen demonstrate quilting, spinning, weaving, soap making, candlemaking, and basket weaving. Stop by the working forge and tour the small museum.

Camp year-round in the fully-equipped 167-site modern campground near the Kentucky River. It has water and electrical hookups, grocery store, and laundry.

Swim in the river from the sandy beach, and go boating from the ramp. Try your luck at fishing for bass, perch, bream, and catfish. Cruise aboard the sternwheeler excursion boat, the *Dixie Belle*. Go swimming in the Olympic-size pool, and slide down the water slide. Concessions are available at the pool. Play 18 holes of miniature golf, and hike the trail.

White Hall, circa 1799, is a 44-room house and state historic site, located 7½ miles northwest of Richmond at 500 White Hall Shrine Road, at Exit 95. Go west ¼ mile on Kentucky 627 to White Hall Street Shrine Road, and continue two more miles following signs. Here, Cassius M. Clay, an emancipationist and Lincoln's minister to Russia, lived. This was the first house in the area to have indoor plumbing and central heating. Tours are offered from April through October. It is closed Mondays and Tuesdays after Labor Day. For information, call 606-623-9178.

Visitors can purchase a combination pass that includes a tour of both Fort Boonesborough and a guided tour of White Hall State Historic Site.

Annual events held in the park include Annual Admiral's Day in September, and the Kentucky Corp of Longriflemen Tournament and Greaser's Car Show in October. In Richmond, attend Kit Carson Days in April, the Madison County Fair in late July, and Main Street Celebration held in mid-October.

Arriving pilots can land at Madison Airport, eight miles southwest of Richmond. Taxis are available. The park is 20 miles from the airport.

INFORMATION
Fort Boonesborough State Park
4375 Boonesborough Road
Richmond, Kentucky 40475-9316
606-527-3131
606-527-6323: marina
606-527-3328: museum

GENERAL BURNSIDE STATE PARK
16

LOCATION   The park is south of Burnside, and eight miles south of Somerset on U.S. 27.

FEATURES   The 400-acre park is on Bunker Hill, formed when the Cumberland River was impounded in 1950. It's the state's only "island park" and is surrounded by Lake Cumberland's 1,255 miles of shoreline. North of the marina, where the Cumberland River and its South Fork combine, Lake Cumberland's great impoundment begins. Here you can see steep cliffs, formed of 300-million-year-old sedimentary sandstone, that shapes a fjord-like section of the lake.

The park was named for Ambrose E. Burnside, who was responsible for keeping eastern Kentucky for the Union in 1863. General Burnside was remembered for his beard and mustache worn with a clean-shaven chin, called a "burnsider."

ACTIVITIES   Boaters can go boating from a six-lane launching ramp, and cruise 45 miles to the east of the island, 25 miles south, and 50 miles west. Anglers have access to more bass, walleye, and crappie fishing than in any other U.S. lake. Rent houseboats, fishing boats, and tackle from the Burnside marina on the mainland.

Five miles from the entrance are two lodges with 88 rooms, and a 110-site campground, which is open seasonally. Here you can play tennis, miniature golf, or golf on the 18-hole course, with a pro shop and rental clubs available. Go swimming in one of two swimming pools, one Olympic-size. Rent a horse from the riding stable, and hike the nature trails. Attend nature programs. Concessions are available.

From mid-November through January 1, General Burnside Island becomes Christmas Island with seasonal lighting. Enjoy a 3.5-mile drive to see the Festival of Lights.

Seven miles south of the park on Kentucky 1275 is the Mill Springs mill. It's one of the world's largest overshot water wheels. Watch the audiovisual presentation on the area's role in Civil War history. For information, call 606-679-6337.

The Big South Fork Scenic Railway is 25 miles south of Burnside, where you can take a 13-mile round trip tour into the backcountry of Big South Fork National Park. The railway operates mid-April through October, and is closed Mondays. For information, call 1-800-GO-ALONG.

Arriving pilots can land at Somerset–Pulaski County Airport, located three miles south of Somerset. Rental cars are available.

INFORMATION
General Burnside State Park
P.O. Box 488
Burnside, Kentucky 42519-0488
606-561-4104 or 606-546-4192
606-561-4104: golf

GENERAL BUTLER RESORT STATE PARK
17

LOCATION   Take I-71 to Kentucky 227 to the park, located 2¼ miles southeast of Carrollton off U.S. 42.

FEATURES   The park is named for General William Orlando Butler, hero of the Battle of New Orleans in the War of 1812.

ACTIVITIES   Stay in the 57-room lodge overlooking the Ohio River Valley, or in one of 23 cottages, open year-round. Dine in the dining room. Camp in the 111-site campground, open year-round, with water and electrical hookups, laundry, and grocery store.

Go swimming in the pool, enjoy fishing for bass, catfish, crappie, and panfish, and rent a pedal boat or rowboat. Play tennis, golf on the nine-hole course, with a pro shop, and hike two miles of hiking trails.

Tour the Butler Turpin House, circa 1859, to see how the family lived during the 19th-century.

During the winter, come to Ski Butler to go downhill skiing on nine runs, with a ski shop and rental equipment available. For a unique experience, go midnight skiing on Friday and Saturday. To get a snow report, call 1-800-456-3284.

Tour Masterson House, circa 1790, located on U.S. 42 east. It's one of the oldest two-story brick houses still standing on the banks of the Ohio River. It's open from Memorial Day through Labor Day on Sundays, from 1:30–4:30. For information, call 502-732-8204.

The Carrollton Historic District features 350 buildings that cover over 25 blocks with homes dating back to the 19th century. For information, call 502-732-8204.

INFORMATION
General Butler Resort State Park
Box 325
Carrollton, Kentucky 41008-0325
502-732-4384
1-800-325-0078: reservations

GRAYSON LAKE STATE PARK
18

LOCATION   The park is located on Grayson Lake, between Carter Caves and Greenbo Lake, off I-64 on Kentucky 7 south. It's also 10 miles south of Grayson, and 25 miles southwest of Ashland.

FEATURES   Grayson Lake covers over 1,500 acres, and was created by damming the Little Sandy River. The area was a favorite camping spot for the Shawnee and Cherokee Indians.

ACTIVITIES   Camp in the 71-site campground, open year-round, with water and electrical hookups, a grocery store, and laundry. Go boating from the launch, and fish for bass, bluegill, and catfish. Hike the .8-mile-long hiking trail.

Tygart State Forest adjoins the state park, and offers additional hiking, picnicking, and hunting.

INFORMATION
Grayson Lake State Park
Route 3, Box 800
Olive Hill, Kentucky 41164-9213
606-474-9727

GREEN RIVER LAKE STATE PARK
19

LOCATION   The 8,200-acre lake is five miles south of Campbellsville. Take Kentucky 55 south to Kentucky 1061.

ACTIVITIES   Camp in the 156-site campground, open year-round, with full hookups, laundry, and grocery store. Go swimming from the beach, and boating from the marina or boat launch, with houseboat, fishing-boat, and pontoon boat rentals available. Enjoy water-skiing, and go stream and lake fishing for bass, catfish, crappie, and muskie.

Play miniature golf, hike the 1.5-mile-long hiking trail, and fly your model airplane from the paved strip. Concessions are available. Spelunkers come here to explore.

Tour the Green River Lake Visitors Center near the state park, and watch its slide show, and see the 20-foot Indian canoe. It's open daily from Memorial Day through Labor Day, and weekdays the rest of the year. For information, call 502-465-4463.

INFORMATION
Green River Lake State Park
179 Park Office Road
Campbellsville, Kentucky 42718-9351
502-465-8255
502-465-2512: marina

GREENBO LAKE STATE RESORT PARK
20

LOCATION   The park is on Kentucky 1, 18 miles north of I-64 from the Grayson exit. It's also 14 miles northwest of Ashland, and eight miles south of Greenup.

ACTIVITIES   Stay in the 36-room Jesse Stuart clifftop lodge, open year-round, with a dining room available. Camp in the 63-site campground, open from April through October, with water and electrical hookups, grocery store, and a laundry. Swim in the lake, and go fishing for bass, bluegill, and catfish.

Go boating from the ramp or marina, with fishing and pontoon boat rentals available. Play tennis, miniature golf, or play on the 18-hole golf course near the park. Hike 25 miles of trails, and participate in planned recreational activities. Rent a bicycle to go bicycling.

Buffalo Furnace is located in the park, where iron production stopped around 1875.

Covered bridges located in the surrounding area include the Oldtown Bridge, nine miles south of Greenbo Lake State Park. The bridge spans the Little Sandy River, and was built in 1880. The two-span bridge is 194 feet long, and listed on the National Register.

Bennett's Mill Bridge is on Kentucky 7, eight miles south of South Shore. The bridge spans Tygarts Creek, and was built in 1855 to accommodate customers at the Bennett Mill. It's one of the state's longest wooded, one-span, covered bridges.

Yatesville Bridge is ½ mile off Kentucky 3, north of Louisa. It spans Blaine Creek, and was built in 1900.

Arriving pilots can land at Ashland–Boyd County Airport, located six miles northwest of Ashland. Rental cars are available.

INFORMATION
Greenbo Lake State Resort Park
H.C. 60, Box 562
Greenup, Kentucky 41144-9517
606-473-7324
800-325-0083: reservations

JEFFERSON DAVIS MONUMENT
STATE HISTORIC SITE
21

LOCATION   The site is in Fairview on U.S. 68, 10 miles east of Hopkinsville.

ACTIVITIES   Ride to the top of the 351-foot memorial, built to honor Jefferson Davis, President of the Confederacy. He was born here in 1808. It's open daily from May through October.

Robert Penn Warren's Birthplace Museum is 25 miles southeast of Hopkinsville in Guthrie. In 1947, he won the Pulitzer Prize for fiction, and the 1958 and 1979 Pulitzer Prizes for his poetry. For information, call 502-483-2683.

Fort Campbell is located 15 miles south of Hopkinsville, at 26th and Tennessee. Tour the Don F. Pratt Museum to learn of the heritage of the 101st Airborne "Screaming Eagles" Division. Walk through 50 indoor exhibits, featuring artifacts from the Civil War until the present day. For information, call 502-798-3215.

Arriving pilots can land at Hopkinsville–Christian County Airport, two miles east of Hopkinsville. Rental cars are available.

INFORMATION
Jefferson Davis Monument State Historic Site
P.O. Box 10
Fairview, Kentucky 42221-0010
502-886-1765

JENNY WILEY RESORT STATE PARK
22

LOCATION   The park is on Dewey Lake, three miles east of Prestonsburg off U.S. 23/460, on Kentucky 3. It's also southeast of Paintsville.

FEATURES   The park is surrounded by the Appalachian Mountains. It was named for Jenny Wiley, a pioneer woman taken captive in 1789, who managed to escape from the Indians following eleven years of captivity.

ACTIVITIES   Stay in the 49-room lodge, with a dining room, or in one of 17 cottages, open year-round. You can also camp year-round in the 123-site campground, with water and electrical hookups, grocery store, and a laundry. Attend naturalists' interpretive programs.

Swim in the pool, ride the sky lift, play golf on the nine-hole course, with a pro shop, and fish in Dewey Lake for crappie and catfish, and for white bass that run in April. Go boating from the boat launch or the marina, with fishing, paddleboat, and pontoon boat rentals available. Hike nine miles of trails including a section of the Jenny Wiley National Recreation Trail, and along the rim of Dewey Lake.

Attend professional productions of Broadway musicals presented in the outdoor Jenny Wiley Summer Music Theater, from mid-June through mid-August, on Tuesday through Sunday at 8:30 P.M. For reservations, call 606-886-9274.

Ride the Mountain Parkway chairlift up Sugar Camp Mountain. Dewey Lake State Forest adjoins the state park, and offers additional hiking and picnicking.

Arriving pilots can land at Big Sandy Regional Airport, nine miles northeast of Prestonsburg. Rental cars are available. The state park is 11 miles away. You can also land at Paintsville–Prestonsburg Combs Field, four miles southeast of Paintsville. The park is three miles away.

INFORMATION
Jenny Wiley Resort State Park
H.C. 66, Box 200
Prestonsburg, Kentucky 41653-9799
606-886-2711
800-325-0142: lodge reservations
606-886-2711, extension 110: marina

JOHN JAMES AUDUBON STATE PARK
23

LOCATION   The park is 3.5 miles north of Henderson, on U.S. 41N.

FEATURES   Audubon was the first artist to depict life-size birds and animals in his paintings. The park's museum contains 126 original prints from the artist's edition of *The Birds of America.*

ACTIVITIES   Camp in the 64-site campground, 54 sites with water and electrical hookups, or stay in one of the five cottages, open year-round. Play tennis, or golf on the nine-hole golf course, with a pro shop. Hike 5½ miles of hiking trails through the 325-acre nature preserve. Go swimming, fishing for bass, bluegill, and catfish, pedal boating, and walking along the beach. Come in the spring to enjoy the wildflowers.

Since the park is located along a main migratory flyway, it offers birders great opportunities to see many bird species, including warblers who pass through here in spring and fall.

Tour the John James Audubon nature center and memorial museum that houses a collection of his original paintings and memorabilia. While the park is open year-round, the museum is open daily from April through October, and weekends only from November through March. It's closed in January. Admission is charged for the museum and beach.

Go to Ellis Park, one of the largest thoroughbred race courses in the U.S. It's open from July through Labor Day. For information, call 800-333-8110. You can also enjoy harness racing in the spring and fall, and quarter horse racing in the early spring, at Riverside Downs. For details, call 502-826-9746.

Arriving pilots can land at Henderson City-County Airport, four miles west of Henderson. Taxi service is available. The park is eight miles from the airport.

INFORMATION
John James Audubon State Park
P. O. Box 576
Henderson, Kentucky 42420-0576
502-826-2247

KENLAKE STATE RESORT PARK
24

KENTUCKY DAM VILLAGE
STATE RESORT PARK
25

LOCATION   Kenlake State Resort Park is on the western shore of Kentucky Lake. It's four miles east of Aurora, via U.S. 68 and Kentucky 80 or Kentucky 94. From Paducah, take I-24 to the Purchase Parkway, then U.S. 68E. From I-24 north, exit U.S. 68/Kentucky 80W.

Kentucky Dam Village State Resort Park is south of Gilbertsville, on the northern tip of Kentucky Lake. From I-24, Exit 27, go 3.5 miles east on U.S. 62.

FEATURES   The 1,200-acre park at Kentucky Dam Village was the first to be constructed on Kentucky Lake. The Kentucky Dam impounding the Tennessee River created the lake. This lake and Lake Barkley are connected by a free-flowing canal to form one of the largest man-made bodies of water in the U.S. Kentucky Lake covers 160,000 acres, and Lake Barkley covers 57,920 acres.

ACTIVITIES   At the 1,400-acre Kenlake State Resort Park, play tennis on one of 5 hard-surface courts, or play at one of the four indoor courts, with a fully equipped pro shop and tennis center. Play golf on the nine-hole course, with a pro shop and rental clubs; rent a horse from the stable; and go swimming from the beach. Go fishing for bass, bluegill, catfish, and crappie. For a daily update on fishing conditions, call 502-527-7665. Hike the .9-mile-long trail, and enjoy boating from the boat launch. Rent a sailboat, houseboat, fishing boat, or ski boat.

Stay in one of 34 cottages or in the 48-room lodge, open year-round. Dine in the dining room. You can also camp in the 92-site campground overlooking the lake, open seasonally, with electrical and water hookups, grocery store, and a laundry.

Saturday Night Jamboree at the Kenlake Music Hall is one mile from the park on U.S. 68. Performances are offered from May through October, on Saturdays at 8:00 P.M. For information, call 502-527-8554.

At Kentucky Dam, overnight year-round in Village Inn's 72-room lodge, overlooking the lake; in the 14-room Village Green Inn; or in one of the 72 housekeeping cottages, and dine in the dining room. Camp in the 225-site campground, with full hookups, a laundry, and grocery store.

Swim in the pool or in the lake, play tennis, or 18 holes of golf on the 6,745-yard golf course, with a pro shop and rental clubs available. Tour the dam powerhouse daily from 9 to 5. For information, call 502-362-4221. Rent a horse and go for a horseback ride. Attend nature programs, or play miniature golf.

The largest state-owned boat dock complex in the state park system, is located adjacent to the park. Boats of many sizes, including houseboats, are available for rent. Go fishing for largemouth bass, white bass, catfish, and crappie. Enjoy inland sailing and windsurfing.

Enjoy the Popular Showboat Outdoor Theatre's musical review, a celebration of the river with songs from the mid-19th century. It runs from mid-June through Labor Day, Friday through Sunday. For information, call 1-800-467-7145. The Kentucky Opry Show is five miles south of the park in Draffenville, and features comedy, country, gospel, and bluegrass music. Performances are offered from May through October on Fridays at 8:00 p.m. For information, call 502-527-3869.

Land Between the Lakes is a 170,000-acre peninsula east of the park. Hikers and backpackers have access to 158 miles of trails. The area is considered to be one of the best spots for hunting, fishing, camping, and seeing wildlife in the United States.

Stop by the Land Between the Lakes Environmental Center to watch their audio-visual program, and see the many natural exhibits, and displays of Indian and Civil War artifacts. Hike interpretive nature trails, and watch for wildlife from the observation station, including raccoons, and white-tailed and fallow deer.

Empire Farms, a 120-acre demonstration farm, provides participatory activities for visitors, including broom making, sheep-shearing, weaving, spinning, and making sorghum molasses.

At Grand Rivers, visit the Barkley Dam and Visitor Center on U.S. 62 and watch commercial barges passing through the huge 1,200-foot locks. Watch audiovisuals depicting life on the Cumberland River during the steamboat era. For information, call 502-362-4236. Stop by the Lakes Area Information Center to pick up a 60-mile scenic lakes driving tour map. For information, call 502-928-4411.

Arriving pilots can land at Kentucky Dam State Park Airport's 4,000-foot lighted airstrip, located one mile northwest of Gilbertsville. Rental cars are available, or a courtesy van can take you into the park or to the lodge. Kentucky Dam Village is 1½ miles from the airport.

INFORMATION

Kenlake State Resort Park
Route 1, Box 522
Hardin, Kentucky 42048-9737
502-474-2211: park
502-474-2245: marina

Kentucky Dam Village State Resort
  Park
P.O. Box 69
Gilbertsville, Kentucky 42044-0069
502-362-4271
800-325-0146: reservations
502-362-8386: marina

KINCAID LAKE STATE PARK
26

LOCATION   The park is four miles east of Falmouth.

ACTIVITIES   The 175-acre lake offers good boating from the ramp, and canoeing in the nearby Licking River. Fishing boat and pontoon boat rentals are available. Go fishing for largemouth bass, bluegill, and channel catfish. Play tennis, explore 2½ miles of hiking trails, participate in planned recreational activities, and attend nature programs, special events, and weekly movies in the 300-seat amphitheater.

Camp in the 84-site campground, open from April through October, with water and electrical hookups, a laundry, and grocery store. Go swimming in the pool.

Attend a professional Broadway musical at the Kincaid Regional Theatre on Chapel Street in Falmouth, from late June through early July, Thursday through Sunday. For theater information, call 606-654-2636.

Rent a canoe to take a trip on the Licking River that has Class I rapids, and enjoy guided moonlight trips during a full moon.

Arriving pilots can land at Gene Snyder Airport, four miles northwest of Falmouth. However, no rental cars are available.

INFORMATION
Kincaid Lake State Park
Route 4, Box 33
Falmouth, Kentucky 41040-9203
606-654-3531

KINGDOM COME STATE PARK
27

LOCATION   The park is in Cumberland near U.S. 119 on Pine Mountain, on the Kentucky-Virginia border.

FEATURES   The park is named for John Fox Jr.'s novel, *The Little Shepherd of Kingdom Come,* a series of books about Appalachian life. It's the state's highest state park, located at an elevation of 2,700 feet.

ACTIVITIES   Go fishing or boating, with pedal boat rentals available. Hike seven miles of trails. Watch for Raven's Rock, a huge stone slab rising 290 feet at a 45-degree angle. Enjoy several overlooks of the mountains. This is an especially colorful spot to visit during the fall "leaf peeping" season. Camp in the campground.

The state park provides access to the scenic 38-mile-long Little Shepherd Trail that winds along the 2,800-foot crest of Pine Mountain.

In Cumberland, tour the Mountain Heritage Museum at 806 East Main, to learn about mountain living, coal mining, and farming. Tour the visitor center. For information, call 606-589-5812.

INFORMATION
Kingdom Come State Park
Box M
Cumberland, Kentucky 40823-0420
606-589-2479

LAKE BARKLEY STATE RESORT PARK
28

LOCATION   The resort is on U.S. 68/Kentucky 80. It's seven miles southwest of Cadiz. From I-24, Exit 65, go west on U.S. 68 along the eastern shore of Lake Barkley. The park is on the Little River Embayment of Lake Barkley. It's also 29 miles west of Hopkinsville.

FEATURES   Lake Barkely, Kentucky's second largest lake, when combined with Kentucky Lake, forms one of the world's largest man-made lakes.

ACTIVITIES   Stay in the 120-room lodge, designed by Edward Durrell Stone, overlooking the lake, or in the 10-room Little River Lodge, open year-round.

Dine in the dining room or coffee shop. Work out in the Executive Fitness Center that has racquetball courts, aerobics instructors, sauna, steam room, and whirlpool. Stay in one of 14 cottages, or camp in the 80-site campground from April through October, with water and electrical hookups, and a laundry.

The 22-mile Little River Canoe Trail that goes between Cadiz and Land Between the Lakes is an easy canoe run, and perfect for canoe camping.

Go boating from the marina, with boat rentals available. Fish for bass, bluegill, catfish, and crappie. Go hiking on nine miles of trails, play golf on the 18-hole golf course, play tennis on one of four courts, enjoy horseback riding, and go to the trapshooting range.

Incoming pilots can land at Hopkinsville–Christian County Airport, two miles east of Hopkinsville. Rental cars are available. You can also land at Lake Barkley State Park Airport, four miles southwest of Cadiz and four miles from the park. A courtesy car provides transportation.

INFORMATION
Lake Barkley State Resort Park
Box 790
Blue Springs Road
Cadiz, Kentucky 42211-0790
502-924-1131
800-325-1708: out-of-state reservations
800-633-6277: in-state reservations
502-924-9954: marina
502-924-9076: pro shop

LAKE CUMBERLAND STATE RESORT PARK
29

LOCATION   The park is 10 miles south of Russell Springs, and 15 miles southwest of Jamestown on U.S. 127. From I-65, exit onto the Cumberland Parkway, then follow U.S. 127 to the east. From I-75, exit onto Kentucky 80 west.

FEATURES   Lake Cumberland is a large man-made lake covering 63,000 acres, with 1,255 miles of shoreline. It's known for some of the best fishing and pleasure boating in the eastern U.S. The resort is located on the north side of the lake.

ACTIVITIES   Stay overnight in 63-room Lure Lodge overlooking the lake, in Pumpkin Creek Lodge with 10 rooms and three suites, or in one of the 30 Wildwood Cottages nestled in the woods, and eat in the dining room. All these facilities are open year-round. Camp in the 150-site campground, with water and electrical hookups, grocery store and laundry, open from April through November.

Go swimming in the indoor or outdoor pools, and go boating from the marina or boat launch, with houseboat, fishing-boat, and pontoon-boat rentals available. Enjoy fishing for bass, crappie, and walleye. For updated fishing information, call 606-679-5655.

Play golf on the nine-hole, par three course, with rental clubs available, or enjoy miniature golf. Play tennis, explore four miles of hiking trails, and go horseback riding. Tour the nature center and attend nature programs. Rent a bicycle to go cycling.

Take a cruise aboard the *Jamestown Queen,* from the Jamestown Resort and Marina on Kentucky 92. The authentic Mississippi River paddlewheeler runs on Sundays from April through October, and on Friday and Saturdays from May through August. For information, call 502-343-LAKE.

Arriving pilots can land at Russell County Airport, located two miles northwest of Jamestown. Taxi service is available. Lake Cumberland is five away. You can also land at Columbia–Adair County Airport, two miles southwest of Columbia. Taxi service is available. The lake is 12 miles away.

You can also land at Somerset–Pulaski County Airport, three miles south of Somerset. This airport is three miles from the park.

INFORMATION
Lake Cumberland State Resort Park
5465 State Park Road
P.O. Box 380
Jamestown, Kentucky 42629-0380
502-343-3111 or 1-800-325-1709: lodge reservations
502-343-2525 or 1-800-234-3625: marina

LAKE MALONE STATE PARK
30

LOCATION   The park is on Kentucky 973, three miles west of Dunmor. From the Western Kentucky Parkway, take Exit 58 to U.S. 431, and go south to Kentucky 973.

FEATURES   Lake Malone covers 826 acres, with cliffs rising 200 feet above the water.

ACTIVITIES   Camp in the 20-site campground, with water and electrical hookups, a laundry and grocery store, open from April through mid-November, or stay in one of 100 primitive sites, open year-round. Go swimming from the beach, and boating from the marina, with fishing and pontoon boat rentals available. Go fishing for bass, crappie, bluegill, and channel catfish. Hike the one-mile hiking trail through the hardwood trees, mountain laurel, and wildflowers.

Arriving pilots can land at Muhlenberg County Airport, two miles northeast of Greenville. Rental cars are available.

INFORMATION
Lake Malone State Park
Star Route 8001
Dunmor, Kentucky 42339-0093
502-657-2111
502-657-9580: marina

LEVI JACKSON WILDERNESS ROAD STATE PARK
31

LOCATION   Levi Jackson is two miles south of London, off I-75, Exit 38.

FEATURES   Levi Jackson State Park was set aside to commemorate the early pioneers' struggle to survive and travel west. Between 1774 and 1800, over 300,000 travelers passed through here along Boone's Trace, and on the Wilderness Trail. This area is also the site of one of the state's bloodiest Indian massacres.

ACTIVITIES   At Levi Jackson State Park, attend corn grinding demonstrations presented from Memorial Day weekend through Labor Day, at McHargue's Mill. Hike along sections of the two pioneer trails. Go camping in the 185-site campground, open year-round, with electrical and water hookups, grocery store, and a laundry.

Tour the Mountain Life Museum to see a restoration of an 1800s village, and learn about the lives of the early settlers. It's open from 9 to 4:30, from April through October. You can also see one of the world's largest millstones at McHargue's Mill.

Swim in the pool, go horseback riding, and hiking on 8½ miles of trails. Play miniature golf, and participate in planned recreational activities.

Yahoo Falls Scenic Area is within the Daniel Boone National Forest, west off Kentucky 27 onto Kentucky 700. Go 3½ miles and turn north onto a forest service road, Kentucky 660. Bring along a picnic and explore several trails, including part of the 250-mile Sheltowee Trace used by backpackers. To reach the falls, follow the signed ¼-mile path that goes through the woods, to the head of a steep gorge. Yahoo Falls drop 113 feet from the Cumberland Plateau into the deep gorge. The best time to see the falls is in the spring and autumn.

Arriving pilots can land at London-Corbin Airport, three miles south of London. However, no rental cars are available.

INFORMATION
Levi Jackson State Park
998 Levi Jackson Mill Road
London, Kentucky 40741-8944
606-878-8000

LINCOLN HOMESTEAD STATE PARK
32

LOCATION   The park is in Springfield at 5079 Lincoln Road, Kentucky 528. From Elizabethtown, take the Blue Grass Parkway to U.S. 150 east, or take Kentucky 555 south.

FEATURES   The park includes three buildings that were important to Abraham Lincoln's father, Thomas. These buildings, brought here for display, include a replica of his childhood home (circa 1782), the Berry House which was the girlhood home of his bride, Nancy Hanks, and a blacksmith and carpenter shop.

ACTIVITIES   Tour historic Berry House from May through September daily, and in October on weekends. Cross the small covered bridge to reach a replica of the Berry's shop where Thomas Lincoln learned woodworking. The park is open daily from May through October. Admission is charged. Play golf on the 18-hole course, with a pro shop available.

The Mt. Zion Covered Bridge, circa 1871, is in Springfield. The bridge is 215 feet long and 16 feet wide.

Arriving pilots can land at Lebanon-Springfield Airport, three miles south of town. Rental cars are available by prior request only. Call 606-336-3818.

INFORMATION
Lincoln Homestead State Park
5079 Lincoln Road
Springfield, Kentucky 40069-9606
606-336-7461

MY OLD KENTUCKY HOME STATE PARK
33

LOCATION   The park is ¼ mile southeast of Bardstown off U.S. 31I/150, on Kentucky 49 south.

FEATURES   The park was established to preserve Federal Hill, the 1818 brick home of the John Rowan family, where Stephen Foster composed his ballad, "My Old Kentucky Home" in 1852.

ACTIVITIES   Camp in the 39-site campground, with water and electrical hookups, open from April through October. Enjoy a picnic, play tennis, or golf on the 18-hole golf course, with a pro shop. Tour the museum. Take a guided tour through the plantation to see rare furnishings, formal gardens, carriage house, and smokehouse.

Ride aboard the tourmobile that departs from the visitor center for a 1½-hour tour which includes a tour of Heaven Hill Distillery. The tourmobile operates Monday through Saturday at 9:30 and 1:30, from June through August. For information, call 502-348-4877.

Attend "The Stephen Foster Story" outdoor musical. The two-hour musical is based on 50 of his most familiar songs. It's offered daily in the park's amphitheater except Mondays, from mid-June through Labor Day. For information, call 1-800-626-1563 or 502-348-5971.

Bicyclists can join Kentucky's Wheelmen to cycle in the "My Old Kentucky Home Bicycle Tour" held in mid-September.

Go to the Kentucky Railway Museum, 12 miles south of Bardstown on US 31-E, Exit 10, off the Bluegrass Parkway. Here you can take a 22-mile round trip train ride through the river valley between New Haven and Boston. For details, call 800-272-1052.

Dine on board the "Old Kentucky Home" dinner train that departs from the depot at 602 North 3rd Street. The railroad cars are restored from the 1940s, and are pulled by two diesel engines. For details on the two-hour round trip, call 502-348-7300.

Take a guided tour of a Green Revival mansion, circa 1851, at 1003 North 3rd Street in Bardstown. Here the first Confederate flag was raised in Kentucky. For details, call 502-348-2586.

You can also tour Wickland off U.S. 61, ½ mile east of Court Square. This Georgian mansion, circa 1817, is where three governors have lived. It's open March through October. For information, call 502-348-5428.

Tour Old Bardstown Village at 210 East Broadway. The village depicts life in the 1800s, where you can observe demonstrations of blacksmithing, spinning, woodworking, and whiskey distilling. Walk through the Civil War museum.

Attend *Kentucky Show!* at 210 East Broadway for a multimedia presentation, featuring 3,600 slides on Kentucky's history and heritage. It's presented from April through October, Thursday through Sunday. For information, call 502-348-6501.

Arriving pilots can land at Samuels Field, two miles west of Bardstown. Rental cars are available.

INFORMATION
My Old Kentucky Home State Park
P.O. Box 323
Bardstown, Kentucky 40004-0323
502-348-3502
1-800-626-1563: information and reservations for musical

NATURAL BRIDGE RESORT STATE PARK
34

LOCATION   The park is near the Red River Gorge Geological Area, 2.5 miles southeast of Slade in the Daniel Boone National Forest. Take Exit 33 off the Mountain Parkway and go 2.5 miles southeast on Kentucky 11.

FEATURES   Natural Bridge, the largest of the natural arches in the park, features 15 million tons of rock suspended across the mountainside. It rises 65 feet in the air and is 78 feet long. The area contains 59 natural sandstone arches, with 12 of them found in the state park.

Red River Gorge features a boulder-strewn area with limestone cliffs, overlooks, three waterfalls, natural arches, and rare plants and animals. Watch for rock "houses"—overhangs originally used as shelter by the Shawnee and other Native American tribes. The gorge itself contains over 150 arches, the most in any area in the eastern U.S. Some are very small, while others, such as Gray's Arch, rise up to 80 feet and is 110 feet across.

ACTIVITIES   Stay in the 35-room lodge or in one of 10 cottages, open year-round. Camp in the 95-site campground, also open year-round with water and electrical hookups, and a laundry. Dine in the dining room. Tour the visitor center, and attend interpretive programs.

Swim in one of the two pools, and play tennis. Hike the ½-mile trail in the state nature reserve to see the arch, or along 18 miles of other trails. Go on an organized backpacking outing. Take the sky lift up for a view of the arch and eastern Kentucky, from May 1 through October 31. Go boating from the launch, or rent a pedal boat. Fish for bass, catfish, crappie, or rainbow trout, and play miniature golf.

Follow a 30-mile driving loop for overlooks of several arches, and views of the Red River coursing through the gorge below. Stop by the Gladie Creek cabin, circa 1884, to see displays on the area's early logging. It's open from Memorial Day through Labor Day. Hike almost 70 miles of trails down into the gorge.

Rock climbers come to scale Tower Rock and Fortress Wall, in the northern part of the gorge. Whitewater rafters come to challenge the Red River that flows along the Cumberland Plateau to the Kentucky River near Boonesborough, and offers Class III and IV rapids in April and May. Backpackers enjoy hiking and camping in the forest, and bushwhacking to 100-foot Big Sandy Falls. For gorge information, call 606-663-2852.

The Red River Gorge National Recreation Trail is a 36-mile system of loop trails, taking you into some of the scenic and historic attractions within the gorge. The trail connects with the Sheltowee Trace National Recreational Trail, a 257-mile path that goes the length of the Daniel Boone National Forest, and extends through the gorge into Tennessee. For information and maps, call 606-745-3100.

The adjoining Clifty Wilderness features rugged cliffs, steep canyons, rock shelters, and more arches. Visitors go hiking, horseback riding, camping, hunting, fishing, and canoeing.

INFORMATION
Natural Bridge Resort State Park
2135 Natural Bridge Road
Slade, Kentucky 40376-9701
606-663-2214
1-800-325-1710 or 606-663-5384: lodge reservations

OLD FORT HARROD STATE PARK
35

LOCATION   The park is 32 miles southwest of Lexington, on U.S. 68 in Harrodsburg.

FEATURES   James Harrod built the first permanent settlement west of the Alleghenies here, in 1774.

ACTIVITIES   Tour the replica of the fort, and watch costumed interpreters demonstrating life of the time. The park includes the Lincoln Marriage Temple, the cabin where Abraham Lincoln's parents were married in 1806. Pioneer Cemetery is the oldest one west of the Allegheny Mountains.

Tour the mansion museum to see Civil War artifacts, paintings, and a Lincoln collection. The museum is open from mid-March through November.

Attend "The Legend of Daniel Boone," an outdoor production, presented in the James Harrod Amphitheater from mid-June through early September, Monday through Saturday at 8:30 P.M. For details, call 606-734-3346.

In Harrodsburg, take a walking and driving tour along trails once followed by Indians and early pioneers. Harrodsburg is the state's oldest town, and the first permanent English settlement west of the Alleghenies. Morgan Row, at 220 South Chiles Street, contains the oldest intact row houses in the state, circa 1807. For details, stop by Harrodsburg's information center at 222 South Chiles. For information, call 606-734-2364.

Take a one-hour riverboat ride aboard the *Dixie Belle* down the Kentucky River, from late April through October. It departs from Shaker Landing off U.S. 68. For a schedule, call 606-734-5411.

Tour Shaker Village of Pleasant Hill, at 3500 Lexington Road, seven miles northeast of Harrodsburg off U.S. 68. Founded in 1805 by the Shakers (a celibate, communal religious sect), it's the largest restored Shaker village in the U.S., with 33 original 19th-century buildings. Listen to Shaker music, and watch dance and farm demonstrations.

Shaker Village is the mid-point for one of Kentucky's scenic byways: U.S. 68. A 2.4-mile section of this road features one of the longest continuous stretches of hand-laid stone fences in central Kentucky.

Arriving pilots can land at Blue Grass Airport, four miles west of Lexington. Rental cars are available.

INFORMATION
Old Fort Harrod State Park
P.O. Box 156
Harrodsburg, Kentucky 40330-0156
606-734-3314

PAINTSVILLE LAKE STATE PARK
36

LOCATION   The park is four miles west of Paintsville. Take U.S. 460 to
Kentucky 40.

ACTIVITIES   The 1,140-acre park is surrounded by steep, rocky cliffs and
wooded coves, and offers fishing (for bass, catfish, bluegill, and rainbow trout),
boating, and water-skiing. Houseboat, fishing-boat and pontoon-boat rentals are
available, and so are groceries.

Arriving pilots can land at Paintsville-Prestonsburg Combs Field, four miles
southeast of Paintsville. Rental cars are available. The park is six miles from the
airport.

INFORMATION
Paintsville Lake State Park
H.C. 66, Box 200
Prestonsburg, Kentucky 41653
606-297-1521 or 1-800-542-5790

PENNYRILE STATE RESORT PARK
37

LOCATION   The park is near Lake Beshear, eight miles south of Dawson
Springs on Kentucky 109, and 20 miles northwest of Hopkinsville on Kentucky
109N.

FEATURES   Pennyrile's 15,000-acre preserve is in the state's largest state forest system, the Pennyrile State Forest. It was named for the pennyroyal, an aro-
matic wildflower that blooms here in May.

ACTIVITIES   Stay in the 435-acre resort park's 24-room lodge overlooking
Pennyrile Lake, or in one of 13 housekeeping cottages, that are open from
March through December 21. Camp in the 68-site campground, with water
and electrical hookups, laundry and grocery store, all open year-round. Dine in
the dining room.

Go swimming in the lodge pool, or rent a paddleboat or rowboat to go boating
from the launch, on the 55-acre lake. Go hiking on seven miles of trails, and
horseback riding from the stable through the park and the adjacent forest. Play
golf on the nine-hole course, with a pro shop and rental clubs available, or play
tennis on one of the courts. Bring along a picnic to eat while overlooking the lake.
The park is open daily from February through December.

Lake Beshear is four miles from the park, where anglers go to fish for crappie,
largemouth bass, channel catfish, and bluegill.

Dawson Springs is on 127 Main, and was once one of the best known spas and health resorts in the South, where thousands came for the curative waters. Tour the Dawson Springs Museum and Art Center, to see photos and memorabilia from the health spa era. For information, call 502-797-3503 or 3891.

Incoming pilots can land at Tradewater Airport, two miles east of Dawson Springs. However, they have no rental cars. For rental cars, land at Hopkinsville–Christian County Airport two miles east of Hopkinsville.

INFORMATION
Pennyrile Forest State Resort Park
20781 Pennyrile Lodge Road
Route 4, Box 137
Dawson Springs, Kentucky 42408-9212
502-797-3421
800-325-1711: out of state reservations
800-633-4447: in-state reservations

PINE MOUNTAIN STATE RESORT PARK
38

LOCATION   The park is 15 miles north of Middlesboro and one mile south of Pineville off U.S. 25E, in the Kentucky Ridge State Forest. It's also 13 miles south of Barbourville.

FEATURES   Pine Mountain State Resort Park became the state's first state park in 1924. Laurel Cove amphitheater was built in a natural forest cove.

ACTIVITIES   Stay in the 30-room lodge overlooking the mountain valleys, or in one of the 20 cottages, open between April and mid-November. You can also camp in the primitive 33-site campground, open from April through October. Dine in the dining room.

Go horseback riding, and hike 8½ miles of trails in the state nature reserve. Play golf on the nine-hole golf course, with a pro shop, or enjoy miniature golf. Go boating and fishing in the 35-acre lake. Tour the nature center. The annual Mountain Laurel Festival is held in late May, when the laurel are in full bloom.

Cumberland Gap National Historic Park is in Middlesboro. Early fur traders, Indians, hunters, and pioneer farmers traveled through this gap going through the Appalachians. Daniel Boone and a crew of axmen opened the Wilderness Road for 200 miles to provide a route for the migration west.

The park has 50 miles of hiking trails including 21-mile Ridge Trail. Camp in one of 4 primitive campsites, accessible only on foot along the trail. Tour the Hensley Settlement along the Ridge Trail on Brush Mountain, reached by hiking four miles, or driving in on the 4-wheel-drive road. Three-hour shuttle tours are offered during the summer. For park information, call 606-248-2817.

Visitors to Cumberland Gap can drive up a road from the visitor center to reach the top of 2,500-foot Pinnacle. Tour the visitor center and pick up a trail map. Hike one of the trails, bordered by phlox and mountain laurel, to reach the overlook of the gap and peaks in three states.

Arriving pilots can land at Middlesboro–Bell County Airport, one mile west of Middlesboro. Rental cars are available. The park is 11 miles from the airport.

INFORMATION
Pine Mountain State Resort Park
1050 State Park Road
Pineville, Kentucky 40977-0610
606-337-3066
606-337-6195: pro shop
800-325-1712: reservations

ROUGH RIVER DAM STATE RESORT PARK
39

LOCATION   The park is on Rough River Lake. Take Western Kentucky Parkway Exit 94 to Kentucky 79 north at Caneyville. It's also 15 miles south of Harned, and 14 miles northwest of Leitchfield.

ACTIVITIES   Stay year-round in the 40-room lodge with private lakeside balconies, or stay in one of the 15 cottages. Camp seasonally in the 66-site campground, with water and electrical hookups, a laundry, and grocery store. Eat in the dining room.

Go swimming from the beach or in the lodge's pool. Enjoy boating from the launch or marina, with fishing-boat and pontoon-boat rentals available. Do some great fishing for walleye, bass, catfish, and crappie in the Rough River.

Play golf on the nine-hole, par three course, with a pro shop and rental clubs available. Play tennis on one of five courts, explore the 1.1-mile-long hiking trail, or work out on the fitness trail. Take a cruise aboard the *Lady of the Lake*. Tour the visitor center and attend interpretive programs.

Attend the "Official Kentucky State Championship Old Time Fiddlers" contest held annually in July.

On Saturday night attend "The Dock Brown Show," at the Pine Knob Outdoor Theater. It's based on the life of a Kentucky outlaw who lived here from 1842 to 1856. You can also watch "Down in Hoodoo Holler" on Friday nights. The theater is open from June through August, at 8:30 P.M. For information, call 502-257-8190 or 502-257-8747.

Arriving pilots can land at the Rough River State Park Airfield's 3,200-foot-long lighted airstrip, within walking distance of the lodge. You can camp on the field. You can also land at Grayson County Airport, four miles southeast of Leitchfield. Taxi transportation is available.

INFORMATION
Rough River Dam State Resort Park
14799 Park Lodge Road
Route 1, Box 1
Falls of Rough, Kentucky 40119-9701
502-257-2311
1-800-325-1713: reservations out of state
1-800-633-9744: in-state reservations

TAYLORSVILLE LAKE STATE PARK
40

LOCATION   From Louisville, take I-64 to the Gene Snyder Freeway south and Kentucky 155 to Taylorsville. Turn east on Kentucky 44 and continue three more miles to reach the park entrance.

ACTIVITIES   Go boating on 3,050-acre Taylorsville Lake, where you can rent houseboats, fishing boats, and pontoon boats from the full-service marina. A six-lane launching ramp is available. Enjoy fishing for stocked black bass, bluegill, and crappie. Go horseback riding along the equestrian trails.

INFORMATION
Taylorsville Lake State Park
1320 Park Road
Mt. Eden, Kentucky 40046
502-477-8713: park
502-477-8766: marina

WAVELAND STATE HISTORIC SITE
41

LOCATION   The site is five miles south of Lexington off U.S. 27, on Higbee Mill Pike.

FEATURES   Joseph Bryan, a descendant of Daniel Boone, built this Greek Revival mansion in 1847.

ACTIVITIES   Tours of the mansion are offered Tuesday through Saturday from 10 to 4, and on Sundays from 2 to 5, from March to mid-December. The ice-house, smokehouse, and servants' quarters have been restored. Bring along a picnic to enjoy.

Visit Kentucky Horse Park, 10 miles north of Lexington at the intersection of I-75 and Iron Works Pike, Exit 120. You can take tours of the grounds either aboard a horse-drawn shuttle or on foot. The International Museum of the Horse tells the history of all breeds of horses. A Parade of Breeds show occurs on the ½-mile track daily from April 1 through October 15. Stop by the visitor center to watch the film. For information, call 606-233-4303. The annual Festival of the Bluegrass is here held in June. For information, contact the Visitor Bureau at 606-233-7299.

Mary Todd Lincoln's House is at 578 West Main Street in Lexington. Built, circa 1803, her home has been restored, and contains personal items from the Lincoln-Todd families. Tours are available. For information, call 606-233-9999.

Ashland, the Henry Clay Estate, is at 120 Sycamore Road. Henry Clay, called "The Great Compromiser," lived in the now- restored family home from 1811 until his death in 1852. It's closed Mondays and all of January. For information, call 606-266-8581. It is listed as a National Historic Landmark.

Arriving pilots can land at Blue Grass Airport, four miles west of Lexington. Rental cars are available.

INFORMATION
Waveland State Historic Site
225 Higbee Mill Road
Lexington, Kentucky 40514-4778
606-272-2611

LOUISIANA

Louisiana's state parks encompass several historical, archeological, cultural, and natural sites. Many of its historic and scenic areas are located along the Mississippi River, and are accessible from the Great River Road, which is marked with pilot wheels. For state park information, write P.O. Drawer 44426, 2500 Shreveport Highway, Baton Rouge, Louisiana 70804-4426, or call 504-342-8111.

Anglers will find plenty of fishing opportunities in Louisiana. Freshwater fishing is available in world-famous Toledo Bend Reservoir, or in one of the state's excellent rivers, lakes, and large coastal marshes. For deep sea fishing, try your skill in the Gulf of Mexico, where you can fish for king mackerel, shark, blue marlin, and tarpon.

For boating opportunities, Louisiana has 7,500 miles of navigable waterways that include the Mississippi, Ouachita, and Red Rivers, and several large lakes such as Pontchartrain, Sabine, Calcasieu, and Bogne.

The state contains some of the largest state-owned wildlife sanctuaries found anywhere in the world. The Atchafalaya Swamp west of Baton Rouge is the nation's largest undeveloped wetlands, where a large crawfish harvest is taken, and where anglers fish for lunker largemouth. Louisiana boasts the nation's only large-scale alligator hunting season.

Southwestern Louisiana is the festival capital of the state, featuring over 75 festivals and special events. These feature Cajun food and music, alligators, historical homes, water sports, and native arts and crafts. Contact the visitor bureau for details at 318-436-9588.

Hikers can obtain trail and backpacking information from the New Orleans section of the Sierra Club, 111 South Hennessey Street, New Orleans, LA 70119.

The weather in the state is semi-humid and subtropical. During the summer, it averages 102 days with temperatures above 90 degrees in the northern region, and 86 days with temperatures going over 90 degrees in the Lake Charles area.

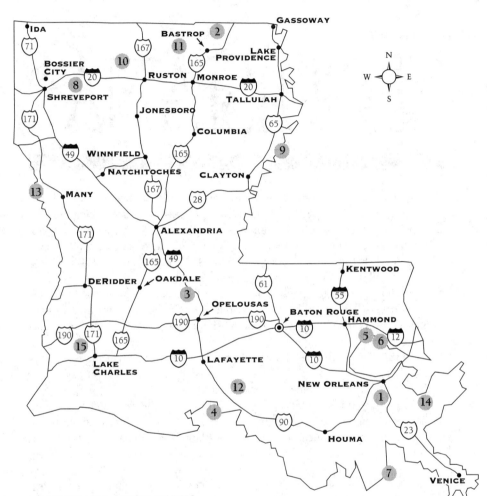

LOUISIANA STATE PARKS

1. Bayou Segnette State Park
2. Chemin-A-Haut State Park
3. Chicot State Park
4. Cypremort Point State Park
5. Fairview Riverside State Park
6. Fontainebleau State Park
7. Grand Isle State Park
8. Lake Bistineau State Park

9. Lake Bruin State Park
10. Lake Claiborne State Park
11. Lake D'Arbonne State Park
12. Lake Fausse Pointe State Park
13. North Toledo Bend State Park
14. St. Bernard State Park
15. Sam Houston Jones State Park

BAYOU SEGNETTE STATE PARK
1

LOCATION The park is in Westwego off the Westbank Expressway, U.S. 90 at its intersection with Drake Avenue. It's across the Mississippi River from New Orleans. Access to the Westbank Expressway is via the Huey P. Long bridge from the west, or from the Greater New Orleans bridge and I-10 from the east.

ACTIVITIES Go swimming in the pool, boating from the ramp, and bass fishing in the bayou's Barataria Basin. Stay in a fully-furnished cabin or the 100-site campground, with water and electrical hookups, and a dump station. Stop by the visitor center, and hike the trails.

The park provides access to an interconnected series of bayous and canals where anglers can fish for redfish, speckled trout, and flounder. Guide services are available at public boat ramps adjacent to the park.

Take a "Cajun Critters" swamp tour from 363 Louisiana Street off the Westbank Expressway, U.S. 90. For information, call 504-436-9999. For a Cypress Swamp tour, go to 501 Laroussini Street, or call 504-581-4501.

Jean Lafitte National Historical Park and Preserve has three units: Barataria, Chalmette, and New Orleans' French Quarter. The park preserves 8,600 acres of the state's coastal wetlands, freshwater marshes, and swamps.

The Barataria Unit is at 7400 Louisiana 45 in Marrero. Tour the visitor center to learn about early area lifestyles. For information, call 504-589-2330. Attend the Louisiana Crawdad Festival in April, in Marrero.

The French Quarter Unit covers 70 blocks between Canal Street, Rampart Street, Esplanade Avenue, and the Mississippi River. The Jean Lafitte National Historical Park and Preserve is located here in the French Quarter. Its Visitor and Folklife Center is at 916–918 North Peters Street on Dutch Alley, where rangers offer guided tours (by reservation) and folk life demonstrations on alternate weekends. For information, call 504-589-2636.

Chalmette National Historic Park is on the east bank of the Mississippi, six miles from New Orleans on St. Bernard Highway. It was the site of the last Battle of New Orleans. Its visitor center is located in the Beauregard home. For information, call 504-271-8186. An annual reenactment of the battle is held in Chalmette on the weekend nearest the actual battle date of January 8. A Tomato Festival is held here in May.

Go for a self-guided canoe trip from Crown Point south of Marrero at Louisiana 45 and 3134. For information, call 504-592-0560 or 504-689-4186. These same bayous were once traveled by the pirate Jean Lafitte. Attend an authentic Cajun dance Sundays from 2 to 6, and enjoy home-cooked gumbo and jambalaya. For information, call 504-589-2330.

Attend the Pirogue Races in Lafitte the third weekend in July, and the Lafitte Seafood Festival the first full weekend in August.

St. Bernard State Park is on Louisiana 39, 18 miles southeast of New Orleans on the banks of the Mississippi River. Go canoeing and fishing in the man-made lagoon, swim in the pool, and camp in the campground. For information, call 504-682-2101.

Hikers and bikers have access to almost 100 miles of trail along the Mississippi River levee. Various trails branch off the levee, including a popular one in Orleans Parish. In New Orleans, you can pick up the trail at the intersection of Carollton and St. Charles Avenues.

For additional information on activities in New Orleans, see St. Bernard State Park.

Arriving pilots can land at Lakefront Airport, four miles northeast of New Orleans. Ground transportation includes taxis and limousines.

INFORMATION
Bayou Segnette State Park
7777 Westbank Expressway
Westwego, Louisiana 70094
504-736-7140

CHEMIN-A-HAUT STATE PARK
2

LOCATION   The park is 10 miles northeast of Bastrop on Louisiana 139. The park is at the confluence of two bayous: Chemin-A-Haut and Bartholomew.

ACTIVITIES   Go camping in the 26-site campground, with water and electrical hookups, and dump station, or stay in one of the fully-equipped cabins. Hike the trails, and go canoeing and boating from the ramp in Big Slough Lake, with rentals available. Enjoy fishing in the lake for stocked bass, and go swimming in the pool.

In Bastrop, tour Snyder Museum and Creative Art Center, 1620 East Madison, U.S. 165 North. For information, call 318-281-8760. Attend Morehouse Parish Farm Fest in January, and the North Louisiana Cotton Fair and Festival in early September. Mer Route hosts a Louisiana Waterfowl Festival in October, and the Bastrop Fall Arts and Crafts Show is in November.

Arriving pilots can land at Morehouse Memorial Airport, two miles southeast of Bastrop. Taxi transportation is available.

INFORMATION
Chemin-A-Haut State Park
14656 State Park Road
Route 5, Box 617
Bastrop, Louisiana 71220-7078
318-283-0812

CHICOT STATE PARK
3

LOCATION   The park is seven miles north of Ville Platte, on Louisiana 3042.

ACTIVITIES   Camp in one of the two campgrounds, 211 sites with water and electrical hookups, and a dump station, or stay in one of 27 fully-furnished cabins. Hike the 7.5-mile backpacking trail. Attend interpretive programs.

Go water-skiing, canoeing, boating from the ramp in Chicot Lake, with rentals available, and swimming in the pool. Go freshwater fishing in the lake stocked with bream, bass, and crappie.

Visit Louisiana State Arboretum on Louisiana 3042, eight miles north of Ville Platte and 1.5 miles from the entrance to the state park. The facilities feature 2.5 miles of nature trails winding through 100 species of native plant life, including an excellent example of a beech-magnolia climax forest. Tours are offered. For information, call 318-363-6289.

Attend the Louisiana Cotton Festival in Ville Platte in October. For details, call 205-925-3860.

INFORMATION
Chicot State Park
Route 3, Box 494
Ville Platte, Louisiana 70586
318-363-2503

CYPREMORT POINT STATE PARK
4

LOCATION   The park is 24 miles south of Jeanerette, off Louisiana 319.

FEATURES   Cypremort provides access to the Gulf of Mexico. A man-made beach is located in the heart of a natural marsh. Enjoy both fresh and saltwater fishing and swimming. Go sailing, and attend one of their annual regattas.

Jeanerette, on the banks of the Bayou Teche, is the home of hot French bread baked in brick ovens, and features spring and fall festivals. For details, call 318-276-4587. Tour the Jeanerette Museum, housed in an all-cypress home. Watch their video on the sugar cane industry. For information, call 318-276-4408.

In Jeanerette, annual events include: the Jeanerette Creole Festival in April, the Mirliton Festival held three days in late June, the annual Country Fair in August, and the Old Country Fair held the second weekend in September. For information, call 205-925-3680.

Take the Jeanerette driving tour along Louisiana 182 east from New Iberia to Jeanerette. You'll pass many historic homes along the Bayou Teche. Maps are available from the New Iberia Tourist Information Center in the Jeanerette

Museum. For information, call 318-365-1540. Tour Albania Mansion, ½ mile east of Jeanerette, built circa 1800, to see an unsupported spiral staircase and doll room. For information, call 318-276-4816.

In Franklin, attend Mardi Gras in February or March, the St. Mary Parish Parade of Homes in March, the Magnolia Festival the fourth weekend in April, and the Festival de Barbue the second weekend in June. Franklin's Cajun Fest is the last week in August, and its International Alligator Festival is held the fourth weekend in October. For information, call 504-925-3860.

Franklin's historic district has over 400 properties located along the main boulevard. For information on walking or driving tours, call 1-800-962-6889 or 318-828-6323. Tour Arlington Plantation, circa 1850, at 56 East Main Street. It's shown by appointment by calling 1-800-256-2931. Darby House, circa 1765, is at 301 Main Street, Louisiana 182, and now houses a branch of the St. Mary Bank. Tours may be arranged by calling 318-828-0560.

Arriving pilots can land at Le Maire Memorial Airport, one mile south of Jeanerette. Rental cars are available.

INFORMATION
Cypremort Point State Park
306 Beach Lane
Star Route B, Box 428AA
Franklin, Louisiana 70538
318-867-4510

FAIRVIEW RIVERSIDE STATE PARK
5

LOCATION   The park is two miles east of Madisonville, on Louisiana 22.

FEATURES   Its 98 acres have moss-draped oaks and woodlands located near the banks of the Tchefuncte River.

ACTIVITIES   Go water-skiing, freshwater fishing from the pier, boating from the dock, or canoeing along the canoe trail on the Tchefuncte River. Enjoy camping in the 85-site campground, with water and electric hookups, and a dump station.

Annual events include: Krewe of Tchefuncte Boat Parade in February, St. Tammany Water Sports Festival in April, Madisonville Wooden Boat Festival in September, Oktoberfest, and Santa on the Tchefuncte in December.

INFORMATION
Fairview Riverside State Park
P.O. Box 856
Mandeville, Louisiana 70447
504-845-3318

FONTAINEBLEAU STATE PARK
6

LOCATION   The park is three miles south of Mandeville on U.S. 190, on the north shore of Lake Pontchartrain.

FEATURES   The northern end of the Lake Pontchartrain Causeway is in the park, and is the world's longest over-water highway bridge. The park contains the ruins of a plantation brickyard and sugar mill.

ACTIVITIES   Drive through an alley of live oaks lining the entrance road. Go water-skiing, swimming from the beach or in the pool, boating, and fresh and salt-water fishing in Lake Pontchartrain. Enjoy camping in the 250-site campground, 186 sites with water and electric hookups, or stay in a cabin. Hike the one-mile nature trail, and enjoy a picnic.

Take a tour of the Mandeville Lakefront to see many of the resort homes, where wealthy New Orleans Creoles spent their summers. Tours are available through the St. Tammany Tour Guide Association. Call 1-800-634-9443 or 504-892-0520 for information.

Annual events include a Mardi Gras Parade, Crawfishman Triathlon in April, Greater Mandeville Seafood Festival in May, Bayou Lacombe Crab Festival in Lacombe the last weekend in June, and All Saints' Day Lighting of the Graves in November. For information, call 504-624-9762.

INFORMATION
Fontainebleau State Park
P.O. Box 152
Mandeville, Louisiana 70470-0152
504-624-4443

GRAND ISLE STATE PARK
7

LOCATION   Grand Isle State Park extends for over a mile along the Gulf of Mexico, and is at the east end of Grand Isle on Louisiana 1. Grand Isle is at the tip of an eight-mile barrier island that is connected to the mainland via a bridge.

FEATURES   Grand Isle is the only inhabited barrier island on the Louisiana Coast, and it provides access to the Gulf of Mexico. The area has a reputation as being one of the top ten fishing spots in the world.

ACTIVITIES   Enjoy camping in the 100-site campground; no hookups are available, but a dumping station is. Go boating from the ramp; swim at your own risk because of the strong undertow. Go saltwater fishing in the Gulf from the 400-foot fishing pier (both day and night) for over 300 different species of fish. Tour the visitor center.

Grand Isle State Park
(courtesy of the Department of Culture, Recreation and Tourism)

Grand Isle Resort features large beaches, lodges, and seafood restaurants, camping with hookups, bird watching, surfing, crabbing, and surf fishing. Go deep sea fishing from a chartered boat. For information, call 504-787-2200.

Watch the Carnival Parade in Grand Isle in February, and attend the Deep South Fishing Rodeo the third weekend in June. Lures and Liars Fishing Rodeo, and the International Grand Isle Tarpon Rodeo, are held the last weekend in July. The Blessing of the Fleet Festival is in July or August, and the Grand Isle Redfish Rodeo is held over the Labor Day weekend.

INFORMATION
Grand Isle State Park
P.O. Box 741
Grand Isle, Louisiana 70358
504-787-2559

LAKE BISTINEAU STATE PARK
8

LOCATION   The park is near Doyline on Louisiana 163, and 20 miles southwest of Minden.

FEATURES   Lake Bistineau is in the heart of a pine forest.

ACTIVITIES   Stay overnight in one of 12 cabins, or camp in one of 67 camp-sites, with water and electric hookups, and a dump station. Swim in one of two swimming pools or in the lake. Go freshwater fishing, boating from the ramp, with rentals available, water-skiing, canoeing, and sailing. Hike the various trails.

Take a Wild America Bayou Tour by taking Exit Dixie Inn/Minden off I-20. Daily tours are offered June through August, and weekends only in September and May. For details, call 318-258-3831.

Visit Germantown Museum and Colony at 500 Museum Road, seven miles northeast of Minden. The colony was established in 1835 under the leadership of "Countess von Leon." For information, call 318-377-4240.

Attend the Germantown Festival in Minden, in May. Triathletes can participate in the annual Caney-Dorcheat Triathlon. For information, call 318-377-4240.

INFORMATION
Lake Bistineau State Park
P.O. Box 589
Doyline, Louisiana 71023
318-745-3503

LAKE BRUIN STATE PARK
9

LOCATION   Lake Bruin is four miles north of St. Joseph on Louisiana 604, and east of U.S. 65.

FEATURES   Lake Bruin has a magnificent cypress growth along its shoreline.

ACTIVITIES   Go water-skiing, swimming from the beach, and freshwater fishing for bass. Enjoy canoeing, sailing and boating from the ramp, with rentals available. Camp in the 25-site campground, with water and electric hookups, and a dump station.

Arriving pilots can land at Tensas Parish Airport, four miles northeast of St. Joseph. However, no rental cars are available.

INFORMATION
Lake Bruin State Park
Route 1, Box 183
St. Joseph, Louisiana 71366
318-766-3530

LAKE CLAIBORNE STATE PARK
10

LOCATION   The lake is seven miles southeast of Homer, on Louisiana 146.

FEATURES   The park features 600 wooded acres along the shore of Lake Claiborne. The lake was formed in the 1960s when Bayou d'Arbonne was dammed.

ACTIVITIES   Go swimming from the beach, freshwater fishing for walleye, largemouth bass, crappie, and bream. Enjoy water-skiing, canoeing, sailing, and boating from the ramp, with rentals available. Camp in the 87-site campground, with water and electrical hookups, and a dump station. Hike the one-mile nature trail.

Stop by the Greek Revival Claiborne Parish Courthouse, circa 1861, on Homer's city square. It's one of only four pre-Civil War courthouses in Louisiana, and is listed on the National Register of Historic Places. Tour Ford Museum at 519 South Main, to see memorabilia from the early settlement days. For information, call 318-258-5863.

Attend the Claiborne Jubilee in Homer, the first weekend in May, the Bluegrass Festival in Athens the first weekend in June, and another one the second weekend in September. Attend the Claiborne Christmas Festival in Homer, in December. For details, call 504-925-3860.

Arriving pilots can land at Homer Municipal Airport, three miles east of the city. However, no rental cars are available.

INFORMATION
Lake Claiborne State Park
P.O. Box 246
Homer, Louisiana 71040
318-927-2976

LAKE D'ARBONNE STATE PARK
11

LOCATION   The park is west of Farmerville, off Louisiana 2.

ACTIVITIES   Go freshwater fishing from the pier, canoeing, sailing, and boating from the ramp, with rentals available. Overnight in a cabin, or stay in the campground. Enjoy hiking and bicycling.

In Farmerville, attend the Watermelon Festival the last weekend in July, and the Marion Mayhaw Festival the first and second weekend in May. For details, call 318-368-9242.

In Bernice, attend the Corney Creek Festival the first weekend in June. For details, call 318-368-9242.

Arriving pilots can land at Farmerville Airport, four miles south of Farmerville. However, no rental cars are available.

INFORMATION
Lake D'Arbonne State Park
P.O. Box 236
Farmerville, Louisiana 71241
318-368-2086

LAKE FAUSSE POINTE STATE PARK
12

LOCATION   The park is 22 miles south of Henderson on West Atchafalaya Basin Protection Levee Road. It's east of St. Martinville via Louisiana 96 and Louisiana 3083.

ACTIVITIES Stay in one of the fully-equipped cabins or in the 50-site campground, with water and electric hookups, a dump station, and limited groceries available. Go boating from the ramp, with rentals available, and catfish fishing in Lake Fausse Pointe. Hike six miles of trails. Tour the visitor center.

Take a swamp tour of the Atchafalaya Swamp. Tours leave from the Whiskey River Landing and from McGee's Landing, 1337 Henderson Levee Road, in Breaux Bridge, Louisiana. For information, call either 318-228-8567 or 318-228-2384. In Breaux Bridge, attend the Crawfish Festival the first weekend in May, and Mulate's Accordion Festival in July.

Go through the Longfellow-Evangeline State Commemorative Area, located along the banks of Bayou Teche. Go north on Louisiana 31 in St. Martinsville. The park commemorates Longfellow's epic poem *Evangeline,* telling of two lovers separated when they were expelled from Canada by the conquering British. Her statue is over the grave, believed to be hers, at nearby St. Martin's Church. Go camping, freshwater fishing, boating from the ramp, swimming, and canoeing. For park information, call 318-394-3754.

Visit Evangeline Oak, a photographer's favorite, located on the bayou at the end of Port Street in St. Martinville. Tour the Acadian House Museum, circa 1780, to see its early Louisiana artifacts. Admission is charged.

While in town, stop by St. Martin De Tours Catholic Church on Main Street, circa 1765. Its Petit Paris Museum has Mardi Gras costumes. For a guided tour reservation, call 318-394-7334.

Attend Mardi Gras in Loreauville. Jeanerette has an Old Country Fair in September. Tour the Jeanerette Museum to learn about 200 years of sugar cane farming. For information, call 318-276-4408.

Visit Shadows-on-the-Tech at 317 East Main Street in New Iberia. It was built by wealthy sugarcane planter David Weeks, circa 1834. For information, call 318-369-6446.

INFORMATION
Lake Fausse Pointe State Park
5400 Levee Road
Route 5, Box 5648
St. Martinville, Louisiana 70582
318-229-4764

NORTH TOLEDO BEND STATE PARK
13

LOCATION   The park is four miles southwest of Zwolle, and one mile south of Louisiana 1215. Access to Zwolle is via U.S. 171 through Mansfield from the north, and through Many from the south.

FEATURES   Toledo Bend Reservoir is located on the Louisiana-Texas border, and offers anglers 1,200 miles of shoreline. Its year-round fishing climate provides good fishing for stocked Florida bass, crappie, and catfish.

ACTIVITIES   Stay overnight in one of the fully-equipped cabins, or in the 63-site campground, with water and electrical hookups, and a dump station. Groceries are available. Hike the trails. Go swimming in the pool, boating from the ramp, and pan fishing in Toledo Bend Lake. Stop by the visitor center.

Toro Hills Resort is a half-hour from the park, on the edge of Kisatchie National Forest, between Many and Leesville on U.S. 171. It features an 18-hole golf course, tennis, and two swimming pools, plus luxury condos. For information, call 1-800-533-5031 or 318-586-4661.

Hodges Gardens, Louisiana's "Garden in the Forest," is across from the resort, and has 4,700 acres of flowers, birds, and wildlife. The gardens feature an Easter Sunrise Service, July 4th celebration, October Fall Fest, and Christmas Festival of Lights. For information, call 318-256-5880.

In Zwolle, attend the Tamale Festival the second weekend in October, the Florien Free State Festival the second weekend in November, the Battle of Pleasant Hill reenactment the nearest weekend to the April 9 conflict, and Fisher Sawmill Days the third weekend in May. Watch tamales being made at the Zwolle Tamale Factory in downtown Zwolle. For information, call 318-645-9086.

In Mansfield, attend the Louisiana Blueberry Festival in June.

Arriving pilots can land at DeSoto Parish Airport, three miles northwest of Mansfield, or at Hart Airport, two miles southwest of Many. Both airports have rental cars.

INFORMATION
North Toledo Bend State Park
P.O. Box 56
Zwolle, Louisiana 71486
318-645-4715

ST. BERNARD STATE PARK
14

LOCATION   The park is 18 miles southeast of New Orleans on Louisiana 39, on the Mississippi River.

ACTIVITIES   Get some good views of the Mississippi River from several over-looks. Go canoeing and fishing in the man-made lagoons. Enjoy hiking, camping in the 51-site campground, with water and electric hookups, and a dump station, and go swimming in the pool. The park is a stop-off point for Chalmette National Historic Park, and the city of New Orleans.

In New Orleans, visit the French Quarter, site of the original city settlement, circa 1718. It's 13 blocks long, bordered by Canal and North Rampart Streets, Esplanade Avenue and the river. The Pontalba buildings, circa 1849, are trimmed with cast iron balconies. The buildings are along Jackson Square. The old Jackson Brewery now houses many shops and restaurants. For a unique tour, ride in a Gay 90s Carriage available at 1824 North Rampart Street. For information, call 504-943-8820.

The Jean Lafitte National Historical Park and Preserve is in the French Quarter. Park naturalists lead free tours, beginning from the park's visitor and folklife center in the French Market, at 916 N. Peters Street. Hike guided and self-guided trails of varied lengths. For information, call 504-589-2636.

Drive across the Lake Pontchartrain Causeway, the world's longest over-water highway bridge. Its northern terminus is in Fontainbleau State Park.

Visit Longue Vue house and gardens at #7 Bamboo Road. The 45-room house, designated as a historic landmark, is located on eight acres, with five gardens designed to celebrate the four seasons. For information, call 504-488-5488.

Take a river plantation and battlefield cruise aboard the *Creole Queen* paddle-wheeler. It departs from the Poydras Street wharf, behind the Hilton Hotel. For information, call 504-524-0814. In late June through early July, participate in the recreation of the famous 1870 steamboat race between the *Natchez* and the *Robert E. Lee,* from New Orleans to St. Louis. For information, call 1-800-543-1949. In addition to these two, you'll find many other paddlewheelers who ply the waters of the Mississippi and Lake Pontchartrain.

To see some Green Revival and mid-Victorian architectural-style homes from the 1800s, drive or take a walking tour through the Garden District from Jackson Avenue to Louisiana Avenue, and from Prytania to Magazine Street. These homes are privately owned. Tour the Beauregard-Keyes house at 1113 Chartres Street. Circa 1827, the home was the birthplace of famous chess champion Paul Morphy, and later became the home of writer Frances P. Keyes. For information, call 504-523-7257.

Tour the Hermann-Grima historic house at 820 St. Louis Street. The French Quarter mansion, circa 1831, has slave quarters, stables, and creole cooking demonstrations on Thursdays, from October through May. It's listed on the National Register of Historic Places. For information, call 504-525-5661.

Jazz lovers should be sure to visit Preservation Hall, 726 St. Peter Street, where jazz is performed nightly. For information, call 504-522-2841 or 504-523-8939. The Jazz and Heritage Festival is held from the last weekend in April through the first weekend in May. For information, call 504-568-0251.

St. Louis Cathedral in Jackson Square is one of the oldest churches in the U.S. You can tour the cathedral Monday through Saturday from 9 to 5, and Sundays from 1 to 5. For information, call 504-861-9521.

For one of the most famous celebrations, come to New Orleans for Mardi Gras, featuring 30 parades. Parades begin rolling 12 days before Shrove Tuesday, (which is the day before Ash Wednesday). On the evening of Shrove Tuesday, two of the festival's most famous parades are held: Rex, King of Carnival and Monarch of Merriment parade, and Comus, God of Revelry parade.

Take a stroll along Lakeshore Drive by Lake Pontchartrain, where you pass the Mardi Gras fountain, which displays color and motion nightly.

New Orleans has other festivities going on year-round, too numerous to mention here. For details, contact the New Orleans City, and Louisiana State, Tourist Information Center at 504-568-5661.

Arriving pilots can land at Lakefront Airport, four miles northeast of New Orleans. Ground transportation includes taxis, limousines, and a courtesy car.

INFORMATION
St. Bernard State Park
P.O. Box 534
Violet, Louisiana 70092
504-682-2101

SAM HOUSTON JONES STATE PARK
15

LOCATION   The park is 12 miles northwest of Lake Charles on Louisiana 378, at the confluence of three rivers.

FEATURES   Sam Houston Jones State Park was originally named for the hero of the Alamo, who is believed to have stayed in the area. Later it was named after the governor who was responsible for preserving the land in the 1940s. It features towering pines, cypress-bordered lagoons, and woodlands.

ACTIVITIES   Go camping in the 73-site campground, with water and electric hookups, and a dumping station. Stay in one of 12 fully-equipped vacation cabins on the Calcasieu River.

Go canoeing, boating from the ramp, with rentals available, water-skiing, and freshwater fishing for perch, bream, or bass, in the Westfork of the Calcasieu River.

Hike the nature trail and the Old Stagecoach Road hiking trail. Attend summer nature interpretive programs. A herd of deer is kept in a special section of the woods. Birders come here during the migration season to count the birds who stop here, as they migrate across the state.

Explore the Creole Nature Trail at 1211 North Lakeshore Drive, featuring a 105-mile driving and walking tour, four national wildlife refuges, and bird sanctuary. The trail begins in Sulphur and follows Louisiana 26 and 81 along the Gulf Coast. Tour historic "Charpentier" District's twenty square blocks of Victorian-era homes. Drive down Shell Beach Drive to see some of the area's most luxurious homes. Maps are available at the State Tourist Center on I-10 near the Texas border, or at the Lake Charles Tourist Center on I-10 in Lake Charles. For information, call 318-436-9588.

Take an airboat tour in Loreauville to see shallow water swamps, bayous, a slough, and coves. For information, call 318-229-4457.

Visit Live Oak Gardens at 5505 Rip Van Winkle Road in New Iberia. The Victorian home, circa 1870, is listed on the National Historic Register. Take a narrated boat tour on Lake Peigneur. For information, call 318-365-3332. The Conrad Rice Mill/Konriko, at 307 Ann Street, is America's oldest rice mill. Tour the mill Monday through Saturday, from 9 to 5. For information, call 318-364-7242.

Take a guided tour of Shadows-on-the-Teche, 317 East Main in New Iberia. It features a plantation home and gardens, circa 1834. It's one of the most authentically restored historic sites in the U.S. For information, call 318-369-6446.

Attend the Mardi Gras parade in February. Contraband Days, Louisiana's second largest festival, featuring approximately 175 events is held city-wide for over two weeks, in May. Attend the Fourth of July Water Festival, and the Louisiana Shakespeare Festival the last weekend in July, and first weekend in August. The Southwest Louisiana State Fair and Expo are in September, and the Annual Gumbeaux Gator Tail Cook Off Craft Fair is in October, in Lake Charles. For further information on these and other festivities, call 1-800-231-4730 outside Louisiana, or 504-925-3860.

Arriving pilots can land at Chennault Industrial Airport, seven miles east of Lake Charles. Rental cars are available.

INFORMATION
Sam Houston Jones State Park
101 Sutherland Road
Route 4, Box 294
Lake Charles, Louisiana 70611
318-855-2665
Cabin reservations: 318-855-7371

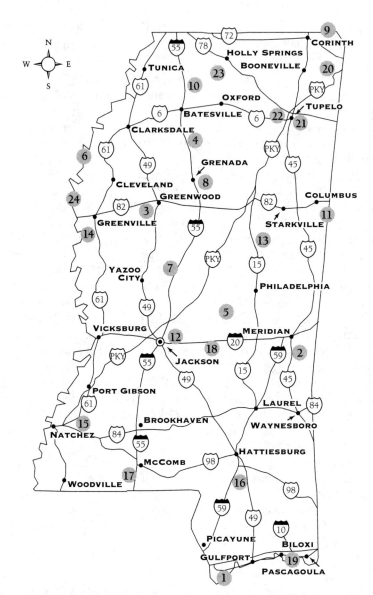

MISSISSIPPI STATE PARKS

1. Buccaneer State Park
2. Clarkco State Park
3. Florewood River Plantation State Park
4. George Payne Cossar State Park
5. Golden Memorial State Park
6. Great River Road State Park
7. Holmes County State Park
8. Hugh White State Park
9. J. P. Coleman State Park
10. John W. Kyle State Park
11. Lake Lowndes State Park
12. LeFleur's Bluff State Park

13. Legion State Park
14. Leroy Percy State Park
15. Natchez State Park
16. Paul B. Johnson State Park
17. Percy Quinn State Park
18. Roosevelt State Park
19. Shepard State Park
20. Tishomingo State Park
21. Tombigbee State Park
22. Trace State Park
23. Wall Doxey State Park
24. Winterville Mounds State Historic Site

MISSISSIPPI

Mississippi has 27 state parks containing hundreds of primitive camping sites. All the parks, including the five historic parks, are open year-round. To overnight in a state park cabin, for which reservations are strongly recommended, call 1-800-467-2527 or 601-364-2140.

The state has 17 million acres of woodlands, providing the perfect spot for camping, hiking, and hunting. For information on its 1.5 million acres of national forests, call 601-965-4391. Because of its mild climate, visitors can enjoy water sports year-round in southern Mississippi, including swimming, sailing, and fishing.

National parks in Mississippi include Vicksburg National Military Park, site of one of the bloodiest battles in the Civil War, Gulf Islands National Seashore, and the Natchez Trace Parkway. For information, contact the National Park Service at 601-875-9057.

The southwestern part of the state has river cities famous for their antebellum mansions. North of Vicksburg are some of the largest cotton plantations in the world.

The famous Natchez Trace, over 8,000 years old, begins at Natchez and goes to Nashville, Tennessee. The trail was first "traced out" by buffalo, then followed by the Indians, and in the 1700s, the French and British founded the network of area trails. By 1785, river trade began when traders from Tennessee and Kentucky floated their wares downriver, and returned home via the Trace, then called the "Boatman's Trail." From 1800 to 1820, the Trace became the busiest highway in the area. However, when steamboats took over the river, the Trace was not in use as much, until it was made into a parkway by the National Parks.

Bicyclists will find excellent riding conditions along the Natchez Trace. At two locations, you can still find part of the sunken Old Trace Road by the Port Gibson Ranger Station. Other original Trace sections are found at Mile Markers 198.6, 221.4, and 260, near the Tupelo Visitor Center. For bicycling information and map, call 601-680-4025.

Over 300 festivals are held throughout the state. Here Jimmie Rodgers, "Father of Country Music," Elvis Presley, and the Blues were born. Award-winning authors also have their roots here. Oxford was William Faulkner's home; Richard Wright and Eudora Welty used Mississippi as the basis for some of their writing. Playwright Tennessee Williams, and puppet master, Jim Henson, were also from here.

BUCCANEER STATE PARK
1

LOCATION   The park is two miles off U.S. 90 on Beach Boulevard in Waveland, on the Gulf Coast. Cross the 1.9-mile-long bridge that spans Bay St. Louis, and turn onto Beach Drive at the end of the bridge to get to the park.

ACTIVITIES   Enjoy playing in the wave pool, on the water slide, and children will enjoy the wading pool, all open seasonally. Go fishing and swimming from the beach. Play tennis, basketball, and hike the nature trail. Attend programs in the outdoor amphitheater.

Go camping at one of the 50 tent sites or on one of the 149 camping pads, 80 with sewer hookups. Laundry facilities are available. Purchase supplies from the camp store and snacks from the snack bar. Tour the visitor center.

Visit the John C. Stennis Space Center for guided tours of NASA's space shuttle main engine testing complex. It's on Highway 607 South, 12 miles northwest of Bay St. Louis. It has a museum and theater. For information, call 601-688-2370.

Enjoy an historic downtown walking tour of Bay St. Louis. Begin at the Historical Society Home on Cue Street. It's an antique-lovers haven. For information, call 601-467-6252.

Arriving pilots can land at Stennis International Airport, located eight miles northwest of Bay St. Louis. Rental cars are available.

INFORMATION
Buccaneer State Park
1150 South Beach Blvd.
Waveland, Mississippi 39576
601-467-3822

CLARKCO STATE PARK
2

LOCATION   The park is 20 miles south of Meridian, off U.S. 45.
FEATURES   Clarkco is located on 65-acre Clarkco Lake.
ACTIVITIES   Hike the marked nature trails, and play tennis on lighted tennis courts. Tour the visitor center and attend interpretive programs. Camp in the 43 improved or 15 primitive campsites, or overnight in one of the 15 cabins, with individual piers. Purchase supplies from the camp store. Laundry facilities are available.

Go swimming from the beach and hike the nature trail. Go boating (launch available), water-skiing, and fishing, with fishing-boat, canoes, and paddleboat rentals available.

Meridian is the hometown of Jimmie Rodgers, where a museum is located with a collection of his memorabilia. It's on 1725 Jimmie Rodgers. From 1-20, take Exit 153 and continue two miles northwest. The Jimmy Rodgers Memorial Festival is held the end of May, a week-long tribute to "The Father of Country Music." For information, call 601-485-1808.

The Frank W. Williams Home, circa 1886, and Merrehope, circa 1858, are at 905 Martin Luther King, Jr. Memorial Drive. For information on either house, call 601-483-8439.

Take a ride aboard the Dentzel Antique Carousel, circa 1890. The only carousel of its kind still operating in the U.S., it's located in Highland Park. It's a National Landmark listed on the National Register of Historic Places. For information, call 601-485-1850.

Peavey Visitors Center at 711-A Street in Meridian has exhibits from Peavey Electronics, the largest manufacturer of amplifiers in the world. Its equipment and instruments are used by musicians all over the world. It features a demo room and a display of its current products including guitars. For information, call 601-484-2460.

Arriving pilots can land at Key Field, three miles southwest of Meridian. Rental cars are available. While there, tour the Key Brothers' Aviation Museum located at the airport to learn more of the history of aviation and the details of the Key Brothers endurance flight.

INFORMATION
Clarkco State Park
386 Clarkco Road
Quitman, Mississippi 39355
601-776-6651

FLOREWOOD RIVER PLANTATION STATE PARK

3

LOCATION   The park is off U.S. 82, two miles west of Greenwood, and south of the intersection of U.S. 82 and U.S. 49E, near the Yazoo River.

FEATURES   Florewood features a working recreation of an 1850s cotton plantation. Two outstanding exhibits are the Whitney gin, and the rare Lane and Bodley side-crank box-bed steamboat engine.

ACTIVITIES The park is closed Mondays. Tour the 100-acre farm, planter's home, slave quarters, sorghum mill, and other plantation buildings. Costumed guides give mansion tours. Come in the autumn to help pick cotton in the fields. Craft activities are demonstrated, except from December to March. A Civil War reenactment is held the first Saturday in November, and a Christmas candlelight tour is held the first Saturday in December.

Tour the Cotton Museum at the grounds entrance, to see the plantation's model and restored cotton gin and steam engine. No camping is available in the park, but snacks are available at the snack bar.

Tour the Cottonlandia Museum ½ mile west of the Yazoo River Bridge on U.S. 82 West Bypass. It shows the history of the Delta region, including exhibits on the early Indians, who used dart and spear points to kill mastadons around 10,000 B.C. Exhibits also tell about the early lumberjacks, trappers, and other local figures. For information, call 601-453-0925.

Visit Cotton Row to see one of nine cotton markets in the U.S. The Row still operates 24 of its original 57 cotton companies. Listed on the National Register, it's on Front, Howard, and Main Streets, in the downtown area. Make an appointment with the Visitors Bureau at 1-800-784-9064.

Attend the Robert Johnson Memorial Blues Festival in Greenwood. He is known as "King of the Delta Blues Singers" and his memorial is on Highway 7 between Itta Bena and Morgan City, at Mt. Zion M. B. Church. For information, contact the Visitors Bureau at 601-453-9197 or 1-800-748-9064.

The four-day Mississippi International Balloon Classic begins the last Thursday in June, and features balloon races, competitions, and a parade. Come the first Saturday in August to attend CROP Day, and Cotton Row on Parade. It features crafts, contests, and entertainment, on downtown Howard Street. For information, call 601-453-9197 or 1-800-748-9064.

Arriving pilots can land at Greenwood-Leflore Airport, six miles east of Greenwood. Rental cars are available. It's eight miles from the state park.

INFORMATION
Florewood River Plantation State Park
P.O. Box 680
Greenwood, Mississippi 38930
601-455-3821

GEORGE PAYNE COSSAR STATE PARK
4

LOCATION The park is five miles northeast of Oakland and I-55, and off Mississippi 32.

FEATURES Cossar is on a peninsula-like area that juts into the Enid Reservoir.

ACTIVITIES Dine in the restaurant that features fried catfish. Go swimming in the pool, and play miniature golf. Hike the nature trails, tour the visitor's center and attend interpretive programs. Pick up a snack at the snack bar. Go boating from the launch, fishing, and water-skiing. Fishing-boat and bicycle rentals are available.

Camp in the 156-site campground, all sites with water and electrical hookups, or in one of the 12 cabins. Laundry facilities and groceries are available. Limited facilities are open during the winter.

INFORMATION
George Payne Cossar State Park
Route 1, Box 67
Oakland, Mississippi 38948
601-623-7356

GOLDEN MEMORIAL STATE PARK
5

LOCATION The park is on Mississippi 492, five miles east of Walnut Grove, off Mississippi 35.

FEATURES Golden Memorial was set aside in memory of the post–Civil War, one-room school originally located on the site.

ACTIVITIES Bring along a picnic to enjoy, and hike the nature trails. Go swimming from the beach, and fishing in the 15-acre, spring-fed lake, stocked with bass and bream. Fishing-boat and canoe rentals are available. Tour the visitor center and attend interpretive programs. No camping is available.

INFORMATION
Golden Memorial State Park
Route 1, Box 8
Walnut Grove, Mississippi 39189
601-253-2237

GREAT RIVER ROAD STATE PARK
6

LOCATION The park is near Rosedale off Mississippi 11, and 35 miles north of Greenville, between the Mississippi River and a levee.

ACTIVITIES Bring along a picnic to enjoy while watching the river traffic. Go water-skiing, fishing, and boating from the launch, in Perry Martin Lake—an oxbow that formed in the Mississippi River. Canoe, fishing-boat, and paddleboat rentals are available.

Camp in the 61-site campground, all sites with water and electrical hookups, or in the primitive camping area. Laundry facilities are available. Limited facilities are open during the winter.

The visitor center has interpretive programs, and fast food available, or you can pick up a snack at the snack bar. Climb the 75-foot, four-level stockade observation tower to get a great overlook of the river. Hike the Deer Meadow Nature Trail through the pecan and mulberry trees.

INFORMATION
Great River Road State Park
P.O. Box 292
Rosedale, Mississippi 38769
601-759-6762

HOLMES COUNTY STATE PARK
7

LOCATION   The state park is four miles south of Durant off I-55, Exit 150.

ACTIVITIES   Go water-skiing, swimming from the beach, boating from the boat launch, and fishing in one of the two fishing lakes, with fishing-boat and paddleboat rentals available. Hike the nature trails. Attend interpretive programs in the amphitheater, and go skating at the skating rink. Test your skill at archery.

Camp in the 28-site campground, with water and electrical hookups, or overnight in one of the 12 cabins. Laundry facilities are available. Pick up a snack at the snack bar, tour the visitor center, and attend an interpretive program.

INFORMATION
Holmes County State Park
Route 1, Box 153
Durant, Mississippi 39063
601-653-3351

HUGH WHITE STATE PARK
8

LOCATION   The park is five miles east of Grenada, off Mississippi 8.

ACTIVITIES   Participate in water sports including sailing, water-skiing and fishing, on 35,000-acre Grenada Reservoir. Go boating from the boat launch, with boat rentals available at the marina. Enjoy swimming from the beach. Tour the visitor center, attend an interpretive program, play tennis, and hike the nature trail.

Stay in one of the 20 cabins, with a pool available for cabin guests. You can also overnight in the 10-unit lodge, or camp in the 200-site campground, with

111 sites equipped with water and electrical hookups. Dine in the restaurant or pick up a snack from the snack bar.

Visit the Grenada Lake Visitors Center Museum in the Corps of Engineers Building. Take Exit 206 from I-55 onto Mississippi 8. Go east four miles to Scenic Route 333. You'll see a display of native animals, plus pictures and videos on the Grenada dam. Hike nearby 2.5-mile Lost Bluff Hiking Trail through the hardwood forest. For information call 601-226-1679.

Arriving pilots can land at Grenada Municipal Airport, three miles north of Grenada. However, no rental cars are available.

INFORMATION
Hugh White State Park
P.O. Box 725
Grenada, Mississippi 39802-0725
601-226-4934

J. P. COLEMAN STATE PARK
9

LOCATION   The park is 13 miles north of Iuka off Mississippi 25 at Pickwick Lake, on the Tennessee River.

ACTIVITIES   Visitors can enjoy all kinds of water sports including boating, fishing, and water-skiing, with a full service marina available. Swim in the pool, and play miniature golf. Pick up a snack from the snack bar, and hike the nature trail. Tour the visitor center and attend interpretive programs.

Overnight in one of the 20 cabins, camp in the 45-site campground, with water and electrical hookups, or on one of the 19 tent camp sites. Laundry facilities are available.

Arriving pilots can land at Iuka Airport, three miles south of Iuka. However, no rental cars are available. The airport is nine miles from the state park.

INFORMATION
J. P. Coleman State Park
613 CR 321
Iuka, Mississippi 38852
601-423-6515

JOHN W. KYLE STATE PARK
10

LOCATION   The park is nine miles east of Sardis off I-55 at Exit 252, and then off Mississippi 315.

ACTIVITIES   Enjoy water activities on the 58,500-acre Sardis Reservoir. Go boating from the launch, water-skiing, and fishing. Fishing-boat rentals are available. Go swimming in the pool.

Camp in the 200-site campground located on Sardis Lower Lake, with adjacent swimming beaches and nature trails. All campsites have water and electrical hookups. Limited facilities are open during the winter.

Pick up a snack from the snack bar. Tour the visitor center and attend an interpretive program. Hike the nature trail, and play tennis.

Tour the Heflin House Museum on 306 South Main Street in Sardis. Circa 1858, the antebellum home has furnishings from the late 1800s. It's open by appointment only. Call 601-487-3451.

Rose Hill Cemetery on North Main Street has many historical markers of veterans from every war since the Civil War.

INFORMATION
John W. Kyle State Park
Route 1, Box 115
Sardis, Mississippi 38666
601-487-1345

LAKE LOWNDES STATE PARK
11

LOCATION   The park is six miles southeast of Columbus, off Mississippi 69.

ACTIVITIES   The lake has a large recreational complex, including a visitor center with a game room, indoor tennis, basketball, and volleyball. Play softball outside under the lights, or tennis on one of six courts. Overnight in one of the four cabins, or camping in the 50-site campground. Hike the self-guided nature trail, and attend interpretive programs.

Pick up a snack at the snack bar, and go swimming, and water-skiing. Enjoy boating from the boat launch, and fishing, with fishing-boat and paddleboat rentals available.

Columbus is the site of many antebellum homes, circa 1835–1857, that may be toured year-round, by appointment only. Twelve of the historic homes are open during the pilgrimage held the first two weekends in April. Tours begin at the Blewett-Harrison-Lee Home at 316 7th Street North. Take a driving tour past some of these historic homes and landmarks, which is marked by blue and white signs. It begins at the Columbus Chamber of Commerce, at 318 7th Street North. For information, call 601-329-1191 or 1-800-327-2686.

Go for a sightseeing excursion or dinner cruise aboard the *Riverboat Julie*. It leaves from Columbus Landing on College Street to cruise along the Tombigbee River. It operates from April through October. For information, call 601-827-2268.

Arriving pilots can land at Golden Triangle Regional Airport, located 10 miles west of Columbus or at Columbus–Lowndes County Airport, three miles southeast of the city. Both have rental cars available.

INFORMATION
Lake Lowndes State Park
3319 Lake Lowndes Road
Columbus, Mississippi 39702
601-328-2110

LeFLEUR'S BLUFF STATE PARK
12

LOCATION   The park is off I-55, Exit 98-B. Go north on Lakeland Drive in Jackson.

ACTIVITIES   Camp in the 30-site campground, with water and electrical hookups, and central dump station. Purchase supplies from the camp store. Go boating from the ramp in Mayes Lake. Swim in the pool, or play tennis on one of the four courts.

The golf course has both a nine-hole and 18-hole course, plus a driving range. Tour the visitor center, attend interpretive programs, and hike the nature trail. Fishing-boat, canoe, and paddleboat rentals are available.

Jackson is the United States' host city for the International Ballet Competition, and is a cultural center with its symphony, operas, and museums. For information, contact the Visitor Bureau at 601-960-1891 or 1-800-354-7695.

Baseball fans can tour the Dizzy Dean Museum at 1204 Lakeland Drive in Jackson. For information, call 601-960-2404.

Attend the Mississippi State Fair at the State Fair Grounds in late September or early October, or the Jackson Zoo Blues, held at the Jackson Zoological Park the first Saturday in April. In late May, you can attend the Jubilee Jam downtown at One Jackson Place. For information, call the Visitors Bureau at 601-960-1891 or 1-800-354-7695.

Historic homes to visit include the Manship House, circa 1857. It was home to Mayor Charles Henry Manship, a painter who lived here during the Civil War. It's at 420 East Fortification Street. For information, call 601-961-4724. Boyd House, "The Oaks," circa 1846, is located at 823 North Jefferson Street. This house served as General Sherman's headquarters while Jackson was under siege. For information, call 601-353-9339.

Flower lovers can tour Mynelle Gardens at 4736 Clinton Boulevard to enjoy flowers throughout the year. For information, call 601-960-1894.

History fans can tour the Mississippi Agriculture and Forestry/National Agricultural Aviation Museum, located 1/4 mile east of I-55 Exit 98B. It's on Lakeland

Drive next to the Smith-Wills Stadium. Stroll through the museum's exhibits that span three eras of transportation, and through the Fortenberry-Parkman Farm, circa 1860s, now restored to illustrate farm life of the 1920s. Explore the crossroads town, circa 1920s. For information, call 601-354-6113.

Arriving pilots can land at Hawkins Field, three miles northwest of Jackson, or at Jackson International Airport, five miles east of the city. Only Jackson International has rental cars available.

INFORMATION
LeFleur's Bluff State Park
2140 Riverside Drive
Jackson, Mississippi 39202
601-987-3923: park
601-987-2998: golf course

LEGION STATE PARK
13

LOCATION   The park is two miles north of Louisville on North Columbus Avenue, old Highway 25.

ACTIVITIES   The park's 1930s Civilian Conservation Corp Legion Lodge is a Mississippi landmark. Overnight in one of the three rustic cabins, or go tent camping. Go boating and fishing in one of the two fishing lakes, with fishing-boat and paddleboat rentals available. Hike the nature trail, and tour the visitor center.

Noxubee National Wildlife Refuge is northeast of the park, and is reached from either Mississippi 25 or from Alternate 45. The 46,000-acre refuge offers fishing in Loakfoma Lake and Bluff Lake for largemouth bass, bluegill, and crappies. Birders come to the Canada Goose Overlook above Bluff Lake to see many giant nesting boxes. Thousands of waterfowl pass through here from November through January. You might also spot an American alligator.

Stop by the refuge headquarters to obtain a hiking map, to use for hiking the narrow gravel roads. Use caution during hunting season in November and December.

Arriving pilots can land at Louisville Winston County Airport, one mile north of Louisville. Rental cars are available.

INFORMATION
Legion State Park
Route 5, Box 32-B
Louisville, Mississippi 39339
601-773-8323

*Mount Locust, a restored early 1800s inn or "stand" on the Old Natchez Trace
(photo by W. L. Sigafoos, courtesy of the National Park Service)*

LEROY PERCY STATE PARK
14

LOCATION   The park is five miles west of Hollandale, off Mississippi 12.

ACTIVITIES   Many animals inhabit this park, including alligators who live in a pond that is fed by 100-degree artesian water. Camp in the 50-site campground by the moss-hung cypress, 16 sites with water and electrical hookups, or overnight in one of the 18 cabins. Laundry facilities are available. Stroll through the small zoo, explore the wildlife interpretive center, and hike the nature trail through the bayou.

Pick up a snack at the visitor center, or enjoy a Sunday buffet in the restaurant. Enjoy swimming in the pool. Go boating from the boat launch, and fishing, with fishing-boat and paddleboat rentals available. The park has a wildlife management area open for hunting.

Arriving pilots can land at Hollandale Municipal Airport, two miles northeast of the city. However, no rental cars are available.

INFORMATION
Leroy Percy State Park
P.O. Box 176
Hollandale, Mississippi 38748
601-827-5436

NATCHEZ STATE PARK
15

LOCATION   The park's 3,411 acres are 10 miles north of Natchez, off U.S. 61 at Stanton.

ACTIVITIES   Natchez Lake features many water sports and excellent fishing, with the state's record largemouth bass caught here. Overnight in one of the two cabins, camp in the 24-site campground, 12 sites with water and electrical hookups, or stay in one of the eight tent campsites. Explore Hamburg Road, an old plantation road that runs through the park. Hike the nature trails, and pick up a snack in the snack bar.

Go boating from the launch, with boat rentals available. Enjoy horseback riding, and tour the visitor center. Bicyclists can enjoy excellent riding conditions along the Natchez Trace. For bicycling information, call 601-680-4025.

Emerald Mound, circa 1300 A.D., was constructed by the ancestors of the Choctaw and Natchez Indians. Covering eight acres, it's the second largest ceremonial mound in the U.S., measuring 770 feet by 435 feet at its base. It's west of the Natchez Trace Parkway near Natchez.

The Grand Village of the Natchez Indians is at 400 Jefferson Davis Boulevard in Natchez. From 1782 to 1729, it served as the center of activity for the Natchez Indians. Tour the visitor center's museum. For information, call 601-446-6502.

Natchez has over 500 antebellum homes, churches, public buildings, and mansions. Many of the homes offer bed and breakfast accommodations. For information, stop by the visitor center at 410 North Commerce Street, on the grounds of historic Stanton Hall, or call 1-800-647-6724 or 601-446-6345. Natchez pilgrimages are held annually each spring and fall, and are among the oldest and largest festivals in North America. Three days are required to tour all the houses.

Tour the Natchez Museum of African-American History and Culture, at 307-A Market Street in Natchez. It highlights their history from 1890 through the 1950s. For information, call 601-445-0728.

Natchez Under-the-Hill is an historic district famous as a 19th-century flat-boat and steamboat landing on the Mississippi River. It was once referred to as the "Barbary Coast of the Mississippi." Today it has restaurants, shops, and riverboat gambling.

Arriving pilots can land at Hardy-Anders Field, six miles northeast of Natchez. Rental cars are available.

INFORMATION
Natchez State Park
230-B Wickliff Road
Natchez, Mississippi 39120
601-442-2658

PAUL B. JOHNSON STATE PARK
16

LOCATION   The park is 15 miles south of Hattiesburg, off U.S. 49.

ACTIVITIES   The park is near spring-fed Geiger Lake, situated beneath towering pine trees. The visitor center has a game room and fast-food service. Attend interpretive programs.

Camp in the 108-site campground, 75 sites with full hookups, or on one of the 25 tent pads, or overnight in one of the 16 cabin units. Laundry facilities are available.

Hike the self-guided nature trail. Pick up a snack from the snack bar, and enjoy water sports including fishing, boating from the boat launch, and water-skiing. Fishing-boat, canoes, and paddleboat rentals are available.

Flower lovers can visit the All-American Rose Garden in Hattiesburg, at the University of Southern Mississippi's front entrance. It features 740 patented rose bushes. They bloom in late spring and during the summer. For information, call 601-266-4491.

Camp Shelby Armed Forces Museum is 12 miles south of Hattiesburg in Camp Shelby. Go in the South Gate, Building #350. It features memorabilia from the Civil War, Mexican War, World Wars, Korea, Vietnam, and the Persian Gulf War. Over 6,000 items are on display. For information, call 601-584-2757.

Make an appointment to see a rare relic of a boat, constructed of cypress and pine using handmade nails and pegs. It's in the Leaf Exhibit on Main Street. The original boat was recovered from a Leaf River sandbar near New Augusta. Call 601-583-1362.

The Turner house, circa 1908, is at 500 Bay Street in Hattiesburg. Listed on the National Register of Historic Places, it contains many original furnishings and oil paintings. For information, call 601-582-4249.

Arriving pilots can land at Hattiesburg Laurel Regional Airport, nine miles north of the city. Rental cars are available.

INFORMATION
Paul B. Johnson State Park
319 Geiger Lake Road
Hattiesburg, Mississippi 39401
601-582-7721

PERCY QUINN STATE PARK
17

LOCATION   The park is six miles south of McComb off I-55, Exit 13 on Lake Tangipahoa.

ACTIVITIES   Visitors enjoy many water sports including swimming in the swimming pool. Camp overnight in the 101-site campground, with water and electrical hookups. Stay in one of the nine lodge rooms with kitchenettes, or in one of the 22 cabins. Groceries and laundry facilities are available. Limited facilities are open during the winter.

Tour the visitor center, and hike the nature trail. Pick up a snack from the snack bar. Play miniature golf. Go water-skiing, boating from the launch, and fishing, with fishing-boat, canoe, and paddleboat rentals available at the marina.

Go to Bogue Chitto Water Park and go canoeing or tubing on the Bogue Chitto Float Trail which is on the Pearl River and its major tributaries. Anglers come in search of outsize catfish. Hike the trails that lead to the banks of the Bogue Chitto, and catch a glimpse of the river below your feet, from the 30-foot cliff.

Arriving pilots can land at McComb–Pike County–John E. Lewis Airport, four miles south of McComb. Rental cars are available.

INFORMATION
Percy Quinn State Park
1156 Camp Beaver Drive
McComb, Mississippi 39648
601-684-3938

ROOSEVELT STATE PARK
18

LOCATION   The park is off I-20, Exit 77, southwest of Morton.

ACTIVITIES   The park offers water sports in its 150-acre lake, including water-skiing, boating, and fishing, with boat rentals available. Enjoy miniature golf, and swimming in the pool.

Tour the visitor center which has a mini-convention center that accommodates up to 200 people. Attend interpretive programs. Play games in the game room, and tennis on the lighted tennis courts. Stop by the nature/wildlife observation area, and hike the nature trail.

Camp in the 109-site campground, with water and electrical hookups, overnight in one of the 20 lodge rooms with kitchenettes, or in one of the 15 cabins. Laundry facilities are available. Purchase your camping supplies in the camp store, or snacks from the snack bar. Limited facilities are available during the winter.

INFORMATION
Roosevelt State Park
2149 Highway 13 South
Morton, Mississippi 39117
601-732-6316: park
601-732-6318: food service

SHEPARD STATE PARK
19

LOCATION   Shepard State Park is three miles west of Pascagoula, south of U.S. 90 at Gautier.

ACTIVITIES   Enjoy a picnic, bicycling the bike trail, and hiking the nature trail through the wild flowers and trees. Go tent camping. Enjoy fishing and boating, with launch and boat rentals available. Tour the visitor center.

Gulf Islands National Seashore stretches 150 miles from Fort Walton Beach, Florida to Gulfport, Mississippi. It protects six of the islands lying off the Mississippi Gulf Coast. To gain access to the beaches on West Ship Island or historic Fort Massachusetts, take a concession boat from Gulfport or Biloxi. The island is 12 nautical miles away, requiring a 1.5-hour trip. Free tours of the fort are conducted twice a day. Walk along the boardwalk, and get a snack. The best time to visit is in spring or fall, to avoid the mosquitoes and fierce heat.

The seashore's visitor center is at 3500 Park Road in Ocean Springs. The other islands are accessible by private boat only. The Davis Bayou Area is accessed off U.S. 90 east of Ocean Springs, where you'll find an information center and 51-site campground. For national seashore information, call 601-875-9057.

Go aboard the Scranton Floating Museum's 70-foot commercial shrimp boat in Pascagoula. It's in River Park on the Pascagoula River, north of U.S. 90. Pascagoula River was called the "Singing River" by the early Indians who camped along its bank. For information, call 601-762-6017, or 601-938-6612. The Old Spanish Fort and museum are at 4602 Fort Drive in Pascagoula. The house, circa the 18th-century, is believed to be the oldest building in the Mississippi Valley, and is open year-round.

Arriving pilots can land at Trent Lott International Airport, six miles north of Pascagoula. Rental cars are available.

INFORMATION
Shepard State Park
1034 Graveline Road
Gautier, Mississippi 39553
601-497-2244

TISHOMINGO STATE PARK
20

LOCATION   Tishomingo is at Mile Marker 304 off the Natchez Trace Parkway, and two miles east of Tishomingo off Mississippi 25.

FEATURES   Tishomingo State Park is Mississippi's only state park located along the Natchez Trace.

ACTIVITIES   From April through mid-October, go for a float trip down Bear Creek. Hike the 13-mile nature trail system and cross the swinging bridge over Bear Creek. Swim in the pool, and enjoy the multi-use playing field.

Go camping in the 62-site campground, 25 sites with water and electrical hookups, or go tent or group camping in the 142-site campground. Laundry facilities are available. Limited facilities are open during the winter.

Purchase a snack from the snack bar. Tour the visitor center and attend interpretive programs. Launch your boat from the ramp and go fishing. Fishing boats, canoes, and paddleboat rentals are available. Take a bike ride along the Natchez Trace Parkway.

Attend the Bear Creek Folklife Fest held the first Saturday in June.

Arriving pilots can land at Iuka Airport, three miles southeast of Iuka. However, no rental cars are available. The airport is 15 miles from the park.

INFORMATION
Tishomingo State Park
Route 2, Box 336 E
Tupelo, Mississippi 38801
601-438-6914

TOMBIGBEE STATE PARK
21

LOCATION   Tombigbee is six miles southeast of Tupelo, off Mississippi 6.

ACTIVITIES   The visitor center has fast-food service, a game room, and offers interpretive programs. Hike three nature trails, play tennis, and test your skill at archery. Go water-skiing and swimming from the beach, and purchase a snack from the snack bar. Launch your boat from the ramp. Enjoy fishing in Lake Lee, with fishing-boat, canoes and paddleboat rentals available.

The group campground accommodates 200. You can also overnight in one of the seven cabins, or on one of the 20 campsites with water and electrical hookups. Groceries and laundry facilities are available.

Elvis Presley, the "King of Rock and Roll," was born in a two-room house in Tupelo, at 306 Elvis Presley Drive. Visit his birthplace and museum with many of his belongings, including the motorcycle boots and jumpsuit he used in his Las Vegas act. For information, call 601-841-1245.

Stop by the Natchez Trace Parkway Visitors Center, six miles north of Tupelo off Mississippi 6 South. Sorghum is made here on the last weekend in September and every weekend in October. Hike the nature trail, and go bicycling along the Trace. Watch the 12-minute audiovisual program on the history of the old trace. For information, call 601-680-4025.

Visit the Tupelo National Battlefield on Mississippi 6, approximately one mile west of its intersection with U.S. 45. It's on West Main Street. This was the site of the last major Civil War battle fought in the state. In July, 1864, Confederate troops led by General Nathan Bedford Forrest attacked General Andrew Jackson Smith's Union forces when he tried to cut the Union supply line. However, the Confederates were defeated in what was one of the war's bloodiest confrontations. For information, call 601-841-6521.

Tour the Tupelo Museum on Highway 6 West, West Main Street. It features exhibits ranging from the Chickasaw Indians to astronauts. For information, call 1-800-533-0611 or 601-841-6438.

Arriving pilots can land at Tupelo Municipal–C. D. Lemons Field, three miles west of Tupelo. Rental cars are available.

INFORMATION
Tombigbee State Park
Route 2, Box 336 E
Tupelo, Mississippi 38801
601-842-7669

TRACE STATE PARK
22

LOCATION   Trace State Park is 10 miles east of Pontotoc, off Mississippi 6.

ACTIVITIES   The park has 2,500 acres, and offers camping in the 25-site campground, with electrical and water hookups. You can also overnight in one of the six cabins. Limited facilities are available during the winter.

Go swimming from the beach, and hike the nature trail. Launch your boat from the ramp and go water-skiing and fishing. Fishing and paddleboat rentals are available. Enjoy cycling along the nearby Natchez Trace Parkway.

Arriving pilots can land at Tupelo Municipal–C. D. Lemon Field, three miles west of Tupelo. Rental cars are available.

INFORMATION
Trace State Park
Route 1, Box 254
Belden, Mississippi 38826
601-489-2958

WALL DOXEY STATE PARK
23

LOCATION   Wall Doxey is seven miles south of Holly Springs off Mississippi 7.

ACTIVITIES   Tour the visitor center, and camp in the 64-site campground, 15 sites with water and electrical hookups, or on one of the 18 tent pads. You can also overnight in one of the nine cabins. Laundry facilities are available.

Purchase a snack from the snack bar. Launch your boat from the ramp, with fishing-boat, canoe, and paddleboat rentals available. Go water-skiing and swimming in the spring-fed lake with a two-level diving platform. Enjoy excellent fishing. Play on the multi-purpose activity field, and hike the nature trail.

Walter Place is one of approximately 90 antebellum homes in Holly Springs. This mansion was used as Grant's wife's quarters during one of the Union occupations. Because the owners of the mansion were so generous, Grant prohibited Federal troops from using the house, resulting in its becoming a haven for Confederate soldiers and spies.

Montrose, a Greek Revival brick mansion, circa 1858, is on Salem Avenue, and today is headquarters for the Holly Springs Garden Club. The grounds are designated a state arboretum. Admission is by appointment only. Call 601-252-2943.

Artist Kate Freeman Clark was born in Holly Springs. She painted over 1,000 paintings that are now housed in the Kate Freeman Clark Art Gallery. During the Holly Springs Pilgrimage held in April, the gallery is open for free tours. While here, also tour several of the historic 19th-century homes such as Greenwood, Hamilton Place, Walter Place and Cedarhurst. To do a self-guided tour, pick up "The Green Line Tour," from the Holly Springs Chamber of Commerce, at 154 South Memphis Street, or call 601-252-2943.

For additional hiking, go to the Holly Springs National Forest . Here you can either follow the one-mile-long Puskus Lake hiking trail, or the 4.5-mile-long Chewalla Lake Trail that circles the lake. You can also do additional camping and bass fishing at Johnston Mill Pond. For information, call 601-252-2633.

Arriving pilots can land at Holly Springs–Marshall County Airport, four miles west of Holly Springs. Rental cars are available.

INFORMATION
Wall Doxey State Park
Route 5, Box 245
Holly Springs, Mississippi 38635
601-252-4231

WINTERVILLE MOUNDS
STATE HISTORIC SITE
24

LOCATION   The site is on Mississippi 1, five miles north of Greenville.

FEATURES   Winterville has ceremonial mounds built by Indians from the Mississippian culture, approximately 1,000 years ago. These Indians were the predecessors of the Choctaw, Tunica, and Chickasaw tribes. Archeologists believe the area was occupied for approximately 600 years before the people were decimated by disease, drought, war, and famine. The 40-acre park contains 12 mounds, with only eight easily seen.

ACTIVITIES   Walk up the steps to the top of the largest mound, rising 55 feet, to get a good overview of the surrounding land. From here you can see the Sacred Plaza where the Indians held their dances and other ceremonies.

Tour the museum in the visitor center to learn more about the mounds and to see the various artifacts including arrowheads, very small carved hands, a dugout canoe, pipes, and pots. The site is open Wednesday through Saturday, and on Sunday afternoons. Admission is charged.

The park has a wildlife management area open for hunting.

Drive along the Million Dollar Mile on the Greenville Harbor Front to watch towboats and barges being constructed. To see some historic fire-fighting equipment, stop by the Old Number One Firehouse Museum at 230 Main Street. It features a children's dress-up area, a 1927 fire engine named Bertha and a 1949 Ford Seagrave pumper. For information, call 601-378-1616.

The Weatherbee House, circa 1873, is at 509 Washington Street. Open by appointment, this classic Victorian Revival cottage has Eastlake furnishings. For an appointment, call 601-378-3141.

Attend Greenville's Delta Blues Festival to see a laid-back way of life, and listen to the Blues being performed. It's held the third Saturday in September. For information, call the Chamber of Commerce at 601-378-3141.

Arriving pilots can land at Greenville Municipal Airport, five miles northeast of Greenville. Rental cars are available.

INFORMATION
Winterville Mounds State Historic Site
Route 3, Box 600
2415 Highway 1 North
Greenville, Mississippi 38703
601-334-4684

NORTH CAROLINA

North Carolina is bounded by the Atlantic Ocean on the east, and the Great Smoky Mountains on the west, giving the state a wide variety of terrain and climate. The Blue Ridge Parkway passes through the state. Its 469 miles extend from Shenandoah National Park in Virginia, to the Great Smoky Mountains National Park in North Carolina and Tennessee. The Appalachian Mountains that run through the state are among the oldest in the world, rising from 4,000 to 6,684 feet above sea level.

Rock climbers have a wide variety of climbing choices. Favorite climbing spots include Table Rock, Looking Glass Rock, and Linville Gorge, all in the Pisgah National Forest. Others are found on Crowders Mountain and in Hanging Rock State Park.

Bicyclists have many options including the 700-mile Mountains-To-Sea Trail, the 200-mile Piedmont Spur, and the 160-mile Cape Fear Run. For a mountain biking challenge, explore a 27-mile loop in the Great Smoky Mountains National Park.

Nantahala Gorge, 12 miles southwest of Bryson City, attracts many river runners, and also provides easy access to the Appalachian Trail that crosses the eastern end of the gorge.

Waterfalls abound in North Carolina. Hike in to see 90-foot Linville Falls, 125-foot High Falls, 441-foot Whitewater Falls, or 404-foot Hickory Nut Falls.

Scuba divers come to dive along the seafloor, where more than 2,000 ships rest on the bottom of the "Graveyard of the Atlantic."

The state parks offer the visitor the opportunity to go fishing, camping, boating, and swimming. However, Mount Jefferson and Mount Mitchell usually close following heavy snowfalls. Trailers are allowed in all the campgrounds except for Mount Mitchell. Hookups are available at Falls Lake, Jordan Lake, and Kerr Lake.

Some of the state's more unusual celebrations include hollering contests, mule days, collard celebrations, chitlins tasting, and a ramp eater convention for those who enjoy the taste of ramps—a cross between garlic and onion.

For leaf-peeping, be sure to drive along the Blue Ridge Parkway. Generally, the leaves peak in mid to late October. For an update on the colors, call 1-800-487-4862.

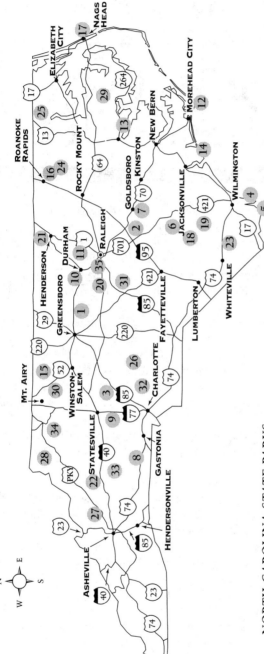

NORTH CAROLINA STATE PARKS

1. Alamance Battleground State Historic Site
2. Bentonville Battleground State Historic Site
3. Boone's Cave State Park
4. Carolina Beach State Park
5. Fort Fisher State Historic Site
6. Cliffs of the Neuse State Park
7. Waynesboro State Park
8. Crowders Mountain State Park
9. Duke Power State Park
10. Eno River State Park
11. Falls Lake State Recreation Area
12. Fort Macon State Park
13. Goose Creek State Park
14. Hammocks Beach State Park
15. Hanging Rock State Park
16. Historic Halifax State Historic Site
17. Jockey's Ridge State Park
18. Jones Lake State Park
19. Singletary Lake State Park
20. Jordan Lake State Recreation Area
21. Kerr Lake State Recreation Area
22. Lake James State Park
23. Lake Waccamaw State Park
24. Medoc Mountain State Park
25. Merchants Millpond State Park
26. Morrow Mountain State Park
27. Mount Mitchell State Park
28. New River State Park
29. Mount Jefferson State Park
30. Pettigrew State Park
31. Pilot Mountain State Park
32. Raven Rock State Park
33. Reed Gold Mine State Historic Site
34. South Mountains State Park
35. Stone Mountain State Park
36. William B. Umstead State Park

ALAMANCE BATTLEGROUND
STATE HISTORIC SITE
1

LOCATION   The site is six miles southwest of Burlington, on North Carolina 62.

FEATURES   On May 16, 1771, three years before the Boston Tea Party, 2,000 of North Carolina's independent western frontiersmen, the "Regulators," were defeated by the royal governor and colonial militia. However, their armed resistance set the stage for America's battle for independence.

ACTIVITIES   Walk through the battleground, where flags mark the position of each side, and look over the bronze map explaining the battle. Guided tours are available. Tour the visitor center to see displays of weapons and uniforms, and watch the audiovisual presentation.

The John Allen House, circa 1780, is on the park grounds, and is typical of the oak and ash log dwellings constructed along North Carolina's western frontier. Colonial Living Week is held here in mid-October.

Attend a performance of *The Sword of Peace* at the Snow Camp Historic Site, 15 miles south of Burlington. You'll learn about the Quakers' struggle during the American Revolution. It's performed from late June through mid-August. For details, call 919-376-6948 or 1-800-726-5115.

Arriving pilots can land at Burlington-Alamance Regional Airport, located three miles southwest of Burlington. Rental cars are available.

INFORMATION
Alamance Battleground State Historic Site
Burlington, North Carolina 27216
1-800-637-3804 or 910-227-4785

BENTONVILLE BATTLEGROUND
STATE HISTORIC SITE
2

LOCATION   The site is 2.5 miles north of Newton Grove; turn right on North Carolina 1008 and go another 2.5 miles.

FEATURES   From March 19–21, 1865, one of the last conflicts of the Civil War occurred here, when Sherman's Union troops defeated Johnston's Confederates in North Carolina's bloodiest land battle. The Harper House was utilized as a hospital by both the Confederate and Union troops during the war. Today it's still furnished as a hospital.

ACTIVITIES   Hike the history trail to see the breastworks, battle trenches, cemetery, and Harper House. Tour the visitor center and watch its slide show. The park is closed on Mondays during the winter.

INFORMATION
Bentonville Battleground State Historic Site
Newton Grove, North Carolina
910-594-0789

BOONE'S CAVE STATE PARK
3

LOCATION   The park is 14 miles west of Lexington via U.S. 64 and North Carolina 150. It's also 15 miles north of Salisbury.

FEATURES   The park is the legendary site by the Yadkin River, where Daniel Boone hid from the Indians.

ACTIVITIES   Explore the 30-foot tunnel in the cave. Come in the spring when over 30 species of wildflowers are in bloom. Go hiking, fishing, and enjoy a picnic.

Arriving pilots can land at Lexington Municipal Airport, located three miles southwest of the city. However, no rental cars are available.

INFORMATION
Boone's Cave State Park
c/o North Carolina State Parks
West District Office
Route 2, Box 224M
Troutman, North Carolina 28166
704-528-6514

CAROLINA BEACH STATE PARK
4

FORT FISHER STATE HISTORIC SITE
5

LOCATION   Carolina Beach State Park is 10 miles south of Wilmington, off North Carolina 421, and one mile northwest of Carolina Beach.

Fort Fisher is five miles south of Carolina Beach, off North Carolina 421. It's also two miles south of Kure Beach.

FEATURES   A Union blockade of southern ports, late in the Civil War, prevented the South from receiving essential war supplies. Fort Fisher was built to provide cover for Confederate seamen entering Cape Fear River, en route to the

Confederacy's major port in Wilmington. Fort Fisher is the South's largest earth-work fort, with a series of redoubts extending for a mile along the Atlantic coast and across a sand peninsula.

ACTIVITIES At Carolina Beach, go hiking along the Flytrap Nature Trail where over 30 trees, shrubs, and flowering plants may be seen. Go fishing and boating (ramp available) in the Cape Fear River and adjoining waterway. A full-service marina is available. Camp in the 83-site campground without hookups, but with a dump station. Attend nature programs, and purchase a snack at the refreshment stand.

At Fort Fisher, only a few mounds are left. Walk through the small museum to learn of the events occurring here between December 1864 to January 1865 when the fort fell to the Union. You'll see excavated artifacts, and a reproduction of a 10-pound Parrot gun. Go swimming in the ocean, fishing, collect seashells, and attend nature programs. Refreshments are available at the refreshment stand. Hike the nature trail.

Tour the nearby Marine Resources Center on U.S. 421 South. Its aquarium has several species of turtles, shark, and fish, found in the Atlantic Ocean. Hike the short nature trails and watch for various birds including heron, brown pelican, egret, and ibis.

Tour the USS *North Carolina* moored at Riverfront Park. Go west on U.S. 17/74/76/421 over the Cape Fear Memorial Bridge on the Cape Fear River in Wilmington. The restored World War II battleship is open daily from 8:00 to 5:30. Watch a 70-minute sound and light spectacular, "The Immortal Showboat" from the grandstand which is built off the port bow. To reach the memorial, take the river taxi from Riverfront Park, located at the corner of Market and Water. For information, call 910-251-5797. Go for a cruise aboard the riverboat, *Henrietta II.* For schedules and information, call 910-343-1611.

Flower lovers can visit Greenfield Park and gardens at the south end of Third Street, which is noted for its azaleas, camellias, and roses. You can take a beautiful drive around Greenfield Lake. You can also stroll through Orton Plantation Gardens, 18 miles south of Wilmington on North Carolina 133.

Festivities in Wilmington include the North Carolina Azalea Festival in early April, Riverfest in early October, and Old Wilmington by Candlelight, featuring a tour of historic homes on the second weekend in December. For details, call 910-762-0492.

Arriving pilots can land at New Hanover International Airport, located three miles northeast of Wilmington. Rental cars are available.

INFORMATION
Carolina Beach State Park
Fort Fisher State Historic Site
P.O. Box 475
Carolina Beach, North Carolina 28428
910-458-5538
910-458-7770: marina

CLIFFS OF THE NEUSE STATE PARK
6

WAYNESBORO STATE PARK
7

LOCATION   The Cliffs of the Neuse State Park is 14 miles southeast of Goldsboro, off North Carolina 111. It's also eight miles south of Seven Springs, on U.S. 70 to North Carolina 1743.

Waynesboro State Park is off the U.S. 117 bypass in Goldsboro.

ACTIVITIES   At the Cliffs, stroll through the visitor center to see dioramas depicting the geology of the cliffs that are layered with sediments containing fossil shells and bones. Camp in the 35-site campground, without hookups, but with a dump station.

Go fishing in the river, swimming, and boating in the 11-acre lake, with rental boats available. Hike the interpretive nature trails, and attend a nature program. Refreshments are available at the refreshment stand.

Waynesboro State Park is open for day use only, where you can enjoy a picnic, go fishing, and hiking along the Neuse River.

The CSS Neuse State Historic Site is 15 miles east on the Neuse River. Here you can see the remains of the Neuse, one of two ironclad gunboats built in the state. Here, too, is the Richard Caswell Memorial, erected to honor North Carolina's first constitutionally elected governor.

Arriving pilots can land at Goldsboro–Wayne Municipal Airport, three miles north of Goldsboro. However, no rental cars are available.

INFORMATION
Cliffs of the Neuse State Park
Waynesboro State Park
Route 2, Box 50
Seven Springs, North Carolina 28578
919-778-6234

CROWDERS MOUNTAIN STATE PARK
8

LOCATION   The park is six miles west of Gastonia off U.S. 29/74, on North Carolina 1125.

FEATURES   The park's 2,586 acres are at the northern end of the ancient King's Mountain range, with its rugged 800-foot peak.

ACTIVITIES   Enjoy primitive camping, picnicking, and fishing in the lake. Go backpacking, hiking, rock climbing, and ride the equestrian trails. Attend the nature programs. Birders come here where over 160 bird species have been spotted.

The Schiele Museum of Natural History and Planetarium is off I-85, the New Hope Road Exit on 1500 East Garrison Boulevard in Gastonia. Besides touring the museum, you can observe living history demonstrations in the log cabin, circa 1754, on the last Sunday of the month, from March through December. For museum information, call 704-866-6900. For the planetarium, call 704-866-6903.

Arriving pilots can land at Gastonia Municipal Airport, located four miles south of the city. Rental cars are available.

INFORMATION
Crowders Mountain State Park
Route 1, Box 159
Kings Mountain, North Carolina 28086
704-867-1181

DUKE POWER STATE PARK
9

LOCATION   The park is located along the northern shore of Lake Norman, 10 miles south of Statesville on North Carolina 1330.

FEATURES   Three-mile-long Lake Norman is the largest man-made lake in the state, covering 1,458 acres.

ACTIVITIES   Enjoy water-based recreational activities including swimming, boating with rentals available, sailing, and windsurfing. The lake boasts excellent fishing for black crappie, bass, catfish, and yellow perch. Numerous sailing regattas are held here. Camp in the 33-site campground, without hookups, but with a dumping station, or stay in a vacation cabin. Attend nature programs, and go hiking. Refreshments are available.

Arriving pilots can land at Statesville Municipal Airport, located three miles southwest of the city. Rental cars are available.

INFORMATION
Duke Power State Park
Route 2, Box 224M
Troutman, North Carolina 28166
704-528-6350

ENO RIVER STATE PARK
10

LOCATION   The park is three miles northwest of Durham, off North Carolina 1569.

FEATURES   Eno River State Park follows a 14-mile stretch of the Eno River. A suspension bridge across the river provides access to both sides of the park.

ACTIVITIES   Go camping in the backcountry by hiking in one mile. Enjoy canoeing, fishing, and rafting on the river. Attend a nature program, and hike the nature trails.

INFORMATION
Eno River State Park
Route 2, Box 436-C
Durham, North Carolina 27705
919-383-1686

FALLS LAKE STATE RECREATION AREA
11

LOCATION   The park is 13 miles north of Raleigh, off North Carolina 50. Falls Lake's main office is seven miles north of Raleigh, off U.S. I-74, then east on Six Forks Road to North Carolina 2003.

FEATURES   The park has three access areas leading to 11,000-acre Falls Lake. North Carolina 50 access is north of North Carolina 50 and 98. Rollingview Marina access is on North Carolina 1807, Baptist Road. Sandling Beach access is 3½ miles north of the intersection of North Carolina 98 and North Carolina 50.

ACTIVITIES   At North Carolina 50's area, go fishing, sailing, and boating from the ramp. At Rollingview Marina, go fishing, sailing, and motor boating, with boat rentals available. Purchase refreshments at the refreshment stand.

Camp in the 117-site campground, with 82 sites providing water and electrical hookups. Tour the visitor center and attend nature programs. Bring along a picnic to enjoy at Sandling Beach, and go swimming, and bass fishing in the lake.

Arriving pilots can land at Triple W Airport, located 11 miles south of Raleigh, or at Raleigh-Durham International Airport, nine miles northwest of the city. Rental cars are available at both airports.

INFORMATION
Falls Lake State Recreation Area
13304 Creedmoor Road
Wake Forest, North Carolina 27587-8505
919-676-1027: park
919-596-2194: marina in Durham
919-833-8584: marina in Raleigh

FORT MACON STATE PARK
12

LOCATION   The fort is on the eastern tip of Bogue Banks, reachable via a causeway from Morehead City. Go two miles east of Atlantic Beach, on North Carolina 1190.

FEATURES   Beaufort Inlet was used by the pirate Blackbeard in the early 1700s. Then, between 1826 and 1834, Fort Macon was constructed to guard the port of Beaufort. It was named for Nathaniel Macon, a North Carolina senator. Lt. Robert E. Lee designed the garrison's jetties.

The fort features a moat that was designed to be flooded with the tidewaters of Bogue Sound. It's considered an unusually good example of 19th-century military architecture. The fort was shelled by Union forces on April 25, 1862, who succeeded in capturing it the next morning. It was later used during the Spanish-American War, and again during World War II.

ACTIVITIES   The fort is closed from Labor Day to June. Tour the museum and the restored commandant's quarters. Guided tours, historical programs, and refreshments are available from Memorial Day through Labor Day.

Hike the nature trail. Enjoy a picnic, surf casting from the shoreline, or swimming in the ocean from the protected beach. The area is known as a deep-sea fishing center.

Theodore Roosevelt Natural Area is seven miles west of Atlantic Beach, on North Carolina 1201. Photographers and nature lovers come to enjoy the many birds and unique plant life. The North Carolina Aquarium offers live exhibits and multimedia programs.

INFORMATION
Fort Macon State Park
P.O. Box 127
Atlantic Beach, North Carolina 28512
919-726-3775

GOOSE CREEK STATE PARK
13

LOCATION   The park is eight miles east of Washington on U.S. 264, on the Pamlico River.

ACTIVITIES   Walk along the two boardwalks to explore the marsh and swamp. Go fishing in the Pamlico River for croaker, bluefish, and flounder. Go canoeing—launch your boats from Dinah's Landing into Upper Goose Creek. Boat rentals are available. Camp in the 12-site campground, without hookups. Attend a nature program, and go swimming.

Arriving pilots can land at Warren Field, located on the northeast side of the city. A courtesy car is available to take you into town.

INFORMATION
Goose Creek State Park
Route 2, Box 372
Washington, North Carolina 27889
919-923-2191

HAMMOCKS BEACH STATE PARK
14

LOCATION   The beach is 4½ miles along Bear Island, which is south of Swansboro, off North Carolina 24 on North Carolina 1151.

FEATURES   The park is only accessible by private boat or ferry. The ferry makes the 2½-mile trip to Bear Island several times a day, from April through October. To reach the ferry from Jacksonville, follow North Carolina 24 for 20 miles to Swansboro. Turn onto North Carolina 1511, and continue for three miles to reach the park headquarters and ferry landing. The ferries run from 9:30 A.M., and the last ferry leaves from the island at 6:00 P.M.

ACTIVITIES   Hammocks Beach boasts a four-mile-long unspoiled beach along the Atlantic Coast. Some of these dunes rise 60 feet. It's a nesting area for the loggerhead sea turtle.

Go surf fishing for bluefish, mullet, and drum. Enjoy shelling, surfing, and swimming in the ocean. Lifeguards are on duty from Memorial Day through Labor Day. Go camping (no hookups) in the 14-site campground, in the dunes and at either end of the beach. However, Bear Island is closed to camping during the full moon phase in June, July and August, to minimize disturbance to the nesting loggerhead turtles.

Hike the nature trail, and attend nature programs. Refreshments are available.

Go kayaking on the two-mile Canoe-Kayak Trail through the salt marsh, to a lagoon. Maps are available at park headquarters. Canoe and kayak rentals are available in Swansboro.

Watch the three-hour musical drama, *Worthy is the Lamb*, in the Crystal Coast Amphitheater, off North Carolina 58, one mile north of its intersection of North Carolina 24. Performances run from mid-June through the Saturday of Labor Day weekend. For information, call 910-393-8373.

INFORMATION
Hammocks Beach State Park
Route 2, Box 295
Swansboro, North Carolina 28584
910-326-4881

HANGING ROCK STATE PARK
15

LOCATION   The park is five miles northwest of Danbury, off North Carolina 89.

ACTIVITIES   Enjoy sparkling mountain streams, waterfalls, and cascades in the 6,340-acre park. Go rock climbing on Moore's and Cook's walls. Rent a boat to go boating, and enjoy fishing and swimming in the lake. The bath-house is open from June 1 through Labor Day. Hike the trails, and attend nature programs. Enjoy the view from the observation tower. Refreshments are available.

Overnight in a vacation cabin, available from April 1 to November 1. You can also camp in the 73-site campground (without hookups) from May 1 through October 31.

INFORMATION
Hanging Rock State Park
Box 186
Danbury, North Carolina 27016
910-593-8480

HISTORIC HALIFAX STATE HISTORIC SITE
16

LOCATION   The site is on U.S. 301 business route in Halifax, at St. David and Dobbs Streets. From I-95, take Exits 154, 160, 168, or 173.

FEATURES   British General Lord Cornwallis stopped here in 1781 on his march north to Yorktown, where he was defeated. "Halifax Resolves," the first for-mal sanction of American Independence, was adopted here in April, 1776.

ACTIVITIES   Stop by the visitor center and watch the audiovisual show. Walk through the adjacent museum to see artifacts from the early local tobacco and fur trade, and learn about the lifestyle of the planter gentry living here in the Roanoke Valley. Another exhibit explains the archeological methods used to dig on the site.

Take a 60-minute guided tour of Constitution-Burgess House, where the first constitution of North Carolina was framed. You'll also see two tavern-hotels, an early jail, town clerk's office, and homes typical of the era. Short tours are available of the 1760 Owens House and of the 1801 Sally-Billy Plan-tation House. You can also take self-guided tours by picking up a map at the visitor center.

Special events are presented throughout the year in honor of the town's historic past as its role as a recruiting center and weapons depot during the Revolutionary War.

INFORMATION
Historic Halifax State Historic Site
St. David and Dobbs Street
Halifax, North Carolina
919-583-7191

JOCKEY'S RIDGE STATE PARK
17

LOCATION　　The park is at the U.S. 158 Bypass in Nags Head.

FEATURES　　The town of Nags Head was named from the early inhabitant's practice of tying lanterns to the necks of ponies, to walk them along the dunes at night. Jockey's Ridge features an area of shifting sands with no vegetation, and has the highest sand dune found on the East Coast.

ACTIVITIES　　Take a 30-minute walk to the top of the 100-foot ridge. Visitors also enjoy hang gliding from the top of Jockey's Ridge and from Engagement Hill. Permits are available at the park office. You can also try your luck at sand skiing. Tour the visitor center and attend a nature program.

Nearby you can visit Fort Raleigh National Historic Site on Roanoke Island, three miles north of Manteo. Here Sir Walter Raleigh tried to establish England's ill-fated first colony in America, over 400 years ago. Tour the visitor center to see displays on when the settlers landed here in 1585. Walk through a reconstruction of the fort, and hike the nature trail to a point overlooking the sound.

During the summer, attend America's oldest symphonic outdoor musical drama, *The Lost Colony,* presented in an outdoor theater overlooking Roanoke Sound. For information, call 919-473-3414 or 1-800-488-5012.

From the historic site, walk to the beautiful Elizabeth Gardens. One of the best times to arrive is in mid to late April, when azaleas and dogwood are in full bloom. The gardens are closed from December to March.

Elizabeth II State Historic Site is across from Manteo's waterfront. Tour a reproduction of the kind of vessel Sir Walter Raleigh sailed over 400 years ago. Tour the visitor center to learn more about the Roanoke voyages. For information, call 919-473-1144.

Another great spot to visit nearby is the Wright Brothers' National Memorial Visitor Center. Here you can see a reproduction of the Wright brothers' first powered flying machine. Walk out to see markers showing the distances covered by the four history-making flights. Their last flight covered 852 feet in 59 seconds, before the craft was destroyed by a sudden gust of wind. Take a look at the reconstruction of their 1901–03 camp and workshop.

The Wright Monument rises above the summit of Kill Devil Hills, where the Wrights launched almost 1,000 flights, as they sought to understand how to keep their craft of cloth, wood, and wire aloft.

Pea Island National Wildlife Refuge is a short distance south of Bodie Island, at Rodanthe. The refuge extends over 12 miles along the Outer Banks. It's a favorite wintering place for large flocks of snow geese, plus 260 species of other waterfowl. Stop by the refuge headquarters to pick up a list of birds found here each season. For information, call 919-987-2394 or 919-473-1131.

Walk the foot trail that goes around North Pond Lake, to one of two observation platforms. Go crabbing, and surf fishing for sea trout, channel bass, pompano, and bluefish. The preserve provides five access points to some Atlantic beaches, plus another access leading to Pamlico Sound.

Beyond this point lies the Cape Hatteras National Seashore, with its five national park service campgrounds and swimming beaches. The seashore extends for 75 miles along North Carolina 12, through the Outer Banks islands of Bodie, Hatteras, and Ocracoke. It's famous for surf fishing, as well as for off-shore fishing expeditions, and has one of the largest sportfishing fleets in the East. For national park information, call 919-473-2111.

South of the state park, you'll come to the Bodie Island Lighthouse, circa 1872, easily distinguished by its horizontal bands of black and white paint. The lighthouse was constructed on the Outer Banks, over a century ago, to warn ships away from the Diamond Shoals, the "Graveyard of the Atlantic." Although the lighthouse is closed to visitors, the visitor center has exhibits telling the history of the lighthouse. Hike the self-guided nature trail, and stop by the bird observation plantation.

Cape Hatteras' Lighthouse, circa 1870, is the tallest in the U.S., rising 208 feet. It's open to the public, but the balcony is closed. Hike the self-guided nature trail. Ocracoke Lighthouse, circa 1823, is closed to the public, and is the state's oldest operating lighthouse. All three islands with lighthouses are connected by North Carolina 12, and the free Hatteras Inlet Ferry.

Jockey's Ridge State Park (photo by David McDaniel, courtesy of the park)

Nags Head Woods Preserve, a National Natural Landmark, is in Kill Devil Hills on Ocean Acres Drive, off North Carolina 158 Bypass. The 640-acre preserve is open Tuesday, Thursday, and Saturday, year-round. It features over 60 different biotic communities, including the sand dunes at Jockey Ridge and Runn Hill, the two largest dunes on the east coast. It also includes over 40 small woodland ponds. The preserve is a habitat for many deer, river otters, as well as for heron, geese, swans, and egrets. Hike the nature trails, and take a guided preserve tour, offered the second and fourth Saturdays of each month.

Arriving pilots can land at Dare County Regional Airport, located one mile northwest of Manteo. Rental cars are available.

INFORMATION
Jockey's Ridge State Park
P.O. Box 592
Nags Head, North Carolina 27959
919-441-7132

JONES LAKE STATE PARK
18

SINGLETARY LAKE STATE PARK
19

LOCATION   Jones Lake State Park is four miles north of Elizabethtown, on North Carolina 242.

Singletary Lake is 12 miles southeast of Elizabethtown, on North Carolina 53.

FEATURES   Jones Lake, shaded by old cypress trees, is next to a tea-colored lake. The lake's shallow oval depression, part of the Bay Lakes of the Southeast, is thought to be the result of a meteorite shower.

ACTIVITIES   At Jones Lake, you can go camping in the 20-site campground (no hookups), boating, with rentals available, swimming, fishing, and hiking the trails. Attend nature programs. Refreshments are available.

At Singletary, enjoy boating, hiking, fishing, and group camping. Campers can also go swimming in the lake. Attend nature programs.

Arriving pilots can land at Elizabethtown Airport, located two miles southeast of town. Rental cars are available.

INFORMATION

Jones Lake State Park
Route 2, Box 945
Elizabethtown, North Carolina 28337
910-588-4550

Singletary Lake State Park
Route 1, Box 63
Kelly, North Carolina 28448
910-669-2928

JORDAN LAKE STATE RECREATION AREA
20

LOCATION Jordan Lake is 20 miles south of Raleigh, off U.S. 1 to U.S. 64 E.
FEATURES Jordan Lake covers 13,900 acres, with 150 miles of shoreline.
ACTIVITIES Visitors have five access points: Crosswinds boat ramp is off U.S. 64 East at B. E. Jordan Bridge; Ebenezer Church is at SR 1008 South; Crosswinds Marina is off U.S. 64 E and north onto SR 1008; Parkers Creek is west of B. E. Jordan Bridge; Vista Point is west of B. E. Jordan Bridge, where you turn south onto SR 1700.

Go boating, with boat rentals available at the full service marina, bass fishing, swimming, and sailing in Jordan Reservoir. Enjoy picnicking, camping in the 750-site campground, 600 sites with hookups. Camping is available at Parkers Creek and Vista Point. Go canoeing, and purchase refreshments at Ebenezer Church. Nature programs and hiking trails are at Vista Point, and Parkers Creek has nature hiking trails.

INFORMATION
Jordan Lake State Recreation Area
Route 2, Box 159
Apex, North Carolina 27502
919-362-0586

KERR LAKE STATE RECREATION AREA
21

LOCATION The area is 11 miles north of Henderson, off I-85 to SR 1319. It's on the border of North Carolina and Virginia.

ACTIVITIES Enjoy water related activities including swimming, bass fishing, boating, sailing, and water-skiing in Kerr Lake. Three commercial marinas have full service facilities for boaters and campers.

Camp in one of the eight campgrounds with over 700 family campsites. Bullocksville has 68 sites without hookups, and County Line has 84 sites with 12 providing electricity and water, and a dump station. Henderson Point has 79 sites, two with electrical and water hookups, and a dump station. Hibernia has 150 sites, 28 with electricity and water, and a dump station. Kimball Point has 91 sites, with 23 providing electricity and water, and a dump station. Nutbush Bridge has 109 sites, 28 with water and electricity, and a dump station. Satterwhite Point has 123 sites, 24 with water and electricity, and a dump station. Steele Creek Marina has 50 sites, 35 with electricity. Hike the trails, and attend nature programs.

Attend special events including a spring art show, an amateur striped bass fishing tournament, and the Governor's Cup Invitational Regatta in June.
INFORMATION
Kerr Lake State Recreation Area
Route 3, Box 800
Henderson, North Carolina 27536
919-438-7791

LAKE JAMES STATE PARK
22

LOCATION   The park is three miles north of Nebo on North Carolina 126, and five miles northeast of Marion.
ACTIVITIES   Camp in the 20-site campground, and go swimming from the beach. Enjoy fishing, boating (ramp available), and hike the trails. Attend the nature programs.
INFORMATION
Lake James State Park
P.O. Box 340
Nebo, North Carolina 28761
704-652-5047

LAKE WACCAMAW STATE PARK
23

LOCATION   The lake is six miles south of Lake Waccamaw, off U.S. 74/76.
FEATURES   Lake Waccamaw is one of the South's largest lakes noted for its black water, so typical of coastal lakes. It's surrounded by cypress trees, and a swamp.
ACTIVITIES   The 10,760-acre park is open for day-use. Enjoy swimming, boating, fishing, and hiking the nature trails. Enjoy primitive camping, and attend nature programs.
INFORMATION
Lake Waccamaw State Park
c/o Singletary Lake State Park
Route 1, Box 63
Kelly, North Carolina 28448
910-669-2928

MEDOC MOUNTAIN STATE PARK
24

LOCATION   The park is 15 miles southeast of Roanoke Rapids, off North Carolina 561.

ACTIVITIES   The park covers 2,287 acres. Come in the spring when the mountain laurel and many wildflowers are in bloom. Go fishing in Little Fishing Creek for bluegill, largemouth bass, pickerel, sunfish, and roanoke bass. Enjoy primitive camping in the campground, and attend nature programs. Go canoeing, and hike the nature trails. Equestrians have access to bridle trails.

Arriving pilots can land at Halifax County Airport, three miles southwest of Roanoke Rapids. Rental cars are available.

INFORMATION
Medoc Mountain State Park
Route 3, Box 2196
Enfield, North Carolina 27823
919-445-2280

MERCHANTS MILLPOND STATE PARK
25

LOCATION   The park is 6 miles northeast of Gatesville on North Carolina 1403, off North Carolina 158.

FEATURES   A dam was built here in 1811, creating a large pond used to provide water power for the area's sawmill and gristmill. The park features a Southern swamp forest dominated by gum and cypress trees.

ACTIVITIES   Anglers come to fish in the 760-acre lake and adjoining swamps for perch, bream, jack, gars, catfish, and largemouth bass. Bird watchers can spot approximately 180 species of birds including white egrets, great horned owls, and eagles. Migrating waterfowl stop over at the millpond during the winter.

Hikers can hike trails where they may come across the harmless white, pink, and black eastern mud snake, and see beaver dams up to six feet in height.

Camp in the 20-site campground under the pine and maple trees (no hookups), or stay in one of the primitive campsites within the swamp. Attend nature programs.

Canoeists can paddle along the Chowan Swamp Canoe Trail, beginning at the millpond and continuing south along a creek. Trips of four or more days are possible. You can also paddle up Bennetts Creek to Lasiter Swamp, to see a stand of virgin cypress trees estimated to be over 1,000 years old. Boat rentals are available.

INFORMATION
Merchants Millpond State Park
Route 1, Box 141A
Gatesville, North Carolina 27938
919-357-1191

MORROW MOUNTAIN STATE PARK
26

LOCATION   The park is five miles east of Albemarle, off North Carolina 24/27/73/740.

FEATURES   The 4,693-acre park lies within the ancient Uwharrie Range, along the Pee Dee River and Lake Tillery. This mountain range even predates the Appalachians.

ACTIVITIES   Enjoy miles of hiking trails, and go horseback riding along the bridle trails. Historic Kron House, utilized as a "hospital" of an early 19th-century physician, is within the park. Go swimming in the pool, camping, fishing, canoeing, sailing, and boating, with rentals available. Rent a vacation cabin, available April 1 to November 1. Camp in the 106-site campground, without hookups, but with a dump station, or overnight in a vacation cabin. Tour the visitor center, and attend summer nature programs. Refreshments are available.

Arriving pilots can land at Stanley County Airport, located four miles northeast of Albemarle. Rental cars are available.

INFORMATION
Morrow Mountain State Park
Route 5, Box 430
Albemarle, North Carolina 28001
704-982-4402

MOUNT MITCHELL STATE PARK
27

LOCATION   The park is at Milepost 355, 35 miles northeast of Asheville, via the Blue Ridge Parkway and North Carolina 128.

FEATURES   Mount Mitchell, rising 6,684 feet, is the highest peak east of the Mississippi River. It was named after Dr. Elisha Mitchell who first measured the peak in 1835, but then fell to his death when he attempted to prove its height. Mount Mitchell is known for its harsh climate, with its bent-over trees due to the high winds. Snow falls from October to May, and winter temperatures of −20 to −25 degrees F. are not uncommon.

North Carolina 128 is famous for the laurel and rhododendron growing along both sides of the road.

ACTIVITIES Tour the visitor center, and go up the observation tower by Dr. Mitchell's gravesite, where you can see as far as the Smoky Mountains on a clear day. Tour the museum, and attend a naturalist's summer talk. Drive to the summit of Mount Mitchell during the summer. The road may be closed during the winter. In spring and fall, you're advised to check road conditions in advance.

Camp in the campground, and hike 18 miles of trails, accessible from mid-May to mid-October. Dine in the rustic mile-high restaurant, open seasonally. Snacks are available at the refreshment stand. Leaf peeping is wonderful here, from mid to late October. For color updates, call 1-800-847-4862.

Nearby Craggy Visitor Center has exhibits of local shrubs and flowers, plus a self-guided nature trail. Three miles further south, stop by Craggy Gardens' picnic area, and stroll through the flowers that bloom from May through September.

To see even more flowers, go to the botanical gardens at the University of North Carolina at Asheville, where garden tours of its 10 acres are available with advance notice.

Take a self-guided tour of the Biltmore Estate, America's largest private home, a 255-room Renaissance chateau, located near Asheville. Circa 1895, the mansion is listed as a National Historic Landmark, and is among the most visited historic residences in the U.S. Entrance to the estate is on U.S. 25, north of the Parkway and I-40. Come in the spring when 50,000 tulips are in full bloom. Biltmore has one of the most complete collections in the U.S. of native azaleas, that generally bloom in early May. Behind-the-scene tours are offered. For information, call 1-800-543-2961 or 704-255-1700.

Ride the 26-story elevator inside 500-million-year-old Chimney Rock, a stone monolith rising 300 feet from the side of the mountain. It's in Chimney Rock Park, southeast of Asheville. Here you'll have a 75-mile vista, and can hike trails leading to a 404-foot waterfall that drops twice as far as Niagara Falls. Guided hikes are offered year-round. The last weekend in April, attend the race cars' Chimney Rock Hillclimb. For information, call 1-800-277-9611 or 704-625-9611.

Tour the Thomas Wolfe Memorial State Historic Site at 48 Spruce Street in Asheville. It's open Tuesday through Sunday, from 10:00 to 5:30. For information on the novelist's childhood home, call 704-253-8304.

The Western North Carolina Nature Center is four miles east of Asheville, on North Carolina 81 at Gashes Creek Road. You'll see both indoor and outdoor exhibits of plants and animals, a petting zoo, and you can hike the self-guided nature trail. For information, call 704-298-5600.

Arriving pilots can land at Asheboro Municipal Airport, six miles southwest of the city. Rental cars are available.

INFORMATION
Mount Mitchell State Park
Route 5, Box 700
Burnsville, North Carolina 28714
704-675-4611: park
704-675-9907: restaurant

NEW RIVER STATE PARK

MOUNT JEFFERSON STATE PARK
28

LOCATION   New River State Park is eight miles southeast of Jefferson off North Carolina 88, on North Carolina 1588.

Mount Jefferson State Park is 1.5 miles south of Jefferson, off U.S. 221.

FEATURES   The New River State Park provides access to the 26.5-mile stretch of the National Wild and Scenic south fork of the New River. The New River is believed to be the second oldest river in the world, surpassed only by the Nile.

Mount Jefferson is a National Natural Landmark because of its oak hickory forest.

ACTIVITIES   At New River State Park, enjoy primitive canoe-camping, or camp in the 16-site campground, without hookups. Enjoy picnicking, boating from the ramp, fishing, and nature study. Attend nature programs.

At Mount Jefferson, enjoy wildflower displays of rhododendron, mountain laurel, and azaleas. Bring along a picnic, hike the trails, and attend nature programs.

Arriving pilots can land at Ashe County Airport, three miles east of Jefferson. Rental cars are available.

INFORMATION
New River State Park   Mount Jefferson State Park
P.O. Box 48   P.O. Box 48
Jefferson, North Carolina 28640   Jefferson, North Carolina 28640
910-982-2587   910-246-9563

PETTIGREW STATE PARK

SOMERSET PLACE STATE HISTORIC SITE
29

LOCATION   The state park and Somerset Place are eight miles south of Creswell, via U.S. 64.

FEATURES   Pettigrew's 17,743 acres feature sections of the old Collins and Pettigrew coastal plantations. Pettigrew State Park is named for General James Pettigrew who is buried here. He played a major role in General George E. Pickett's famous charge at Gettysburg, on July 3, 1863. Lake Phelps is a wildlife sanctuary.

Somerset was built for its English owner, Josiah Collins III. His 14-room plantation house, circa 1830s, has Greek Revival architecture, and was the gathering place for the upper class.

ACTIVITIES   Hike over five miles of trails through the park's virgin forest of oaks, swamp chestnuts, and hardwoods, making this a colorful spot to visit in the fall.

Go camping in the 13-site campground (no hookups), hiking, boating, and fishing for bass, perch, and panfish. Go sailing and wind surfing on the lake, where wind conditions are ideal. Attend summer nature programs. Enjoy a picnic in the picnic grove.

Tour restored Somerset Place, and stroll through its gardens and restored outbuildings. See Indian artifacts displayed during the park's Indian heritage celebration in September.

INFORMATION
Pettigrew State Park   910-797-4475
Route 1, Box 63
Kelly, North Carolina   Somerset Place State Historic Site
                                      910-797-4560

PILOT MOUNTAIN STATE PARK
30

LOCATION   The park is 24 miles north of Winston-Salem, off US. 52.

FEATURES   The 1,400-foot quartzite monadnock was used as a landmark by early pioneers and Indians.

ACTIVITIES   Pilot Mountain State Park has two sections, connected by a five-mile, 300-foot-wide woodland hiking and horseback riding corridor. You can park your horse trailer at either end of the corridor.

Drive to the summit of nearby Little Pinnacle, where you can take short trails to get to scenic overviews of Pilot Mountain and the Blue Ridge Mountains in the distance. Rock climbing is permitted on Little Pinnacle Wall. Attend nature programs.

In the Mount Airy section of the park, camp in the 85-site campground, with a dump station and coin laundry available. Swim in the pool, go fishing, enjoy the waterslide, and rent a paddleboat to go boating.

In the Pinnacle section, camp in the 49-site campground. Attend a nature program, hike the trails, and go fishing, or horseback riding.

Arriving pilots can land at Smith Reynolds Airport, three miles northeast of Winston-Salem. Rental cars are available.

INFORMATION
Pilot Mountain State Park
Route 1, Box 21
Pinnacle, North Carolina 27043
910-325-2355

RAVEN ROCK STATE PARK
31

LOCATION   Raven Rock is six miles northwest of Lillington off U.S. 421, on North Carolina 1314.

FEATURES   The park is known for its massive rock outcrop that rises 152 feet, and juts out at a 45-degree angle above the Cape Fear River.

ACTIVITIES   The park covers 3,058 acres where you can picnic, go canoeing, primitive camping in the campground, or canoe camping. Enjoy fishing for catfish, largemouth bass, and sunfish in both the river and creek. Hike the trails and attend nature programs. Equestrians have access to bridle trails. Refreshments are available.

INFORMATION
Raven Rock State Park
Route 3, Box 1005
Lillington, North Carolina 28448
910-893-4888

REED GOLD MINE STATE HISTORIC SITE
32

LOCATION   The site is on North Carolina 200, west of Stanfield, and 14 miles southeast of Concord, on U.S. 601.

FEATURES   In 1799, John Reed's young son, Conrad, found a shiny rock in Little Meadow Creek, and used it as a doorstop. In 1802, a jeweler offered to pay him $3.50 for it. The rock was made of gold, weighed around 17 pounds, and was the first authenticated gold "find" in the U.S. The state historic site contains the first placer gold mine operated in the U.S.

ACTIVITIES   Visitors can take a guided tour of a maze of restored mine shafts, and see a restored 1895 stamp mill, still being used to demonstrate how gold is extracted. Pay a fee and pan for your own gold in the panning area.

Follow the self-guided nature trail through the fields and forests, and enjoy a picnic under the tall pines. Tour the visitor center.

Arriving pilots can land at Midland Airpark, 12 miles north of Concord, but no rental cars are available.

INFORMATION
Reed Gold Mine State Historic Site
Concord, North Carolina 28026
704-786-8337

SOUTH MOUNTAINS STATE PARK
33

LOCATION   The park is 18 miles south of Morganton, on North Carolina 1904.

FEATURES   Come to see High Shoals Waterfall that tumbles 80 feet into a mountain stream.

ACTIVITIES   Go primitive camping in the 11-site campground, hiking, and trout fishing in the river. Cycle the bicycle trail, and attend nature programs. Bridle trails are available.

INFORMATION
South Mountains State Park
Route 1, Box 206
Connelly Springs, North Carolina 28612
704-433-4772

STONE MOUNTAIN STATE PARK
34

LOCATION   The park is seven miles southwest of Roaring Gap off U.S. 21, on North Carolina 1002 to John P. Frank Parkway.

FEATURES   The park features a 600-foot-high granite dome, resembling a moonscape.

ACTIVITIES   Tour the visitor center and enjoy a spectacular view from the deck. Hike along the various trails, some twisting through rhododendron and mountain laurel. Trails lead to the 2,300-foot summit of Stone Mountain, and to Stone Mountain Falls, Cedar Rock, and Wolf Rock. Rock climbers have access to 13 of Stone Mountain's ascent routes, many rated as difficult, and not recommended for beginners.

Enjoy camping in one of the 37 sites, without hookups, but with a dump station. Anglers come to fish for stocked trout in 17 miles of streams. Tour the visitor center, ride the bridle trails, and attend nature programs. Refreshments are available.

INFORMATION
Stone Mountain State Park
Star Route 1, Box 17
Roaring Gap, North Carolina 28668
910-957-8185

WILLIAM B. UMSTEAD STATE PARK
35

LOCATION   The park is 11 miles west of Raleigh on I-40, or 10 miles northwest off U.S. 70.

ACTIVITIES   The 5,000-acre park has two separate areas. Crabtree Creek has both family and group camping. Enjoy lake fishing, hiking, and swimming, open to group campers only. Ride the bridle trails, and attend interpretive programs. Rent a boat to go boating on the lake.

Reedy Creek also has interpretive programs, lake fishing, hiking trails, and camping, in the 37-site campground, without hookups.

Arriving pilots can land at Raleigh-Durham International Airport, located nine miles northwest of the city. You can also land at Raeford Municipal Airport, three miles northeast of town. Rental cars are available at both airports.

INFORMATION
William B. Umstead State Park
Route 8, Box 130
Raleigh, North Carolina 27612
919-787-3033

OKLAHOMA

The name Oklahoma comes from two Choctaw Indian words: "okla" meaning people, and "humma" meaning red. Oklahoma became our 46th state, and was known as "the place to strike it rich" by drilling for oil. The first commercial oil well was drilled in 1897.

The state has the second largest Indian population of any state in the Union, with descendants of the original 67 tribes still living there. Each year in Anadarko, 10,000 Plains Indians from 14 different tribes, celebrate one of the state's most colorful festivals. The Exposition features a six-day renewal of tribal customs and rituals, including World Championship War Dance finals, Plains Indians war dances, Apache fire dances, and the Kiowa Eagle Dance.

Oklahoma has 63 state parks and recreation areas, and its forests cover 24 percent of the state. An unusual feature of five of these parks is the availability of either motorcycle trails, or a combination of motorcycle and ORV trails. These trails are found in Lake Murray, Beaver State Park, Little Sahara, Quartz Mountain, and Keystone Lake.

Visitors can stay in one of five Oklahoma resort parks: Lake Murray, Lake Texoma, Quartz Mountain, Roman Nose, or Western Hills Guest Ranch.

Oklahoma has 200 man-made lakes, more than any other state. Its 2,000 miles of combined shoreline is more than the Atlantic and Gulf coasts. The lakes and reservoirs are known for their bass, walleye, crappie, catfish, and trout fishing. The state's highest point, 4,973 feet, is located at Black Mesa. Its lowest point is 287 feet, due east of Idabel.

For viewing fall foliage, one route begins in Miami near Twin Bridges State Park and goes south on Oklahoma 10. It passes Honey Creek State Park, Upper Spavinaw State Park, Tahlequah State Park, with a side trip to Sequoyah State Park. From here, pick up Oklahoma 82 to drive past the Cherokee Heritage Center, passing Tenkiller State Park, and end up in Greenleaf State Park. For information, contact the Tahlequah Chamber of Commerce at 918-456-3742 or 1-800-652-6552, or in Oklahoma, 405-521-2409.

For further details, contact the various park authorities listed throughout the text, or call the Oklahoma Tourism and Recreation Department at 1-800-652-6552, or in Oklahoma, 405-521-2409.

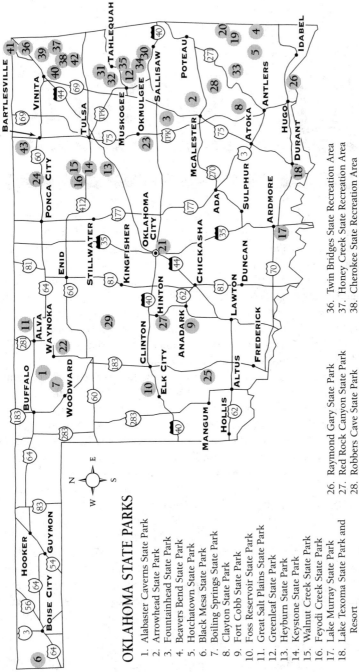

OKLAHOMA STATE PARKS

1. Alabaster Caverns State Park
2. Arrowhead State Park
3. Fountainhead State Park
4. Beavers Bend State Park
5. Hotchatown State Park
6. Black Mesa State Park
7. Boiling Springs State Park
8. Clayton State Park
9. Fort Cobb State Park
10. Foss Reservoir State Park
11. Great Salt Plains State Park
12. Greenleaf State Park
13. Heyburn State Park
14. Keystone State Park
15. Walnut Creek State Park
16. Feyodi Creek State Park
17. Lake Murray State Park
18. Lake Texoma State Park and Resort
19. Lake Wister State Park
20. Heavener Runestone State Park
21. Little River State Park
22. Little Sahara State Park
23. Okmulgee Lake State Park
24. Osage Hills State Park
25. Quartz Mountain State Park
26. Raymond Gary State Park
27. Red Rock Canyon State Park
28. Robbers Cave State Park
29. Roman Nose State Park and Resort
30. Sallisaw State Park
31. Sequoyah State Park
32. Sequoyah Bay Recreation Area
33. Talimena State Park
34. Tenkiller State Park
35. Cherokee Landing State Park
36. Twin Bridges State Recreation Area
37. Honey Creek State Recreation Area
38. Cherokee State Recreation Area
39. Bernice State Park
40. Little Blue State Park
41. Spring River Canoe Trail State Park
42. Spavinaw State Park and Upper Spavinaw State Park
43. Wah-Sha-She State Park

The Ouachita National Forest stretches from southeastern Oklahoma almost to Little Rock, Arkansas. This is the oldest and largest national forest in the South, and is laced with dozens of wooded trails and 33 recreation areas. Pronounced "wash-i-ta," it means "hunting trip" in Choctaw. The Ouachitas are one of the few mountain ranges in the U.S. that run east to west. Be sure to come here in the fall, especially the third week in October, when the sweet gums, maples, sumacs, and red oaks turn into a colorful mosaic.

ALABASTER CAVERNS STATE PARK
1

LOCATION   The park is six miles south of Freedom, on Oklahoma 50, and then go another mile east on Oklahoma 50A. The cave entrance is in Cedar Canyon.

FEATURES   Alabaster Caverns is the world's largest gypsum cave. Its 2,300-foot-long cavern has selenite, alabaster, and onyx-like rock formations. Eight kinds of bats inhabit the cave.

ACTIVITIES   Take a cavern tour to see a wonderland of pink, white, and multi-colored alabaster and sparkling crystals. The cavern has three distinct areas: a collapsed section where large rooms are filled with huge boulders of gypsum, shale and selenite; a dome section with many small domes; and a channel section that has been smoothed and polished by an underground stream. Some interesting formations include Elephant Rock, Echo Dome, Gun Barrel Tunnel, Devil's Bathtub, and Cathedral Dome. For information, call 405-621-3381. Take the special Halloween Cavern Tour.

Camp in one of 10 campsites with full hookups, and a dumping station. Food service is available. Swim in the pool. Hike 1/4-mile Canyon Trail along Cedar Canyon to reach the park's natural bridge, an arch rising 150 feet above the canyon floor.

While in town, stroll through No Man's Land Historical Museum on Sewell Street to see area artifacts. It's closed Mondays. For information, call 405-349-2670.

INFORMATION
Alabaster Caverns State Park
Route 1, Box 32
Freedom, Oklahoma 73842
405-621-3381

ARROWHEAD STATE PARK
2

FOUNTAINHEAD STATE PARK
3

LOCATION   Arrowhead State Park is on the south shore of Lake Eufaula, 15 miles north of McAlester off U.S. 69 between Enterprise and Porum. It's also four miles east of Canadian, off Oklahoma 69.

Fountainhead State Park is 14 miles southwest of Checotah, off I-40. Fountainhead Resort is located on Lake Eufaula, and overlooks the two rivers that converge to form the lake.

FEATURES   Lake Eufaula has 600 miles of shoreline, and is noted for its black bass and catfish fishing. It was formed when a dam was constructed across the Canadian River. At the far end of the dam, look for the large rock wall with black anthracite that is intersected with orange-red granite layers. A winding road goes through the park, leading to lakeside picnic groves, a beach, and boat ramps.

ACTIVITIES   Arrowhead Resort and Hotel are owned and operated by the Choctaw Indian Nation of Oklahoma. It has 96 guest rooms, plus camping is available in 246 sites, 65 sites with electricity, and 20 with water and sewer hookups. The resort has a cafe, grocery store, and 102 cottages. Play tennis, golf on the 18-hole golf course, and go horseback riding. Enjoy boating from the ramp, or take a guided fishing tour. A heated marina is available for year-round fishing.

At Fountainhead Resort, you can stay in the hotel, in cottages, in tree houses with kitchenettes, or camp in the campground, with full hookups. Another option is to rent a vacation houseboat from the marina.

Go fishing from an enclosed fishing dock, and go boating, with rental boats available. Play golf on the 18-hole course, and swim in the pool or in the lake. Go water-skiing, play tennis, and enjoy horseback riding from the stable. Tour the nature center, and hike three-mile Outlaw Nature Trail. Eat in the restaurant or purchase supplies in the grocery store.

An airstrip is located at the resort, with an asphalt runway and lights. Another strip is located at McAlester Regional, three miles southwest of the city, where rental cars are available. A third strip, Eufaula Municipal, is located two miles west of town where a courtesy car is available to take you to the resort.

Indian powwows, art and craft fairs, Choctaw Indian Princess pageants, and other Indian tribal events, are held throughout the year. Attend the Italian Festival in McAlester in May, when Italian immigrants celebrate their proud heritage.

In September, attend the Oklahoma State Prison Rodeo held "behind the walls," when approximately 150 inmates, representing teams from Oklahoma's correctional institutions, vie for the four top places.

In Eufala, attend the annual Indian Powwow, Chili Cook-off, and on the last weekend in July, the Whole Hawg Day Festival which attracts thousands who come to watch, and to sample barbecue sauces prepared by competing cooks. For information, contact the city of Eufaula: 918-689-2534.

In the first two weeks of September, hunters seek doves that flock to the area by the thousands.

In Muskogee, located north of Lake Eufaula, attend the azalea festival in April, and the fall festival in October.

INFORMATION

Arrowhead State Park
H.C. 67, Box 57
Canadian, Oklahoma 74425
Park office: 918-339-2204
Pro shop: 918-339-2769
Fountainhead State Park

Park Manager
H.C. 60, Box 1340
Checotah, Oklahoma 74426
Park office: 918-689-5311
Pro shop: 918-689-3209

Fountainhead Resort Hotel: 1-800-345-6343 (in Oklahoma)
  or 1-800-826-3973

BEAVERS BEND STATE PARK
4

HOTCHATOWN STATE PARK
5

LOCATION   Beavers Bend State Park is seven miles north of Broken Bow, on U.S. 259A. It's in southeastern Oklahoma, off U.S. 259, adjacent to Broken Bow Lake.

Hotchatown State Park is four miles north of Beavers Bend State Park, off U.S. 259A, and seven miles northeast of Broken Bow. This park has three access entrances: Stephens Gap, Carson Creek, and Cedar Creek. The park office is located at Carson Creek, and the golf course is at Cedar Creek.

FEATURES   Beavers Bend is often referred to as the "Little Smokies," and encompasses over 3,500 acres in the Ouachita Mountains. It was named for John Beavers who owned much of the land.

ACTIVITIES   In Beavers Bend State Park, you can fish for rainbow trout in Mountain Fork River, or for stocked bass, trout, catfish, crappie, and perch in Broken Bow Reservoir. Go swimming from the beach, boating, water-skiing, paddle boating, whitewater canoeing, bumper-boating, jet skiing, yakanoeing, and scuba diving.

Enjoy horseback riding, tennis, or bring along a picnic. Play golf on the nine-hole or 18-hole course. Attend a naturalist program, and rent a party barge or bicycle.

Tour Forest Heritage Center Museum to see their exhibit on the local trees, petrified wood, and artifacts from the forest industry. The center is open from March 15 to December 31.

Stay overnight in one of 47 cabins, or in one of the 8 campgrounds with 179 campsites available, 110 sites with full hookups, and a trailer dump site. Groceries and snacks are available, or you can dine in the Beavers Bend Restaurant.

Hike the one-mile Beaver Lodge Nature Trail that begins near the spillway or from River Bend Road. Big Oak Nature Trail passes through the white oak woods.

The David L. Boren Trail is 24 miles long, has numerous access points, and goes to Hotchatown State Park's Cedar Creek Area. If you hike here from November through March, watch for the great blue heron and bald eagles that winter here.

In June, attend the "Festival of the Forest," a celebration commemorating the culture of the Choctaw Indians, and features the skills of lumberjacks, and artisan crafts.

The Ouachita National Forest has 53 miles of scenic trails for hikers and equestrians, following old logging roads. An undeveloped campsite for equestrians is at the Cedar Lake Recreation Area.

Ouachita Trail's 192 miles traverse the entire length of the 1.6-million acre forest, which straddles the border between Arkansas and Oklahoma. Besides its 192 miles, you can explore side loops and spur trails, including 23-mile Boardstand and Old Military Road Trails, which pass through the Indian Nations National Scenic and Wildlife Area. The six-mile Black Fork Mountain Trail leads into a designated wilderness, and provides great views of the Ouachita Mountains. For information on the trail, contact Hot Springs National Park, Arkansas 71902, at 501-321-5202.

Besides hiking, you can also go canoeing on the Ouachita River, and go fishing for four-pound bass. The best fishing is during the cooler months between October and March.

Hotchatown State Park has 49 campsites, with water and electrical hookups. Go swimming, water-skiing, and bass fishing in Broken Bow Lake, and rent a boat from the marina to go boating. Play 18 holes of golf on the Cedar Creek golf course.

Attend the Owachito Festival of the Forest in June, and the Riverfront Arts and Crafts Festival in October. Participate in eagle watches from November through February, and fly-fishing clinics from November through April.

For a colorful fall drive, begin in Broken Bow. One route goes northeast on Oklahoma 3 to Antlers, where the route turns northeast onto Oklahoma 2 to Clayton, passing Clayton Lake State Park. This drive takes you through the heart of the state's timber-growing region.

A second route also begins in Broken Bow, and goes north along U.S. 259 with a loop through Beavers Bend State Park, and then continues on U.S. 259 to Big Cedar. This scenic route is south of the well-known Talimena Skyline Drive, and follows several rapidly flowing rivers. For information, call Talimena State Park at 918-567-2052.

Incoming pilots can land at Broken Bow Municipal Airport, located two miles southwest of town. Rental cars are available.

INFORMATION

Beavers Bend State Park
P.O. Box 10
Broken Bow, Oklahoma 74728
Park office: 405-494-6300
Cabins: 405-494-6538
Restaurant: 405-494-6551
Hotchatown State Park

P.O. Box 218
Broken Bow, Oklahoma 74728
Park office: 405-494-6452
Cabin reservations: 1-800-522-8568
  (in Oklahoma)
Pro shop: 405-494-6456

BLACK MESA STATE PARK
6

LOCATION   In the extreme northwestern Oklahoma Panhandle, the park is 35 miles northwest of Boise City.

FEATURES   Black Mesa extends for approximately 45 miles, from Oklahoma into Colorado and New Mexico. Its highest point in Oklahoma rises to 4,972 feet. In Colorado, it rises to 6,600 feet.

ACTIVITIES   Black Mesa State Park is nine miles southeast of the mesa. Go boating and fishing in the small lake. Enjoy camping in the campground, and hiking among large rock pinnacles. It's open year-round.

INFORMATION

Black Mesa State Park
c/o Oklahoma Tourism and Recreation Department
500 Will Rogers Building
Oklahoma City, Oklahoma 83105-4492
405-521-2409

BOILING SPRINGS STATE PARK
7

LOCATION   The park is six miles east of Woodward, on Oklahoma 34C in northwestern Oklahoma.

FEATURES   The park has some natural springs, producing nearly 60 gallons of water per minute, that bubble up through sparkling white sands.

ACTIVITIES   Camp in one of 56 campsites. Area Three has electrical and water hookups, while Area Four has full hookups. You can also stay in one of four cabins. Enjoy fishing for catfish in Boiling Springs Lake, and go swimming in the pool. Enjoy picnicking, hiking, or playing golf on the 18-hole golf course, located adjacent to the park. To reserve a tee time, call 405-256-1206.

Hike the trail that has three sections: the one-mile Seven Bridges Trail, the .5-mile River Trail, and the 1.5-mile Springs Trail.

In July, attend Woodward Elks Rodeo in Woodward. While there, tour nearby Alabaster Caverns State Park.

For a colorful fall drive, where you'll pass dense stands of hardwood trees, begin in Woodward and follow Oklahoma 34C, passing Boiling Springs State Park. Intersect Oklahoma 50B and continue on to Mooreland. Turn north on Oklahoma 50 and drive to 50A and Alabaster Caverns State Park. For additional information, contact Boiling Springs State Park.

The huge sand dunes of the Little Sahara Recreation Area are nearby, and range from 25 to 75 feet in height. Called the "walking hills" by the early explorers, the off-road vehicle area is open year-round, 24 hours a day. Dune buggy riders especially enjoy cruising the dunes at night. Caution should be exercised because of shifting sands and sharp drop-offs. For information, call 405-824-1471.

Have you ever gone rattlesnake hunting? Every year, on the weekend after Easter, the Waynoka Saddle Club sponsors such a hunt, and thousands come out to enjoy the carnival, watch prize snakes being weighed and measured, and to taste snake meat. For details, contact the saddle club, or the Waynoka Chamber of Commerce, Box 173, Waynoka, Oklahoma 73860.

For water sports, go 10 miles to the northwest to Fort Supply Lake.

Incoming pilots can land at West Woodward Airport, located seven miles west of town. Rental cars are available.

INFORMATION
Boiling Springs State Park
Box 965
Woodward, Oklahoma 73802
Park office: 405-256-7664
Cabin reservations: 1-800-522-8565 (in Oklahoma)
Pro shop: 405-256-1206

CLAYTON STATE PARK
8

LOCATION   The park is five miles south of Clayton, on Oklahoma 271.

ACTIVITIES   Camp in the 59-site campground, 10 sites with water, 25 with electrical hookups, and a dumping station. Swim in Clayton Lake from the beach, and go bass fishing, and boating from the ramp, with boat rentals available.

INFORMATION
Clayton State Park
Route 1, Box 33-10
Clayton, Oklahoma 74536
918-569-7981

FORT COBB STATE PARK
9

LOCATION   The area is seven miles northwest of Fort Cobb off Oklahoma 9, and northwest of Anadarko.

ACTIVITIES   Camp in the large campground with 303 campsites with full hookups. Try your luck at bass fishing from the enclosed fishing dock in Fort Cobb Reservoir. Go swimming from the beach, water-skiing, or boating from the ramp, with boat rentals available at the marina. Play golf on the 18-hole golf course.

Fort Cobb Reservoir also contains a large public hunting area along its shores. In late October, approximately ten million crows descend on the area. During the winter, as many as 60,000 ducks arrive.

Each year, 10,000 Plains Indians, from 14 different tribes, arrive in Anadarko to attend one of the state's most colorful festivals. The Exposition features a six-day renewal of tribal customs and rituals, with the World Championship War Dance finals, Plains Indians war dances, and Apache fire dances.

INFORMATION
Fort Cobb State Park
P.O. Box 297
Fort Cobb, Oklahoma 73038
Park office: 405-643-2249
Pro shop: 405-643-2398

FOSS RESERVOIR STATE PARK
AND WILDLIFE REFUGE
10

LOCATION   The reservoir is 15 miles northwest of Clinton. From the junction of I-40 and Exit 53, go north six miles on Oklahoma 44.

ACTIVITIES   Foss Lake is the largest lake in western Oklahoma, with 63 miles of shoreline. The lake is divided into Foss Reservoir Recreation Area and the Washita National Wildlife Refuge.

Camp in the 76-site campground, with water and electrical hookups. Go fishing for catfish, sand bass, and walleye, from an enclosed fishing dock. Enjoy water-skiing, swimming from the beach, and boating from the ramp or dock, with boat rentals available at the marina.

The area surrounding the park is known for its fine deer, quail, and turkey hunting.

INFORMATION
Foss Reservoir State Park
H.C. 66, Box 111
Foss, Oklahoma 73647
405-592-4433

GREAT SALT PLAINS STATE PARK
11

LOCATION   The park is eight miles north of Jet, on Oklahoma 38, in north-western Oklahoma.

FEATURES   The Salt Flats are one of the state's most unusual geological phenomena, and geologists believe they're the remnants of a prehistoric sea. The park is a natural wildlife refuge for over 250 bird species. Great Salt Plains Reservoir and Salt Flats are adjacent to the park.

ACTIVITIES   This park is the only place in the world where visitors can dig for hourglass selenite crystals (from April 1 to October 15). These crystals emerge from the large salt flats, and may be found just below the surface. Selenite crystals are found off the dirt access road going north off Oklahoma 64, six miles west of Jet.

Rent one of their 6 cabins, or stay in one of the three campgrounds with 155 campsites, 63 sites with full hookups. Sandy Beach Area 2 has primitive camping.

Go fishing for catfish in the Great Salt Plains Lake, swim from the beach, go hiking, water-skiing, and boating. Hike Nescatunga Trail, named for the Osage Indian word meaning "big salt water."

For viewing spectacular fall foliage, begin from the park and follow Oklahoma 38, going south to Jet. For additional route information, call the park at 405-623-4215.

Visit the restored Homesteader's Original Sod House, circa 1894, in Aline/Cleo Springs. It's one of the few remaining sod homes in the U.S. See early-day farm machinery, a blacksmith shop, and interpretive displays.

Visit the Museum of the Cherokee Strip in Enid, featuring Indian and pioneer artifacts. It's open Tuesday through Friday from 9 to 5, and on the weekends from 2 to 5. For information, call 405-237-1907.

INFORMATION
Great Salt Plains State Park
Route 1, Box 28
Jet, Oklahoma 73749
Park office: 405-626-4731
Cabin reservations: 1-800-522-8585 (in Oklahoma)

GREENLEAF STATE PARK
12

LOCATION   The park is in eastern Oklahoma, three miles south of Braggs, on Oklahoma 10A.

ACTIVITIES   The park is named for Greenleaf Creek, which was dammed to form the lake. Stay in the lodge, in one of the 14 cabins, or camp in one of 139 campsites, 89 with full hookups.

Tour the visitor center, and go swimming in the pool or in the lake. Fish for bass in Greenleaf Creek from an enclosed heated fishing dock, motorcycle along the trails, or enjoy boating from the boat ramp. Boat rentals and food service are available.

Hike 20-mile Greenleaf Lake Trail that circles the lake. It's closed from October 15 through December 1. Ticks are very abundant, so bring along plenty of insect repellent.

While you're in the area, visit Five Civilized Tribes Museum, and Submarine USS *Batfish* in Muskogee.

INFORMATION
Greenleaf State Park
Route 1, Box 119
Braggs, Oklahoma 74423
918-487-5196
Cabin reservations: 1-800-522-8565 (in Oklahoma)

HEYBURN STATE PARK
13

LOCATION   The park is 12½ miles west of Sapulpa, off Oklahoma 33, and 3½ miles south on County Road.

FEATURES   Sapulpa was named for Jim Sapulpa, a Creek Indian who settled along Rock Creek in 1850.

ACTIVITIES   Camp in the campground with 74 campsites, 52 sites with water and electrical hookups. Limited groceries are available. Go fishing for catfish, swimming, water-skiing, and boating (from the ramp) in Heyburn Lake, where boat rentals are available.

In Sapulpa, tour Sapulpa Historical Museum, at 100 E. Lee. It's open Tuesday through Sunday from 1 to 4, or by appointment. Call 918-224-4871. Also tour one of the largest potteries in the Southwest. Plant tours are offered Monday through Friday from 8:00 to 3:15, or you can walk through the showroom, open 7 days a week. For information, call 918-224-5511.

Veteran's Memorial in Sapulpa has the Michael Knight Memorial collection of shoulder patches, plus other military artifacts.

INFORMATION
Heyburn State Park
Bristow, Oklahoma 74010
918-247-6695

KEYSTONE STATE PARK
14

WALNUT CREEK STATE PARK
15

FEYODI CREEK STATE PARK
16

LOCATION   Keystone State Park is 15 miles west of Tulsa, on the south end of Keystone Lake. Take the Keystone Expressway, U.S. 64/U.S. 412. It's also five miles southeast of Mannford, then 1.5 miles on Oklahoma 151.

Walnut Creek State Park is also 15 miles west of Tulsa, on the north side of Keystone Reservoir. It's off the Cimarron Turnpike in Sand Springs, 13 miles east of the 209th Street exit, on Prue Road.

Feyodi Creek State Park is 2½ miles south of Cleveland, on U.S. 64.

ACTIVITIES   Keystone Lake has 330 miles of shoreline, with over 30 parks scattered around its shores. Its wide sandy beaches, some over a mile long, are great for jogging and beach walking. Yachtsmen and wind surfers are treated to delightfully windy conditions.

The lake is known as the striped bass capital of Oklahoma. You can also fish for walleye and catfish. Attend the Striped Bass Festival (held the second weekend in June)—a parade, carnival, ski show, fish fry, and children's games.

Keystone Dam is located on the Arkansas River, two miles downstream from the junction of the Cimarron and Arkansas Rivers, 15 miles west of Tulsa. For information about touring the powerhouse, stop by the office at the north end of the dam on weekdays.

Watch for bald eagles diving and soaring by the river below the dam. The best viewing spot is from an access area on the north side of the river.

The lake has a separate area set aside at White Water Park, where both motorcycle and ORV activities are allowed. Appalachia Bay is for motorcycle riding only. For information, call 918-865-2621.

Keystone State Park has 21 housekeeping guest cabins. Camping is available in one of the three campgrounds, with a total of 143 campsites, 75 sites with electrical hookups, and dumping station.

The park has rental bicycles and a fitness trail. Grab a bite to eat at the Hard Dock Cafe, located inside the marina, where rental boats are available. Purchase food at the grocery store, and go fishing year-round from the heated fishing dock. For information, call 918-865-2197.

Hike Whispering Hills Trail, located east of Sand Springs. Its 1.4-mile loop takes you along the shoreline of Keystone Lake. During the winter months, watch for eagles migrating through the area.

Walnut Creek State Park has camping in 66 sites, all sites with water and electrical hookups, and a trailer dump station. Go fishing for catfish, boating from the ramp, swimming from the beach, and water-skiing in Keystone Lake.

Feyodi Creek State Park has 43 campsites, 18 with full hookups, and a disposal station. Go swimming, boating from the ramp, and fishing.

Annual events in Tulsa include the Pecan Festival in mid-June. For information, call 918-756-6172. The Creek Nation features an all-Indian rodeo in June. For information, call 918-756-8700.

Other events include the Rendezvous Fair and Mayfest in May, featuring native Oklahoma artwork, a juried art fair, and children's art exhibition. Several horse shows are presented throughout the spring and summer. The Tulsa Powwow is held in August, and Labor Day festivities, a Chili bake-off and Bluegrass Festival, and the state fair, are featured in September. For information, contact the Chamber of Commerce at 918-585-1201.

Stop by Discoveryland, located west of Tulsa on West 41st Street, where the Rodgers and Hammerstein musical *Oklahoma!* is performed from early June through late August, in a natural outdoor-theater setting. The theater is closed Sundays. For information, call 918-245-OKLA.

Flower lovers can visit Woodward Park and municipal rose garden, located at Peoria and 23rd Street in Tulsa. The garden center is open Monday through Friday from 9 to 4.

Incoming pilots can land at Richard Lloyd Jones Airfield, located five miles south of Tulsa. Rental cars are available.

INFORMATION

Keystone State Park
Box 147
Mannford, Oklahoma 74044
Park office 918-865-4991
Cabin reservations: 1-800-522-8568
or 918-865-4991

Walnut Creek State Park
New Prue, Oklahoma 74060
918-242-3362

Feyodi Creek State Park
P.O. Box 258
Cleveland, Oklahoma 74020
918-358-2844

LAKE MURRAY STATE PARK
17

LOCATION   Lake Murray State Park is two miles east of I-35, south of Ardmore, halfway between Oklahoma City and Dallas.

FEATURES   The park is the state's largest, and lies on the edge of Lake Murray.

ACTIVITIES   The park is open year-round. Enjoy fishing from their indoor fishing arena, or take guided fishing trips. It has a snack bar, and a drive-up boat gasoline pump.

Water sports include sailing, canoeing, paddle boating, water-skiing, and water cruises from the marina. Swim in the lake or pool. Play on the lighted miniature golf course adjacent to the lake, open from March to October.

Rent a horse from the stable to go riding, enjoy a hayride, or cookout. They're open from March to November. Hike 3-mile Buckhorn Trail along the shoreline, connecting Lake Murray Lodge with Tipps Point campground.

The park also has rental bikes, tennis courts, a nine-hole golf course, and supervised recreational programs. Tucker Tower Museum, an historic landmark, has an observation platform and nature center.

Lake Murray's Pear Orchard Motorcycle Use Area is in the northwest part of the park, near Ardmore. For information, call 405-223-4044.

Stay in the 236-site campground, with full hookups, and trailer dumping station, in one of 54 rooms in the Pioneer Heritage Resort's inn, or in one of 88 cottages. Dine at Quilts Restaurant.

Country Inn features year-round Heritage Arts and Crafts workshops. Learn to quick-piece an old fashioned quilt, paint delicate china, weave on a loom, or the art of good storytelling.

For good fall foliage viewing, begin in Ardmore and travel south on U.S. 77, passing Lake Murray State Park. For information, call 405-223-4044. Visit nearby Turner Falls and Arbuckle Wilderness.

At Easter, attend Heritage Festival in the park. Annual events held in Ardmore include the Shrine Rodeo in April, Ardmore Birthday in July, Championship Bull Riding, and the Ardmore Trade Show in October. Stop by the Charles B. Goddard Center for the Performing Arts, to see one of their traveling exhibits.

A 2,500-foot paved and lighted airstrip is located near the state park resort. A unicom call to the Country Inn will bring you free ground transportation. Pilots can also land at Ardmore Municipal Airport, located 10 miles northeast of town. Rental cars are available.

INFORMATION

Lake Murray State Park
P.O. Box 1329
Ardmore, Oklahoma 73402
405-223-4044
Water sports: 405-223-6600, Ext. 163

Fishing Arena: 405-223-6600,
    Ext. 161
Riding Stables: 405-223-8172
Resort Inn: 405-223-6600
Park office: 405-223-4044

LAKE TEXOMA STATE PARK AND RESORT
18

LOCATION   The area is 10 miles west of U.S. 69, on Oklahoma 70 between Durant and Kingston.

FEATURES   Lake Texoma, Oklahoma's second largest lake, is impounded by Denison Dam. The dam was the largest earth-fill dam in the country when it was built in the early 1940s.

The state recreation area has 425 miles of shoreline, is 40 miles long, and lies in both Oklahoma and Texas.

The lake supports two wildlife refuges, two state parks, almost 100 campgrounds and resort areas, and over 22,000 boats. It is one of the few inland lakes in the country rated for ocean-going sailing craft.

Water depths range up to 90 feet, and because of the lake's size, many yachts compete here year-round. Some events include the Easter Regatta, Saint Patrick's Day and Memorial Day Regatta, and in June, the Ladies' Regatta. For information, call 214-465-1551.

ACTIVITIES   Wind surfers come to Walnut Creek II, area C, where lessons and rentals are available on weekends. Here, too, is the site of the annual Sailboat Madness fun races, held the first part of June, and the Oklahoma Board Sailing Championships held in September. The Tulsa Board Sailing Association also sponsors wind surfing activities here.

Each Labor Day, over 2,000 people enter the Sand Springs "Great Raft Race" to race down the Arkansas River, from Sand Springs to Tulsa. "Rafts" include rubber inner tubes to elaborate multi-man Olympic racing shells. In September, you can also attend the State Chili Cook-off.

Water skiers will find great conditions at Mud Creek, Dry Lake Cove, Black Jack Cove, and House Creek.

In late September, attend the National Aerobatics Meet, where aerobatic pilots from all over the U.S. compete to become members of the American flying team, that goes on to participate in the World Competition.

The lake is an anglers' paradise, ranked nationally for record-setting fish, including big striper, catfish, smallmouth bass, and sunfish. If you're fishing below the dam, watch for the warning devices and red flashing lights, warning of changes in water releases. Attend Striper Camp to discover better techniques for landing the striped bass. After two days of fishing with a professional guide, participate in a fishing tournament with other camp guests.

Bird watchers will have a heyday at the lake since it's located in the Central "flyway," and hosts millions of migrating birds every spring and fall, plus countless shore birds.

Lake Texoma Resort has a 99-room lodge, 67 cottages, the Bayview Lodge with accommodations for 40, three camping areas with 509 campsites, groceries, and a dining room. Play golf on the 18-hole golf course. Enjoy playing tennis on the tennis courts, horseback riding, and hiking the trails. Go swimming in the pool or in the lake, and rent boats from the full-service marina.

Tishomingo, north of Lake Texoma, has the Arrowhead Museum containing 9,000 Indian stone artifacts, and many early-day household items. Tour the Original Council House of the Chickasaw Indians, built in 1838 when the tribe moved to Oklahoma from Mississippi and Alabama.

Tour the Denison Dam Powerhouse to see paleontological specimens. Take a guided tour at 1:00 P.M., Monday through Friday.

Tishomingo National Wildlife Refuge, three miles south of the dam, is on the Upper Washita arm of Lake Texoma. Its headquarters is open Monday through Friday from 8:00 to 5:00.

The 24-mile Platter-Lakeside Trail, located near Cartwright at Lake Texoma, is a multi-use trail enjoyed by both hikers and equestrians. Primitive camping is permitted at both ends of the trail, accessible from either the Platter or Lakeside Recreation Areas. For information, call 214-465-4990.

Equestrians can book a moonlight ride, cowboy breakfast, or a western cookout, at the Texoma stable. For information, call 405-564-3961.

Boaters have access to Catfish Bay Marina, complete with its own airstrip, launch ramp, restaurant, and swimming beach. They also provide a full-service gas dock, groceries, boat rentals, and striped bass fishing guides. For information, call 405-564-2307.

Go into Durant in mid-July to attend the Oklahoma Shakespeare Festival. For schedules and tickets, call Southeastern Oklahoma State University, 405-924-0121, extension 217.

Other nearby attractions include the Cedarvale Gardens on U.S. 77, outside of Davis, and touring the Lake Texoma Fisheries Station, four miles north of Pottsboro, Texas. Take a float-plane ride from the floating dock near Grandpappy Point. Hunt for fossils after seeing the paleontology exhibits at Denison Dam, and trek along the water line where dinosaur tracks have been found in the shale and limestone.

Enjoy exploring the eight-mile Winding Trail, or the Crosstimbers Hiking Trail near Gordonville, Texas. For information, call 214-465-4990.

The one-mile-long Washington Irving Scenic Nature Trail begins on the northern end of the Washington Irving Cove South public-use area, and winds along the sandstone bluffs.

Enjoy a picnic where the early pioneers did. Go to Flowing Wells Resort, where an historical marker shows where 5 flowing artesian wells, now covered over by the lake, attracted earlier visitors to picnic under the oak trees. Snacks are available from a nearby store.

Are you a triathlete? If so, check out the annual Tulsa National YMCA Triathlon, held in August. For information, call 918-583-6201.

Bicyclists have access to many limited-access, hard-surfaced, service roads along the lake's 330-mile-long shoreline.

Fifteen airstrips surround the lake. Visitors can land at Kingston–Lake Texoma State Park's strip, located four miles east of Kingston. The strip offers courtesy rides. Larger aircraft can land at the commercial airport at Durant's Eaker Field, three miles southwest of town. It has a courtesy car.

INFORMATION
Lake Texoma Resort
Box 248
Kingston, Oklahoma 73439
Resort Lodge: 405-564-2311
Reservations: 1-800-522-8568 (in Oklahoma)
Pro Shop: 405-564-3333
Park office: 405-564-2566

LAKE WISTER STATE PARK
19

HEAVENER RUNESTONE STATE PARK
20

LOCATION   Lake Wister State Park is two miles south of Wister, on U.S. 270, in the Ouachita National Forest in southeastern Oklahoma.

Heavener Runestone is two miles north of Heavener, half-way up 1,200-foot Poteau Mountain. Cross the railroad tracks in the center of Heavener, take the first turn north and follow signs. The park itself is three miles from the railroad.

ACTIVITIES   At Lake Wister, enjoy water-skiing, boating, with boat rentals available, excellent fishing for bass, bluegill, catfish, crappie, and walleye, in Lake Wister, and touring the state waterfowl refuge. Go swimming in the lake from the beach, or in the pool.

Stay overnight in one of the 15 housekeeping cabins, or camp in one of the five campgrounds with 172 campsites, 100 sites with full hookups, and trailer dumping station. Purchase groceries, or eat in the restaurant, open year-round.

Hikers and equestrians have access to 53 miles of old logging roads now used as trails, within the Ouachita Forest. Come in the fall when the foliage is in full color. Adjacent lands are available to hunt deer, dove, quail, and turkey.

From the park, take a scenic tour along the 55-mile-long Talimena Skyline Drive that goes from Mena, Arkansas to Talihina, Oklahoma.

Stop at the Spiro Mountains State Archeological Park, located three miles east of Spiro on Oklahoma 9, and then four miles north on Spiro Mounds Road. From Oklahoma 271, go north 4½ miles on Lock and Dam Road 14. This world-renowned prehistoric site has been referred to as the "King Tut of the West." Examine its earthen mounds and remnants of an Indian culture that flourished here from 1200–1300 A.D. Hike the 1.5-mile trail to see the nine mounds, and the Spiro Culture House reproduction. For information, call 918-962-2062.

Heavener Runestone State Park, three miles north of Heavener, features a 12-foot high, 10-foot wide, stone with runic alphabet carvings. The eight weathered symbols have been translated to read," November 11, 1012," and are believed to have been carved by Viking explorers 500 years before Columbus' arrival.

Hike up the steep path to reach the stone, enclosed in a stone building. A visitor center is at the entrance to a trail leading down the side of the ravine, to the museum 50 feet below. A hilly one-mile nature trail takes you through the 50-acre park.

INFORMATION

Lake Wister State Park
Route 2, Box 6B
Wister, Oklahoma 74966
Cabin reservations: 918-655-7212
Park office: 918-655-7756
Grocery store: 918-655-9472

Heavener Runestone State Park
Route 1, Box 1510
Heavener, Oklahoma 74937
918-653-2241

LITTLE RIVER STATE PARK
21

LOCATION   Little River State Park is 13 miles east of Norman, on Oklahoma 9.

ACTIVITIES   Little River State Park is on 4,641-acre Lake Thunderbird. Visitors have access to swimming beaches, bathhouses, boat-launching ramps, sail boats, and water-skiing. Wind surfers and boat rentals are available at the marina. Fish for bass from an enclosed fishing dock. Go for a hayride, ride the equestrian trails, with rentals available at the stables, and check out the bicycle and hiking trails.

Camp in one of 447 campsites, many with both water and electrical hookups. Groceries and trailer dumping stations are available.

In April, attend the Medieval Fair in Norman, and enter the Kingdom of Avalon to savor the pleasures of the Middle Ages.

Incoming pilots can land at the University of Oklahoma Westhelmer Airpark, located three miles northwest of town. Rental cars are available.

INFORMATION

Little River State Park (Clear Bay Area)
Route 4, Box 277
Norman, Oklahoma 73019
405-321-2395
Little River State Park (Indian Point Area)
405-364-7634

LITTLE SAHARA STATE PARK
22

LOCATION   The park is four miles south of Waynoka, on U.S. 281.

ACTIVITIES   Little Sahara is a mecca for dune buggy enthusiasts, who have access to constantly-moving sand dunes. Go for a hike on the nature trails.

Camp in the campground with 41 campsites, 21 with electrical and water hookups. Snacks are available.

INFORMATION
Little Sahara State Park
P.O. Box 132, Route 2
Waynoka, Oklahoma 73860
405-824-1471

OKMULGEE LAKE STATE PARK
23

LOCATION   The park is five miles southwest of Okmulgee, on Oklahoma 56.

ACTIVITIES   Camp in the 46-site campground, with water and electrical hookups, and a trailer dumping station. Go swimming, water-skiing, bass fishing, or boating from the ramp, in Lake Okmulgee. Hike the trails.

Attend the Pecan Festival in Okmulgee in June, when the locals vie for a listing in the *Guinness Book of World Records*, by baking the world's largest pecan pie.

To learn more about the Creek Indians, tour the Creek Nation Council House, located in the town square in Okmulgee. It's closed Sundays and Mondays.

Incoming pilots can land at Okmulgee Municipal Airport, located three miles north of town. Rental cars are available.

INFORMATION
Okmulgee Lake State Park
210 Dripping Spring Lake Road
Okmulgee, Oklahoma 74447
918-756-5971

OSAGE HILLS STATE PARK
24

LOCATION   The park is five miles north of Pawhuska on Oklahoma 99, then 10 miles east on U.S. 60. The park is also 11 miles west of Bartlesville on U.S. 60, and two miles south on Oklahoma 35.

FEATURES   The Osage Indians settled in northeastern Oklahoma's woodlands in 1796. Pawhuska means "White Hair," named for a legendary Osage Indian chief.

ACTIVITIES   The park is densely wooded and has an 18-acre lake, eight stone cabins, two campgrounds, with 20 paved sites with full hookups, and a dump station. Go bass fishing and boating in Lake Lookout, and hike the trails. Go horseback riding, swimming in the pool, or play tennis.

If you're here in the fall, be sure to drive from the park along U.S. 60 to Bartlesville, and then southwest on Oklahoma 123 to Barnsdall, to see the fall foliage.

Go to Bartlesville's Community Center's Marie Foster Performing Arts Hall to attend performances by the Bartlesville Civic Ballet and the Bartlesville Symphony. In June, the OK Mozart Festival, a 10-day affair, is presented.

In early June, attend the National Biplane Fly-in at the Bartlesville Airport, when hundreds of multi-wing aircraft are flown in and displayed. The Antique Airplane Association Fly-in is held in September, and features many beautifully restored antique planes. For details, contact the Chamber of Commerce at 1-800-364-8708.

Incoming pilots can land at Frank Phillips Airport at Bartlesville. Rental cars are available.

INFORMATION
Osage Hills State Park
Red Eagle Route, Box 84
Pawhuska, Oklahoma 74056
Cabin office: 918-336-4141 or 1-800-522-8565 in Oklahoma
Park office: 918-336-5635

QUARTZ MOUNTAIN STATE PARK
25

LOCATION   The park is 17 miles north of Altus, on Oklahoma 44A.

FEATURES   The area overlooks Lake Altus-Lugert, and was once a winter camp and sacred ground for the Kiowa and Comanche Indians. Altus Reservoir has a 49-mile-long shoreline.

The red granite, forming the mountains beyond the park entrance, has been eroded over millions of years, producing rounded blocks and boulders sometimes called "devil's marbles" or "woolsocks."

ACTIVITIES   The area is a favorite for hikers. Hike the ½-mile-long New Horizon Trail that begins near Group Camp number 1, to scale the park's highest peak. If you're in the area from November to February, watch for American bald eagles who winter here.

Quartz Mountain State Park swimming beach
(photo by Fred W. Marvel, courtesy of Oklahoma Tourism)

Go walleye, bass, crappie, and catfish fishing in Lake Altus-Lugert. Rent boats from the marina, enjoy a picnic, and swim from the swimming beach or in an enclosed pool that remains open during the winter.

You can also go water-skiing, boating from the ramps, rock hounding, play tennis, or golf the nine-hole or 18-hole course. A skating rink and water slide are located near the park.

Camp in the 128-site campground, or in Quartz Mountain Resort overlooking the lake, with 45 lodge rooms and 16 cottages, or stay in the Mountainview Lodge, with a 64-person dormitory. Attend plays in the outdoor amphitheater, and purchase something to eat at the Finale Restaurant. Quartz Mountain Grocery Store provides "almost anything you forgot." For information, call 405-563-2270.

Quartz Mountain is home to the Summer and Fall Arts Institutes, and you can participate in an "Outdoor Adventure" vacation package offered year-round, that includes lodging, meals, and outings with a park naturalist. For information, contact the park supervisor.

The park maintains an ORV area characterized by shifting sand dunes, located on the north shore of Lake Altus-Lugert.

Annual events include Eagle Watch in January, State Wildflower Festival in May, and the Christmas Arts and Crafts Bazaar.

Tour the nearby Museum of the Western Prairie to learn more about 18th-century life in the region, with artifacts from the early French, Spanish, English, Indian, and cowboy residents.

Anadarko is east of Quartz Mountain Resort, and is the home of Indian City. The outdoor museum features authentic villages depicting the daily lives and cultures of seven American Indian tribes. Take a regularly scheduled conducted tour, and watch Indian dances performed daily during the summer, and on Saturdays and Sundays year-round.

Held annually, two days before and including Veteran's Day, is the Kiowa Veteran's Day Celebration, with a reenactment of an actual battle that occurred in the early 1800s.

The American Indian Exposition is held annually in mid-August, and features a parade, pageant, ceremonial dances, and the National Championship War Dance contest. As early as two weeks before the event, members of the Plains Indian tribes gather, camping out in their teepees, brush arbors, tents, and even in modern-day campers.

Tour the National Hall of Fame for Famous American Indians, adjacent to the Southern Plains Indian Museum and Crafts Center.

In Altus, attend the annual Jackson County Fair, and the Great Plains Stampede and Rodeo, held in September. Each spring you can attend a livestock show, plus a farmers' market. Each October, the Annual Shortgrass Arts Festival is held. Altus Air Force Base is also home to the free world's largest airplane, the C-5.

Pilots flying into the area can land at Altus, two miles north of the city. Free ground transportation is available.

INFORMATION
Quartz Mountain State Park
Route 1, Box 40
Lone Wolf, Oklahoma 73655
Park office: 405-563-2238
Resort office: 405-563-2424
Pro shop: 405-563-2520

RAYMOND GARY STATE PARK
26

LOCATION   The park is 1.5 miles south of Fort Towson, on Oklahoma 209.

ACTIVITIES   Go swimming, boating, and bass fishing in Raymond Gary Lake. Camp in one of 115 campsites, 15 with electrical hookups.

INFORMATION
Raymond Gary State Park
H.C. 65, Box 127
Fort Towson, Oklahoma 74735
405-873-2307

RED ROCK CANYON STATE PARK
27

LOCATION   The park is ½ mile south of Hinton, off Oklahoma 8, on Oklahoma 281.

FEATURES   During the mid-1800s, the California Road, a major wagon trail, passed through the canyon. Ruts carved by the wagon wheels are still visible in the sandstone. The canyon bottom is lined with a forest of sugar maples, an unusual occurrence since it is 175 miles farther west than they are usually found.

ACTIVITIES   Camp in the campground, located down a short, steep road leading to the floor of the canyon. It has 78 sites, 56 with water and electricity, five with full hookups, and a dump station. Enjoy a picnic in their picnic shelter, or hike a two-mile trail around the canyon rim. Go bicycling, fishing, swimming in the pool, rock climbing, and rappelling.

Stop by Oklahoma's most prominent landmark, Rock Mary, on the California Road.

When fall colors abound, begin your drive in Binger and follow Oklahoma 8 to Hinton, where you intersect U.S. 281. Attend the rodeo held each July in Hinton.

INFORMATION
Red Rock Canyon State Park
P.O. Box 502
Hinton, Oklahoma 73047
405-542-6344

ROBBERS CAVE STATE PARK
28

LOCATION   The 8,500-acre park is four miles north of Wilburton, on Oklahoma 2 in southeastern Oklahoma.

FEATURES   Robbers Cave is one of the state's largest state parks, nestled in the San Bois Mountains. The cave was used as a hideout by Jesse James, the Dalton gang, and the Younger Brothers. It was also utilized during the early 1700s by French traders and trappers, who stored their provisions, furs, and hides here.

In 1830, the area was part of the Choctaw Nation, when the Indians hunted in the game-filled forest.

ACTIVITIES   Stay overnight in one of the 26 housekeeping cabins, or camp in one five campgrounds, with dump stations, and 117 campsites. Whispering Pines has full hookups, and Old Circle has electrical hookups. Two other campgrounds offer primitive camping. An equestrian campground has water and electrical hookups, plus access to 25 miles of riding trails.

Enjoy dining in the cafe, or purchase groceries for your picnic. Tour the nature center, and go bass fishing in Lake Carlton. Enjoy swimming from the swimming beach (life guards on duty), or in the indoor pool. Rent a bicycle to go cycling.

The park has three lakes: Carlton, Wayne Wallace, and Coon Creek. Go canoeing and boating, from the ramps or from the dock. Rentals are available. Boating is also available from the ramp on the Wayne Wallace Reservoir.

Robbers Cave's network of hiking trails includes a nature walk near the famous cave, plus a backpacker/hiking trail accessing approximately 12 miles of trails. Rock climbers have a place to practice their technical climbing and rappelling.

A beautiful fall drive begins near Robbers Cave State Park, and continues south on Oklahoma 2, to intersect U.S. 270 heading to Wilburton.

In late October, attend the Robbers Cave Fall Festival, where over 100 exhibitors place their arts and crafts on sale.

INFORMATION
Robbers Cave State Park
P.O. Box 9
Wilburton, Oklahoma 74578
Park office: 918-465-2565
Cabin and campsite reservations: 918-465-2562
Grocery: 918-465-2562
Cafe: 918-465-3005

ROMAN NOSE STATE PARK AND RESORT
29

LOCATION   The park is near Lakes Watonga and Boecher, seven miles northwest of Watonga via Oklahoma 8 and 8A.

FEATURES   Roman Nose was once a favorite retreat of the Cheyenne Indians, because of its location nestled within a canyon, and also because of the water from the Spring of Everlasting Waters, which pours out at the rate of 600 gallons per minute.

ACTIVITIES   Camp in the 74-site campground, with hookups and a dump station. Go trout fishing in Lake Watonga. Hike the trails, play badminton, swim in the natural rock swimming pool, and go horseback riding. Go boating on the lakes, with paddleboat rentals available. Eat in the cafe.

The park's theme resort highlights the rich Cheyenne and Plains Indian heritage of the area. It has 47 rooms, 10 cottages, and the Redbird Restaurant. Swim in the pool, attend interpretive program, go bicycling, play golf on a nine-hole golf course, and play tennis on the tennis courts.

An unusual resort feature is a two-night, three-day package, featuring lodging and meals, an Indian Taco cookout, interpretive sightseeing, and an Indian crafts class. Contact the resort for details.

Annual events include Cheyenne Summerfest in May, Oakerhater Powwow in August, Watonga Cheese Festival in November, and Traders Fest in December.

For a scenic fall drive, begin in Watonga and follow Oklahoma 8 past Roman Nose, or take Oklahoma 8A for a short distance.

In nearby Watonga, visit the home of Oklahoma's sixth territorial governor, T. B. Ferguson, which was built in 1901. Behind the home, you can see a city jail, circa 1893, an 1870 U.S. calvaryman's log cabin, and a remount station. In November, attend the Watonga Cheese Festival.

INFORMATION
Roman Nose State Park and Resort
Box 61
Watonga, Oklahoma 73772
Park office: 405-623-4215
Resort Lodge: 405-623-7281
Pro Shop: 405-623-7989

SALLISAW STATE PARK
30

LOCATION   The park is eight miles north of Sallisaw, on Oklahoma 17.

ACTIVITIES   Go boating and bass fishing in Brushy Lake. Camp in the 60-site campground, 19 sites with water and electrical hookups, and a trailer dump station.

Sequoyah's Home Site is 11 miles northeast of Sallisaw, on Oklahoma 101. It's the original log cabin home of Sequoyah, inventor of the Cherokee alphabet. Watch a film on Sequoyah's life. The cabin, museum, and grounds are closed Mondays.

Faulkner's Cabin, circa 1845, is in downtown Sallisaw on West Cherokee. Judge Frank Faulkner was a pioneer lawyer in early Sequoyah.

Attend a horse race at Blue Ribbon Downs, two miles west of Sallisaw, on Oklahoma 64 West. Races are held Thursday through Sunday, and on holidays from late February through late November. For times, call 918-775-7771.

INFORMATION
Sallisaw State Park
P.O. Box 527
Sallisaw, Oklahoma 74955
918-775-6507

SEQUOYAH STATE PARK
31

SEQUOYAH BAY RECREATION AREA
32

LOCATION   Sequoyah State Park is on Fort Gibson Lake, 52 miles east of Tulsa on Oklahoma 58, and six miles east of Wagoner, on Oklahoma 51.

Sequoyah Bay Recreation Area is on a peninsula in Fort Gibson Lake, five miles southeast of Wagoner, on Oklahoma 16, then five miles east on Grey Oaks Road.

ACTIVITIES   At Sequoyah State Park, camp in the 316-site campground, 159 sites with electricity, and 26 with water and sewer hookups. Enjoy a picnic, and go boating from the ramp in Lake Gibson, with boat rentals available. Go bass fishing from the indoor fishing dock.

In Sequoyah Bay Recreation Area, you can camp in the 82-site campground, 32 sites with electrical hookups. Go boating, fishing, water-skiing, and swimming in Lake Gibson. The park has a state waterfowl refuge.

If you prefer staying in fancier surroundings, stay in the Western Hills Guest Ranch, with an American Cowboy theme. The ranch has 101 rooms, 54 cottages, and a dining room. Enjoy horseback riding, covered wagon rides, bicycling, and golfing on the 18-hole golf course. Fish from the fishing piers, take a lake tour, go water-skiing, and hike the nature trails.

The ranch also has a nature center, campground, marina with boat rentals and boat ramps, grocery store, tennis courts, and swimming pool.

Learn how to ride horseback western-style, rope calves, sharp-shoot with air rifles, bows and arrows, and sling shots. Participate in a mini-Wild West show and competition.

Annual events on the lake include a crappiethon, a 60-day, tagged-crappie fishing promotion, held from mid-March to mid-May. Events are planned for every June weekend, including Summerfest, fishing tournaments, and sailing regattas. Other events include a Winter Bluegrass Festival   January, Eagle Watch and the American Fiddlers Festival in February, Pelican Tours of Ft. Gibson Lake from October through November, Three Forks Rendezvous in November, and Waterfowl Tours on Ft. Gibson Lake in December and January.

Less than three miles west of Fort Gibson Lake is the city of Wagoner, Indian Territory's first incorporated town (1896). Tour some early territorial homes, particularly the one housing the Historical Fashion House Museum and Research Center. It's stocked with over 2,000 vintage garments and accessories from the early 1800s. For information, call 918-485-4623.

Arriving pilots can land on Sequoyah Park Airport's 3,400-foot strip, six miles southeast of Wagoner, inside the park. A Unicom call gets you free ground transportation.

INFORMATION

Sequoyah State Park
Box 509
Wagoner, Oklahoma 74477
Park office: 918-772-2046
Resort: 918-772-2545
Pro shop: 918-772-2297

Sequoyah Bay Recreation Area
Route 2, Box 252
Wagoner, Oklahoma 74441
918-683-0878

Western Hills Guest Ranch
918-772-2545 or 918-772-2046
Pro shop: 918-772-2297

TALIMENA STATE PARK
33

LOCATION   The park is seven miles north of Talihina on Oklahoma 271, in the foothills of the Stair Mountains.

ACTIVITIES   Camp at one of 22 campsites. Go hiking, and enjoy a picnic.

The Talimena Scenic Drive goes along the crest of the Ouachita Mountains, through the Ouachita National Forest. It has frequent turn-outs to get a closer look at the brilliant colors of the hardwoods, or you can stop to go hiking in the woods.

If you continue beyond the park on the Talimena Scenic Byway, you'll reach almost 3,000 feet, where you can look out over the Holson Valley. This drive spans the highest mountain range between the Appalachians and the Rockies, and is particularly beautiful in the fall, around the third week in October, when the sweet gums, sugar maples, sumacs, and red oaks turn the forest into a mosaic of color.

INFORMATION
Talimena State Park
P.O. Box 318
Talihina, Oklahoma 74571
918-567-2052

TENKILLER STATE PARK
34

CHEROKEE LANDING STATE PARK
35

LOCATION   Tenkiller State Park is 10 miles north of the Vian exit on Oklahoma 82, on the southeast side of Tenkiller Lake. The lake lies between the cities of Gore and Tahlequah. Ten miles north of I-40, take the Webber-Falls-Gore Exit onto Oklahoma 100. From Tahlequah, continue south for 10 miles on Oklahoma 82.

Cherokee Landing State Park is 10 miles south of the intersection of U.S. 62 and U.S. 82, south of Tahlequah. It's on the northwest side of Tenkiller Lake.

FEATURES   Lake Tenkiller was formed in the 1950s when Tenkiller Ferry Dam, the state's second largest dam, was built across the Illinois River.

The lake was named for the Cherokee family from whom the land was obtained to build the dam. The park was named after a warrior who was given this name by the white soldiers of Ft. Gibson because of the ten notches on his bow.

ACTIVITIES   Tenkiller State Park is nestled below limestone cliffs and wooded hills, and has 11 marinas, 13 parks with campgrounds, 19 launching ramps, and a 130-mile-long shoreline. It's a mecca for water sports, where visitors can go water-skiing, jet skiing, or touring Tenkiller Lake on a tour boat. It has a full-service marina.

Go fishing in Tenkiller Lake for bass, crappie, catfish, and stocked rainbow trout, from the enclosed fishing dock, and participate in one of their bass tournaments. The Lower Illinois River, from the dam to Gore Landing, is a designated trout stream, that is stocked annually for year-round fishing.

Rent one of the 40 native-stone cabins, or stay in one of the 10 camping areas with a total of 221 campsites, 89 sites with full hookups.

Dine in the restaurant, purchase supplies in the grocery store, hike the trails, or swim either in the pool or in the lake.

The lake's clear water is world famous among scuba divers. The best diving spot is at the south end of the lake. A favorite for locals is Crappie Point, where divers find such interesting items as false teeth and jewelry, lost by boaters and swimmers. An unusual feature of the lake is the Aqua Park playground, located beneath Gene's Aqua Pro Shop, where divers can explore a school bus, car, and even swing on the underwater swing set.

Annual events include canoe racing on the Upper Illinois in April, a bass fishing tournament in late April at the Sixshooter Resort and Marina, and a parade of boats in August.

Go canoeing on the Upper Illinois River, an easy-flowing river with several stretches of mild rapids. Canoes and boats may be rented along the river. The 12-mile stretch of water on the Lower Illinois River offers a challenge for the more experienced canoer.

Cherokee Landing State Park offers boating from the ramp, picnicking, and camping in the 145-site campground, with hookups. Go fishing, water-skiing, scuba diving, swimming from the beach, and hike the nature trails.

Tahlequah is the Cherokee Indian's capital city. To learn more about their heritage, tour Tsa-La-Gi, located 2.5 miles south and one mile east of Tahlequah, off Oklahoma 62.

It's a recreated Cherokee village from the 17th-century, and staffed by Cherokees living as their ancestors did 300 years ago. It's open from early May through early September.

In September, attend the Cherokee National Holiday, when thousands of Cherokees assemble to celebrate the establishment of the Cherokee Nation, and the signing of the first Cherokee constitution in 1839. Blowgun making, the art of fashioning bows and arrows, gig making, and games of Cherokee marbles, are included in the weekend activities.

The Cherokee Heritage Center is nestled between Lake Tenkiller and the Illinois River, three miles south of Tahlequah, on U.S. 62. It presents the history and culture of America's second largest Indian tribe. Tour the Cherokee National Museum, and attend the historic outdoor drama, the "Trail of Tears," from early June through mid-August. For information, call 918-456-6007.

Tour the Ft. Gibson Stockade, circa 1824, located one mile north of Ft. Gibson on Oklahoma 80. Fort Gibson National Cemetery is one mile east of Ft. Gibson on Oklahoma 62, and contains the graves of some famous Oklahomans, early pioneers, and explorers.

The Murrell Mansion, circa 1844, is located three miles south of town on U.S. 82, and one mile east. It's one of the most imposing antebellum structures in Oklahoma, with antique furnishings and manuscripts. It's closed Mondays.

Arriving pilots can land at Cookson Airport, located on the east side of the lake, one mile southwest of town. Watch for deer on the runway in the early morning or late evening. Rental cars are available, and often an attendant is on hand to run visitors to the lake. Incoming pilots can also land at Tahlequah Municipal Airport, located two miles northwest of town. Rental cars are available.

INFORMATION

Tenkiller State Park
HCR 68, Box 1095
Star Route
Vian, Oklahoma 74962
918-489-5643
Restaurant: 918-489-2394
Cabins: 918-489-5641

Cherokee Landing State Park
H.C. 73, Box 510
Park Hill, Oklahoma 74451
918-457-5716

Lake Tenkiller Association
P.O. Box Ten K
Cookson, Oklahoma 74427
918-457-4403

TWIN BRIDGES STATE RECREATION AREA
36

HONEY CREEK STATE RECREATION AREA
37

CHEROKEE STATE RECREATION AREA
38

BERNICE STATE PARK
39

LITTLE BLUE STATE PARK
40

SPRING RIVER CANOE TRAIL STATE PARK
41

SPAVINAW STATE PARK AND
UPPER SPAVINAW STATE PARK
42

LOCATION   All three state recreation areas are located on Grand Lake O' the Cherokees, with 1,300 miles of shoreline, in northeastern Oklahoma.

Twin Bridges is six miles northeast of Fairland at the intersection of U.S. 60 and Oklahoma 137, at the junction of Neosho and Spring Rivers. It's on the northern end of the lake.

Honey Creek is two miles southwest of Grove on Oklahoma 10.

Cherokee State Recreation Area is east of Langley, on Oklahoma 20. Cherokee I is south of Langley, below Pensacola Dam on the Grand River. Cherokee II is located at the east end of the mile-long Pensacola Dam. Cherokee III is one mile east of the dam by the spillway.

Bernice State Park is ½ mile east of Bernice off Oklahoma 85A on Horse Creek.

Little Blue is two blocks east of Disney, close to the Cherokee parks, and one mile south of Tiajuana, off Oklahoma 28.

Spring River Canoe Trail State Park is located six miles east of Miami, on Oklahoma 10.

Spavinaw State Park is ¾ mile south of Spavinaw, on Oklahoma 20. Upper Spavinaw State Park is five miles south of Jay, off Oklahoma 10 and 59.

ACTIVITIES   Twin Bridges State Recreation Area has a 176-site campground, with electrical hookups, dump station, picnic shelters, motorboat rentals, enclosed fishing, boating ramps, a swimming beach, bathhouses, and a concession stand.

Honey Creek State Recreation Area has 52 sites, all with electrical hookups, picnicking, a dump station, boat ramp, boat rentals, a city swimming pool, and bathhouse. Go water-skiing and bass fishing in Grand Lake.

Cherokee State Recreation Area has 119 campsites, a swimming beach, boating, water-skiing, scuba diving, and fishing.

Bernice State Park has 53 campsites, boating, and fishing.

Little Blue State Park has a 40-site campground, boating, fishing, and water-skiing.

Spring River Canoe Trail State Park has three small state parks located on the Spring River. Here you can picnic, camp in the 50-site campground, fish, and go canoeing and boating from the ramp.

Spavinaw State Park has 56 campsites, swimming, and fishing in Spavinaw Lake. Upper Spavinaw State Park accesses Lake Eucha and Lake Spavinaw, and has swimming, boating, and fishing.

In Grove State Park, cruise aboard the *Cherokee Queen*, docked at Honey Creek Bridge, two miles south of U.S. 59. Trips are available from May through October, Tuesday through Sunday. For information, call 918-786-4272.

Tour Har-Ber Village is located 3½ miles west of Grove, on Har-Ber Road. In this recreated early-day frontier town, you'll find over a hundred 19th-century structures, housing a huge collection of antiques and artifacts. Food service is available. It's closed November through April. For information, call 918-786-4272.

Music buffs can attend a music show at the Kountry Kuzins Jamporee. Visitors to Grove can also see Satsuki, featuring a touch of the Orient in a Japanese garden.

Take a trip to Pensacola Dam to see the world's longest multiple-arch dam. Tours of this hydro-generating plant are offered from May through September, on Wednesday through Sunday, from 8 to 4.

Watch a live performance of "Jonah and the Whale" at the Picture in Scripture Amphitheater.

For details on Grand Lake area activities, contact the Grand Lake Association at 918-786-2289.

Incoming pilots can land at Grove Municipal Airport, located two miles northeast of town. Rental cars are available.

INFORMATION

Twin Bridges State Recreation Area
Route 1, Box 170
Fairland, Oklahoma 74343
918-540-2545

Honey Creek State Recreation Area
Route 5, Box 209
Grove, Oklahoma 74344
918-786-9447

Cherokee State Recreation Area
P.O. Box 220
Disney, Oklahoma 74340
918-435-8066

Bernice State Park
Route 5, Box 209
Grove, Oklahoma 74344
918-786-9447

Little Blue State Park
P.O. Box 220
Disney, Oklahoma 74340
918-435-8066

Spring River Canoe Trail State Park
Route 1, Box 170
Fairland, Oklahoma 74343
918-540-2545

Spavinaw State Park and
   Upper Spavinaw State Park
P.O. Box 220
Disney, Oklahoma 74340
918-435-8066

WAH-SHA-SHE STATE PARK

43

LOCATION   The park is four miles west of Hulah, on Oklahoma 10. It's also 15 miles northeast of Pawhuska on Oklahoma 99, and then 10 miles east on Oklahoma 10.

ACTIVITIES   Enjoy camping in the 68-site campground, 47 sites with water and electrical hookups, and a dump station. Enjoy picnicking, hiking the trails, water-skiing, boating from the ramp, swimming from the beach, or bass fishing in Lake Hulah.

INFORMATION

Wah-Sha-She State Park
Route 1, Box 301
Copan, Oklahoma 74022
918-532-4627

SOUTH CAROLINA

South Carolina has 53 state and historic parks. Learn about the state's history at Hampton, Redcliffe, and Rose Hill plantations. Landsford Canal has the remnants of one of the state's earliest public works projects. At Rivers Bridge, you'll see where Confederate soldiers attempted to halt General Sherman's march to Columbia. Kings Mountain has a living history farm, and exhibits at Keowee-Toxaway help you to learn about the Cherokee Indians who once inhabited the area.

Restaurants and/or snack bars are located at Charlestowne Landing, Hickory Knob, Santee, and Table Rock State Parks. Golfers can play on an 18-hole championship course at both Cheraw and Hickory Knob State Parks, or nine holes at Goodale State Park. Most of these parks offer swimming, nature walks, and campfire programs during the summer months. For general state park information, call 803-734-0156.

U.S. 17 follows a pre-Colonial Indian trail that headed south from Massachusetts. Today this route takes you past many oceanside communities, including Myrtle Beach, Atlantic Beach, and Surfside. Visitors can go deep-sea fishing and crabbing along the inland waterway. Tennis players have access to over 200 tennis courts, and divers can dive to several charted shipwrecks.

The Grand Strand, a 55-mile chain of beaches, is located on South Carolina's northern-most Atlantic coast. The Strand is famous for its fishing villages, such as Murrells Inlet and Little River. It's also known as the "Seaside Golf Capital of the World" with over 70 courses open to the public.

Cherokee Foothills Scenic Highway, South Carolina 11, follows an ancient Cherokee path. It leaves I-85 at Gaffney to make a 130-mile loop past Cowpens Battlefield, several state parks, over to Lake Keowee, and rejoins I-85 at the Georgia line. This is an especially colorful drive during the spring and fall.

Foothills Trail is an 85-mile-long woodland hiking trail, that goes over the ridges along the North Carolina–South Carolina state line, from Table Rock to Oconee State Park. Primitive campsites are located along the trail. For a map and information, contact the Foothills Trail Conference, P.O. Box 3041, Greenville, South Carolina 19602, or call 803-268-8456.

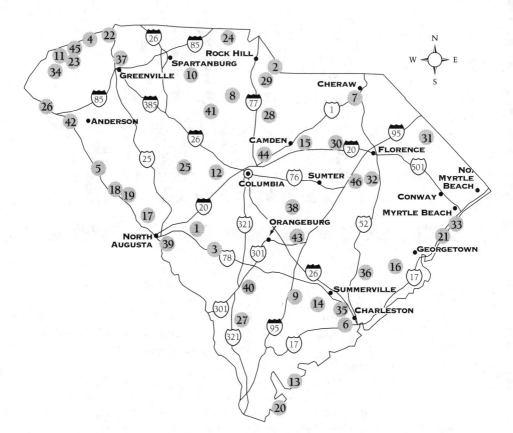

SOUTH CAROLINA STATE PARKS

1. Aiken State Park
2. Andrew Jackson State Park
3. Barnwell State Park
4. Caesar's Head State Park
5. Calhoun Falls State Park
6. Charlestowne Landing State Park
7. Cheraw State Park
8. Chester State Park
9. Colleton State Park
10. Croft State Park
11. Devils Fork State Park
12. Dreher Island State Park
13. Edisto Beach State Park
14. Givhans Ferry State Park
15. Goodale State Park
16. Hampton Plantation State Park
17. Hamilton Branch State Park
18. Hickory Knob State Resort Park
19. Baker Creek State Park
20. Hunting Island State Park
21. Huntington Beach State Park
22. Jones Gap State Park
23. Keowee-Toxaway State Park

24. Kings Mountain State Park
25. Lake Greenwood State Park
26. Lake Hartwell State Park
27. Lake Warren State Park
28. Lake Wateree State Park
29. Landsford Canal State Park
30. Lee State Park
31. Little Pee Dee State Park
32. Lynches River State Park
33. Myrtle Beach State Park
34. Oconee State Park
35. Old Dorchester State Park
36. Old Santee Canal State Park
37. Paris Mountain State Park
38. Poinsett State Park
39. Redcliffe Plantation State Park
40. Rivers Bridge State Park
41. Rose Hill Plantation State Park
42. Sadlers Creek State Park
43. Santee State Park
44. Sesquicentennial State Park
45. Table Rock State Park
46. Woods Bay State Park

Five lakes, located in the northwest corner of the state, were created to provide the area with hydroelectric power, resulting in some of the best boating and fishing to be found in the Southeast. Over 3,000 miles of these lakes and rivers shoreline provide water-based activity for 12 of the state parks. Lakes Jocassee and Keowee exchange water, when water from the upper lake spills into the lower one. Then, when the demand for power lessens, water is pumped back up from the Keowee to the Jocassee.

Lake Keowee, in turn, flows into Hartwell Lake which then feeds Richard B. Russell Lake. The water continues on to J. Strom Thurmond Lake, before spilling into the Savannah River, and ends up in the Atlantic Ocean.

Fall colors arrive late in South Carolina, near the southern end of the Appalachians. The season runs from mid to late October through the first week or two in November. Visit the upcountry of western South Carolina, where the Cherokee Foothills Highway (South Carolina 11), runs east and west, to north of Spartanburg. For details, contact the South Carolina Division of Tourism, 1-803-734-0122.

AIKEN STATE PARK
1

LOCATION   The park's 1,067 acres are 16 miles east of Aiken, off U.S. 78, on the South Edisto River. It's also off South Carolina 302 from Columbia.

FEATURES   The park was named for William Aiken, Sr., president of the Charleston-Hamburg Railroad, which was the longest railroad line in the world in the 1830s. Four park lakes were formed from sands left behind by an ancient sea, and later filled by natural springs.

ACTIVITIES   Go lake and stream fishing for bass and catfish, and swim in the spring-fed pond. Go boating, with fishing boat and paddle boat rentals available. Additional fishing is available in the south fork of the Edisto River, bordering the park.

Camp in the 25-site campground, with water and electrical hookups, and a dump station. Bring along a picnic to enjoy. Hike the three-mile jungle nature trail. Take a conducted walk during the spring, to learn more about the many wildflowers blooming here. Birders come here, particularly in the spring and fall, where over 160 species have been spotted.

See some restored vintage carriages in Aiken, at 100 Berrie Road. Visits are free. While in Aiken, stroll through Hopeland Gardens, at Whiskey Road and Dupree Place. Concerts and plays are presented Monday evenings during the summer. For information on the gardens, or for an appointment to see the carriages, call 803-642-7630.

Aiken is the site of the raising and training of race horses during the winter months, in preparation for the spring races. Tour the Thoroughbred Hall of Fame at Hopeland Gardens, featuring a collection of the state's finest racing memorabilia. It's open Tuesday through Sunday afternoons, from October through May.

Tour the Montmorenci Vineyards, five miles east of Aiken on U.S. 78. Wine tasting follows the tour. For an appointment, call 803-649-4870.

Arriving pilots can land at Aiken Municipal Airport, five miles north of Aiken. Rental cars are available.

INFORMATION
Aiken State Park
1145 State Park Road
Aiken, South Carolina 29856
803-649-2857

ANDREW JACKSON STATE PARK
2

LOCATION   The park is nine miles north of Lancaster, on U.S. 521.

FEATURES   The park commemorates Andrew Jackson, our seventh President, often referred to as "Old Hickory."

ACTIVITIES   Attend concerts or interpretive programs, presented year-round in the amphitheater. Tour the museum on weekends from 1 to 5, or by appointment on weekdays, to learn more about the frontier period. Look through the one-room log schoolhouse's exhibits.

Camp in the 25-site campground, with water and electrical hookups, and a dump station. Hike the nature trail, and go fishing and boating in the park lake, with fishing boat rentals available.

Arriving pilots can land at Lancaster County McWhirter Field located four miles west of Lancaster. Rental cars are available.

INFORMATION
Andrew Jackson State Park
198 Andrew Jackson Park Road
Lancaster, South Carolina 29720
803-285-3344

BARNWELL STATE PARK
3

LOCATION   Barnwell State Park is seven miles northeast of Barnwell, on South Carolina 3, and 3.3 miles south of Blackville.

FEATURES   The park has two lakes in its center.

ACTIVITIES   Camp in the 25-site campground, with water and electrical hookups, and a dump station. Hike the nature trail, and go boating, with fishing-boat and paddle boat rentals available. Enjoy fishing and swimming. Overnight in one of the five vacation cottages.

In Barnwell, stop by the courthouse square to see the vertical sundial that's over 150 years old, and still keeps perfect time.

Many come to Healing Springs, five miles north of Barnwell State Park, off South Carolina 3, to fill their containers with the artesian water.

INFORMATION
Barnwell State Park
Route 2, Box 147
Blackville, South Carolina 29817
803-284-2212

CAESAR'S HEAD STATE PARK
4

LOCATION   The park's 7,476 acres are 16 miles northwest of Greenville, on U.S. 276, on the South Carolina–North Carolina state line.

FEATURES   The park is at an altitude of 3,208 feet, and covers 10,000 acres. It's at the top of the state's Mountain Bridge Recreation and Wilderness Area.

ACTIVITIES   Hike the trails, attend interpretive programs, and tour the visitor center. Food service is available at the trading post. Another store is located in the gift shop. Go up the lookout tower for a great view of the Blue Ridge Mountains. Hike the two-mile trail to Raven Cliff Falls. Go fishing in the river.

If you're here during the week of July 4th, attend Freedom Weekend Aloft, when over 200 balloons are sent soaring above Greenville.

Mountain Bridge Recreation and Wilderness Area has scenic vistas and hiking trails. The Middle Saluda River flows through the area, and is the state's only designated State Scenic River.

Arriving pilots can land at Greenville Downtown Airport, three miles east of Greenville. Rental cars are available.

INFORMATION
Caesar's Head State Park
8155 Geer Highway
Cleveland, South Carolina 29635
803-836-6115

CALHOUN FALLS STATE PARK
5

LOCATION   The park is one mile north of Calhoun Falls, off South Carolina 81.

ACTIVITIES   Go fishing from the fishing pier, and swimming in Richard B. Russell Lake. Enjoy picnicking, camping in the 41-site campground (with a dump station), and go boating from the 13 boat ramps. A tackle shop is available. Go to the Richard B. Russell Dam for a good overlook of both the lake, and the dam that impounds the Savannah River. Hike the nature trails.

The Savannah River Scenic Highway is an especially beautiful drive, particularly during the spring and fall.

Arriving pilots can land at Hester Memorial Airport, one mile east of Calhoun Falls. No rental cars are available. The state park is two miles from the airport.

INFORMATION
Calhoun Falls State Park
Route 1, Box 360-A
Calhoun Falls, South Carolina 29628
803-447-8267

CHARLESTOWNE LANDING STATE PARK
6

LOCATION   The state park is at 1500 Old Town Road, west of the Ashley, and three miles northwest of Charleston, off South Carolina 171.

FEATURES   The landing marks the original site of the state's first permanent English settlement, established in 1670.

ACTIVITIES   Board a replica of the *Adventure,* a 17th-century trading vessel. Walk through the Settler's Life replica village and participate in the various activities. Take a narrated tram tour through the park grounds that has 80 acres of lush gardens. Rent a bicycle to take a ride, and stroll through the Animal Forest, a natural habitat zoo. Food is available in the park. Tour the interpretive center, and attend interpretive programs. Purchase souvenirs from the gift shop.

While in Charleston, stop by the visitor center, at 85 Calhoun Street, to pick up maps for the local attractions. Take a guided boat tour of the ruins at Fort Sumter National Monument, constructed from 1829–60, in Charleston Harbor. It was here that the first shot was fired which began the Civil War. To reach the monument, boats leave from both the Charleston City Marina and Patriots Point. For information on the fort, call 803-883-3123. For boat schedules, call 803-722-1691.

Fort Moultrie is across the channel from Fort Sumter, on Sullivan's Island. Take South Carolina 703 from U.S. 17 in Mt. Pleasant, and follow signs to the visitor center on Middle Street. The fort was the site of the first decisive victory of the Revolutionary War, that involved both land and naval forces. It was also active during the Confederate bombardment of Fort Sumter. Tour the museum and watch the film. For information, call 803-883-3123.

To learn more about Charleston, watch *Forever Charleston* in the theater next to the Charleston Visitor Center, at 375 Meeting Street. For information, call 803-724-

7474. Charleston has many buildings listed in the National Register of Historic Places, with 77 buildings dating from before the American Revolution, 136 from the late 18th-century, and over 600 others that were constructed prior to 1940.

Drayton Hall, a plantation home built between 1738 and 1742, is nine miles from Charleston. Listed on the National Trust for Historic Preservation, the home has never been modernized, and is an excellent example of early 18th-century architecture. For information, call 803-766-0188.

Magnolia Plantation and Gardens, circa 1680, is 10 miles northwest of Drayton, at the intersection of U.S. 17 and South Carolina 61, on Ashley River Road. Wander along the garden paths, with camellias and azaleas in full bloom during the spring. The plantation also includes the country's oldest colonial estate garden, where plants are in bloom year-round. Tour the plantation house. Bicycle and canoe rentals are available.

Middleton Place, circa 1741, is the oldest, and one of the most beautifully landscaped, gardens in America. It's northwest of Magnolia Plantation, and 14 miles northwest of the intersection of U.S. 17. The gardens were designed with a symmetry generally found in English and French gardens. It required 100 slaves working for 10 years to be completed. The Middleton Place House, circa 1755, provides the visitor with a history of the renowned Middleton family, from 1741 through 1865. Henry Middleton served as president of the First Continental Congress, and his son, Arthur, signed the Declaration of Independence. For information, call 803-556-6020 or 1-800-782-3608.

Tour Calhoun Mansion, at 16 Meeting Street. Circa 1876, the Victorian mansion is furnished with period pieces, and is considered an elaborate showplace in the Old South. Tours are offered Wednesday through Sunday from 10 to 4. For information, call 803-722-8205.

Attend a performance at the Dock Street Theater, at Church and Queen. Circa 1736, the theater was constructed around the ruins of the original theater. Tours of the theater are free, and it's open Monday through Friday, from noon to 6:00. Performances are presented in the theater and foyer. For information, call 803-723-5648.

Purchase a combination ticket to see the Charleston Museum, the Heyward-Washington House, and the Joseph Manigault House. For information, call 803-722-2996.

Visitors can tour several other beautiful gardens in the Charleston area, including Boon Hall Plantation, eight miles north of town at 1054 Long Point Road, on U.S. 17.

Arriving pilots can land at Charleston Executive Airport, six miles southwest of the city. Rental cars are available.

INFORMATION
Charlestowne Landing State Park
1500 Old Town Road
Charleston, South Carolina 29407-6099
803-556-4450

CHERAW STATE PARK
7

LOCATION   The park is four miles southwest of Cheraw, on U.S. 1.

FEATURES   Cheraw was named after a local Indian tribe. It was the state's first state park, and is also one of the largest, encompassing 7,361 acres.

ACTIVITIES   Camp in the 17-site campground, with water and electrical hookups, and a dump station, or overnight in one of eight vacation cabins. Hike the nature trail, and ride the bridle trail. Go canoeing and boating, with rentals available. Go to the upper end of the lake where you'll find towering cypress trees. Enjoy swimming and fishing in the lake. Play golf on the 18-hole championship golf course, with a full-service pro shop.

Attend the Palmetto Regatta the first weekend in May. The Cheraw Spring Festival is held the first or second weekend in April. Attend interpretive programs, presented year-round.

Cheraw is an historic town, with over 50 antebellum houses located within the historic district. Pick up a self-guiding map of the district from the Chamber of Commerce, 221 Market Street. For information, call 803-537-7681.

Stop by the Cheraw Fish Hatchery on U.S. 1, six miles south of Cheraw, to see the warm-water fish that are raised here. For information, call 803-537-7628.

Arriving pilots can land at Cheraw Municipal Airport, three miles northwest of the city. Rental cars are available.

INFORMATION
Cheraw State Park
Route 2, Box 888
Cheraw, South Carolina 29520
803-537-2215

CHESTER STATE PARK
8

LOCATION   The park is three miles southwest of Chester, on South Carolina 72.

ACTIVITIES   Camp in the 25-site campground, with water and electrical hookups, and a dump station. Hike the nature trails, go boating, and fishing in the park lake, with rentals available. Try your skill on the archery range. A horse show ring is available, and bridle paths surround the 160-acre fishing lake.

Tour the Cruse Vineyards and Winery, four miles north of Chester, to watch the production of wine. Sample the wines in the tasting room. It's open Friday from 3 to 6, and Saturday from 12 to 6. Admission is free.

Arriving pilots can land at Chester Municipal Airport, five miles north of the city. Rental cars are available.

INFORMATION
Chester State Park
Route 2, Box 348
Chester, South Carolina 29706
803-385-2680

COLLETON STATE PARK
9

LOCATION   The park is 12 miles north of Walterboro, on U.S. 15, and 5 minutes from I-95, Exit 68.

ACTIVITIES   Colleton State Park is the headquarters for the Edisto River Canoe and Kayak Trail, a 56-mile black water river. Go canoeing, and camp in the 25-site campground, with water and electrical hookups, and a dump station. Hike the nature trail, go fishing and boating from the ramp. This section of the Edisto River is designated as the state's first canoe and kayak trail. Canoeists often paddle from here to Givhans Ferry State Park.

Arriving pilots can land at Walterboro Municipal Airport, two miles northeast of the city. Rental cars are available.

INFORMATION
Colleton State Park
Canadys, South Carolina 29433
803-538-8206

CROFT STATE PARK
10

LOCATION   The park is three miles southeast of Spartanburg, off South Carolina 56.

FEATURES   The park is an old World War II training ground, that has been converted into a state park.

ACTIVITIES   Camp in the 50-site campground, with water and electrical hookups, and a dump station. Hike the nature trails, go boating, with pedal boat and fishing boat rentals available, and swim in the Olympic-size pool. The park has tennis courts, equestrian facilities, and a 160-acre fishing lake.

Spartanburg, circa 1785, is the largest peach-producing area in the state. Historic houses in town include the Price House, circa 1795. To reach it, go southwest on U.S. 221, off I-26, to Switzer and follow signs. It's open Tuesday through Saturday from 11 to 5, April through October, and Sunday afternoons year-round.

The Jammie Sea House, circa 1790, is believed to be Spartanburg's oldest house. It's at 106 Darby Road, and is open by appointment. Call 803-576-5646. You can also tour the Walnut Grove Plantation, whose restored manor house dates back to 1765. From I-26, go north on U.S. 221, and follow signs for approximately 1½ miles. It's open from 11 to 5 Tuesday through Saturday, from April through October, and Sunday afternoons year-round.

Arriving pilots can land at Spartanburg Downtown Memorial Airport, three miles southwest of the city. Rental cars are available.

INFORMATION
Croft State Park
450 Croft State Park Road
Spartanburg, South Carolina 29302
803-585-1283 or 803-583-2913

DEVILS FORK STATE PARK
11

LOCATION   The park is 16 miles northwest of Pickens, off South Carolina 11, the Cherokee Foothills Scenic Highway. It's also six miles north of South Carolina 11, on South Carolina 25 at Lake Jocassee, north of Salem.

FEATURES   Lake Jocassee is the state's coldest, deepest, and most pristine mountain lake. It holds three state records for the bass and trout, caught in its over 300-foot depth.

ACTIVITIES   Camp in the 60-site lakeside campground, with a dumping station, and purchase your supplies from the park store. Hike the trails; go boating from the ramp, with rentals available; fish, with supplies from the tackle shop; and swim in the park lake. Overnight in one of 20 mountain villas, and tour the visitor center.

Whitewater Falls are 11 miles north of South Carolina 11, above Salem, and off South Carolina 130. These two sets of falls drop over 400 feet.

The Cherokee Foothills Scenic Highway follows a 130-mile crescent, from I-85 close to the North Carolina border, down to I-85 at the Georgia border. Come in the spring when the peach trees, dogwood, and mountain laurel are in full bloom, or in the fall in mid-October, when the leaves take on their fall hues. The highway follows a path once used by Cherokee Indians, frontier traders, and bootleggers, and passes through the Blue Ridge foothills.

Take a short trip south of the park to Duke Power Company's World of Energy. Follow signs off South Carolina 11, to the intersection of South Carolina 130 and 183. Watch their audio-visual program and hike the ¼-mile nature trail.

For a unique horseback ride, follow the Chattooga National Wild and Scenic River that runs south from North Carolina's Blue Ridge foothills. The river carves a 40-mile border between South Carolina and Georgia. While there, you can also go for a challenging whitewater rafting trip.

Arriving pilots can land at Pickens County Airport, four miles south of the city. A courtesy car is available.

INFORMATION
Devils Fork State Park
161 Holcombe Circle
Salem, South Carolina 29676
803-944-2639

DREHER ISLAND STATE PARK
12

LOCATION   The park is six miles southwest of Chapin, off U.S. 176, or you can take Exit 91, off I-26.

FEATURES   The island park is on Lake Murray, a 50,000-acre impoundment above what was once the world's largest earthen dam. Lake Murray has 520 miles of shoreline, and the park has 12 miles of shoreline.

ACTIVITIES   Camp in the 112-site campground, with water and electrical hookups, and a dump station. Hike the nature trails, go boating from the ramp, water-skiing, and fishing from the park lake. Participate in a fishing tournament. Supplies are available from the trading post and tackle shop.

Visit the Lake Murray visitor and information center, on South Carolina 6 near the dam, to see its exhibits.

INFORMATION
Dreher Island State Park
Route 1, Box 351
Prosperity, South Carolina 29127
803-364-4152

EDISTO BEACH STATE PARK
13

LOCATION   The beach is 50 miles southwest of Charleston, on South Carolina 174, on Edisto Island. It's also 22 miles off U.S. 17.

FEATURES   Edisto Beach boasts some of the tallest Palmetto trees to be found in South Carolina.

ACTIVITIES   Go shelling in this beachcomber's paradise, along three miles of beach. Camp in the 75-site campground by the ocean, with water and electrical hookups, and a dump station. Overnight in a vacation cabin by the marsh, and go fishing and swimming in the ocean. Go boating from the boat ramp, and hike the hiking trails. Attend an interpretive program, and purchase a souvenir in the gift shop.

Arriving pilots can land at Charleston Executive Airport, six miles southwest of the city. Rental cars are available.

INFORMATION
Edisto Beach State Park
8377 State Cabin Road
Edisto Island, South Carolina 29438
803-869-2156 or 803-869-2756

GIVHANS FERRY STATE PARK
14

LOCATION   The park is 16 miles west of Summerville, off South Carolina 61.

ACTIVITIES   Camp in the 25-site campground, with water and electrical hookups, and a dump station. Overnight in one of the four vacation cabins situated under Spanish moss-draped oak trees and high bluffs that overlook the Edisto River. Go river fishing, and hike the nature trail. Canoeists often paddle to here, from Colleton State Park.

Arriving pilots can land at Dorchester County Airport, five miles northwest of Summerville. Rental cars are available.

INFORMATION
Givhans Ferry State Park
Route 3, Box 327
746 Givhans Ferry Road
Ridgeville, South Carolina 29472
803-873-0692

GOODALE STATE PARK
15

LOCATION   The park is five miles northeast of Camden, off U.S. 1, on Old Wire Road.

ACTIVITIES   Go boating, with fishing boat and paddleboat rentals available. Enjoy swimming and fishing in the 140-acre lake that's surrounded by cypress trees. Play golf on the nine-hole course, that's particularly enjoyed by novice golfers. Hike the nature trail.

Historic Camden village, circa 1732, is located north of I-20, on U.S. 521, and north of Camden. It's the oldest inland city in South Carolina. It features several historic homes including the Cravin House, circa 1790, the 1840s Cunningham House, and the reconstructed Kershaw-Cornwallis House, circa 1770. Camden was the site of the major British garrison of Lord Cornwallis, where the battles of Hobkirk Hill and Camden were fought during the Revolutionary War. Hike the park trails.

The city of Camden hosts one of the nation's richest steeplechase races, "The Carolina Cup." It's held around Easter.

Arriving pilots can land at Woodward Field, three miles northeast of Camden. Rental cars are available.

INFORMATION
Goodale State Park
650 Park Road
Camden, South Carolina 29020
803-432-2772

HAMPTON PLANTATION STATE PARK
16

LOCATION   The plantation is eight miles north of McClellanville, off U.S. 17. It's also 15 miles southwest of Georgetown, and adjacent to the Santee River.

FEATURES   The plantation house, circa 1735, was the ancestral home of Archibald Rutledge, Poet Laureate of South Carolina. The plantation grew rice and cotton from the early 1700s until 1860. However, after slavery was abolished, the plantation system was no longer profitable. The 15-room house, listed on the National Register of Historic Places, has been restored, and features a Greek Revival facade and two-story columns.

ACTIVITIES   Tour the plantation grounds, open year-round. The house is open for tours Thursday through Monday from 1 to 4, April 1 through Labor Day, and on weekend afternoons after Labor Day through March 31, or by appointment. Admission is charged.

INFORMATION
Hampton Plantation State Park
1950 Rutledge Road
McClellanville, South Carolina 29458
803-546-9361

HAMILTON BRANCH STATE PARK
17

HICKORY KNOB STATE RESORT PARK
18

BAKER CREEK STATE PARK
19

LOCATION   Hamilton Branch State Park is on Thurmond Lake, 12 miles southeast of McCormick, off U.S. 221 near Modoc.

Hickory Knob State Resort Park is eight miles southwest of McCormick, off U.S. 378, on the South Carolina/Georgia border.

Baker Creek State Park is in Sumter National Forest, three miles southwest of McCormick, on U.S. 378.

ACTIVITIES   Hamilton Branch offers 200 lakeside campsites, with water and electrical hookups, and a dump station. Go boating from the ramp in the park lake, fishing, and enjoy a picnic.

At Hickory Knob, overnight in one of the 18 modern lakefront cabins, or in the 80-room lodge located in the woods, beside the lake. Go camping in the 75-site campground, with water and electrical hookups. Overnight in the motel, or rent the restored Guillebeau House, a 200-year-old French Hugenot house. Dine in the restaurant, and go swimming in the pool. Play tennis, visit the skeet range, and bring your bird dog to the four-mile bird dog field trial area.

Hike the nature trail, or play 18 holes of championship golf along the lakeshore, with a pro shop available. Test your skill at archery. Go boating from the ramp, and fishing in Thurmond Lake for bass, crappie, and catfish. Boat rentals are available. Tour the visitor center and attend interpretive programs. Supplies are available at the trading post or gift shop.

At Baker Creek State Park, play miniature golf, and bring along a picnic. Go boating from the ramp, with paddleboat rentals available, and swimming and fishing in Thurmond Lake. Enjoy camping in the 100-site campground, with water and electrical hookups, and a dump station. Hike the nature and hiking trails, or go horseback riding on the equestrian trails.

Strom Thurmond Lake has 600 miles of shoreline, easily accessible from U.S. 378, U.S. 221, South Carolina 81, and South Carolina 28. Visitors can also enjoy water-skiing, sailing, and motor boating, with many free-access ramps.

Stop by the Thurmond Lake Visitor Center, on U.S. 221 at Thurmond Dam. Here you can see a collection of artifacts, an aquarium, and hands-on exhibits. Take a tour of the power plant. For information, call 803-333-2476.

Take a drive a long the Savannah River Scenic Highway, particularly beautiful in the spring and fall.

Arriving pilots can land at McCormick County Airport, one mile southeast of the city. A shuttle bus, courtesy car, and van are available for transportation.

INFORMATION

Hamilton Branch State Park
Route 1, Box 97
Plum Branch, South Carolina 29845
803-333-2223

Baker Creek State Park
Route 1, Box 219
McCormick, South Carolina 29835
803-443-2457

Hickory Knob State Resort Park
Route 1, Box 199-B
McCormick, South Carolina 29835
803-391-2450

HUNTING ISLAND STATE PARK
20

LOCATION   The park is 16 miles east of Beaufort, on U.S. 21.

FEATURES   The barrier island was once the hunting ground for both Indians and the early settlers, who hunted here for deer, raccoon, and waterfowl.

ACTIVITIES   Climb to the top of the 136-foot-high, 19th-century lighthouse, for a great overlook of the Atlantic coastline. It was abandoned in 1933 after it had served as a beacon for ships entering St. Helena Sound. On the west side of the island, walk along the elevated boardwalk over the salt marsh, where you can observe the wildlife. Watch for swarms of fiddler crabs that come ashore under the walkway at low tide.

Rent one of the 15 vacation cabins, or overnight in the 200-site campground, with electrical and water hookups, a dump station, and a camp store. Go fishing from the 1,120-foot fishing pier, and enjoy swimming in the ocean. Equestrians can ride the bridle trail. Tour the visitor center and attend interpretive programs.

Beaufort has many stately homes built by Southern plantation owners, who came here to escape the summer heat and malaria of the mainland. When the city was taken over by the Yankees, these mansions escaped being burned, like so many others, when General Sherman marched from Atlanta to the sea. Take a walking tour of the old 36-block section that includes "The Point," where the English built the first permanent settlement in 1711. Begin on Bay Street overlooking the river. For information, call the Chamber of Commerce at 803-524-3163.

Arriving pilots can land at Beaufort County Airport, three miles southeast of the city. You can also land at Laurel Hill Plantation Airport, six miles northeast of the city. Both airports have rental cars available.

INFORMATION
Hunting Island State Park
1775 Sea Island Parkway
St. Helena Island, South Carolina 29920
803-838-2011

HUNTINGTON BEACH STATE PARK
21

LOCATION   The park is three miles south of Murrells Inlet, on U.S. 17, adjacent to Brookgreen Gardens on the Grand Strand.

ACTIVITIES   Huntington Beach has almost 2,500 acres of natural habit to explore. Hike the nature trails and walk along the boardwalks, to spot the native wildlife. Camp in the 127-site campground, with water and electrical hookups, and a dump station. Ride the bridle trail, or go fishing and swimming in the ocean. Tour the visitor center and attend interpretive programs. Purchase supplies in the trading post.

Take a guided tour during the spring or summer, through the 55-room mansion, Atalaya, Spanish for "watchtower." It was once the castle-like studio of famed sculptor Anna Hyatt Huntington. The mansion's 40-foot tower originally held a 3,000 gallon water tank, that provided an early version of running water. For information, call 803-237-4440.

Stroll through Brookgreen Gardens, located four miles southwest of Murrells Inlet, off U.S. 17. Over 500 of America's finest 19th- and 20th-century sculptures are exhibited among 2,000 plant species. Artists include Frederic Remington, Daniel Chester French, plus over 200 of the greatest names in American sculpture. Programs and tours are offered daily. For information, call 803-237-4218.

Take a cruise along the Intracoastal Waterway from Murrells Inlet. Anglers have a choice of going fishing from the pier, in the surf, river, or inlet, or deep-sea fishing for blue crabs, channel bass, and trophy-size bill fish.

INFORMATION
Huntington Beach State Park
Murrells Inlet, South Carolina 29567
803-237-4440

JONES GAP STATE PARK
22

LOCATION   The park's 3,346 acres are 11 miles northwest of Marietta, off U.S. 276.

FEATURES   Jones Gap was named for pioneer Solomon Jones, who founded the early road to North Carolina that went through the Middle Saluda River Gorge. The park is a river and wilderness haven. Jones Gap is included in the 10,000-acre Mountain Bridge Wilderness Area.

ACTIVITIES   Go fishing in the Middle Saluda River. Tour the interpretive center and attend interpretive programs. The park is the trailhead for the Jones Gap Trail, including a five-mile hike to Caesar's Head. You can enjoy primitive camping along the trail. The park also provides access to the Foothills Hiking Trail.

INFORMATION
Jones Gap State Park
303 Jones Gap Road
Marietta, South Carolina 29661
803-836-3647

KEOWEE-TOXAWAY STATE PARK
23

LOCATION   The park's 1,000 acres are on Lake Keowee, at the western end of South Carolina 11, and 15 miles northwest of Pickens.

FEATURES   White explorers came upon the capital of the Lower Cherokee Nation, located south of the park. Here the Cherokee lived until they were forced to move to Oklahoma, along the "Trail of Tears," where over 4,000 of them died before reaching their destination. Their tribal council site, now several hundred feet under Lake Keowee, was also an 18th-century center where British and colonial traders gathered from hundreds of miles, to trade their trinkets for animal skins.

The Toxaway River once flowed a few miles to the north, but now much of its river bed, plus the town of Keowee, have been covered by the lake.

ACTIVITIES   Camp in the 24-site campground, 14 sites with water and electrical hookups, and a dump station, or enjoy primitive camping along the trail. Hike the trails, and go boating and fishing in the park lake. Overnight in the large vacation cabin overlooking Lake Keowee, and tour the park museum to learn more about the Upper Cherokees, who originally owned this land.

Arriving pilots can land at Pickens County Airport, four miles south of the city. A courtesy car is available.

INFORMATION
Keowee-Toxaway State Park
108 Residence Drive
Sunset, South Carolina 29685
803-868-2605

KINGS MOUNTAIN STATE PARK
24

LOCATION   The park's 6,141 acres are 14 miles northwest of York, between South Carolina 161 and I-85, along the foothills of the Appalachian Mountains. It's adjacent to Kings Mountain National Military Park.

FEATURES   Historians believe the Battle of Kings Mountain, fought on October 7, 1780, was a Revolutionary War turning point. The British defeat resulted in an increase in American resistance, that culminated in the British surrendering at Yorktown in 1781.

ACTIVITIES   The park has a restored 1840s homestead called the "Living Farm." Attend Pioneer Days, a two-day event held in September. You can observe competitive shooting, and hear authentic folk music presented by regional artists. Camp in the 118-site campground, with water and electrical hookups, and a dump station, and purchase supplies in the trading post.

Hike 16 miles of nature and hiking trails,, or follow three-mile Clarks Creek Hiking Trail to reach the national park. Come in the spring when the wild azalea and mountain laurel are in bloom. Go horseback riding on 20 miles of bridle trails, with a stable and rental horses available. Go boating, with rentals available. Go fishing in Lake York that is stocked with bass, bream, crappie, and catfish, and go swimming in Lake Crawford. Tour the visitor center and attend interpretive programs. Play carpet golf, or rent a bicycle to go for a bike ride.

Kings Mountain National Military Park is south of Kings Mountain State Park, off I-85. The national park is one of the largest military parks in the country. Walk the self-guiding trail to see the significant battlefield sites. Both the state and national parks include part of the Over Mount Victory Trail, a national historic motor trail. For national park information, call 803-936-7921.

Arriving pilots can land in Charlotte-Douglas Airport, in Charlotte, and Greenville-Spartanburg Airport, between Greenville and Spartanburg. Car rentals are available.

INFORMATION
Kings Mountain State Park
Route 2, Box 230
1277 Park Road
Blacksburg, South Carolina 29702
803-222-3209 or 803-222-9363

LAKE GREENWOOD STATE PARK
25

LOCATION   The park is 17 miles east of Greenwood: from South Carolina 34, go two miles north on South Carolina 702.

*Kings Mountain National Military Park, near Kings Mountain State Park
(photo by Richard Frear, courtesy of the National Park Service)*

ACTIVITIES   The park, spread over five peninsulas, is on the shoreline of 200-mile-long Lake Greenwood. Camp in the 125-site campground, with water and electrical hookups, and a dump station. Hike the nature trail, go swimming, water-skiing, boating from the ramp, and fishing in Lake Greenwood. Supplies are available in the trading post and tackle shop.

Flower lovers can visit the gardens of Park Seed Company, located seven miles north of Greenwood on South Carolina 254. The seeds from these test gardens are sent all over the world. The gardens are at their best during June and early July. Guided tours are available at 9:00, 10:30, 1:00 and 2:30. For information, call 803-941-4213 or 1-800-845-3369.

From the intersection of South Carolina 34 and 248, follow signs south to reach the Ninety Six National Historic Site. This settlement became an important military objective during the Revolutionary War. Two village sites dating from the French and Indian War, and fortifications built during the Revolutionary War, are being restored by the National Park Service. Hike a loop trail to see the settlements and redoubts, to learn more about the history of the region.

Arriving pilots can land at Greenwood County Airport, three miles north of the city. Rental cars are available.

INFORMATION
Lake Greenwood State Park
302 State Park Road
Ninety Six, South Carolina 29666
803-543-3535

LAKE HARTWELL STATE PARK
26

LOCATION   The park is west of Fair Play at the southern end of South Carolina 11, which is the Cherokee Foothills Scenic Highway, near its intersection with I-85 at Exit 1. It's near the South Carolina/Georgia border.

ACTIVITIES   Camp in the 148-site campground, with water and electrical hookups, and a dump station, and purchase supplies from the camp store. Hike the nature trails, go boating from the ramp, and fishing in Lake Hartwell. Purchase fishing supplies in the tackle shop. Tour the visitor center.

The Cherokee Foothills Scenic Highway follows a 130-mile crescent, from I-85 close to the North Carolina border, down to I-85 at the Georgia border. Come in the spring when the peach trees, dogwood, and mountain laurel are in full bloom, or in the fall in mid-October when the leaves take on their fall hues. The highway follows a path once followed by the Cherokee Indians, frontier traders, and bootleggers, and passes through the Blue Ridge foothills.

INFORMATION
Lake Hartwell State Park
19138 A South Highway 11
Fair Play, South Carolina 29643
803-972-3352

LAKE WARREN STATE PARK
27

LOCATION   The park is five miles southwest of Hampton, off South Carolina 363.

ACTIVITIES   Hike the nature trail, go boating from the ramp, and fish in the 200-acre lake. Tour the visitor center.

Arriving pilots can land at Hampton-Varnville Airport, one mile east of the city. No rental cars are available.

INFORMATION
Lake Warren State Park
Route 1-A, Box 208-D
Hampton, South Carolina 29924
803-943-5051

LAKE WATEREE STATE PARK
28

LOCATION   The park is between Columbia and Great Falls, off U.S. 21. It's also 15 miles east of Winnsboro, and eight miles off I-77, Exit 41.

FEATURES   Lake Wateree is the oldest impoundment in the state, and has several hundred miles of shoreline.

ACTIVITIES   Camp in the 72-site campground, with water and electrical hookups, and purchase supplies from the park store. Hike the nature trail, go boating from the ramp, and fishing in Lake Wateree, with a tackle shop available.

In Columbia, tour the Hampton-Preston Mansion and gardens, located on 1615 Blanding Street. Nearby at 1616 Blanding Street is Robert Mills' house and gardens, circa 1823. For information on both houses, call 803-252-1770.

Arriving pilots can land at Fairfield County Airport, three miles southwest of Winnsboro. Rental cars are available.

INFORMATION
Lake Wateree State Park
Route 4, Box 282E-5
Winnsboro, South Carolina 29180
803-482-6126

LANDSFORD CANAL STATE PARK
29

LOCATION   The park is 10 miles south of Rock Hill, on U.S. 21, and six miles northwest of Lancaster, off U.S. 21.

FEATURES   Architect Robert Mills designed a series of canals, including this one, at what was originally called "Land's Ford." This two-mile stretch of navigable water was created to bypass the Catawba River's rapids, which made it impassable to boats and barges. However, the railroad soon put the canal out of business after a few years. This section parallels the Catawba River and is still intact.

ACTIVITIES   The park is open Thursday through Monday. The interpretive center has displays depicting the development of the canal system, and it's also open Thursday through Monday. Bring along a picnic to enjoy beside the Catawba River, and stroll along the 1.5-mile towpath. Walk the nature trail through the hardwoods. Go fishing in the river. Tour the lock-keeper's house on the banks of the Catawba River, to learn how the adjacent early 19th-century canal was built, beginning in 1820.

Stroll through the Glencairn Gardens at Charlotte Avenue and Crest Street, in Rock Hill.

Arriving pilots can land at Lancaster County McWhirter Field, four miles west of Lancaster. Rental cars are available.

INFORMATION
Landsford Canal State Park
Route 1, Box 423
Catawba, South Carolina 29704
803-789-5800

LEE STATE PARK
30

LOCATION   The park is seven miles east of Bishopville, off I-20, on South Carolina 22.

ACTIVITIES   Go camping in the 50-site campground, with water and electrical hookups, and a dump station. Go swimming and boating, with pedal boat rents available. Enjoy fishing for redbreast bream in the Lynches River. The park is also the site of many equestrian events. Hike the nature and hiking trails, or ride the bridle trail. Explore the preserved floodplain swamp.

Arriving pilots can land at Lee County Airport, two miles north of Bishopville. No rental cars are available.

INFORMATION
Lee State Park
Route 2, Box 202
Bishopville, South Carolina 29010
803-428-3833

LITTLE PEE DEE STATE PARK
31

LOCATION   The park is 11 miles southeast of Dillon, off South Carolina 57.
FEATURES   Stephen Foster's original lyrics for his famous song about the Swannee River first read: "Way down upon the Pee Dee River."
ACTIVITIES   Go camping in the 50-site campground, with water and electrical hookups, and a dump station. Hike the nature trail. Go boating, with fishing and pedal boat rentals available. Enjoy fishing for bream in the black water of the Little Pee Dee River, or in the 55-acre lake.

Arriving pilots can land at Dillon County Airport, three miles north of the city. Rental cars are available.
INFORMATION
Little Pee Dee State Park
Route 2, Box 250
Dillon, South Carolina 29536
803-774-8872

LYNCHES RIVER STATE PARK
32

LOCATION   The park is 12 miles southwest of Florence, on U.S. 52.
ACTIVITIES   Camp in the 50-site campground, or overnight in one of the four cabins. Go hiking on the nature and hiking trails, fishing in the Lynches River, and swimming in the Olympic-size pool. Birders enjoy coming here to go bird watching. Go boating, with fishing and pedal boat rentals available. Tour the interpretive center and attend interpretive programs.

Arriving pilots can land at Florence Regional Airport, three miles east of the city. Rental cars are available.
INFORMATION
Lynches River State Park
Route 1, Box 223
Lake City, South Carolina 29560
803-389-2785

MYRTLE BEACH STATE PARK
33

LOCATION   The park is three miles south of Myrtle Beach, on U.S. 17. It's opposite Myrtle Beach Air Force Base, on the Grand Strand.

ACTIVITIES   Camp in the 300-site campground, with water and electrical hookups, and a dump station, or overnight in one of the five vacation cabins. Purchase supplies from the trading post.

Tour the visitor center and attend interpretive programs, presented year-round. Hike the nature trails, and enjoy surfing, excellent deep-sea and surf fishing from the 730-foot fishing pier. Go swimming in the ocean or in the pool.

Myrtle Beach is known as a golf and tennis resort community. Over 80 championship golf courses are located within a half hour's drive of the area. In 1991, *Golf Digest* magazine named North Myrtle Beach's Tidewater Golf Club as America's best new golf course. For information, call 803-626-7444. Attend the annual Canadian-American Days Festival in mid-March, and the Myrtle Beach Sun Fun Festival in early June. Tennis players can participate in the annual Myrtle Beach Tennis Festival. Contact the Chamber of Commerce at 1-800-356-3016, Extension 110, for information.

Attend performances at the Alabama Theatre at Barefoot Landing, at 4750 U.S. 17 South. Reservations are required. Call 803-272-1111. You can also go to the Carolina Opry at the intersection of U.S. 17 and the U.S. 17 Bypass, south of Restaurant Row. For required reservations, call 803-238-8888 or 1-800-843-6779. The "Dixie Stampede" is also located at the intersection of U.S. 17 and the U.S. 17 Bypass. For performance reservations, call 803-497-9700.

Tonight Mark Twain! is a live theater matinee presentation at 2:00 P.M. on Wednesday afternoons, from mid-March through the end of September, at the Southern Country Nights Theater in Surfside Beach. Call 803-238-8888 or 1-800-843-6779 for information.

Tour Brookgreen Gardens, located four miles southwest of Murrells Inlet, off U.S. 17, to see the world's largest collection of outdoor statuary. Over 500 of America's finest 19th- and 20th-century sculptures, done by artists including Frederic Remington and Daniel Chester French, are exhibited among 2,000 plant species. Programs and tours are offered daily. For information, call 803-237-4218.

Myrtle Beach Opry's 600-seat theater features a family music show that combines the best of comedy, country, gospel, and 50's rock and roll. Other theaters in the area include Dixie Jubilee, Alabama Theater, Gatlin Brothers Theatre, Legends in Concert Theatre, Euro Circus, Magic on Ice, and Medieval Knights Dinner Theater. Contact the Chamber of Commerce at 1-800-356-3016, for further information.

Arriving pilots can land at Myrtle Beach Jetport International Airport, three miles southwest of the city. Rental cars are available.

INFORMATION
Myrtle Beach State Park
U.S. No. 17-S
Myrtle Beach, South Carolina 29577
803-238-5325

OCONEE STATE PARK
34

LOCATION   The park is 12 miles northwest of Walhalla, off South Carolina 28. It's also near Mountain Rest on South Carolina 107.

FEATURES   Look for some of the stonework laid in the park during the 1930s by the Civilian Conservation Corps. You can still see an old overshot waterwheel, that was used to supply power in the earlier days.

ACTIVITIES   Take the self-driving auto tour. Camp in the 140-site campground, with water and electrical hookups, and a dump station, or overnight in one of the 19 vacation cabins. Purchase your camping supplies from the park store. Hike the nature and hiking trails, and go boating, with fishing-boat, pedal boat, and canoe rentals available. Go fishing and swimming in the park lake. Tour the visitor center and attend interpretive programs. Play carpet golf.

The Foothills Trail ends here after following the ridges of the North Carolina–South Carolina line from Table Rock. You can camp along the trail in primitive campsites.

Oconee Station State Park is four miles off South Carolina 11, onto South Carolina 95. Here you'll see the oldest structure in the state, built in the early 1790s, used to protect frontier families from the Indians.

Stumphouse Mountain Tunnel, and 200-foot Issaqueena Falls, are off South Carolina 28, five miles north of Walhalla. No steam locomotive ever passed through this 1,600-foot tunnel, built to link the Port of Charleston to the Midwest, when its builders went broke. Bring along a flashlight if you decide to go exploring. Hike the nature trail to reach the 200-foot falls.

Walhalla National Fish Hatchery is north of the park, off South Carolina 107. You'll see where the trout are raised that later wind up in the streams of several Appalachian states.

Walhalla's Main Street is lined with many majestic antebellum homes. The town was originally settled by the Germans in the mid-19th century, and was named after the mythical Norse paradise of Valhalla.

INFORMATION
Oconee State Park
624 State Park Road
Mountain Rest, South Carolina 29664
803-638-5353

OLD DORCHESTER STATE PARK
35

LOCATION   The park is six miles south of Summerville on South Carolina 642, and northwest of Charleston.

FEATURES   The park preserves the remnants of the former community of Dorchester, settled in 1696 by Congregationalists from Massachusetts. The villagers moved away following the Revolution, and unfortunately the village was destroyed by retreating British soldiers in 1781. Today you can still see the ruins of the fort, the bell tower of St. George's Church, and village excavations.

ACTIVITIES   Go boating from the ramp, hike the trails, and enjoy fishing in the Ashley River. Picnic near the ruins of the 18th-century town. Archeological relics are on display in the small museum.

Arriving pilots can land at Dorchester County Airport, five miles northwest of Summerville. Rental cars are available.

INFORMATION
Old Dorchester State Park
300 State Park Road
Summerville, South Carolina 29485
803-873-1740

OLD SANTEE CANAL STATE PARK
36

LOCATION   The park is one mile east of Moncks Corner, off the U.S. 52 bypass. It's three miles south of Lake Moultrie.

FEATURES   Old Santee Canal, circa 1800, runs for over a mile along Lake Moultrie's Tail Race Canal. It contains the southern end of the Santee Canal, the first channel canal that was dug in America.

ACTIVITIES   Go boating from the ramp, rent a canoe to go canoeing along the southern end of the canal, and go fishing in the river. Tour the visitor center and attend interpretive programs. Walk along the boardwalks through the Biggin Creek Basin, or go horseback riding on the bridle trail.

Lake Moultrie offers some of the state's best fishing for landlocked striped bass, and is stocked with bream, crappie, and catfish.

Arriving pilots can land at Berkeley County Airport, one mile southwest of Moncks Corner. Rental cars are available.

INFORMATION
Old Santee Canal State Park
900 Stoney Landing Road
Moncks Corner, South Carolina 29461
803-899-5200

PARIS MOUNTAIN STATE PARK
37

LOCATION   The park is nine miles north of Greenville, off U.S. 25. Go right on South Carolina 253 and follow signs.

FEATURES   The park encompasses three lakes.

ACTIVITIES   Rent a pedal boat on Lake Placid, or drive along its four miles of mountainous roads. Camp in the 50-site campground, with both modern and primitive sites. It has 50 sites with water and electrical hookups, and a dump station. Go canoeing, with rentals available, swimming in the crystal-clear water, or fishing in the three stocked lakes. Hike the trails.

Arriving pilots can land at Greenville Downtown Airport, three miles east of the city, or at Donaldson Center Airport, six miles south of the city. Rental cars are available at both airports.

INFORMATION
Paris Mountain State Park
2401 State Park Road
Greenville, South Carolina 29609
803-244-5565

POINSETT STATE PARK
38

LOCATION   The park's 1,000 acres are on the edge of the Wateree Swamp, 18 miles southwest of Sumter near Wedgefield, off South Carolina 261.

FEATURES   Rhododendron and mountain laurel grow here beside the moss-draped oak trees.

ACTIVITIES   Camp in the 50-site campground, with water and electrical hookups, and a dump station. Hike the nature and hiking trails, go boating, with fishing and pedal boat rentals available. Go fishing and swimming in the park lake. Overnight in one of the four vacation cabins, tour the visitor center and attend interpretive programs, presented year-round.

Congaree Swamp National Monument is 20 miles southeast of Columbia, off South Carolina 48, west of the park. Follow its self-guided canoe trail, walk the 3/4-mile boardwalk, or explore 18 miles of hiking trails. The area is known for its record-size trees. For information, call 803-776-4396.

Arriving pilots can land at Sumter Municipal Airport, four miles north of the city. Rental cars are available.

INFORMATION
Poinsett State Park
Route 1, Box 38
6660 Poinsett Park Road
Wedgefield, South Carolina 29168
803-494-8177

REDCLIFFE PLANTATION STATE PARK
39

LOCATION   Redcliffe is three miles southeast of Beech Island, off U.S. 278.
FEATURES   Redcliffe was the home of Governor, Congressman, and Senator Hammond, and later of John S. Billings, a journalist and former editor for Time-Life.
ACTIVITIES   Tour the Southern antebellum plantation, where you can see many of the original furnishings. The house is open for tours weekends and by appointment. Hike the nature trail, go fishing in the small pond. Tour the interpretive center.
INFORMATION
Redcliffe Plantation State Park
181 Redcliffe Road
Beech Island, South Carolina 19841
803-827-1473

RIVERS BRIDGE STATE PARK
40

LOCATION   The park is seven miles southwest of Ehrhardt, off South Carolina 64, and 13 miles east of Allendale, one mile off U.S. 601.
FEATURES   In February, 1865, the Confederate cavalry attempted to stop General William Sherman's march from Savannah, north to Virginia. A Georgia Confederate colonel then boasted that he could hold his position here at Rivers Bridge "until next Christmas if you can keep them [Sherman's army] off my flanks." The effort failed. The park is the only one commemorating the Confederacy, and the bodies of the Confederate soldiers who died here were later brought back for reburial. Today you can still see the ruins of the old Confederate fortifications.
ACTIVITIES   Go camping in the 25-site campground, with water and electrical hookups, and a dump station. Enjoy a picnic, and go swimming in the pool. Hike the mile-long nature trail through the oaks, that are covered with Spanish moss. If you come in early April, you can see the wisteria, dogwood, and native azalea in bloom. Go fishing along the river and in the creek for crappies, catfish, gar, and largemouth bass. Go boating from the ramp.

Wander through the small brick museum, open Monday through Friday, and weekend afternoons.

Arriving pilots can land at Allendale County Airport, two miles southeast of the city. Rental cars are available.

INFORMATION
Rivers Bridge State Park
Route 1
Ehrhardt, South Carolina 29081
803-267-3675

ROSE HILL PLANTATION STATE PARK
41

LOCATION   The state park is off U.S. 176, seven miles north of Whitmire, on Sardis Road. It's also accessible off South Carolina 2, eight miles southwest of Union.

FEATURES   The stucco mansion was constructed between 1818 and 1832, and is enhanced by its 160-year-old magnolia trees. It was immortalized in Margaret Mitchell's classic, *Gone with the Wind.* William Henry Gist, the Secessionist Governor, lived here in 1858.

ACTIVITIES   Go through the clapboard building housing exhibits from the local cotton culture, and 19th-century life. The grounds are open Thursday through Monday. Tour the mansion on weekends, or during the week by appointment. Attend interpretive programs. Bring along a picnic to enjoy, and hike the 1/4-mile nature trail. Admission is charged for mansion tours.

Arriving pilots can land at Union County–Troy Shelton Field, one mile southwest of Union. Rental cars are available.

INFORMATION
Rose Hill Plantation State Park
Sardis Road, Route 2
Union, South Carolina 29379
803-427-5966

SADLERS CREEK STATE PARK
42

LOCATION   The park is on a peninsula extending into Lake Hartwell, 12 miles southwest of Anderson, off U.S. 29. It's also 12 miles from I-85, Exit 14.

ACTIVITIES   Camp in the 100-site campground, with water and electrical hookups, open year-round. Go walking along the nature paths, or go boating and fishing for trophy-size bass in Lake Hartwell.

INFORMATION
Sadlers Creek State Park
940 Sadlers Creek Park Road
Anderson, South Carolina 29642
803-226-8950

SANTEE STATE PARK
43

LOCATION   The park is 1½ miles west on South Carolina 6 from I-95, Exit 98, on the northwest shore of Lake Marion. It's also three miles northwest of Santee, off U.S. 301.

ACTIVITIES   Hike the nature trails, camp in the 150-site campground, with water and electrical hookups, and a dump station, or rent one of 30 cabins. Go boating in the lake from the ramp, with fishing and pedal boat rentals available. Enjoy swimming, tour the visitor center, and attend interpretive programs. Play tennis, and dine in the restaurant. You can also purchase supplies in the camp store or tackle store. Rent a bicycle to go cycling.

Lake Marion boasts some of the state's finest fishing. Anglers try their luck at landing landlocked striped bass, plus stocked bream, crappie, and catfish. Participate in a fishing tournament.

Across Lake Marion is the Santee National Wildlife Refuge, five miles north of Santee on U.S. 15/301, or from I-95, take Exit 102. As many as 20,000 geese come to winter here. Hike the nature trail, and go up the observation tower to get a look at the wildlife. Fort Watson, a British outpost used during the Revolutionary War, is located within the refuge. The refuge is open for day-use only. For information, call 803-478-2217.

INFORMATION
Santee State Park
Route 1, Box 79
Santee, South Carolina 29142
803-854-2408

SESQUICENTENNIAL STATE PARK
44

LOCATION   The park is in the middle of the sandhills region, 13 miles northeast of Columbia on U.S. 1, and three miles from I-20.

ACTIVITIES   Go camping in the 87-site campground, with water and electrical hookups, and a dump station. Hike the nature trail, or work out on the exercise trail. Go lake fishing, swimming, and boating, with canoe, fishing and pedal boat rentals available. Tour the visitor center and attend year-round interpretive programs. A log house on the park grounds dates back to 1756.

Arriving pilots can land at Columbia Metropolitan Airport, five miles southwest of the city, or at Columbia Owens Downtown Airport, two miles south of the city. Both airports have rental cars.

INFORMATION
Sesquicentennial State Park
9564-D Two Notch Road
Columbia, South Carolina 29223
803-788-2706

TABLE ROCK STATE PARK
45

LOCATION   The park's 3,083 acres are 16 miles north of Pickens, off South Carolina 11.

FEATURES   Table Rock was revered by the Cherokee as the dining spot of the Great Spirit. A nearby mountain called "The Stool" was believed to be where the Great Spirit sat. Table Rock rises 1,000 feet, and has black mineral deposit stains flowing down its steep sides.

ACTIVITIES   The rounded dome of Table Rock shelters this park, where you can go camping in the 100-site campground, with water and electrical hookups, and a dump station, or overnight in one of the 14 cabins. Purchase supplies in the camp store, and play carpet golf.

Hike 14 miles of nature and hiking trails, including one leading to the summit of Table Rock Mountain. The Carrick Creek Nature Trail takes you through rhododendron and mountain laurel. The South Carolina portion of the Foothills Trail begins here in the park. Hikers can continue for almost 85 miles to Oconee State Park via this trail, with primitive campsites located along its route. For trail information, write the Foothills Trail, P.O. Box 3041, Greenville, South Carolina 29602, or call 803-268-8456.

Go boating, with fishing-boat, canoe, and pedal boat rentals available. Enjoy fishing from the pier, and swimming in the park lake. Tour the visitor center and attend interpretive programs. Dine in the Table Rock Lodge Restaurant, famous for its country-style Sunday buffets, and enjoy dancing at one of their summer dances.

Arriving pilots can land at Pickens County Airport, four miles south of the city. A courtesy car is available.

INFORMATION
Table Rock State Park
246 Table Rock State Park Road
Pickens, South Carolina 29671
803-878-9813: park
803-878-9065: restaurant

WOODS BAY STATE PARK
46

LOCATION   The park is three miles west of Olanta, off I-95 and U.S. 301.

FEATURES   A unique feature, Carolina Bay, is located in the park and contains an unusual depression that holds enough water for an alligator pond. Many believe that a cataclysmic meteor shower came down upon the Southeast centuries ago, creating hundreds of these indentations in the earth's crust.

ACTIVITIES   Follow the boardwalk out into the watery, 1,541-acre forest, or explore the canoe trail through the bayoulike bay. Go fishing and boating, with canoe rentals available. Hike the nature trail and attend interpretive programs. Equestrians can ride the bridle trail.

INFORMATION
Woods Bay State Park
Route 1, Box 208
Olanta, South Carolina 29114
803-659-4445

TENNESSEE

Tennessee has over 50 state parks that were established to preserve some of the state's finest scenery, including majestic waterfalls dropping into ancient river gorges. Historic areas are preserved at Pinson Mounds, Old Stone Fort, and the Chucalissa Indian Village at T. O. Fuller State Park. Visit Davy Crockett's birthplace, and follow in the footsteps of the state's early settlers at Sycamore Shoals and Fort Loudoun. Civil War history is featured at Fort Pillow and Nathan Bedford Forrest State Historic Areas.

The parks have over 2,600 campsites. Although reservations aren't accepted for the campgrounds, you can make advance reservations for their inns and cabins. Priority is given to requests for weekly cabin reservations from Memorial Day through Labor Day.

Senior citizens are given a 10 percent year-round discount for overnight lodging in state park inns. Seniors are also given free green fees on all state park golf courses on Mondays, excluding holidays. Seniors who reside in Tennessee are also provided with a 50 percent discount, when the vehicle is registered in your name. Non-resident camping seniors are given discounts at Cove Lake, Fall Creek Falls, Harrison Bay, Roan Mountain, and Warrior's Path. To contact the state parks, write to 401 Church Street, Nashville, TN 37243-0446, or call 1-800-421-6683 or 615-532-0001.

For a scenic drive, follow the Tennessee Scenic Parkway System. It covers over 2,300 miles of highways, and connects the state parks, major lakes, historic sites, and recreational attractions. The parkway is marked with Tennessee's state bird, the mockingbird.

Hikers have access to many trails through the state including the Trail of the Lonesome Pine. Section I of this trail traverses 35 miles along the crest of the Clinch Mountains, north of Knoxville. Primitive camping is permitted along its length.

Come in the fall to drive through the Great Smoky Mountains, where some of the best color to be found anywhere, is located. The season usually begins in the high country of the east during the last week of September, and runs through mid-November in the lowlands along the Mississippi River. Peak color in the Smokies occurs the last half of October. For color updates, call the hotline at 1-800-697-4200, from the end of September through mid-November.

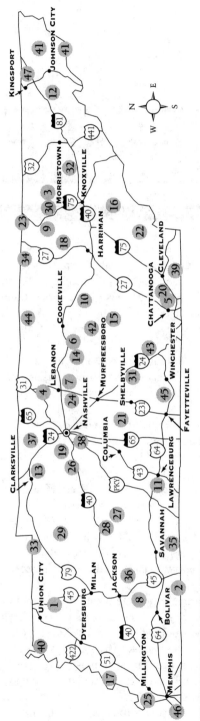

TENNESSEE STATE PARKS

1. Big Cypress Tree State Natural Area
2. Big Hill Pond State Area
3. Big Ridge State Park
4. Bledsoe Creek State Park
5. Booker T. Washington State Park
6. Burgess Falls State Natural Area
7. Cedars of Lebanon State Park
8. Chickasaw State Park
9. Cove Lake State Park
10. Cumberland Mountain State Park
11. David Crockett State Park
12. Davy Crockett Birthplace State Park
13. Dunbar Cave State Park
14. Edgar Evins State Park

15. Fall Creek Falls State Park
16. Fort Loudoun State Historic Area
17. Fort Pillow State Park
18. Frozen Head State Natural Area
19. Harpeth Scenic River/Narrows of the Harpeth State Historic Area
20. Harrison Bay State Park
21. Henry Horton State Park
22. Hiwassee Scenic River State Park
23. Indian Mountain State Park
24. Long Hunter State Park
25. Meeman-Shelby Forest State Park
26. Montgomery Bell State Park
27. Mousetail Landing State Park
28. Natchez Trace State Park

29. Nathan Bedford Forrest State Historical Area
29. Johnsonville State Historic Park
30. Norris Dam State Park
31. Old Stone Fort State Archeological Area
32. Panther Creek State Park
33. Paris Landing State Park
34. Pickett State Park
35. Pickwick Landing State Park
36. Pinson Mounds State Archeological Park
37. Port Royal State Historical Park
38. Radnor Lake State Natural Area
39. Red Clay State Historical Park

40. Reelfoot Lake State Park
41. Roan Mountain State Park
41. Sycamore Shoals State Historical Area
42. Rock Island State Park
42. Bone Cave State Natural Area
43. South Cumberland State Recreation Area
44. Standing Stone State Park
45. Tims Ford State Park
46. T. O. Fuller State Park
47. Warrior's Path State Park

Memphis is called the home of "King Cotton" and "The King" after Elvis Presley, whose estate, Graceland, is visited by millions of fans from around the world. Nashville is also referred to as "Music City USA," and Chattanooga is famous for its Lookout Mountain attractions and Civil War battlefields.

BIG CYPRESS TREE STATE NATURAL AREA
1

LOCATION   The area is off U.S. 45E/Kimery Road, northwest of Greenfield.

FEATURES   The 283-acre natural area is in the flood plain of the Middle Fork of the Obion River.

ACTIVITIES   Go hiking through the bottomland hardwood forest. Contact the local ranger for a tour of the area. Bring along a picnic to enjoy.

INFORMATION
Big Cypress Tree State Natural Area
U.S. Highway 45E/Kimery Road
Greenfield, Tennessee 38230
901-235-2700

BIG HILL POND STATE AREA
2

LOCATION   The park is 15 miles south of Selmer, and 10 miles west of Eastview, on Tennessee 57. It's at the junction of the Tuscumbia and Hatchie State Scenic Rivers.

FEATURES   Big Hill has a cypress-lined pond, created during levy construction for the Memphis-Charleston Railroad.

ACTIVITIES   The 4,218-acre park has a 30-site campground, without hookups. Enjoy backpacking and hiking on the nature trails. Go boating from the ramp, with rentals available, and bass fishing in Traviss McNatt fishing lake. Tour the visitor center and attend interpretive programs. Follow the boardwalk through the scenic wetland.

Arriving pilots can land at Robert Sibley Airport, six miles northeast of Selmer. Rental cars are available.

INFORMATION
Big Hill Pond State Area
Route 1, Box 150 C
Pocahontas, Tennessee 38061
901-645-7967

BIG RIDGE STATE PARK
3

LOCATION   The park is at 1015 Big Ridge Road in Maynardville. It's 14 miles northeast of Norris, and east of I-75, on Tennessee 61.

FEATURES   The area includes 3,642 acres along the shore of beautiful Norris Reservoir.

ACTIVITIES   Rent a horse to go riding. Camp in the 48-site campground, all sites with water and electrical hookups, or overnight in one of the 19 cabins. Hike the nature trails. Go canoeing and boating from the ramp, with boat rentals available. Enjoy bass fishing and swimming in Norris Reservoir. Tour the visitor center, attend interpretive programs, and get a snack at the snack bar.

INFORMATION
Big Ridge State Park
1015 Big Ridge Road
Route 1
Maynardville, Tennessee 37807
615-992-5523

BLEDSOE CREEK STATE PARK
4

LOCATION   The park is four miles east of Gallatin, on Tennessee 25.

FEATURES   The park is along the Bledsoe Creek Embayment of Old Hickory Reservoir, near the old 1780s settlement of Cairo.

ACTIVITIES   Camp in the 133-site campground, 100 sites with water and electrical hookups, dump station, and a laundry. Enjoy hiking six miles of trails, including the 1.5-mile-long nature trail. In Old Hickory Lake, go catfish fishing, water-skiing, and boating from two ramps. Enjoy a boat cruise.

Tour the historic site of Wynnewood in Castalian Springs, eight miles east of Gallatin, on Tennessee 25. Circa 1828, the structure was probably the largest log structure ever erected in the state, and was used as a stagecoach inn and mineral springs resort. It's open daily from April through October, and is closed Sundays from November through March, except by appointment. Call 615-452-5463.

Cragfont is seven miles east of Gallatin on Tennessee 25. Circa 1802, the three-story home was lived in by frontiersman James Winchester. For information, call 615-452-7070. The Trousdale Place, circa the early 1800s, is at 183 West Main, and is a National Registered Historic Landmark. For information, call 615-452-7854.

Arriving pilots can land at Sumner County Regional Airport, located two miles east of Gallatin. Rental cars are available.

INFORMATION
Bledsoe Creek State Park
400 Zieglers Fort Road
State Highway 25/Route 2, Box 60
Gallatin, Tennessee 37066
615-452-3706

BOOKER T. WASHINGTON STATE PARK
5

LOCATION   The park is six miles northeast of Chattanooga, off Tennessee 58, on the shore of Chickamauga Reservoir.

FEATURES   The park was named for Booker Taliaferro Washington, born a slave in 1856, in Virginia. He began as a laborer and then went on to become the president of Tuskegee Institute. He is particularly remembered for his hard efforts toward helping his people find equality through achieving economic independence.

ACTIVITIES   Hike the nature trails in the 250-acre park. Go boating from the ramp, with rentals available at the marina. Anglers come to fish in Lake Chickamauga for bass, walleye, sauger, and catfish. Camp in the group campground, or overnight in a cabin. No individual campsites are available. Swim in the lake or pool, and purchase snacks in the concession building.

Falling Water Falls is nearby on Signal Mountain, nine miles north of town, on U.S. 127. The mountain was named during the Civil War, when it was utilized as a signaling point by the Confederate army.

Chickamauga-Chattanooga Battlefield is the nation's oldest, largest, and most visited military park. The railroad made Chattanooga an important Civil War objective, and battles for its possession were among the bloodiest in history. For more detail, see Harrison Bay State Park.

Watch the 3-D display that recreates the Civil War battle of Chickamauga-Chattanooga, at Confederama. It's on 3742 Tennessee Avenue. For information, call 615-821-2812.

Tour Rock City Gardens, five miles southwest of town on Lookout Mountain, via Tennessee 58 and Georgia 157. The gardens feature 10 acres of lichen-covered sandstone formations. Stop by Lover's Leap and Observation Point, for a panoramic view of seven states. For information, call 706-820-2531.

Take a riverboat cruise from March through December on the Tennessee River, beginning at Ross' Landing on Broad Street. For information, call 615-266-4488.

Ride the Lookout Mountain Incline Railway, boarding either on St. Elmo Avenue or on top of the mountain, three blocks from Point Park. The railway is the world's steepest, reaching a grade of 72.7 percent. For information, call 615-821-4224 or 615-629-1411.

To see a 145-foot natural waterfall, that flows 1,120 feet beneath the surface of Lookout Mountain, go to the Lookout Mountain Caverns located west of town. Take Exit 174 or 179A, off I-24 and follow signs. Guided tours cover .8-mile. For information, call 615-821-2544.

Arriving pilots can land at Dallas Bay Sky Park, located 11 miles north of Chattanooga. Rental cars are available.

INFORMATION
Booker T. Washington State Park
5801 Champion Road
Route 2, Box 369
Chattanooga, Tennessee 37416
615-894-4955

BURGESS FALLS STATE NATURAL AREA
6

LOCATION   The area is on Burgess Falls Road, Route 6, in Sparta. It's also eight miles south of I-40, near Cookeville.

FEATURES   Falling Water River contains some of the most beautiful cascading waterfalls in the state, the remnants of historic waterworks.

ACTIVITIES   Bring along a picnic, and hike the trails along the gorge of the Falling Water River. Guided tours are available. Go boating from the ramp.

The Rock House, now a National Shrine, is five miles east of town on Tennessee 70E. This 1840s stagecoach stop was visited by Andrew Jackson when he traveled to Washington D.C. It's open by appointment. Contact the Chamber of Commerce at 615-738-8830.

Virgin Falls, 11 miles east of Sparta on Tennessee 70, is formed by an underground stream that emerges to drop over a 110-foot cliff, and returns to a cave located at its base. You can go backpacking, and hike eight miles along the National Recreation Trail.

Arriving pilots can land at Upper Cumberland Regional Airport, located nine miles northwest of Sparta. It's five miles from the state park. Rental cars are available on request.

INFORMATION
Burgess Falls State Natural Area
4000 Burgess Falls Drive
Route 6
Cookeville, Tennessee 38502
615-432-6568

CEDARS OF LEBANON STATE PARK
7

LOCATION   The park is eight miles south of Lebanon, on U.S. 231. It's also south of I-40.

FEATURES   During the Depression, the pencil industry logged all the cedar from the area, but it was replanted by the WPA. Now the park contains the largest remaining red cedar forest in the U.S. The park was named for the Cedars of Lebanon that once lived on King Solomon's land.

ACTIVITIES   Go hiking on the nature trails, and camp in the 166-site campground, 90 sites with water and electrical hookups, and a laundry. Go swimming in the Olympic-size pool, and tour the interpretive center. Overnight in one of the nine cabins. Food is available at the snack bar and in the camp store. Rent a horse at the stable, play Frisbee golf, and tennis. Rent a bicycle to go cycling. The park also has a recreation center.

Enjoy the annual wildflower tours in April, when over 20 native wildflowers burst into bloom.

Arriving pilots can land at Lebanon Municipal Airport, two miles southwest of Lebanon. Rental cars are available.

INFORMATION
Cedars of Lebanon State Park
328 Cedar Forest Road
Route 6
Lebanon, Tennessee 37087
615-443-2769

CHICKASAW STATE PARK
8

LOCATION   The park is eight miles west of Henderson, on Tennessee 100.

ACTIVITIES   The park and forest cover 14,280 acres, making it one of Tennessee's largest state parks. Enjoy hiking through the Chickasaw State Forest, and rent a horse to go horseback riding. Camp in the 75-site campground, 54 sites with water and electrical hookups, and pick up supplies in the camp store. Go bass fishing, and boating, with rentals available, and swim in one of the two lakes.

Rent one of the 13 air-conditioned cabins, nestled under the tall pines. Dine in the restaurant or get a snack from the snack bar, and purchase a souvenir from the gift shop. Try your skill at archery, and play tennis.

INFORMATION
Chickasaw State Park
20 Cabin Lane
State Highway 100
Henderson, Tennessee 38340
901-989-5141

COVE LAKE STATE PARK
9

LOCATION   The park is one mile north of Caryville, off U.S. 25W.

FEATURES   Cove Lake is at the eastern edge of the Cumberland Mountains. During the winter, several hundred Canadian geese come here to feed.

ACTIVITIES   Enjoy camping in the 97-site campground, with water and electrical hookups, and a dumping station. Rent a bicycle to go biking along bike trails, passing through the grasslands and mountains. Go boating in Cove Lake (rentals available), bass fishing, and swimming. Attend interpretive programs, and play tennis. Dine in the restaurant or pick up a snack at the snack bar, both open seasonally. Purchase a souvenir in the gift shop, or try your skill at archery.

Hike along Section II of the Cumberland State Scenic Trail. This section of the trail goes for 30 miles along the Cumberland Plateau, from Oliver Springs to Caryville. You can do primitive camping along the way.

Go to nearby Devil's Race Trace that has a steep pinnacle rock, providing a great panoramic view of the area.

INFORMATION
Cove Lake State Park
Route 2, Box 108
Caryville, Tennessee 37714
615-566-8355 or 615-566-9701

CUMBERLAND MOUNTAIN STATE PARK
10

LOCATION   The park is six miles south of Crossville, on U.S. 127.

FEATURES   The park features a 50-acre lake, stone dam, and seven-arch stone bridge that spans Byrd Lake. The bridge is the largest masonry structure constructed by the CCC. The 1,400-acre park is on the largest remaining timberland plateau in the U.S., 2,000 feet above sea level.

ACTIVITIES   Enjoy a picnic, and go camping in the 147-site campground, all sites with water and electrical hookups, and a camp store. Go swimming, boating, with rentals available, and fishing in the 50-acre lake. Overnight in one of the 36 cabins located within the hardwoods, and dine in the restaurant overlooking the lake.

Purchase a snack from the snack bar, and a souvenir from the gift shop. Hike the nature trails, including one beside the lake, and rent a horse from the stable to go horseback riding. Play tennis on one of the three courts, play disc golf, and go backpacking.

Nearby you can visit the historic Cumberland Homestead's tower, and tour its museum. Also nearby are the Piney and Ozone Falls Natural Areas, the Sequatchie Valley, and the Catoosa Wildlife Management Area. The Catoosa Refuge is the state's largest refuge, where spelunkers can explore many caverns.

In Crossville, attend a performance presented at the Cumberland County Playhouse, three miles west of town on Tennessee 70S. Take Exit 317 off I-40. Productions are given Friday through Sunday, from March through November, with Thursday performances during the summer. For reservations, call 615-484-5000 or 615-484-2300. Attend the Cumberland Mountain Spring Festival in Crossville, in early May.

Arriving pilots can land at Crossville Municipal Airport, three miles west of the city. Rental cars are available.

INFORMATION
Cumberland Mountain State Park
Route 8, Box 322
Crossville, Tennessee 38555
615-484-6138

DAVID CROCKETT STATE PARK
11

LOCATION   It's one mile west of Lawrenceburg, on U.S. 64, on the banks of Shoal Creek.

FEATURES   David moved his family here, to the head of Shoal Creek, in September, 1817. Today the state park is located where Crockett once operated his powder mill, grist mill, and distillery. Unfortunately, they were all washed away by floods. Today you can still see an exhibit of the water-powered grist mill.

ACTIVITIES   Play tennis on the lighted courts. Enjoy camping in the 107-site campground, all sites with water and electrical hookups. Hike the trails, or rent a bike to ride the bicycle trails. Go swimming in the Olympic-size pool. Go fishing and boating in the stream, with boat rentals available. Purchase a souvenir from the gift shop, and try your skill at archery.

Attend summer dinner theater performances. Reservations are required. Call 615-762-9541. Tour the visitor center, staffed summers. Dine year-round in the 200-seat restaurant, or pick up a snack from the snack bar, open seasonally.

Explore the 2.5-mile, one-way road along the original Old Natchez Trace, at Mile Marker 375.8. You'll get several overlooks from the ridge of the surrounding countryside.

Arriving pilots can land at Lawrenceburg Municipal Airport, three miles northeast of the city. It's five miles from the park. A courtesy car is available for transportation into town.

INFORMATION
David Crockett State Park
1400 West Gaines
P.O. Box 398
Lawrenceburg, Tennessee 38464
615-762-9408

DAVY CROCKETT BIRTHPLACE STATE PARK
12

LOCATION   The park is midway between Jonesborough and Greeneville, 3.5 miles off U.S. 11E. It's along the bank of the Nolichucky River. Take U.S. 11-E for nine miles to Tennessee 107. Turn left, heading toward Tusculum.

FEATURES   Davy Crockett wasn't born on a mountaintop as the ballad says. However, his birthplace on the Nolichucky River contains a replica of the cabin where he was born, on August 17, 1786.

Davy Crockett was known for his hunting skills, tall tales, and courageous volunteer spirit.

ACTIVITIES   Tour the visitor center and museum, and take a self-guided tour of the bluff-top trail through Crockett's woods. The museum is closed weekends from Labor Day through Memorial Day. Camp in the 75-site campground, open year-round, all sites with water and electrical hookups, and 38 with sewer hookups. Look for the limestone marker and cabin where Crockett was born.

Swim in the pool, go fishing for catfish in the river, or go canoeing. Take a guided raft trip down the Nolichucky River. It has Class I, II, III, and IV rapids. It's more difficult to raft above Ervine, but more pastoral below.

Jonesborough, Tennessee's oldest town that was founded in 1779, is listed on the National Register. Stop by the visitor center at 117 Boone Street, to arrange for a tour of four historic houses: Chester Inn, Sister's Row, Gammon-Sterling House, and the Mansion House.

Special events in Jonesborough include the Old Time Country Radio Reunion in mid-May, Jonesborough Days over the 4th of July, a national storytelling festival in early October, and Christmas in Olde Jonesborough featuring a tour of homes. For information, call 615-753-5961. Come to the area in the fall when the Appalachian Mountains take on their many fall colors. For an unforgettable flight, go flying over these mountains when the colors reach their peak, to see an incomparable fairyland.

In Greeneville, visit Andrew Johnson National Historic Site, set aside to honor the 17th President of the U.S. It's at the corner of Depot and College Streets, one block east of Main Street. His tailor shop forms part of the interpretive museum, and the park also has his two Greeneville residences. The cemetery in which he is buried is at the end of Monument Avenue, one block south of West Main Street. For historic site information, call 615-638-3551.

You can also visit the Samuel Doak-Johnson Museum at Tusculum College, on the outskirts of East Greeneville. Circa 1818, the house has period furniture, and craft demonstration studios. It's open Tuesday through Saturday, March through December. For information, call 615-639-4681.

Arriving pilots can land at Greeneville Municipal Airport, two miles north of Greeneville. Rental cars are available.

INFORMATION
Davy Crockett Birthplace State Park
1245 Davy Crockett Park Road
Route 3, Box 103A
Limestone, Tennessee 37681
615-257-2167

DUNBAR CAVE STATE PARK
13

LOCATION   The park is three miles northeast of Clarksville, and south of U.S. 79, on Tennessee 13.

FEATURES   Monthly square dances were once held in the cave mouth, attended by many Grand Ole Opry stars. This area is laced with caves and sinkholes, and Dunbar Cave is its most prominent. It's been occupied for thousands of years because of its stream and natural air conditioning.

ACTIVITIES   Take a one-hour guided tour of the cave, offered by reservation only. Call for a tour schedule. The cave is open for groups Monday through Friday year-round, and for individuals on weekends from April through September. Go fishing in the small lake near the cave entrance, hike the nature trail, and tour the visitor center.

Much of downtown Clarksville is listed on the National Register of Historic Places. Pick up a walking-tour map from the Chamber of Commerce at 312 Madison Street, or call 615-647-2331. Take a free tour of the Beachhaven Vineyards and Winery, off I-24 at Exit 4. For information, call 615-645-8867. Take a walk beside the Cumberland River on Riverside Drive.

Tour the Smith-Trahern Mansion, off U.S. 79 on Smith Street. Circa 1858, it overlooks the Cumberland River, and has a curved staircase, and widow's walk along the roof. It's open Monday through Friday from 9:30 to 2:30, and closed major holidays. For information, call 615-648-9998.

Take a cruise on the Cumberland River aboard the *Queen of Clarksville* Riverboat. Board it at McGregor Park on Riverside Drive. For schedules, call 615-647-5500 or 615-552-2442. Attend the Old Time Fiddlers' Championship in Clarksville in early April, the Mayfest at the Beachhaven Winery, and the National Rodeo, both held in May.

Arriving pilots can land at Outlaw Field, six miles northwest of Clarksville. Rental cars are available.

INFORMATION
Dunbar Cave State Park
401 Old Dunbar Cave Road
P.O. Box 580
Clarksville, Tennessee 37043
615-648-5526 or 615-645-3015

EDGAR EVINS STATE PARK
14

LOCATION   The park's 6,000 acres are on Center Hill Reservoir, north of Smithville. It's south of I-40, Exit 273, on Tennessee 96. It's also 7.2 miles south of Silver Point.

ACTIVITIES   Edgar Evins State Park encompasses 6,290 acres. Enjoy camping in the 60-site campground, all sites with water and electrical hookups. The campground has a coin laundry, and camp store. Overnight in a rustic cabin. Go hiking on the nature trails, swimming, water-skiing, and boating from the ramp or marina, with rentals available. Enjoy fishing for walleye, bass, and bream. Tour the visitor center. Take a cruise in the fall, going 50 miles upstream to Rock Island State Park.

In Smithville, attend the Fiddlers' Jamboree and Crafts Festival in early July.

Arriving pilots can land at Smithville Municipal Airport, three miles northeast of the city. However, no rental cars are available.

INFORMATION
Edgar Evins State Park
Route 3
Silver Point, Tennessee 38582
615-858-2446: park
615-858-2114: campground

FALL CREEK FALLS STATE PARK
15

LOCATION   The park is 14 miles northwest of Pikeville, off Tennessee 30 and Tennessee 111.

FEATURES   Fall Creek Falls are the highest falls east of the Rockies, dropping 256 feet. The park also features two other waterfalls: Cane Creek and Piney Falls, each dropping 85 feet, and the 45-foot Cane Creek Cascades. It also has deep chasms, gorges, and virgin timber. The park, with over 16,000 acres, is the state's largest state park.

ACTIVITIES   Play golf on the championship 18-hole course, with a pro shop. The course is ranked by *Golf Digest* magazine as one of the top 20 public courses in the U.S. Call 615-881-5706 for a tee time. You can also play disc golf.

Stay in the 73-room resort inn, and dine in the restaurant. Overnight in one of the 20 vacation cabins, or camp in the 227-site campground, all sites with water and electrical hookups. It has a coin laundry, and supplies are available in the camp store.

Pick up a snack at the snack bar, or a souvenir from the gift shop. Explore the nature center, and go swimming in the Olympic-size pool. Tour the interpretive center, and watch naturalist's programs in the amphitheater.

Rent a boat to go boating, or go for a boat cruise on Fall Creek Lake. Enjoy pan fishing, and rent a horse at the stable to go riding. Bike the bicycle trails with bike rentals available, and play tennis. Go backpacking on one of the two 25-mile Cane Creek overnight loops.

Hikers can explore one of the eight nature trails, or, for a remote backcountry hike, go to Virgin Falls Pocket Wilderness, north of Fall Creek Falls. The eight-mile trail passes Big Laurel Falls, which drop 30 feet, and then they flow backward into a sinkhole. Sheep Cave's creek drips water down a steep cliff into a cave system, and Virgin Falls emerges from a cave to fall 110 feet into a sinkhole.

You can also hike a 12-mile section of the 200-mile Cumberland Trail, from Black Mountain across Brady Mountain.

Arriving pilots can land at Upper Cumberland Regional Airport, located nine miles northwest of Sparta. It's 15 miles from the state park. Rental cars are available on request.

INFORMATION
Fall Creek Falls State Park
Route 3
Pikeville, Tennessee 37367
615-881-5569: park
615-881-3241: campground

FORT LOUDOUN STATE HISTORIC AREA
16

LOCATION   The area is 18 miles east of Vonore, on Tennessee 72, and north on U.S. 411.

FEATURES   The fort contains a replica of the 18th-century British palisade fort, built to prevent the French from penetrating the Appalachian frontier. The fort overlooks the Tellico Reservoir and Appalachian Mountains.

ACTIVITIES   Hike the nature trails. Go fishing from the pier for bass, crappie, catfish, and bluegill. The lake holds the state record for a 130-pound blue cat. Enjoy boating from the ramp. Tour the reconstructed fort and the interpretive center's museum, and enjoy a breathtaking view of the Smokies. Camp in the 40-site campground, with a laundry, or go backpacking. Bring along a picnic to enjoy. Purchase a souvenir from the gift shop.

Tour the Sequoyah Birthplace Museum located on the tribal grounds. The museum is a memorial to Sequoyah, the Cherokee who invited a writing system for his people in the early 1800s. It's open daily from March through December. For information, call 615-884-6246.

INFORMATION
Fort Loudoun State Historic Area
338 Fort Loudoun Road
Vonore, Tennessee 37885-9756
615-884-6217

FORT PILLOW STATE PARK
17

LOCATION   The park's 1,650 acres are 18 miles west of Henning via Tennessee 207, off Tennessee 87.

FEATURES   The fort is located on the Chickasaw Bluffs, overlooking the Mississippi River. Here, in 1861, the Confederates constructed an extensive fortification, which they named after General Gideon J. Pillow. The fort was taken over by the Union Army, who controlled it during most of the war. Today only remnants of the earthworks remain.

ACTIVITIES   Camp in the 40-site campground, with water hookups, and laundry facilities. Go hiking or backpacking on the trails, fishing and boating from the ramp, with rentals available. Tour the interpretive center and museum, and enjoy a picnic in the pavilion. Purchase a souvenir in the gift shop. Watch for wildlife in the hardwood slough, fed by Cold Creek.

INFORMATION
Fort Pillow State Park
Route 2, Box 109 A
Henning, Tennessee 38041
901-738-5581

FROZEN HEAD STATE NATURAL AREA
18

LOCATION   The 11,869 acres are six miles east of Wartburg, on Tennessee 62.

FEATURES   The area is a true wilderness area that encompasses 11,869 acres, enjoyed primarily by hikers, backpackers, and picnickers. It's named for one of the highest peaks found in the Cumberland Mountains, whose summit is always surrounded with ice and snow.

ACTIVITIES   The area has 10 blazed trails of varying difficulty, covering 50 miles. Take the 2.8-mile hike to Frozen Head fire tower, rising to 3,324 feet. Here you can see the Cumberland Plateau and Tennessee River valley. Go backpacking, or camp in the 20-site campground, with a camp store. Purchase a souvenir in the gift shop, and a snack from the snack bar. Go fishing in the river.

If you come in April, you can enjoy the many blooming wildflowers, and flowering trees. Take a guided weekend flower walk. Come in August for the Folk Life Festival, featuring dancing, arts and crafts. Equestrians come in October to enjoy a colorful horseback trail ride.

INFORMATION
Frozen Head State Natural Area
964 Flat Ford Road
Route 2, Box 321
Wartburg, Tennessee 37887
615-346-3318

HARPETH SCENIC RIVER/NARROWS OF THE HARPETH STATE HISTORIC AREA
19

LOCATION   The area is off Tennessee 70, at Kingston Springs.

FEATURES   The Narrows contain a 100-yard, man-made tunnel, chiseled through solid rock where an early 1800s industrial complex was located.

ACTIVITIES   Canoeists come to canoe the Harpeth Scenic River. River accesses include the U.S. 100 bridge, the 1862 Newsom's Mill ruins, and the McCrory Lane Bridge at Hidden Lake. If you go downstream to the narrows, you can either put in to go both upstream or downstream. Explore Bell's Bend five-mile float, with its unique 1/4-mile portage. The Harpeth River features Class I and II waters, with a low flow occurring during the summer. It's suitable for beginners.

Take an interpretive tour of the historic area of Mound Bottom, located one mile upstream. It preserves an ancient Indian ceremonial center. Enjoy hiking or backpacking, swimming and fishing. Rent a horse to go horseback riding.

INFORMATION
Harpeth Scenic River/Narrows of the
Harpeth State Historic Area
Route 2
Kingston Springs, Tennessee 37082
615-797-9052 or 797-2099

HARRISON BAY STATE PARK
20

LOCATION   The park's 1,300 acres are 10 miles northeast of Chattanooga,
off Tennessee 58, along the shore of Chickamauga Reservoir.

ACTIVITIES   Lookout Mountain Trail is two miles south of Chattanooga, off
I-24. Follow signs to Point Park. Hikers have access to over 20 miles of trails
winding around the historic, scenic park. Trails interconnect with the top of the
mountain tourist attraction, Point Park, a Civil War battlefield located above the
clouds. For information, call 615-821-7786.

Go camping in the 260-site campground, either in the woods or beside the lake.
The campground has a camp store, laundry, and 136 sites with water and electrical
hookups. Go swimming in the pool, play tennis, and dine in the marina restaurant, open March through October. Pick up a snack at the snack bar.

The park has the most complete docking facility found on any of the TVA
lakes. Go water-skiing, bass fishing, and rent a boat from the marina to go boating or canoeing from the canoe access points. Try your skill at archery, or play disc
golf. Purchase a souvenir in the gift shop.

Visit the Chickamauga-Chattanooga Battlefield, the nation's oldest, largest, and
most visited national military park. Its visitor center is on U.S. 27, off I-75, 10
miles south of Chattanooga. The park includes the Civil War battlefields of
Chickamauga, Orchard Knob, Lookout Mountain, and Missionary Ridge. Hike the
self-guiding trails, walk through the interpretive exhibits, take an auto tour,
observe living history demonstrations, and go horseback riding. For information, call 404-866-9241.

In Chattanooga, attend the June Jaunt, the Autumn Leaf Special in mid-October, and the Fall Color Cruise and Folk Festival in late October.

Arriving pilots can land at Dallas Bay Sky Park, 11 miles north of Chattanooga.
Rental cars are available.

INFORMATION
Harrison Bay State Park
8411 Harrison Bay Road
Route 2, Box 118
Harrison, Tennessee 37341
615-344-6214

HENRY HORTON STATE PARK
21

LOCATION   The park's 1,150 acres are two miles south of Chapel Hill, on U.S. 31 Alternate.

FEATURES   Henry Horton was the 36th governor of Tennessee, and the park is located on his old estate on the Duck River. The river has the longest remaining stretch of free-flowing water in the state, and supports the most diverse mussels in the world.

ACTIVITIES   Play golf on the 18-hole championship course, with a pro shop and putting green. For a tee time, call 615-364-2319. Enjoy tennis on the lighted courts, and utilize their skeet and trap range, play disc golf, or test your skill at archery. Pick up a snack at the snack bar. Hike the nature trails, and rent a horse to go horseback riding.

Overnight in the 72-room resort inn, or stay in one of the five vacation cabins. Camp in the 90-site campground, 54 sites with water and electrical hookups, and a dumping station. Dine in the restaurant, and purchase a souvenir in the gift shop.

Enjoy swimming in the pool, boating from the ramp, and fishing and canoeing in the Duck River. The river has Class I and II water, with some turbulent shoals. It's suitable for beginners.

INFORMATION
Henry Horton State Park
P.O. Box 128
Chapel Hill, Tennessee 37034
615-364-2222

HIWASSEE SCENIC RIVER STATE PARK
22

LOCATION   The park is on Maggie Mill Road, and covers a 23-mile river section from the Tennessee–North Carolina state line, to U.S. 411 north of Benton.

FEATURES   The Hiwassee was the first designated State Scenic River in the state.

ACTIVITIES   The river is rated as Class III, where canoers, rafters, and anglers seeking trout come to enjoy their sports. Go swimming, and boating from the boat launching ramps. Rent horses from the corral, and camp in the 41-site Gee Creek primitive campground. Enjoy hiking, backpacking, and nature photography. Part of the John Muir Trail winds through the river gorge.

The Ocoee River, on U.S. 64, is a premier whitewater river with Class III, IV, and V rapids, and also has some difficult, powerful rapids. Only advanced paddlers should attempt to navigate the river in canoes or kayaks. Water is released by the Tennessee Valley Authority on scheduled days, from late March to early November. Many outfitters provide three-hour guided raft trips, mainly on weekends in spring and fall, and almost daily in the summer.

Arriving pilots can land at Chilhowee Airport, four miles northeast of Benton. However, no rental cars are available.

INFORMATION
Hiwassee Scenic River State Park
Box 255
Delano, Tennessee 37325
615-338-4133

INDIAN MOUNTAIN STATE PARK
23

LOCATION   The park's 213 acres are between Jellico and the Kentucky state line. From Jellico, take Exit 160 off I-75, and go 1.5 miles north on Tennessee 25W, one mile west on Tennessee 297, and another mile on Indian Mountain Road.

FEATURES   Indian Mountain was developed on some old strip mining land, and has two lakes.

ACTIVITIES   Camp in the 50-site campground, with water and electrical hookups, and a dump station. Hike the ¾-mile nature trail adjacent to the campground. Go boating and fishing, with rowboat and paddleboat rentals available. Bike the bicycle trails.

INFORMATION
Indian Mountain State Park
Jellico, Tennessee 37762
615-784-7958

LONG HUNTER STATE PARK
24

LOCATION   The 2,400-acre park is located along the shore of the Percy Priest Reservoir near Mt. Juliet. It's off I-40 and I-24, on Tennessee 171.

FEATURES   Percy Priest Reservoir encompasses 14,200 acres of water.

ACTIVITIES   Enjoy hiking and backpacking on the 28 miles of hiking trails. Enjoy swimming, boating from the ramp, with rentals available, and fishing from the fishing pier. The Couchville Area is barrier-free, and features a 110-acre lake with a fishing pier. No camping is available.

Tour the visitor center, and purchase a souvenir in the gift shop.

INFORMATION
Long Hunter State Park
2910 Hobson Pike
Route 3
Hermitage, Tennessee 37076
615-885-2422 or 615-459-8194

MEEMAN-SHELBY FOREST STATE PARK
25

LOCATION   The forest is 13 miles north of Memphis, off U.S. 51, and borders the Mississippi River. From Millington, take the North Watkins Exit from U.S. 51, and go northwest for 10 miles.

FEATURES   The 14,500-acre park contains two lakes, and two-thirds of the park contain bottomland hardwood forests.

ACTIVITIES   Camp in the 50-site campground, all sites with water and electrical hookups. Go hiking, bicycling, backpacking, or rent a horse to go horseback riding, along many miles of trails. Go bass fishing, and boating from the ramp, in the Mississippi River, with boat rentals available. Go for a cruise along the mighty river.

Enjoy swimming in the Olympic-size pool. Attend interpretive programs, and tour the visitor center and Meeman Museum. Stay overnight in a cabin, and pick up a snack at the snack bar. Purchase a souvenir in the gift shop, and try your skill at archery. Rent a bicycle to go cycling.

Arriving pilots can land at General Dewitt Spain Airport, six miles northwest of Memphis, or at Memphis International Airport, located three miles south of the city. Both airports have rental cars available.

INFORMATION
Meeman-Shelby Forest State Park
Route 3
Millington, Tennessee 38053
901-876-5215

MONTGOMERY BELL STATE PARK
26

LOCATION   The park is eight miles east of Dickson, on U.S. 70. It's also 10 miles northwest on Tennessee 46, to U.S. 70, then east for four miles.

FEATURES   The wooded hills are the birthplace of the Cumberland Presbyterian Church. It has the remains of the Laurel Furnace, circa 1810, which was part of the iron manufacturing operation of early Tennessee industrialist, Montgomery Bell. Laurel Furnace and the old ore pits are still visible.

Hall Spring, located in the park, produces 1,100 gallons of water per minute.

ACTIVITIES   Go camping in the 120-site campground, all sites with water, and 115 with electrical hookups. Overnight in one of eight cabins, or stay in the 36-room resort inn. Pick up camping supplies in the camp store, dine in the restaurant, or pick up a snack from the snack bar.

Enjoy a picnic. Go canoeing, boating, pan fishing, and swimming in Acorn Lake, with rentals available. Play golf on the 18-hole golf course, with a pro shop. For a tee time, call 615-797-2578.

Play tennis, and tour the visitor center. Hike the nature trails, go backpacking, and pick up a souvenir in the gift shop. Test your skill in archery.

In Nashville, home of country music, musical opportunities abound. For example, you can go to the Grand Ole Opry, 2804 Opryland Drive, on Friday or Saturday night, to listen to some of country music's famous singers perform. For information, call 615-889-6611. Opryland, U.S.A., located at 2802 Opryland Drive and Briley Parkway, presents 12 fully-staged musicals, plus acres of entertainment. For information, call 615-889-6611. For additional country music, check with any local hotel.

Take a cruise on the Cumberland River from the docks at First Avenue at Broadway, or from the end of McGavock Pike West. General Jackson Showboat's dinner cruises include a musical revue, besides its other cruises. For information, call 615-889-6600.

Tour the Belle Meade Mansion at 110 Leake Avenue, known as one of the finest antebellum plantations of the Old South. Tours include the Victorian Carriage Museum. For information, call 615-352-7350.

The Belmont Mansion, circa 1850, is located at Acklen Avenue and Belmont Boulevard, on the Belmont College Campus. For hours and information, call 615-383-7001. Flower lovers should go to Cheekwood/Tennessee Botanical Gardens and Fine Arts Center, at Forest Park Drive, off Tennessee 100. The 55-acre site features beautiful gardens, a Georgian-style mansion, and restaurant. It's open Tuesday through Sunday. For information, call 615-352-5310.

Tour the Tennessee State Museum at Fifth Avenue, between Union and Deaderick Streets. Closed Mondays, the museum has reproductions and artifacts from early area history, including Davy Crockett's rifle. For information, call 615-741-2692.

The Hermitage, home of Andrew Jackson, is at 4580 Rachel's Lane. The National Historic Landmark was home to our nation's seventh president. The mansion grounds include a formal garden, the Old Hermitage Church, and a visitor center with a restaurant. For information, call 615-889-2941.

Annual events include the Iroquois Steeplechase in early May, Summer Lights Festival from late May to early June, International Country Music Fan Fair in early June, Tennessee State Fair in mid-September, Tennessee Grassroots Days in late September, and Trees of Christmas during December.

Arriving pilots can land at Dickson Municipal Airport, three miles north of the city. Rental cars are available.

INFORMATION
Montgomery Bell State Park
Route 1, P.O. Box 684
Burns, Tennessee 37029
615-797-3101
615-797-9052: campground

MOUSETAIL LANDING STATE PARK
27

LOCATION   The park is on the east banks of the Tennessee River, off U.S. 100 near Parsons.

FEATURES   Mousetail Landing was named during the Civil War, when one of the area's tanning companies caught fire, and large numbers of mice were forced to scatter.

ACTIVITIES   Go camping in the 26-site campground, 19 sites with water and electrical hookups, or backpack in to a backcountry site. Enjoy hiking the trails, pan fishing, water-skiing, swimming, and boating from the boat launch, in the Tennessee River.

Arriving pilots can land at Scott Field, one mile southwest of Parsons. Rental cars are available. The state park is six miles from the airport.

INFORMATION
Mousetail Landing State Park
P.O. Box 280-B
Linden, Tennessee 37096
901-847-0841

NATCHEZ TRACE STATE PARK
28

LOCATION   The park is south of I-40, Exit 116/Wildersville, and three miles south on Tennessee 114. It's also 15 miles northeast of Lexington.

FEATURES   The Natchez Trace was a southwesterly path that headed west from Nashville, and extended 500 miles as it passed through Mississippi, to Natchez. During the early 1800s, early pioneers followed this old Indian trace en route to their settlements in the lower Mississippi Valley. The old trail is now preserved as the Natchez Trace Parkway, and a western spur of the Trace is located here in the state park.

Natchez Trace State Park is the state's largest, and covers 14,073 acres within the 48,000-acre Natchez Trace State Forest. Besides the trace, it also has four lakes encompassing 1,015 acres, including Pin Oak and Cub Lakes.

ACTIVITIES   Go hiking and backpacking on 45 miles of trails along the old trace, through the scenic woods. Play tennis, and go camping in the 146-site campground, all sites with water and electrical hookups, and pick up your supplies at the camp store. Overnight in a cabin, or in the 20-unit inn at the resort. Dine in the restaurant.

Enjoy boating from the ramp in Cub Creek Lake, with rentals available. Go bass fishing, water-skiing, and swimming. Tour the visitor center, and purchase a souvenir from the gift shop. Test your skill at archery and tennis, or play disc golf.

Arriving pilots can land at Franklin Wilkins Airport, one mile east of Lexington. Rental cars are available.

INFORMATION
Natchez Trace State Park
Route 1, Box 265
Wildersville, Tennessee 38388
901-968-7526

Buffalo River at Metal Ford where the Old Trace crosses the river
on the Natchez Trace Parkway, near Natchez Trace State Park
(photo by Guy Braden, courtesy of the National Park Service)

NATHAN BEDFORD FORREST
STATE HISTORICAL AREA

JOHNSONVILLE STATE HISTORIC PARK

29

LOCATION   Nathan Bedford Forrest's 840 acres are seven miles northeast of Camden via Eva Road, on the western shore of Kentucky Lake, and north of I-40, on Tennessee 191.

Johnsonville State Historic Park is off U.S. 70, is on the eastern side of Kentucky Lake north of New Johnsonville.

FEATURES   Confederate General Nathan Bedford Forrest was responsible for destroying Union boats and supplies with his camouflaged artillery, in 1864. He made one of the most famous Civil War quotations when he said, "Get there first with the most men."

Johnsonville's 550-acre park overlooks the site of the Battle of Johnsonville, where cavalry under General Nathan Bedford Forrest successfully sank four Federal gunboats downstream, and destroyed a Union Army supply depot at Johnsonville.

Pilot Knob, located within Nathan Bedford Forrest's area, is the highest point in western Tennessee, and was named because of its use as a landmark by riverboat pilots.

ACTIVITIES   At Nathan Bedford Forrest State Historical Area, tour the Tennessee River Folklife Center on top of Pilot Knob, and watch their presentations on log rafting, commercial fishing, and river music. Go to the top of 741-foot Pilot Knob for a great view of the western valley of the Tennessee River. For information, call 615-584-6356.

Trace Creek, across Kentucky Lake, is a park annex, and has a museum with information on the battle. Camp in the 50-site campground, 38 sites with water and electrical hookups, and a dump station. Stay overnight in a cabin, and enjoy a picnic in the pavilion.

Go fishing for white bass, sauger, catfish, and crappie. Call the TWRA at 1-800-624-7406 for a fish locator map. Enjoy water-skiing, canoeing, and boating from the ramp, in Kentucky Lake. Hike the nature trails or go backpacking. Play tennis on the tennis courts.

At Johnsonville State Historic Park, you can still see four of the original breastworks, and take an interpretive tour.

Arriving pilots can land at Benton County Airport, three miles south of Camden. Rental cars are available.

INFORMATION
Nathan Bedford Forrest State
    Historical Area
Star Route
Eva, Tennessee 38333
901-584-6356

Johnsonville State Historic Park
Route 1, Box 3704
New Johnsonville, Tennessee 37134
615-535-2789

NORRIS DAM STATE PARK
30

LOCATION   The park is one mile south of Norris Dam, on U.S. 441, and east of I-75, Exit 128, on the Norris Reservoir.

FEATURES   Norris Dam was begun in 1933, and was the first Tennessee Valley Authority project. The park's 4,000 acres include virgin forest land.

ACTIVITIES   The state park offers camping in two campgrounds with 90 campsites, 50 sites with water, and 85 with electrical hookups, a camp store, and coin laundry. You can also overnight in one of the 45 cabins. Enjoy hiking along miles of trails through the forest. Go boating from the boating ramps, with rentals available from the marina. Go swimming in the Olympic-size pool, and go water-skiing, canoeing, and fishing for trout, bass, crappie, and walleye, in Norris Lake.

Tour the visitor center and attend interpretive programs. Play tennis, and test your skill at archery. Purchase a snack at the snack bar, or a souvenir from the gift shop. A grist mill, circa 1795, still grinds corn daily during the summer, and is sold in the restored country store.

Tour the Lenoir Museum, open daily from May through October, and weekends only during November through April. You'll see memorabilia from eastern Tennessee, including rifles and ammunition, fossils and arrowheads, plus Civil War newspapers, and Confederate scrip. For information, call 615-494-9688.

Take a self-guided tour of TVA's Norris Reservoir, including stops to see the dam, powerhouse, and the old fish hatchery. Hike along the Songbird Trail.

While in the area, tour the Museum of Appalachia, located two miles east of I-75. Take Exit 122 onto Tennessee 61. Stroll through the 35-structure village that includes a working farm, blacksmith and cobbler shop, church, school, and mule-powered molasses mill. Attend musical performances, and observe pioneer skills, presented periodically. Special events include the July 4th celebration, Tennessee Fall Homecoming in October, and Christmas in Old Appalachia. For information, call 615-494-0514.

In Norris, attend the Fall Homecoming and Fiddle Contest in mid-October.

INFORMATION
Norris Dam State Park
1261 Norris Freeway
P.O. Box 27
Lake City, Tennessee 37769
615-426-7461

OLD STONE FORT
STATE ARCHEOLOGICAL AREA
31

LOCATION   The historic site is 4.5 miles north of Manchester on U.S. 41, 1.5 miles off I-24, Exit 114.

FEATURES   The park is located by an ancient walled structure, constructed along the bluffs above the forks of the Duck River. This sacred site dates back almost 2,000 years ago, to prehistoric Woodland Indians.

ACTIVITIES   Play golf on the nine-hole course. Go camping in the 51-site campground, all sites with water and electrical hookups. Hike the 1.25-mile nature trail along the old fort wall. Go fishing, tour the visitor center and museum, and attend interpretive programs. Purchase a souvenir in the gift shop. Go bass fishing in the Duck River.

Go to nearby May Prairie for an interpretive tour of the prairie remnant, where you can see many rare plants.

INFORMATION
Old Stone Fort State Archeological Area
Route 7, Box 7400
Manchester, Tennessee 37355
615-723-5073

PANTHER CREEK STATE PARK
32

LOCATION   The park's 1,290 acres are six miles west of Morristown, on U.S. 11E, on the Cherokee Reservoir, and west of I-81.

FEATURES   Panther Creek was named for nearby Panther Creek Springs, a pioneer landmark.

ACTIVITIES   Camp in the 50-site campground, all sites with water and electrical hookups, a laundry, and dump station. Hike the nature trails, and climb the 1,460-foot ridge for a great view of the valley below. Go bass fishing, water-skiing, boating from the ramp, and swimming in Cherokee Reservoir. Rental boats are available nearby. Purchase a souvenir in the gift shop. Play tennis, and tour the visitor center.

In Morristown, stop by the Davy Crockett Tavern and Museum, on Morningside Drive. It's a reproduction of the one operated by Davy's father, in the 1790s. It's open Monday through Saturday, from May through October. For information, call 615-586-6382. Attend the Mountain Makin 's Festival in late October.

Arriving pilots can land at Moore-Murrell Airport, four miles southwest of Morristown. Rental cars are available through prior request. Call 615-586-2483.

INFORMATION
Panther Creek State Park
2010 Panther Creek Road
Route 1, Box 624
Morristown, Tennessee 37814
615-587-7046

PARIS LANDING STATE PARK
33

LOCATION   The park's 1,200 acres are 17 miles northeast of Paris, on U.S. 79, on Kentucky Lake.

FEATURES   Paris Landing was named for its steamboat and freight landing, circa mid-1800s.

ACTIVITIES   Play 18 holes of golf on the championship course, with a pro shop. For a tee time, call 901-644-1332 or 901-642-4311, extension 133. Camp in the 80-site campground, 46 sites with electrical hookups, 12 with water, and 19 with sewer hookups. A camp store and laundry are available. Overnight in the 100-room inn or in a vacation cabin, and dine in the restaurant.

Go boating from the ramp on Kentucky Lake, with houseboat and fishing-boat rentals available at the full-service marina. Here you can enjoy water-skiing, bass fishing or swimming in one of the two pools. Play tennis on the lighted courts. Hike the nature trails. Purchase a snack from the snack bar, and a souvenir from the gift shop.

Annual events include the World's Biggest Fish Fry in late April.

Fort Donelson National Battlefield is on Tennessee 79 near Dover. Here the North had its first major Civil War victory, in February of 1862, when General Simon Buckner was forced to surrender 13,000 troops as prisoners of war to General Ulysses S. Grant. At that time, this number of prisoners was the largest ever to surrender in the U.S.

Tour the visitor center on U.S. 79, 1.5 miles west of the Cumberland River Bridge at Dover, and watch the slide show describing the battle. During the summer, observe living history programs presented by the park staff. For information, call 615-232-5348.

Take the six-mile auto tour of the battlefield, past the trenches and two reconstructed Confederate huts. Near the lower gun battery you can see the barrels of eight 32-pound guns, and a cannon that was able to fire a 10-inch cannonball for four miles at the Union ironclads.

The Big Sandy Unit of the Tennessee Wildlife Refuge, and the Land Between the Lakes' 170,000 acres, are located between Kentucky Lake and Lake Barkley, on Tennessee 79, west of Dover. Enjoy camping, fishing, hunting, and hiking. Tour the Homeplace's living history farm, circa 1850, and attend a performance at the planetarium and multi-media theater. For information, call 502-924-5602.

Arriving pilots can land at Henry County Airport, four miles northwest of Paris. Rental cars are available.

INFORMATION
Paris Landing State Park
Highway 79E
Paris, Tennessee 38242
901-644-7358

PICKETT STATE PARK
34

LOCATION   The park is 13 miles northeast of Jamestown, on Tennessee 154.

FEATURES   The park is located in an 11,700-acre wilderness in the upper Cumberland Mountains, with natural bridges and caves.

ACTIVITIES   Arch Lake's dark green water provides great boating opportunities, trout fishing and swimming. Canoers also enjoy excellent whitewater canoeing. Camp in the 32-site campground, with water and electrical hookups, and a dumping station, or overnight in a cabin. The park has a network of nine marked hiking trails. Lake View Trail is accessed by a swinging bridge and passes through the laurel, dogwoods, and magnolias. Natural Bridge Trail is five miles long, and winds through the forest before descending to Natural Bridge.

Pickett State Park is the southern end of the Sheltowee Trace Hiking Trail. This trail ranges in difficulty from moderate to difficult, and is marked with white diamond-shaped blazes and white turtles. Enjoy backpacking, with camping permitted along the trail unless otherwise posted. Another trail goes to the nearby home and grist mill of World War I hero, Alvin York.

Purchase souvenirs in the gift shop, and go boating (rentals available), fishing, and swimming. Snacks may be purchased at the snack bar. Tour the interpretive center, and test your skill at archery, or play tennis.

Nearby Twin Arches is the second largest arch found in southeastern U.S.

Arriving pilots can land at Jamestown Municipal Airport, five miles south of the city. However, no rental cars are available.

INFORMATION
Pickett State Park
Rock Creek Route, Box 174
Jamestown, Tennessee 38556
615-879-5821

PICKWICK LANDING STATE PARK
35

LOCATION   The park is at Pickwick Dam, on the shore of Pickwick Reservoir, 15 miles south of Savannah off Tennessee 128, on Tennessee 57.

ACTIVITIES   Pickwick Landing has a 75-room resort inn and restaurant that overlook the lake. Enjoy swimming in the pool. You can also overnight in one of the 10 modern cabins, or camp in the 48-site campground, all sites with water and electrical hookups, or camp at one of the 100 tent sites. The campground has a laundry.

The park features a full-service marina, with boat rentals. Take a scenic cruise down the Tennessee River. Enjoy tennis, water-skiing, and fishing. Play 18 holes of golf on the championship course, with a pro shop available. For a tee time, call 901-689-3149. Pick up a souvenir at the gift shop, and a snack from the snack bar. Hike the nature trails.

In Savannah, attend the Tennessee River Bluegrass Festival in late June to early July.

Arriving pilots can land at Robert Sibley Airport, six miles northeast of Selmer. The airport is 20 miles from the state park. You can also land at Savannah–Hardin County Airport three miles southeast of Savannah. It's 10 miles from the state park. Both airports have rental cars.

INFORMATION
Pickwick Landing State Park
P.O. Box 10
Pickwick Dam, Tennessee 38365
901-689-3135

PINSON MOUNDS
STATE ARCHEOLOGICAL PARK
36

LOCATION   Pinson Mounds are three miles east of U.S. 45 on Ozier Road, and approximately 10 miles south of Jackson.

FEATURES   The 32 Indian ceremonial and burial mounds include the second largest Indian ceremonial mound in the U.S.

ACTIVITIES   Tour the interpretive center and museum, open daily, but closed weekends during the winter. Walk the self-guided and nature trails, including a boardwalk along the Forked Deer River. Observe archeological research being conducted frequently on the site. Bring along a picnic. Group camping facilities are available.

In Jackson attend the West Tennessee State Fair in mid-September.

Arriving pilots can land at McKellar-Sipes Regional Airport, four miles west of Jackson. Rental cars are available.

INFORMATION
Pinson Mounds State Archeological Area
460 Ozier Road
Route 1
Pinson, Tennessee 38366
901-988-5614

PORT ROYAL STATE HISTORICAL PARK
37

LOCATION   Port Royal is near Adams, at the confluence of Sulfur Fork Creek and the Red River, off Tennessee 76.

FEATURES   The area was one of the state's earliest communities and trading centers.

ACTIVITIES   Hike the trails, go fishing, and take an interpretive tour (available on request). Go boating from the ramp, and canoeing in the river. Tour the museum, and cross the covered bridge that spans the Red River.

INFORMATION
Port Royal State Historical Park
3300 Old Clarksville Highway
Route 1
Adams, Tennessee 37010
615-358-9696

RADNOR LAKE STATE NATURAL AREA
38

LOCATION   Radnor Lake State Natural Area is six miles southwest of Nashville in the Overton Hills.

ACTIVITIES   At Radnor Lake, often referred to as "Nashville's Walden Pond," enjoy bird watching, take an interpretive tour, and attend scheduled interpretive programs. Hike along six miles of hiking trails.

For additional activities in the Nashville area, look under Montgomery Bell State Park.

Arriving pilots can land at Cornelia Fort Airpark, five miles northeast of Nashville, or at John C. Tune Airport, located one mile northwest of the city. However, only John C. Tune has rental cars.

INFORMATION
Radnor Lake State Natural Area
1050 Otter Creek Road
Nashville, Tennessee 37220
615-373-3467

RED CLAY STATE HISTORICAL PARK
39

LOCATION   The area is off Tennessee 60, 12 miles southwest of Cleveland, along the Georgia border.

FEATURES   Red Clay is the site of the last Eastern Cherokee Indian Nation's council grounds, before the Indians were sent away on the "Trail of Tears."

ACTIVITIES   Tour the interpretive center's museum, the Indian council house, and the reconstructed Indian farmstead. Attend interpretive programs in the large amphitheater. Hike several miles of trails, including those leading to the Eternal Flame, and Blue Spring. Bring along a picnic to enjoy, and purchase a souvenir in the gift shop.

Arriving pilots can land at Hardwick Field, four miles northeast of Cleveland. Rental cars are available.

INFORMATION
Red Clay State Historical Area
1140 Red Clay Road SE
Route 6
Cleveland, Tennessee 37311
615-478-0339

REELFOOT LAKE STATE PARK
40

LOCATION   The park is 5.2 miles east of Tiptonville, on Tennessee 21.

FEATURES   On February 7, 1812, a violent earthquake struck, causing the land to sink as much as 10 feet. Then water from the Mississippi River entered the depression and created a 14-mile-long lake. Today this shallow 18,000-acre lake is dotted with islands, and its partially submerged forest provides ideal conditions for one of the most abundant fish hatcheries in the U.S.

ACTIVITIES Launch your canoes and boats into Reelfoot Lake from the ramp, with boat rentals available. Take a 3½-hour cruise from the jetty by the visitor center, available from April through October. You'll stop at Caney Island, where you can hike the nature trail and see some Indian mounds. In mid-summer, the American lotus blooms in parts of the lake, and the cruise boat then stops to let visitors pick the flowers.

Birders come to Lake Reelfoot because it is the site of many migrating waterfowl that fly along the "Mississippi Flyway." Many bald eagles winter here, between December and mid-March. Take a daily bus tour to get a look at these wonderful creatures. The two-hour tour leaves from the Reelfoot Lake State Airpark Inn at 10:00 A.M. Reservations are required. Call 901-253-6862.

Explore the marshlands of the lake, and see the fish hatchery. Fishing is obviously very good. Enjoy swimming, tennis, and purchase a souvenir from the gift shop.

Overnight in the 20-room resort inn, in one of the 5 cabins, or in one of the 120-site campsites, all sites with water and electrical hookups. In addition, 25 tent sites are located along the lake shore. Pick up supplies in the camp store, dine in the restaurant, or pick up a snack in the snack bar. Purchase a souvenir from the gift shop.

Tour the visitor center in Tiptonville to see Indian artifacts. The visitor center and museum are open from Tuesday through Saturday, and Sunday afternoons.

Arriving pilots can land at Reelfoot Lake Airport, nine miles northeast of Tiptonville. However, no rental cars are available. You can camp next to the strip.

INFORMATION
Reelfoot Lake State Park
Route 1
Tiptonville, Tennessee 38079
901-253-6862

ROAN MOUNTAIN STATE PARK

SYCAMORE SHOALS
STATE HISTORICAL AREA
41

LOCATION Roan Mountain's 2,000 acres are 20 miles southeast of Elizabethton on U.S. 19E, via Tennessee 143. It's seven miles east of the town of Roan Mountain.

Sycamore Shoals State Historic Area is on U.S. 321, two miles south of Elizabethton.

FEATURES   Roan Mountain State Park has the world's largest rhododendron garden, covering over 600 acres. The park was named for 6,285-foot Roan Mountain, one of the highest peaks in the eastern U.S., and is surrounded by the Cherokee National Forest.

Sycamore Shoals State Historical Area played a significant role during the 18th-century when the first permanent American settlement outside the 13 colonies was formed, in 1772. The Watauga Association, the first majority-rule system of American democratic government was also formed. The Overmountain Men gathered to march to the Battle of King's Mountain here in 1780, where they defeated the British. As a result of this skirmish, the British retreated to Yorktown.

ACTIVITIES   At Roan Mountain, enjoy camping in the 87-site campground, all sites with water and electrical hookups, or in one of the 20 tent sites. The campground has a laundry, and dump station. You can also overnight in one of the 20 cabins. Enjoy hiking, trout fishing in the Doe River, and swimming in the pool. Attend interpretive programs, and tour the visitor center and museum. Dine in the restaurant. Play tennis.

Hike to the top of 6,313-foot Roan Mountain. Attend an annual Rhododendron Festival in late June. Hikers also have access to the Appalachian Trail that crosses through the park.

Go cross-country skiing during the winter in the South's only cross-country skiing resort park. Ski rentals are available. Nordic guides are available at the ski center for guided trips to the summit of Roan Mountain.

The 154-foot white clapboard covered bridge in Elizabethton spans the Doe River. It was originally built for $3,000. It's one of the few covered bridges still in use in the Southeast. A covered bridge celebration is held in late June, and the Overmountain Victory Trail Celebration is held in early September. Winterfest is celebrated in December.

At Sycamore Shoals, tour the museum, and watch the 30-minute movie featuring the Overmountain Men's history. Attend the outdoor drama, *The Wataugans*, presented evenings in mid-July. Walk through reconstructed Fort Watauga, which was originally erected on the shore of the Watauga River. The museum and fort are open daily from sunup to sunset. Hike the loop trail.

Annual reenactments are held each September, when history buffs dress as the Overmountain Men to march 220 miles to King's Mountain, along the King's Mountain Victory Trail. For historical area information, call 615-543-5808.

Tour the nearby John and Carter Mansion. It's three miles north on the Broad Street extension, off U.S. 321. Circa 1780, the mansion still has 90 percent of its original building material. It's open Wednesday through Sunday from 9:00 to 5:30, from mid-May to mid-September. For information, call 615-543-6140.

Arriving pilots can land at Elizabethton Municipal Airport, three miles northeast of the city. Rental cars are available.

INFORMATION

Roan Mountain State Park
Route 1, Box 236
Roan Mountain, Tennessee 37687
615-772-3303: park and
  campground
615-772-3314: cabin reservations

Sycamore Shoals State Historical
  Area
1651 West Elk Avenue
P.O. Box 1198
Elizabethton, Tennessee 37643
615-543-5808

ROCK ISLAND STATE PARK

BONE CAVE STATE NATURAL AREA
42

LOCATION   Rock Island State Park is one mile west of Rock Island off U.S. 70S, at the upper end of Center Hill Lake. Bone Cave State Natural Area is nearby.

ACTIVITIES   Come in the spring to see Great Falls of the Caney Fork River. Enjoy camping in the 50-site campground, all sites with water and electrical hookups, or at one of the nine tent sites. Laundry facilities and a camp store are available. Limited camping facilities are available during the winter.

Go canoeing, and boating from the ramp, with boat rentals available. Go bass fishing, water-skiing, and swimming from the natural sand beach on the Center Hill Reservoir. Hike the nature trails, and tour the interpretive center. Test your skill at archery, or play tennis.

Tour nearby Bone Cave where Pleistocene mammal fossils were discovered. The cave was mined for saltpeter during the War of 1812, and later during the Civil War.

INFORMATION

Rock Island State Park
Bone Cave State Natural Area
Route 2, Box 20
Rock Island, Tennessee 38581
615-686-2471

SOUTH CUMBERLAND

STATE RECREATION AREA
43

LOCATION   The area's 12,000 acres are 4.5 miles east of Monteagle, on Tennessee 56. Take Exit 134 from I-24.

ACTIVITIES   The park has eight separate areas. Stop by the visitor center on Tennessee 41, between Monteagle and Tracy City, to learn about the Lone Rock Coke Ovens located in the Grundy Lakes Recreation Area, and the 150-foot-high Great Stone Door. Visit the Sewanee Natural Bridge, rising 27 feet; Foster Falls near Grundy Lakes; and Lost Cove Caves in the Carter Natural Area.

The Stone Door/Savage Gulf area has waterfalls, and many miles of hiking and backpacking trails. Fiery Gizzard Trail connects Foster Falls with Grundy Forest.

Camp in the campground, hike the trails, go boating, fishing, and swimming in Fiery Gizzard Creek. Pick up a souvenir from the gift shop, or play tennis.

For a scenic drive, follow I-24 for 40 miles southeast to Chattanooga.

Franklin Forest's 7,000 acres are south of St. Andrews, off Tennessee 41/64. Here you can go hunting, camping, swimming, and hiking.

Wonder Cave is four miles north of Monteagle, off Tennessee 41. One of the oldest commercial caves in the U.S., visitors need to carry hand-held Coleman lanterns to light the way. For information, call 1-800-572-6363.

INFORMATION
South Cumberland State Recreation Area
Route 1, Box 2196
Monteagle, Tennessee 37356
615-924-2980

STANDING STONE STATE PARK
44

LOCATION   The park's 11,000 acres are eight miles northwest of Livingston, on Tennessee 52.

FEATURES   Standing Stone stands eight feet tall, and was once a boundary between Indian nations.

ACTIVITIES   Play tennis or disc golf. Go camping in the 35-site campground, all sites with water and electrical hookups. Overnight in one of the 23 rustic cabins, or stay in the timber lodge. Hike the trails, and go backpacking in the primitive woods.

Go boating, rent a canoe, enjoy swimming and trout fishing, in the park's 69-acre Standing Stone Lake. You can also travel five miles to fish for bass, walleye, catfish, and tailwater trout in the Dale Hollow Reservoir. Tour the interpretive center, and play tennis on the tennis court. Purchase a snack from the snack bar.

Come in September for the National Rollyhole Marbles Championship.

Arriving pilots can land at Upper Cumberland Regional Airport, located nine miles northwest of Sparta. It's 20 miles from the state park. Rental cars are available on request.

INFORMATION
Standing Stone State Park
1674 Standing Stone Park Highway
Livingston, Tennessee 38570
615-823-6347

TIMS FORD STATE PARK
45

LOCATION   The park is 11 miles west of Winchester, on Tennessee 50W, on Tims Ford Lake. It's also south of Tullahoma. Take Tennessee 130 to Old Tullahoma Highway, and then go left on Mansford Road.

ACTIVITIES   Camp in the 50-site campground, all sites with water and electrical hookups, and laundry facilities. Purchase supplies in the camp store. Hike the trails, and go boating from the ramp, with rentals available at the marina. Enjoy fishing for bass, bream, catfish, trout, and walleye, and purchase supplies from the small bait shop.

Go swimming in the Olympic-size pool, and play tennis and disc golf. Overnight in one of the 20 cabins. Go bicycling on five miles of paved bike trails, with rentals available. Dine in the restaurant, or pick up a snack at the snack bar.

Tour the historic towns of nearby Lynchburg, Cowan, and Sewanee. In Lynchburg, tour Jack Daniel's Distillery, on Tennessee 55. Circa 1866, it's listed on the U.S. Register of Historic Sites. For information, call 615-759-4221.

Arriving pilots can land at Winchester Municipal Airport, three miles southeast of the city. Rental cars are available.

INFORMATION
Tims Ford State Park
Route 4
Winchester, Tennessee 37398
615-967-4457

T. O. FULLER STATE PARK
46

LOCATION   The park's 1,000 acres are 11 miles southwest of Memphis, off U.S. 61, near I-40 and I-50.

FEATURES   The historic Chucalissa Indian Village is located within the park, which was named for Dr. Thomas Oscar Fuller, a well-known Memphis clergyman and educator. The prehistoric Indian village has been reconstructed with grass-thatched huts, a temple, and ceremonial burial ground. Chucalissa in Choctaw language means "abandoned houses." Archeologists believe it was abandoned in the 1500s, probably prior to the arrival of the Spanish conquistador Hernando de Soto.

ACTIVITIES   Go fishing, play tennis, test your skill at archery, or golf on the 18-hole course. For a tee time, call 901-785-7260. Camp in the 54-site campground, 51 sites with water and electrical hookups, and laundry facilities. Pick up a trail guide and hike the Honeysuckle Nature Trail. Go swimming in the pool. Tour the visitor center, and pick up a snack from the snack bar.

The Chucalissa Village, one-half mile from the state park, is reached via a passageway decorated with traditional snake images. You can see the strata that the archeologists have worked through, as they uncovered this historic village. The Burial Exhibit contains 37 skeletons lying as they were found, surrounded by their burial objects. Today Choctaw Indians and native craftsmen demonstrate how the area's earlier people lived. You can tour native houses, an historic Indian temple, covered excavation, and the museum. The village is closed on Mondays.

In Memphis, tour Graceland, home of Elvis Presley, at 3764 Elvis Presley Boulevard. Tours of his mansion are available. It's closed Tuesdays from November 1 to March 1. Admission is charged. For information, call 901-332-3322 or 1-800-238-2000.

Drive down Beale Street, off Riverside Drive. The area is known as the "Birthplace of the Blues," and features outdoor events at Handy Park, and performances in the old Daisy Theater. For information, call 901-526-4880 or 901-523-9782.

Davies Manor, at 9336 Davies Plantation Road, has a two-story structure considered to be the oldest house in Shelby County. It's open Tuesday afternoons, from May through October. Admission is charged. For information, call 901-386-0715.

Flower lovers can tour the Memphis Botanic Gardens, at 760 Cherry Street in Audubon Park. Be sure to come when the dogwood are in bloom. For information, call 901-685-1566.

Take a riverboat cruise down the Mississippi, beginning at Riverside Drive. Excursions depart daily from March through November, and in December, weather permitting. For information, call 901-527-5694.

While down on Riverside, tour the Mississippi River Museum on Mud Island. You'll see full-scale reproductions of riverboats, an aquarium, plus sight and sound exhibits. It's open daily, but closed Monday and Tuesday during the winter. You can reach Mud Island via monorail from Front Street in town. Attend live entertainment performances in the 4,500-seat amphitheater, from Memorial Day weekend through Labor Day. For monorail schedules and museum information, call 901-528-3595. For other information, call 901-576-7241.

History buffs can tour the Victorian Village Historic District on Adams Street. Tour the Mallory-Neely House, (901-523-1481), Fontaine House (901-526-1469), and the Magevney House.

To learn more about the Civil Rights Movement, tour the National Civil Rights Museum, between Vance and Calhoun, at 450 Mulberry Street. Here you can also see the motel room and balcony where Martin Luther King was assassinated. For information, call 901-521-9699.

Annual events in Memphis include the Memphis in May International Festival, Great River Carnival in late May to early June, Elvis International Tribute Week in mid-August, the Mid-South Fair in mid-September, and the Liberty Bowl Football Classic in late December.

Arriving pilots can land at General Dewitt Spain Airport, six miles northwest of Memphis, or at Memphis International Airport, three miles south of the city. Both airports have rental cars.

INFORMATION

T. O. Fuller State Park
3269 Boxtown Road
Memphis, Tennessee 38109
901-543-7581

Chucalissa Museum
901-785-3160

WARRIOR'S PATH STATE PARK
47

LOCATION   The park's 1,500 acres are on the shore of Fort Patrick Henry Reservoir, five miles southeast of Kingsport on U.S. 23. From I-81, take Exit 59 to Tennessee 36.

FEATURES   The park was given its name because of its location, near ancient Cherokee war and trading paths.

ACTIVITIES   Play golf on the 18-hole course, with a pro shop, driving range, and snack bar. For a tee time, call 615-323-4990. You can also play miniature golf or disc golf. Attend interpretive programs, and camp in the 160-site campground, open year-round, with 94 sites providing water and electrical hookups. Purchase your supplies from the camp store. You can also overnight in a vacation cabin.

Hike nine miles of trails through the woods, and up the Holston Bluffs to Devil's Backbone. Enjoy horseback riding. Go boating in Ft. Patrick Henry Lake from the ramp or marina, with rentals available. Go trout fishing, or swim in the pool that has a water slide. Bike the trails, and play tennis.

In Kingsport, tour Exchange Place at 4812 Orebank Road. The restored 19th-century farm was once a facility for changing horses, and Virginia currency for Tennessee currency. It's open weekends from May through October. For information, call 615-288-6071. Situated on the Holston River, the Netherland Inn, circa 1818, (on Netherland Inn Road) has been restored, and is open Sunday afternoons. For information, call 615-274-3211.

Come in late July to early August for the Fun Fest in Kingsport.

Six miles from downtown Kingsport is Bays Mountain Park and Planetarium. The 3,000-acre preserve overlooks the city, and features a 44-acre lake, 25 miles of nature trails, and a planetarium. For information, call 615-229-9447.

INFORMATION

Warrior's Path State Park
P.O. Box 5026
Kingsport, Tennessee 37663
615-239-8531

TEXAS STATE PARKS

1. Abilene State Recreation Area
2. Admiral Nimitz State Historical Park
3. Atlanta State Park
4. Balmorhea State Park
5. Bastrop State Park
6. Bentsen-Rio Grande Valley State Park
7. Blanco State Recreation Area
8. Bonham State Park
9. Brazos Bend State Park
10. Buescher State Park
11. Caddo Lake State Park
12. Caprock Canyons State Park
13. Cassels-Boykin State Park
14. Cleburne State Park
15. Copper Breaks State Park
16. Daingerfield State Park
17. Davis Mountains State Park
18. Dinosaur Valley State Park
19. Eisenhower State Recreation Area
20. Enchanted Rock State Park
21. Fairfield Lake State Recreation Area
22. Falcon State Recreation Area
23. Fort Griffin State Historical Park
24. Fort Parker State Park
25. Fort Richardson State Historical Park
26. Galveston Island State Park
27. Garner State Park
28. Goose Island State Recreation Area
28. Copano Bay Pier State Park
28. Fulton Mansion State Park
29. Guadalupe River State Park
30. Huntsville State Park
31. Inks Lake State Park
32. Kerrville State Recreation Area
33. Lake Arrowhead State Rec. Area
34. Lake Brownwood State Rec. Area
35. Lake Colorado City State Park
36. Lake Corpus Christi State Rec. Area
37. Lake Lewisville State Park
38. Lake Mineral Wells State Park
39. Lake Somerville State Rec. Area
40. Lake Texana State Park
41. Lake Whitney State Recreation Area
42. Lockhart State Recreation Area
43. Longhorn Cavern State Park
44. Lost Maples State Park
45. Lyndon B. Johnson State Historical Park
45. Pedernales Falls State Park
46. Martin Dies Jr. State Park
47. McKinney Falls State Park
48. Monahans Sandhills State Park
49. Mustang Island State Park
50. Palmetto State Park
51. Palo Duro Canyon State Park

52. Possom Kingdom State Rec. Area
53. Rusk/Palestine State Park
54. San Jacinto Battleground State Historical Park
55. Sea Rim State Park
56. Seminole Canyon State Park
57. Tyler State Park

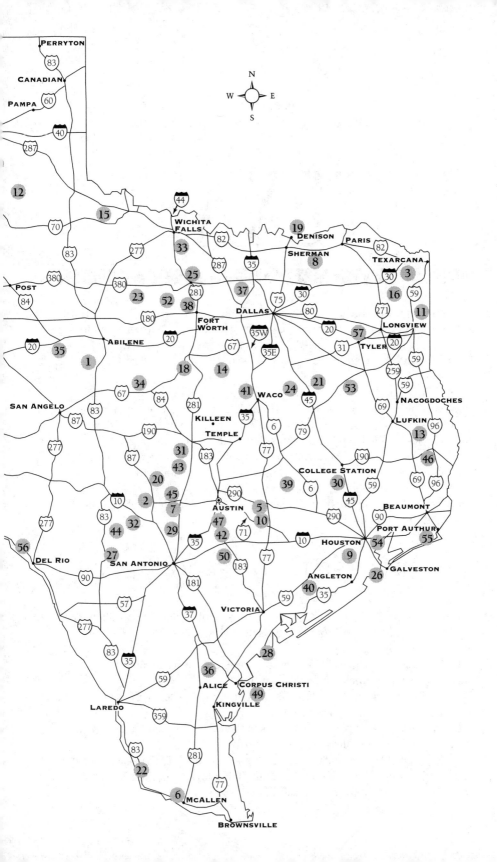

TEXAS

Texas is big! It's large enough to fit 15 of the 50 states within its borders and still have 1,000 square miles left over. Its north-south border extends 801 straight-line miles and stretches 773 miles from east to west. The Rio Grande River forms a long section of the boundary separating the U.S. and Mexico, and measures 1,248 miles.

The climate is generally mild, with an average rainfall ranging from 59 inches along the Sabine River (more than in New Orleans), to under eight inches in the extreme part of western Texas. The state boasts 91 mountains rising one mile above sea level. Guadalupe Peak is the highest at 8,749 feet.

Texas ranks second only to Alaska in its volume of inland water. It features several large bodies of water including Lake Sam Rayburn, Lake Livingston, Lake Texoma, plus the Falcon and Amistad Reservoirs. The state ranks first among states in its production of oil and natural gas, and leads all the states in its number of livestock.

ABILENE STATE RECREATION AREA

1

LOCATION   The park is 19 miles southwest of Abilene near Buffalo Gap, adjacent to Lake Abilene. From U.S. 84, follow Texas 89 south for 14½ miles to reach Park Road 32.

FEATURES   The park has a large grove of 4,000 native pecan trees, and was once a popular Comanche Indian campground.

ACTIVITIES   Camp in the 95-site campground, 83 sites with electrical and water hookups. Limited groceries are available.

Go swimming in the pool, fish for bass in the pond, and hike the nature trails. Watch for buffalo and a Texas Longhorn herd.

Buffalo Gap Historical Village is located off Texas 89 at Buffalo Gap, and contains a collection of 19th-century buildings, including a courthouse, jail, stores, and a log cabin. For information, call 915-572-3365.

Incoming pilots can land at Abilene Regional Airport, three miles southeast of the city. It has rental cars, and is 15 miles from the state park.

INFORMATION
Abilene State Recreation Area
Route 1
Tuscola, Texas 79562
915-572-3204

ADMIRAL NIMITZ STATE HISTORICAL PARK
2

LOCATION   The park is at 340 East Main in Fredericksburg, at the intersection of U.S. 290 and U.S. 87.

FEATURES   It's dedicated to the two million men and women who served with the admiral in the Pacific during World War II.

ACTIVITIES   The park is open from 8 to 5, Monday through Sunday.

The Steamboat Hotel, built in the 1850s, houses the Museum of the Pacific War, and has a restored kitchen, dining room, and ballroom. The second floor has restored rooms from 1850, 1860, 1880, and 1915. The third floor contains artifacts from Nimitz' career, from after World War II until his death.

The Nauwald building next door contains the Nimitz Gallery of Combat Art. Behind the hotel is the Garden of Peace, donated by the people of Japan.

Follow the Nimitz Trail, which connects the garden with the History Walk of the Pacific. An anchor chain takes you past memorabilia from some of the major battles, including large relics of planes, tanks, guns, vehicles, and the "Fat Man," a Nagasaki-type atomic bomb.

Many of the exhibits are "hands-on" displays, where visitors can get the feel of what it's like to steer a submarine, or turn on a ship's searchlight.

In the combat information center, built from a World War II destroyer, witness the light and sound presentation of the "nearly perfect" destroyer battle in the Pacific War—the Battle of St. George.

Camp in Lady Bird Johnson Municipal Park, three miles from Fredericksburg off Texas 16 South. For information, call 512-997-4202.

Fredericksburg Historic District is known for its "Sunday Houses," small structures with a sleeping loft accessed via an outside stairway. Here early farmers and ranchers stayed overnight when they came to town, since it was too far to travel back and forth in one day. Several of these stone houses still remain, and are marked by historical medallions. They are now privately owned, and are only open for tours five times a year. To walk by them, pick up a map of the district from the Chamber of Commerce.

Incoming pilots can land at Gillespie County Airport, located three miles southwest of Fredericksburg.

INFORMATION
Admiral Nimitz State Historical Park
P.O. Box 777
Fredericksburg, Texas 78624
210-997-4379

ATLANTA STATE PARK
3

LOCATION   The park is on the southern shore of 20,300-acre Wright Pat-
man Lake, on the Sulphur River in northeast Texas. It's 12 miles southwest of
Texarkana, off U.S. 59, and 12 miles northwest of Atlanta via F.M. 1154, off U.S.
59 north, or via F.M. 96, off Texas 77 west. It's also accessible from Douglassville,
Linden, Maud, and Queen City.
ACTIVITIES   Camp in the 59-site campground, 51 sites with water and elec-
tric hookups, plus eight with sewer hookups, and a trailer dump station.
   Go pan fishing, swimming, water-skiing, and boating from the ramp in Lake
Wright Patman. Hike the nature trails.
   Incoming pilots can land at Atlanta Municipal Airport, two miles southwest of
the city. It has rental cars, and is 10 miles from the lake.
INFORMATION
Atlanta State Park
Route 1, Box 116
Atlanta, Texas 75551
903-796-6476

BALMORHEA STATE PARK
4

LOCATION   The park is four miles south of Balmorhea, off U.S. 290.
FEATURES   The famous San Solomon Springs were once an important
watering place for buffalo, Indians, and early pioneers.
ACTIVITIES   Go camping in the 34-site campground, all sites with water
hookups, 28 with electrical hookups, and a dump station. You can also overnight
in a vacation cabin.
   Most visitors come here to swim in one of the world's largest pools fed by
springs, providing 26 million gallons of water daily. Lifeguards are on duty from
the fourth Friday in May through Labor Day.
   Balmorhea Lake also offers boating and fishing.

INFORMATION
Balmorhea State Park
Box 15
Toyahvale, Texas 79786
915-375-2370

BASTROP STATE PARK

5

LOCATION   The park is one mile northeast of Bastrop, off Texas 21, on Lake Bastrop.

FEATURES   The park is shaded by the strange "Lost Pines," an isolated area of pines located far from the vast woods of East Texas.

ACTIVITIES   Camp in one of the 78 campsites, with 25 offering full hookups. You can also stay in the lodge or cabins, and food service is available. Swim in the pool, fish in the lake, hike the nature trails, or play golf on the golf course.

In Bastrop, attend year-round performances of an opera presented in the Bastrop Opera House, circa 1889. Performances are usually offered Friday and Saturday evenings. The first Thursday of each month features audience participation in the "Mister Ree Murder Production" at 9 A.M. For information, call 512-321-6283.

Car buffs can tour the Central Texas Museum of Automotive History, 12 miles south of Bastrop on Texas 304. See 85 vintage cars covering eight decades. For information, call 512-237-2635.

INFORMATION
Bastrop State Park
Box 518
Bastrop, Texas 78602
512-321-2101

BENTSEN–RIO GRANDE VALLEY STATE PARK

6

LOCATION   The park is six miles southwest of Mission, off U.S. 83, on the Rio Grande. From the junction of U.S. 83 and F.M. 2062, drive south five miles on F.M. 2062, to Park Road 43.

FEATURES   Bentsen–Rio Grande was set aside to preserve the native flora and fauna of the lower Rio Grande Valley. Several hundred species of birds have been sighted here, including the rare Audubon oriole, zone-tailed hawk, and red-eye cowbird.

Look for evidence of the route of the old U.S. Army Military Road, from Fort Ringgold to Brownsville, near the present park entrance.

ACTIVITIES   Camp year-round in the campground with 142 sites, 77 with full hookups, and a dump station.

Go bass fishing, boating from the ramp, and hiking the trails. Birders come to this river-bottom woodland to search for over 270 species of birds. Hikers can stroll mile-long Singing Chaparral Nature Trail, or follow the longer hiking trail located at the south end of the park.

Each Christmas season, the annual all-poinsettia show is held in Mission, the only one of its kind in the U.S. In even-numbered years, the banks in town display the flowers, and in odd-numbered years, poinsettias are displayed in public buildings and private homes.

Capilla de la Lomita, Chapel of the Little Hill, is three miles south of town. Take F.M. 1016 to Madero, then go ¼ mile west. The chapel was built by the Oblate Fathers in 1865, and is one of the oldest missions still being used today. Enjoy a picnic, or hike along the nature trails.

To tour some colorful grounds, visit the Shary Estate, four miles north of Mission on Shary Road, F. M. 494.

INFORMATION
Bentsen–Rio Grande Valley State Park
Box 988
Mission, Texas 78572
210-585-1107

BLANCO STATE RECREATION AREA
7

LOCATION   The park is one mile south of Blanco, off U.S. 281, on the Blanco River.

ACTIVITIES   Camp in the 31-site campground, 10 with full hookups, and a trailer dump station. Go swimming in the river, fishing, boating (with motors under 12 horsepower), and hike the nature trails.

Enjoy a scenic drive along F.M. 32, two miles south of Blanco from U.S. 281. Follow the ridge called the "Devil's Backbone."

INFORMATION
Blanco State Recreation Area
Box 493
Blanco, Texas 78606
210-833-4333

BONHAM STATE PARK
8

LOCATION   The park is 3.5 miles southeast of Bonham, on F.M. 271.

ACTIVITIES   Camp year-round in the 31-site campground, with water and electrical hookups. Go boating on Blanco River, where boat rentals are available. Enjoy pan fishing, swimming, and playing golf on the miniature golf course. A snack bar operates during the summer.

In Bonham, tour Fort Inglish Park on Sam Rayburn Drive, a replica of a log blockhouse and stockade, built in 1837. Here you can see 3 original, restored log cabins, pioneer furnishings, and artifacts. The park is open Tuesday through Sunday, from April 1 through September 1, from 10 to 5. For information, call 903-583-3441.

Tour Sam Rayburn's house on U.S. 82, 1.5 miles west of town, and watch the film on this well-known statesman. "Mister Sam" served as speaker of the U.S. House of Representatives longer than anyone in American history. His house has been restored to its 1961 condition, with original furniture, and his personal effects on display. Tours are conducted hourly on Tuesday through Friday from 10 to 4, Saturdays from 1 to 5, and Sundays from 2 to 5. For information, call 214-583-5558.

The Sam Rayburn Library, on U.S. 82, four miles west of Bonham, is an exact duplicate of Speaker Rayburn's U.S. Capitol office. It contains many gavels used on historic occasions, and a 2,500-year-old Grecian urn, given to him by the Athens Palace Guard in appreciation for American economic aid. For information, call 214-583-2455.

Arriving pilots can land at Jones Field, two miles north of Bonham. It has rental cars, and is three miles from the park.

INFORMATION
Bonham State Park
Route 1, Box 337
Bonham, Texas 75418
903-583-5022

BRAZOS BEND STATE PARK
9

LOCATION   The park is 20 miles south of Richmond-Rosenberg, via F.M. 762.

FEATURES   Brazos Bend is one of the state's largest parks, covering almost 5,000 acres of aquatic Brazos River, with its bottomland's wetlands, oak forests with wild grape vines, Spanish moss, and coastal prairies. It has abundant wildlife including many migratory waterfowl, shore, and wading birds, and a large population of American alligators.

ACTIVITIES   Enjoy fishing from the pier, hiking and bicycling the trails, visiting wildlife observation platforms, and camping in the campground. On Saturday night, go star gazing at George Observatory.

In Richmond, tour historical buildings found in Decker Park, located in the 500 block of Preston in Richmond. Included is a 1901 railroad depot, a log cabin replica of the original Fort Bent, the McNabb house, built in 1850 and occupied by Carrie Nation's daughter, and an 1896 county jail.

The Fort Bend County Historical Museum is believed to be one of the state's smallest museums, featuring a special exhibit on local resident Jane Long, "Mother of Texas." The Moore home, a Victorian mansion built in 1883 for Texas Congressman John N. Moore, is on the museum grounds, and is open Sundays from 1 to 5.

George Ranch Historical Park is on F.M. 762, eight miles south of Richmond. Visit the 1820s Jones farmstead, tour the 1890s Victorian museum, and watch living history featuring cowboys working the ranch in the 1930s style of ranching. For information and schedules, call 713-545-9212.

Three historic homes to visit in Richmond include the Long-Smith Cottage, circa 1840s; the Moor home, circa 1883 (both on 500 Houston); and the McFarlane house at 410 Jackson.

INFORMATION
Brazos Bend State Park
21901 F.M. 762
Needville, Texas 77641
713-553-5101

BUESCHER STATE PARK
10

LOCATION   The park is three miles north of Smithville on Lake Buescher, via Texas 71/95, F.M. 2104.

FEATURES   The scenic park is located in the "Lost Pines" region, and includes groves of huge live oaks, laden with Spanish moss.

ACTIVITIES   Go camping in the 70-site campground, 40 with electrical and water hookups, and a trailer dump station. Go pan fishing, boating, hiking, enjoy a picnic, and go swimming.

Scenic Park Road 1 connects the park with Bastrop State Park, 15 miles to the west.

Incoming pilots can land at Smithville Municipal Airport, two miles north of Smithville. Taxis are available. The park is one mile from the airport.

INFORMATION
Buescher State Park
Box 75
Smithville, Texas 78957
512-237-2241

CADDO LAKE STATE PARK
11

LOCATION   Drive 15 miles northeast of Marshall on Texas 43. It's two miles north of Karnack.

FEATURES   The area was once occupied by the Caddo Indians, a tribe quite advanced in civilization. Indian legends tell of a lake formed at night, in the dark of the moon, by powerful shaking earth spirits angered at a Caddo Indian chief. Steamboats from New Orleans and other ports once crossed the lake in the mid-1800s. Pioneers arrived at the turn of the century hunting for pearls in the freshwater mussels.

ACTIVITIES   Camp in the 48-site campground, 20 sites with water and electrical hookups, eight with full hookups, and a trailer dump station. Tour the visitor center, stay in the lodge or cabins, and purchase food from the store. Hike the scenic trails.

Go bass fishing in the Big Cypress River or in Caddo Lake. Since the lake is 25,400 acres, covering portions of both Texas and Louisiana, it has a maze of channels. The state has marked 42 miles of "boat roads" to explore on the lake.

Arriving pilots can land at Harrison County Airport, three miles southeast of Marshall. Rental cars are available.

INFORMATION
Caddo Lake State Park
Route 2, Box 15
Karnack, Texas 75661
903-679-3351

CAPROCK CANYONS STATE PARK
12

LOCATION   The park is 3.5 miles north of Quitaque, off Texas 86. From Texas 86, go north 3.5 miles on F.M. 1065.

FEATURES   The park is located in one of the state's most scenic regions, where erosion has carved spectacular landscapes in the cliffs and canyons.

ACTIVITIES   Honey Flats campground has 35 campsites, 25 with water and electrical hookups, and is ¼ mile from Lake Theo. South Prong has 20 tent sites, and is four miles from Lake Theo. Off-trail camping is permitted.

The lake area has picnic shelters, an amphitheater, an interpretive center, and hiking and equestrian trails. Thirty miles of designated trails wind through the 14,000 acres of canyons, river bottoms, and rolling panhandle plains. Come in the spring and early summer when wildflowers peak. Park trails range in length from 1.5-mile Canyon Loop Trail to 5.5-mile Upper Canyon Trail.

Go fishing for bass, catfish, bluegill, and crappie; go boating from the ramp, and swimming in Lake Theo.

Park elevations vary from 2,000 to 3,000 feet. Summers can be blistering hot, but September to May is delightful.

Caprock Canyons Trailway is a multi-use trail. It's 64.25 miles long, and goes through the fields of the Texas High Plains, before dropping into the canyons of the Caprock Escarpment and the Red River Valley. Watch for a 1,000-foot abandoned railroad tunnel, listed in the Register of Historic Places.

INFORMATION
Caprock Canyons State Park
Box 204
Quitaque, Texas 79255
806-455-1492

CASSELS-BOYKIN STATE PARK
13

LOCATION   The park is located on Sam Rayburn Lake, seven miles northeast of Zavalla. From Texas 69, go east 6.1 miles on Texas 147, and north .8-mile on F.M. 3123.

FEATURES   Sam Rayburn Lake is the largest body of water found wholly within the state. It has a 560-mile-long shoreline, located in the heart of the Angelina National Forest. It's considered one of the most popular recreation areas in East Texas.

ACTIVITIES   The lake is open for all types of boating activities. Anglers will find prime fishing for several species of bass, crappie, walleye, catfish, and bream. Go water-skiing. The state park campground has 30 campsites.

INFORMATION
Cassels-Boykin State Park
Route 2, Box 154
Zavalla, Texas 75980
409-897-2144

CLEBURNE STATE PARK
14

LOCATION   The park is 12 miles southwest of Cleburne, via U.S. 67 and Park Road 21. The park is also accessible from Glen Rose.

ACTIVITIES   Enjoy camping in the 58-site campground, with water and electrical hookups, and a trailer dump station. Go swimming, power boating, water-skiing, sailing, or bass fishing in Lake Pat Cleburne. Boat rentals and groceries are available. Hike the trails. The park contains a wildlife refuge, and 116-acre Cedar Lake.

In Cleburne, tour Layland Museum at 201 North Caddo. The museum features the history of our Native Americans. You can also see a 12-foot mammoth tusk, and a gun collection, with weapons dating from the 1750s.

Arriving pilots can land at Cleburne Municipal Airport, two miles northwest of Cleburne. However, no rental cars are available.

INFORMATION
Cleburne State Park
Route 2, Box 90
Cleburne, Texas 76031
817-645-1021

COPPER BREAKS STATE PARK
15

LOCATION   The 1,933-acre park is 13 miles south of Quanah, on Texas 6, on the Pease River.

FEATURES   Quanah was named for Quanah Parker, the last great war chief of the Comanche Indians.

ACTIVITIES   Camp in the 46-site campground, with water hookups, 25 sites with electrical hookups, and a trailer dump station.

Go bass fishing in Lake Copper Breaks, and swimming or boating from the ramp or dock. Tour the visitor center, and hike the trails.

Drive by Medicine Mounds, five miles south of Texas 283. The four cone-shaped hills rise 350 feet above the plains, and were held in reverence by the Comanche Indians.

Arriving pilots can land at Quanah Municipal Airport, two miles southwest of Quanah. A courtesy car is available. The airport is eight miles from the park.

INFORMATION
Copper Breaks State Park
Route 3
Quanah, Texas 79252
817-839-4331

DAINGERFIELD STATE PARK
16

LOCATION   From Daingerfield, go three miles east on Texas 49, Park Road 17.

ACTIVITIES   Camp in the 40-site campground, nine with full hookups, and 16 with water and electricity. You can also stay in the group lodge, or in one of the two cabins.

A snack bar is open during the summer. Go swimming, fishing, and boating in the lake. There is a five mph limit, and a ramp is available. Come in the spring when the dogwood are in bloom. Tour the visitor center, attend a nature program, and hike the trails.

Nearby Lake O' the Pines offers fishing for huge smallmouth buffalo fish, sometimes weighing 97 pounds, for bass weighing 12 pounds, and for spotted bass weighing six pounds. Enjoy boating, sailing, water-skiing, swimming, and camping.

Incoming pilots can land at Greater Morris County Airport, seven miles north of town. However, no rental cars are available.

INFORMATION
Daingerfield State Park
Route 1, Box 286-B
Daingerfield, Texas 75638
903-645-2921

DAVIS MOUNTAINS STATE PARK
17

LOCATION   The park is four miles northwest of Fort Davis, via Texas 118 and Park Road 3.

FEATURES   The volcanic mountains, named for Jefferson Davis, the U.S. Secretary of War, are Texas' most extensive. They range in elevation from 4,900-5,500 feet. Because of their elevation, the winters are mild and the summers cool.

Fort Davis, located on the east side of the park, was active from 1854 to 1891 as a military post to provide protection for gold seekers, settlers, and traders. The park protects the Montezuma quail, a rare Texan bird.

ACTIVITIES   Hike 4.5 miles of trails that begin at the interpretive center, including one connecting with the trail leading to the Fort Davis National Historical Site.

Tour the park's interpretive center, and attend campfire programs from June through August. Camp in the 108-site campground, 78 sites with water, 27 with sewer, and 47 sites with electrical hookups. You can also stay in the Indian Lodge, with 39 guest rooms and a restaurant. For reservations, call 915-426-3254.

Drive Skyline Drive following the highest ridges in the park, with two scenic overlooks at 6,000 feet. Another spectacular drive follows Texas 170 between Presidio, 80 miles south of the Davis Mountains, and Study Butte.

Take the 74-mile scenic loop on Texas 118 to follow Texas' highest road. The loop returns through Fort Davis. Thirteen miles west of the park, tour McDonald

Observatory located on top of Mt. Locke. The 82-inch telescope is the largest in the world available to the public. If you want to use the telescope—limited to the last Wednesday night of the month—make advance arrangements at least six months in advance by writing the Visitor Center, McDonald Observatory, Box 1337, Fort Davis, TX 79734. For information, call 915-426-3640. The least-crowded months to tour are January and February.

While at the summit, follow the short self-guided walking tour to the white dome, housing the University of Texas' 107-inch reflecting telescope.

The W. L. Moody Jr. Visitor Center, at the foot of Mt. Locke, presents programs throughout the day, Monday through Saturday, and Sunday afternoons. The dome is open to the public and may be viewed from the visitors' gallery. Take a self-guided tour, or join a guided tour that leaves at 9:30 and 2:00, from June through August, and at 2:00 the rest of the year. From June through August, the center conducts Star Parties at the state park amphitheater, on Tuesday and Friday at 9:30 P.M.

Nearby Fort Davis National Historic Site is located on the north edge of town. From I-10 from the north, or U.S. 90 from the south, follow Texas 17 and 118. The site is a good example of a Texas frontier fort, with many restored buildings. Look for the 13 homes along Officers' Row that stand in a precise arrangement. Tour the visitor center and walk through the museum located in the reconstructed barracks. Watch a replica of a 19th-century military parade, with music from the band manuals of 1875.

Hike extensive nature trails, including Tall Grass Trail, during the summer. Costumed interpreters conduct tours, and present demonstrations in the commanding officer's quarters, officers' kitchens, servants' quarters, and commissary.

INFORMATION

Davis Mountains State Park	Fort Davis National Historic Site
Box 786	P.O. Box 1456
Fort Davis, Texas 79734	Fort Davis, Texas 78734
915-426-3337	915-426-3225

DINOSAUR VALLEY STATE PARK
18

LOCATION   The park is 17 miles south of Granbury, on the Paluxy River. From Texas 67, go east four miles on F.M. 201 to Park Road 59, and then continue east one mile. It's also five miles west of Glen Rose.

FEATURES   The Paluxy River flows over solid rock containing the best-preserved dinosaur tracks in Texas. Tracks of the plant-eating sauropods who were over 60 feet long, and weighed 30 tons, and theropods, 12-foot-tall meat-eaters, have been found here. During their lifetime, this area was a coastal swampland.

ACTIVITIES   See dinosaur replicas on exhibit in the museum. Hike the nature trails. Camp in the campground, with water and electrical hookups. Go fishing and swimming. Watch for the herd of Texas Longhorn.

Drive through Fossil Rim Wildlife Ranch, home to 30 rare and endangered species of African wildlife. The ranch is off U.S. 67, 3.5 miles west of Glen Rose. For information, call 817-897-2960.

Incoming pilots can land at Granbury Municipal Airport, two miles west of the city. A courtesy car is available.

INFORMATION
Dinosaur Valley State Park
Box 396
Glen Rose, Texas 76043
817-897-4588

EISENHOWER STATE RECREATION AREA
19

LOCATION   The park is seven miles northwest of Denison, on Lake Texoma. From U.S. 75-A, go west 1.8 miles on F.M. 1310, and then 20 miles north on Park Road 20.

ACTIVITIES   Camp in the 180-site campground, 50 sites with full hookups, and 45 with electricity and water. A trailer dump station, and food are available.

Swim in Lake Texoma, go trail biking in the trail bike area, hike the trails, fish for bass, boat from the ramp, with rental boats available from the marina.

Tour Denison Dam, north of town on U.S. 75A. Short tours are offered Monday through Friday at 1 P.M. See their fossils on exhibit that were unearthed during construction of the dam that impounds Lake Texoma.

Eisenhower's Birthplace State Historic Site is at 208 E. Day Street, in Denison. It's been restored to its 1890 appearance. For information, call 903-465-8908.

Tour Hagerman National Wildlife Refuge northwest of Sherman, on the south end of the Big Mineral Arm of Lake Texoma. From U.S. 75 between Denison and Sherman, take F.M. 691 west to F.M. 1417, and go north for 1.5 miles. Go fishing, boating, hiking, and enjoy a picnic. Approximately 250 bird species have been recorded here. Pick up a bird list at the refuge headquarters. For information, call 903-786-2826.

In Loy Lake Park, walk through Grayson County Frontier Village, circa 1840–1900, open Sunday afternoons May through November. You'll see a collection of rustic structures from the 19th-century including a log cabin, circa 1839, and log schoolhouse with the teacher's sleeping loft.

Incoming pilots can land at Grayson County Airport, four miles west of Sherman-Denison.

INFORMATION
Eisenhower State Recreation Area
Route 2, Box 50K
Denison, Texas 75020
903-465-1956

ENCHANTED ROCK STATE PARK
20

LOCATION   The park is 18 miles north of Fredericksburg, and 22 miles south of Llano, via Texas 16, F.M. 965.

FEATURES   Enchanted Rock is 500 feet high, one billion years old, and is among the oldest exposed rocks in North America. Indian legends tell of human sacrifices, and some tribes feared to even set foot here. Still other Indians believed ghost fires flickered on the rock's crest on moonlit nights.

ACTIVITIES   Camp in the primitive campground where only tent camping is permitted. Campground reservations are accepted. Hike the trail to the crest of Enchanted Rock, designated a National Natural Landmark. Many visitors come for the rock climbing and rappelling.

Enchanted Rock State Park contains this massive dome of solid granite covering over 600 acres and standing 500 feet high. The rock is the subject of Indian legends due to the glittering lights and strange creaking sounds often witnessed on summer nights.
(photo by Richard Reynolds, courtesy of TTDA)

For an unusual tour, visit the dulcimer factory at 715 South Washington in Fredericksburg. Visit Admiral Nimitz Museum State Historical Park and Museum of the Pacific War, at 340 E. Main. For details, see the information found under Admiral Nimitz State Historic Park.

Take a scenic drive on R.M. 965 north, U.S. 87 to R.M. 648 to Doss, follow Texas 16 northwest for 13 miles, and go west on F.M. 1323 to Willow City.

Incoming pilots can land at Gillespie County Airport, three miles southwest of Fredericksburg. However, no rental cars are available.

INFORMATION
Enchanted Rock State Park
Ranch Road
965 North Fredericksburg
Route 4, Box 170
Fredericksburg, Texas 78624
915-247-3093

FAIRFIELD LAKE STATE RECREATION AREA
21

LOCATION   The area is seven miles northeast of Fairfield, on Lake Fairfield. From U.S. 84, go northeast of F.M. 488, 1.3 miles northeast of F.M. 1124, and east 3.2 miles on F.M. 3285.

ACTIVITIES   Camp in the 135-site campground, 99 sites with water and electrical hookups, and a trailer dump station.

Swim in the lake, fish for bass, catfish, and stocked perch from the fishing pier, and boat from the ramp. Hike 4.5 miles to reach a primitive camping area. Attend nature programs.

INFORMATION
Fairfield Lake State Recreation Area
Route 2, Box 912
Fairfield, Texas 75840
903-389-4514

FALCON STATE RECREATION AREA
22

LOCATION   The park is 14 miles northwest of Roma, on the Falcon Reservoir. From U.S. 83, follow F.M. 2098 northwest for 3.2 miles, to Park Road 46.

FEATURES   The reservoir is owned jointly by the U.S. and Mexico. The dam is almost five miles long, and is 100 feet high.

ACTIVITIES   Fish for black bass and catfish in the reservoir, go water-skiing, swimming, and boating.

The campground has 117 campsites, 31 sites offering full hookups, 31 with water and electricity, and a trailer dump station. You can also overnight in a cabin. Groceries and a snack bar are available.

Pilots can land at the area's 3,500-foot lighted air strip.

INFORMATION
Falcon State Recreation Area
Box 2
Falcon Heights, Texas 78545
210-848-5327

FORT GRIFFIN STATE HISTORICAL PARK
23

LOCATION   The park is on the Clear Fork of the Brazos River. From U.S. 180, drive north from Albany 14.4 miles on U.S. 283, to reach Park Road 54E.

FEATURES   The site includes the ruins of the 1867 fort and townsite, which once served as the base for sorties sent out against the Comanches. The surrounding town grew up in the 1870s and 1880s, and for over 12 years, was a wild, rough settlement with many gunfights that resulted in 34 killings. After the fort was abandoned, the town's population declined, and today you can see rural homes scattered along the Brazos River.

ACTIVITIES   Camp in the 20-site campground, 15 with electrical and water hookups, and a trailer dump station.

Go pan fishing in the Brazos River, and tour the visitor center. Observe the Texas Longhorn herd, maintained by the state from which Bevo, the University of Texas' mascot, is selected. Several old fort buildings still stand, and historical plaques provide details of their former existence.

INFORMATION
Fort Griffin State Historical Park
Route 1
Albany, Texas 76430
915-762-3592

FORT PARKER STATE PARK
24

LOCATION   The park is five miles north of Groesbeck, and seven miles south of Mexia. From the junction of Texas 14 and U.S. 84, go south six miles on Texas 14 to Park Road 28, and continue west .8-mile.

FEATURES   The park features both open and wooded land, along the Navasota River and 750-acre Lake Springfield.

ACTIVITIES   Camp in one of the 25 campsites, with water and electrical hookups, and a trailer dump station. Go bass fishing, swimming, and boating on Fort Parker Lake. Hike the nature trails.

Tour Old Fort Parker State Historic Site, four miles north of Groesbeck via Texas 14 and Park Road 35. It was established in 1834 to protect the settlement of the early homesteads. In 1836, the entire Parker family was killed, except for 9-year-old Cynthia Ann Parker. She married a Comanche chief and was the mother of the last great Comanche chief, Quanah Parker. The fort has been restored and contains pioneer memorabilia, and an authentic log blockhouse and stockade. It's open daily from 8 to 5.

The Navasota River and other streams combine to form Lake Mexia, where excellent year-round fishing, boating, swimming, camping, and water-skiing is available. One of the streams feeding the lake is Baines Creek, named for George Washington Baines, great-grandfather of the late president Johnson, who served as a circuit-riding Baptist preacher during the Civil War.

Incoming pilots can land at Mexia–Limestone County Airport, three miles southwest of Mexia. A courtesy car and taxis are available.

INFORMATION
Fort Parker State Park
Route 3, Box 95
Mexia, Texas 76667
817-562-5751

FORT RICHARDSON
STATE HISTORICAL PARK
25

LOCATION   From Jacksboro, follow U.S. 281 southwest for one mile. The park is on an eight-acre lake.

FEATURES   The fort was the most northerly in a line of federal posts, established to halt Comanche and Kiowa Indian attacks following the Civil War. It was named for Union General Israel B. Richardson, killed in the battle of Antietam. Col. Ranald S. Mackenzie of the famed Mackenzie's Raiders, was one of its regimental commanders. The enlisted men's barracks is now used as the museum. The fort was abandoned in May, 1878.

ACTIVITIES   Tour the historic site, museum, barracks, and see the original wooden officers' quarters, morgue, and the bakery that once produced 600 loaves of bread daily. The barracks is open daily from Memorial Day through Labor Day, Friday through Sunday, and by special request the rest of the year. The park itself is open year-round.

Camp year-round in the 23-site campground, with water and electrical hookups, and a trailer dump station. Fish in the lake, and hike the 1.7-mile hiking trail that loops through the park. Attend a military reenactment, presented each November.

Jacksboro Lake is off Texas 59, northeast of town. Fish for bass, catfish, bluegill, and go swimming, boating, and water-skiing.

Incoming pilots can land at Jacksboro Municipal Airport, one mile northeast of the city. However, it has no rental cars. The park is two miles from the airport.

INFORMATION
Fort Richardson State Historical Park
Box 4
Jacksboro, Texas 76056
817-567-3506

GALVESTON ISLAND STATE PARK
26

LOCATION   The park is six miles south of Galveston, on Galveston Island. It extends from the Gulf of Mexico to West Galveston Bay. From Texas 45, follow 61st southeast for two miles, to Texas 3005, Seawall Boulevard, and continue 11 more miles.

FEATURES   The park spans the width of Galveston Island, with 32 miles of sandy beaches. It includes a salt marsh, elevated boardwalks, and observation platforms to observe the birdlife.

ACTIVITIES   Camp in the 170-site campground, with electrical and water hookups, and a trailer dump station. Enjoy boating, hiking the nature trails, birding, swimming, and surfing from 1.6 miles of beach.

Try "wade fishing" in the salt marsh, west of West Galveston Bay. Excellent fishing is available both in the Gulf of Mexico and in the Bay. Charter boats are available.

Drive along the ten-mile seawall, built after the Galveston flood of 1900, one of the most destructive hurricanes in current history, in which 6,000 people lost their lives.

Attend summer dramas of *The Lone Star,* and a Broadway musical, presented on alternate nights except Sundays, from late June through late August. The 1,700-seat amphitheater is 12 miles southwest of town on Seawall Boulevard, then ¼ mile north on 13 Mile Road. A Texas-style barbecue is available from 6 to 8 P.M. on show nights. For information, call 409-737-3441 in Galveston, or 713-486-8052 in Houston.

Galveston is often called the "Queen City of the Southwest" because of its hundreds of Victorian homes, lining the streets of the Silk Stocking and the East End Historical districts. Tour Aston Villa at 2328 Broadway, and Bishop's Palace at 1402 Broadway. Moody mansion and museum is at 2618 Broadway. Powhatan house is at 3427 Avenue O, and Samuel May Williams home is at 3601 Avenue P.

Take a one-hour narrated tour on the Galveston Flyer, a hand-crafted trolley that runs between Seawall, the Port of Galveston, and the East End. Obtain your tickets at the Strand Visitor Center at 2016 Strand in Hendley Row.

Enjoy a one-hour free walking tour of the Strand, once called the "Wall Street of the Southwest," beginning at noon and 2:00 on Sundays. This National Historic Landmark District is on Strand and Mechanic Streets, between 20th and 25th. It features "Dickens on the Strand" in December, and Mardi Gras celebrations in early spring. For information, call 409-765-7834.

The *Elissa* is moored near the Strand at Pier 21, at the end of 22nd Street. This restored iron barque was built in 1877 in Scotland, and has masts rising over 100 feet. It is one of the oldest merchant ships. Tour the ship, and watch the orientation film at the Strand Visitor Center. Once a year, the ship goes sailing. For information, call 409-763-1877.

Take a one-hour sightseeing cruise on the *Colonel,* a triple-deck paddle-wheel boat. It departs from Moody Gardens, at One Hope Boulevard. For information, call 409-740-7797. While there, tour Moody Gardens.

Tour the David Taylor Classic Car Museum, featuring antique, classic, and muscle cars, at 1918 Mechanic Street.

Visit Sea-Arama Marine World, at 91st and Seawall Boulevard. Sea Rim State Park is at 75 East Galveston, via Texas 87.

Incoming pilots can land at Scholes Field, three miles southwest of Galveston. It has rental cars.

INFORMATION
Galveston Island State Park
Route 1, Box 156A
Galveston, Texas 77551
409-737-1222

GARNER STATE PARK
27

LOCATION   From Texas 127, the park is on the Frio River, 7.2 miles north of Concan, off U.S. 83, on Park Road 29.

ACTIVITIES   Camp in the large campground with 354 campsites, 143 sites with water and electrical hookups, 211 with water, and a trailer dump station. Eighteen cabins are also available. Snacks and groceries are sold, and a restaurant is open during the summer.

Go swimming and fishing in the river, hike and bicycle along the trails. Play miniature golf, and rent a pedal boat.

Take a scenic drive through Frio River Canyon, along U.S. 83, F.M. 1050, and Texas 127.

INFORMATION
Garner State Park
Concan, Texas 78838
512-232-6132 and 512-232-6133

GOOSE ISLAND STATE RECREATION AREA

COPANO BAY PIER STATE PARK

FULTON MANSION STATE PARK
28

LOCATION   Goose Island State Recreation Area is on Aransas Bay, 12 miles northeast of Rockport. From F.M. 3036, go north 5.9 miles on Texas 35, to Park Road 13. Then continue east 1.5 miles and south 1.2 miles.

Copano Bay Pier State Park is north of Rockport, near present Texas 35's causeway.

Fulton Mansion State Park is 3.5 miles north of Rockport, on Fulton Beach Road.

FEATURES   Goose Island is situated on an old sand ridge called Live Oak Ridge, a remnant of a barrier island formed 120,000 years ago when sea level was higher. The recreation area has two units—mainland and island. It got its name because of the wild geese who live here during the winter.

Two miles northeast of the park is the site of 44-foot "Big Tree," an immense live oak certified as the largest one in Texas, estimated to be 2,000 years old.

ACTIVITIES   Go camping in one of 102 sites, located both near the waterfront and in the woods, with 57 sites providing water and electrical hookups, and a dump station. Go fishing in the ocean for redfish, drum, flounder, oysters, and crabs. Enjoy hiking the nature trails, swimming, boating from the ramp, and water-skiing. The park has a dining hall, and a lighted fishing pier.

In July, attend the annual art festival. On the weekend preceding Columbus Day, attend the annual Sea Fair in Rockport.

At Copano Bay Causeway State Park, go fishing from piers extending from the north and south sides of Rockport. Concessions on both sides provide tackle and food. A public boat ramp is located on the south side.

Tour the Fulton Mansion State Historical Structure. Completed in 1876 after four years of construction, the house was a showplace of its time. The restored house and grounds are open Wednesday through Sunday. For information, call 512-729-0386.

Across the St. Charles Bay from the park, and 36 miles northeast of Rockport, is the Aransas National Wildlife Refuge, famed as the principal wintering ground for the nearly extinct whooping crane. Its interpretive center offers a slide show and mounted specimens. To get a good look at the "whoopers," take a ride aboard the *Whooping Crane,* from the Rockport yacht basin, Tuesday through Sunday, from mid-October through mid-April. Hike the nature trails, go fishing, and drive the self-guided auto route.

Our Lady of the Sea Catholic Chapel is located west of the park. Begun in 1854, it was originally constructed of cement made from the local oyster shells.

The jetty sheltering the Rockport Yacht Basin is a popular spot for bay fishing. Deep-sea charter cruises are available. A public fishing pier is at Fulton Yacht Basin, four miles north.

Tour Texas Maritime Museum, near the center of Rockport, on Texas 35. It's open Tuesday through Sunday. For information, call 512-729-1271.

Arriving pilots can land at Aransas County Airport, five miles north of Rockport. It has rental cars.

INFORMATION

Goose Island State Park
Star Route 1, Box 105
Rockport, Texas 78382
512-729-2858

Copano Bay Pier State Park
Rockport, Texas 78382
512-729-8633
Aransas Refuge Manager
P.O. Box 100
Austwell, Texas 77950
512-286-3559

Fulton Mansion State Park
Fulton Beach Road
Rockport, Texas 78382
512-729-0286

GUADALUPE RIVER STATE PARK
29

LOCATION   The park is 13 miles east of Boerne. From Texas 46, follow U.S. 281 north for eight miles, to Park Road 31, and continue west three miles.

FEATURES   The 1,900 acre park is cut by a cypress-edged river that flows through the park.

ACTIVITIES Go hiking, swimming in the river, canoeing, and fishing for catfish. Camp in the campground with 105 sites, 48 with electrical and water hookups, and a dump station.

Visit nearby Cascade Caverns located on Cascade Caverns Road, three miles southeast of Boerne, off I-10. One-hour interpretive tours leave every 30 minutes.

Old Kendall Inn, circa 1859, in the downtown plaza in Boerne, was originally a stagecoach inn, and later served as a gathering place for lawmen, army officers, and cattle drovers. Today it houses a bed and breakfast, shops, and restaurants.

INFORMATION
Guadalupe River State Park
Route 2, Box 2087
Bulverde, Texas 78163
210-438-2656

HUNTSVILLE STATE PARK
30

LOCATION The park is on Lake Raven, 10 miles south of Huntsville, in the Sam Houston National Forest. From Texas 30, drive south 6.9 miles on I-45 to Park Road 40, and continue southwest .2-mile.

ACTIVITIES Camp in the 191-site campground, 64 sites with water and electrical hookups, and a dump station. Limited groceries and snacks are available.

Swim or go boating on the lake, and go fishing for bass from the fishing pier. Boats and canoes are available for rent. Hike the trails including a marked botany trail, and go bicycling along the bike trails. The national forest has 140 miles of trails, where you can see dogwood and wild plum blooming in the spring. For information, call 409-344-6205.

Tour the Sam Houston Memorial Museum Complex at 1836 Sam Houston Avenue, to see two period-furnished homes, and a museum.

Take a scenic drive through Sam Houston National Forest on F.M. 1374, not shown on most road maps. It goes to Stubblefield Lake Recreation Area, and F.M. 1375 goes east from New Waverly to Walker Lake Recreation Area.

Arriving pilots can land at Huntsville Municipal Airport, two miles northwest of town. It has rental cars.

INFORMATION
Huntsville State Park
Box 508
Huntsville, Texas 77340
409-295-5644

INKS LAKE STATE PARK
31

LOCATION   The park is nine miles west of Burnet, off Texas 29, and then south on Park Road 4. It's southeast of Buchanan Dam.

ACTIVITIES   Go water-skiing, canoeing, and golf their nine-hole course on the shore of Inks Lake. Camp in the 189-site campground, 54 sites with electricity and water, and 135 with only water hookups, and a dump station. Groceries are available. Go boating, with rentals available, swim in the lake, and go fishing for catfish.

INFORMATION
Inks Lake State Park
Box 117
Buchanan Dam, Texas 78609
512-793-2223

KERRVILLE STATE RECREATION AREA
32

LOCATION   Kerrville is on the Guadalupe River, three miles southwest of Kerrville. From Texas 16, go southeast 2.1 miles on Texas 173, to Park Road 19.

FEATURES   Because the area is believed to have the most ideal climate in the nation, it's one of Texas' most popular health and recreation centers.

ACTIVITIES   Camp year-round in the 120-site campground, 30 sites with full hookups, 55 sites with both water and electricity, 65 sites with water only, and a dump station.

Swim, fish for bass, go boating in the river from the dock or ramp, and hike the trails.

In April, the Hill Country Chili Classic is held at Camp Verde, 11 miles south of town on F.M. 689. Come to Kerrville over Memorial Day weekend and the first weekend in June, for Texas State's Arts and Crafts Fair. Musical festivals are held on Memorial Day, July 4th, and Labor Day weekends, and bluegrass festivals are held at Quiet Valley Ranch south of town, in August and September.

Tour the Classic Car Showcase and Wax Museum on F.M. 783 at I-10, Harper Road, Exit 505. Here you see a collection of cars from the 1920s through the 1940s, complete with wax figures of their owners. It's open Monday, and Wednesday through Saturday from 10 to 5, and Sunday from noon to 5. For information, call 210-895-5655.

The Cowboy Artists of America Museum is one mile south of town, on Bandera Highway, Texas 173. It features works of living western American artists. For information, call 210-896-2553.

Visit Texas Heritage Music Museum at Inn of the Hills, 1001 Junction Highway, Suite F. It contains memorabilia of Texas musicians, and sponsors the Jimmie Rogers Jubilee in September. For information, call 210-895-4442.

Arriving pilots can land at Kerrville Municipal–Louis Schreiner Field, five miles southeast of Kerrville. It has rental cars.

INFORMATION
Kerrville State Recreation Area
2385 Bandera Highway
Kerrville, Texas 78028
210-257-5392

LAKE ARROWHEAD
STATE RECREATION AREA
33

LOCATION　　The park is 15 miles southeast of Wichita Falls, via U.S. 281 and F.M. 1954.

FEATURES　　The earthen dam is three miles long, and has over a dozen steel derricks erected over oil wells, located in the lake.

ACTIVITIES　　Camp in the 67-site campground, 48 sites with water and electricity. Go bass fishing, swimming, and water-skiing in Lake Arrowhead. Enjoy boating from the ramp, with boat rentals available at the marina. Purchase a snack or groceries, and attend summer programs in the amphitheater.

Tour historic Kell house at 900 Bluff Street in Wichita Falls, Tuesday through Friday, and on Sunday. Explore the river walk trail along the Wichita River, connecting Lucy Park to 54-foot-high Wichita Falls. To reach the trail, take U.S. 277 west, and turn north on Sunset Drive.

Arriving pilots can land at Kickapoo Downtown Airpark, two miles southeast of Wichita Falls. It has rental cars.

INFORMATION
Lake Arrowhead State Recreation Area
Route 2, Box 260
Wichita Falls, Texas 76301
817-528-2211

LAKE BROWNWOOD
STATE RECREATION AREA
34

LOCATION   The lake is 22 miles northwest of Brownwood. From U.S. 67/377, follow Texas 279 northwest for 15.2 miles, to Park Road 15. Go east 5.2 more miles.

ACTIVITIES   Camp in one of 89 campsites, 20 sites with full hookups, 55 with electricity and water, and a trailer dump station. You can also stay in one of 17 cabins, or two lodges. Go swimming in the lake, ride trail bikes, and go boating from the ramp, with boat rentals available. Hike the trails, or fish for bass from the lighted fishing pier. Skiing is available during the winter.

In Brownwood, visit the Douglas MacArthur Academy of Freedom, located on Austin Avenue, F.M. 2524 at Coggin St. The school, an affiliate of Howard Payne University, has a display dedicated to MacArthur, including a 3,500-foot mural and electric map featuring his Pacific campaigns. Tours are offered Monday through Saturday, when school is in session. For information, call 915-646-2502, extension 406.

Incoming pilots can land at Brownwood Municipal Airport, five miles north of Brownwood. It has rental cars.

INFORMATION
Lake Brownwood State Recreation Area
Route 5, Box 160
Brownwood, Texas 76801
915-784-5223

LAKE COLORADO CITY STATE PARK
35

LOCATION   The park is seven miles southwest of Colorado City, off I-20 west or Texas 163 south.

ACTIVITIES   The park has 128 campsites with water hookups, 78 with electricity, a dump station, and limited groceries.

Enjoy year-round bass, catfish, and walleye fishing, swimming. and boating in the lake. Ride minibikes in the special area set aside for them.

Tour Colorado City Historical Museum in downtown Colorado City, off U.S. 80 at 3rd and Locust. It's open from 2 to 5 except Mondays, and contains artifacts of early West Texas, and 19th century pictures and archives.

INFORMATION
Lake Colorado State Park
Route 2, Box 232
Colorado City, Texas 79512
915-728-3931

LAKE CORPUS CHRISTI
STATE RECREATION AREA
36

LOCATION   The area is 35 miles northwest of Corpus Christi, on the southeast shore of Lake Corpus Christi. Follow Farm Road to Market Road #1068. It's also six miles southwest of Mathis off Texas 359.

FEATURES   The Nueces River was once a disputed boundary between Mexico and the U.S. However, following the Mexican War which ended in 1848, the Rio Grande, located 120 miles south, was declared to be the official border. The Nueces River was then dammed, creating Lake Corpus Christi.

The lake is 27 miles long, and has over 200 miles of shoreline, making it one of the largest artificial bodies of fresh water in Texas. The park surrounds a large protected cove, providing protection against the prevailing southeast winds.

Summer temperatures average 84 degrees, and in winter 64 degrees. The heaviest rainfall occurs in late summer and early fall. The annual rainfall averages 28.5 inches.

ACTIVITIES   Enjoy water sports: rent a boat from the marina, go water-skiing, swimming, and fishing for catfish, perch, crappie, and record-size bass and flathead, from the fishing pier (rental boats available).

Camp in one of the 48 sites, with water and electrical hookups, 25 sites with full hookups and screened shelters, or in one of the 60 tent sites. Groceries are available seasonally. Hike the ½-mile nature trail, where birders come to search for 300 species of birds that have been spotted here.

Attend the 10-day Buchaneer Days Festivities held in late April through early May. They feature 2 parades, 11 carnivals, 3 nights of fireworks, sailboat races, a model airshow, and a music festival. For information, call 512-882-5603.

The port of Corpus Christi and Harbor Bridge is one of the 10 busiest in the U.S., with ships coming here from all over the world. The harbor entrance is spanned by an impressive bridge on U.S. 181, that rises 235 feet over the water. Under the bridge is an observation platform where you can get close-up views of ships entering and leaving the port.

Arriving pilots can land at Corpus Christi International Airport, five miles west of the city, and eight miles from the bay. It has rental cars.

INFORMATION
Lake Corpus Christi State Recreation Area
Box 1167
Mathis, Texas 78368
512-547-2635

LAKE LEWISVILLE STATE PARK
37

LOCATION   The state park is on the eastern shore of Lake Lewisville. From the Junction of I-35 and Texas 121, go east six miles on Texas 121 to F.M. 423, north 5.25 miles to Hackberry Road, west two miles, and then south a quarter-mile to reach the lake. It's also 27 miles north of downtown Dallas.

FEATURES   This huge 23,280-acre lake provides opportunities for water sports and outdoor recreation for the Dallas–Fort Worth area. The lake is home to the Dallas Corinthian Yacht Club, and two Coast Guard auxiliary flotillas.

ACTIVITIES   The lake has many facilities on its eastern shore, including the state park. It has marinas, boat rentals, launching ramps, and anglers' supplies. Fishing is excellent for largemouth bass, crappie, catfish, white bass, and hybrid white/striped bass.

Enjoy swimming, water-skiing, sailing, and camping year-round in the 50-site state park campground, with water and electrical hookups.

INFORMATION
Lake Lewisville State Park
Route 2, Box 353H
Frisco, Texas 75034
214-292-1442

LAKE MINERAL WELLS STATE PARK
38

LOCATION   The park is four miles east of Mineral Wells, on Lake Mineral Wells. Follow U.S. 180 east for 3.9 miles, and then go north on the park road for .6 mile.

FEATURES   Crazy Water Well, located at the intersection of U.S. 281 and 180, marks the site of the first mineral-water well in the county. The water made the city nationally famous in the late 19th to early 20th century because it was believed to cure mental illness, along with many other maladies.

ACTIVITIES   Extensive picnic facilities are located on the south side of the lake, and camping facilities are on the north side. The campground has 108 camp-sites, 77 with electrical and water hookups, and a dump station.

Equestrians will find 20 campsites with water. A 10-mile equestrian/hiking trail leads to a primitive camp area. However, no horse rentals are available. Go swimming in the lake, fishing for catfish, and boating from the ramp.

For a scenic drive, take Texas 4, 12 miles west of Mineral Wells at Palo Pinto, south to I-20, to see spectacular bluffs and the Palo Pinto Mountains. If you follow U.S. 281 north from I-20, you pass through the Brazos River Valley.

INFORMATION
Lake Mineral Wells State Park
Route 4, Box 39C
Mineral Wells, Texas 76068
817-328-1171

LAKE SOMERVILLE
STATE RECREATION AREA
39

LOCATION   Lake Somerville State Recreation Area has two recreation areas, both located on Lake Somerville. Birch Creek Unit is on the north shore and reached from Texas 36. Go west 7.6 miles on F.M. 60, and 4.3 miles south on Park Road 57.

Nails Creek Unit is on the south shore, reached from U.S. 290 in Burton. Drive 11 miles northwest on F.M. 1697, and east three miles on F.M. 180.

FEATURES   Lake Somerville has 85 miles of shoreline, with numerous camping areas plus commercial marinas, scattered around its shores.

ACTIVITIES   Birch Creek Unit has 133 sites, with 103 offering electrical and water hookups. Go swimming in the lake, boating from the ramp, bass fishing, water-skiing, and hike the trails.

Nails Creek Unit has 40 campsites, with water and electrical hookups, and a dump station. Go swimming, fishing and boating in the lake, and hike the trails. A 23-mile hiking/equestrian trail, with primitive campsites, connects Birch Creek and Nails Creek Units.

INFORMATION
Lake Somerville State Recreation Area
Birch Creek Unit
Route 1, Box 499
Somerville, Texas 77879
409-535-7763

Nails Creek Unit
Route 1, Box 61C
Ledbetter, Texas 78946
409-289-2392

LAKE TEXANA STATE PARK
40

LOCATION   The lake is 6.5 miles east of Edna. Take Texas 111 east for 5.8 miles, and then go north on the local road.

ACTIVITIES   Go camping in the 141-site campground, all sites with electricity, 55 with water hookups, and a dump station. Go boating from the ramp, swimming, water-skiing, and fishing for catfish in Lake Texana.

Arriving pilots can land at Jackson County Airport, three miles northeast of Edna. It has a courtesy car and is 10 miles from the park.

INFORMATION
Lake Texana State Park
Box 666
Edna, Texas 77957
512-782-5718

LAKE WHITNEY STATE RECREATION AREA
41

LOCATION   The park is on the eastern shore of Lake Whitney. From Texas 22, go north .6-mile on F.M. 933, then west 2.5 miles on F.M. 1244, to Park Road 47 SW.

FEATURES   Lake Whitney is one of the nation's most popular water recreation areas. It stretches 45 miles up the Brazos River Valley, and has many campsites, marinas, parks and recreation areas around its shoreline.

ACTIVITIES   Camp in the 187-site campground, all sites with water, 35 sites with full hookups, and 7 with water and electrical hookups, and dumping stations.

Swim or water ski in Lake Whitney, and ride minibikes in the area provided. Fish for bass, scuba dive in the clear water down to depths of almost 100 feet, or go boating from the ramp.

Motorcyclists can go to Lake Whitney Cycle Ranch. Go west on Texas 22 to F.M. 2960, Iron Springs Road, which is not shown on most highway maps. Races are held beside the Brazos River the first, third, and fifth Sundays, at 10 A.M.

Tour Old Fort Graham, north of Whitney on F.M. 933 to F.M. 2604, to Pioneer Cove. The military post was established in 1849, and the one-room rock building is open weekends, Memorial Day through Labor Day.

Arriving pilots can land at Lake Whitney State Recreation Area Airport, three miles southwest of Whitney.

INFORMATION
Lake Whitney State Recreation Area
Box 1175
Whitney, Texas 76692
817-694-3973

LOCKHART STATE RECREATION AREA
42

LOCATION   Lockhart State Recreation Area is four miles southwest of Lockhart. From U.S. 183, follow F.M. 20 west for two miles, to the park road.

ACTIVITIES   Camp in the 20-site campground, 10 with full hookups, and ten with water and electrical hookups.

Go swimming in the pool, hike the trails, and play nine holes of golf. Fish for panfish in the stream.

Arriving pilots can land at Lockhart Municipal Airport, two miles south of Lockhart. It has rental cars.

INFORMATION
Lockhart State Recreation Area
Route 3, Box 69
Lockhart, Texas 78644
512-398-3479

LONGHORN CAVERN STATE PARK
43

LOCATION   The park is 11 miles southwest of Burnet, off U.S. 281, on Park Road 4.

FEATURES   It's located in the Backbone Ridge, in Ellenburger limestone left behind by a shallow sea, which occupied the area over 450 million years ago.

The cavern was once home to cavemen who left their tools behind. Later it served as a Rebel retreat during the Civil War. Then, during the 1870s, it was used as a hideout for bandits.

ACTIVITIES   Tour the cave featuring two miles of trail, with lights. Most visitors enjoy seeing the Cathedral Room, and five other rooms, featuring transparent crystal. Snacks are available.

Hike the half-mile-long trail through the oak-juniper hill country.

Take a Vanishing Texas River Cruise. Go 3 miles west on Texas 29, and then 13.5 miles north on F.M. 2341. Watch for bald eagles that winter here from November through April. For information and reservations, call 512-756-6986.

Arriving pilots can land at Burnet Municipal Kate Craddock Field, one mile southwest of Burnet. It has rental cars.

INFORMATION
Longhorn Cavern State Park
Route 2, Box 23
Burnet, Texas 78611
512-756-6976

LOST MAPLES STATE PARK
44

LOCATION   The park is four miles north of Vanderpool, on Ranch Road 187.

ACTIVITIES   Hike and backpack along 11 miles of trails, ranging in difficulty from moderate to strenuous, through canyons and on ridge tops, along the Sabinal River. They lead you to some primitive campsites, or you can camp in the park's 30-site campground, with water and electrical hookups, and a trailer dump station.

Tour the visitor center. Go pan fishing and swimming in the Sabinal River. Come in November when the bigtooth maples reach their color peak.

Bird watchers will find abundant bird life in the park, including the rare golden-cheeked warbler. Over 90 different plant families are represented here.

For a scenic drive, follow F.M. 337 through the woods. Another pretty drive is along F.M. 187 north of Vanderpool, up 2,300-foot Edwards Plateau. To see a good sinkhole, drive 8.9 miles north of the park on F.M. 187. The sinkhole is on the west edge of the road.

INFORMATION
Lost Maples State Park
HCO 1, Box 156
Vanderpool, Texas 78885
210-966-3413

LYNDON B. JOHNSON
STATE HISTORICAL PARK

PEDERNALES FALLS STATE PARK
45

LOCATION   The park is 15 miles west of Johnson City, on U.S. 290, near LBJ National Historic Site, and east of Stonewall. It's also 16 miles east of Fredericksburg.

Pedernales Falls is nine miles east of Johnson City, via Ranch Road 2766, then north three miles on an access road.

FEATURES   The state park, plus the LBJ National Historic Park, provide background to the man who served as our 36th president.

ACTIVITIES   The visitor center is located in Behren's "Dogtrot Cabin," built in the 1840s. Observe buffalo and Texas Longhorn cattle, as well as demonstrations of early 1900s farming techniques, at the Sauer-Beckman Homestead. Bring along a picnic, hike the nature trails, play tennis, and go fishing, or swimming. The park has a dining hall. The visitor center provides films, displays, and memorabilia on Johnson's life.

The only way you can get to the LBJ National Historic Park is via a free bus that leaves from the state park's visitor center. The 90-minute ranch tour goes through the "Texas White House," to the old Junction School, the birthplace and Johnson family cemetery, and to the LBJ Ranchlands. If heat and humidity are too high, the tours are shortened. For information, call 512-644-2241 or 512-868-7128.

Lyndon B. Johnson National Historical Park has two units. One is in Johnson City, one block south of U.S. 290, and the other is 50 miles west of Austin, in Stonewall. The visitor center in Johnson City, 2 blocks south of U.S. 290, has guided tours and living history programs in the boyhood home, and on his grandparents' ranch. See the almost 100-year-old frame structure where Johnson lived while attending public school. Johnson Settlement is one block west, and access is via a quarter-mile footpath from Johnson's boyhood home. For information, call 512-868-7128.

At Pedernales Falls State Park, camp in the 69-site campground, with water and electrical hookups, and a trailer dump station. Go fishing, boating, swimming, hiking, or enjoy a picnic.

In nearby Fredericksburg, many historic structures remain, including the Pioneer Museum on Main Street. The Admiral Nimitz Center commemorates the life of World War II Fleet Admiral Chester Nimitz.

Local festivities include the Stonewall Peach Jamboree and Antique Machines Show in June. In July, attend the Fourth of July festivities, an antique car show and swap meet, and in October, attend Oktober Fest and Karate Fest.

Arriving pilots can land at Gillespie County Airport, three miles southwest of Fredericksburg, 15 miles from the park. However, it has no rental cars.

INFORMATION

Lyndon B. Johnson State Historical
  Park
Highway 290, East of Fredericksburg
P.O. Box 238
Stonewall, Texas 78624
210-644-2252

Lyndon B. Johnson National
  Historical Park
P.O. Box 329
Johnson City, Texas 78671
512-868-7128

Pedernales Falls State Park
Route 1, Box 31 A
Johnson City, Texas 78636
512-868-7304

MARTIN DIES JR. STATE PARK
46

LOCATION   The park is 15 miles east of Woodville, along the eastern shore of Steinhagen Lake, impounding the Neches River. From U.S. 96, follow U.S. 190 west 11 miles to Park Road 485. It's also 13 miles west of Jasper, on U.S. 190.

ACTIVITIES   Enjoy hiking the trails, or picnicking among the trees. Go bass fishing, boating, and swimming.

Hen House Ridge Unit is on the east side of the lake, and on the south side of U.S. 190. It has 100 sites. The Walnut Ridge Unit is on the north side of U.S. 190, and has 78 campsites. Between both units, you'll find 63 sites with water, and 115 with electrical hookups. Hike over the nature trail's bridge to an island on Walnut Ridge, where you can watch for woodpeckers and several kinds of water birds. Food service is available.

Cherokee Units North and South are located on the west side of the lake, and offer overnight camping only when the other units have filled. These units have boat ramps, boat rentals, hiking, swimming in the lake, water-skiing, and a minibike area.

INFORMATION
Martin Dies Jr. State Park
Route 4, Box 274
Jasper, Texas 75951
409-384-5231

McKINNEY FALLS STATE PARK
47

LOCATION   The park is seven miles southeast of Austin, at the confluence of Onion and Williamson Creeks. To reach the park from U.S. 183 south, follow Scenic Loop Road, reached via W. 35th and Old Bull Creek Road.

ACTIVITIES   Tour the visitor center, and hike the interpretive trails. Camp in the 84-site campground, 70 sites with water and electrical hookups, and a dump station. Explore the ruins of Thomas F. McKinney's homestead, one of Stephen F. Austin's original 300 colonists. Go bass fishing from the stream bank, and ride the bicycle trails.

In Austin, tour the short story writer's home of O. Henry, at 409 E. 5th Street. He lived here from 1885 to 1895. It's open Tuesday through Saturday from 11:00 to 4:30, and on Sunday 2:00 to 4:30 P.M. Each May the museum sponsors the O. Henry "Punoff." For information, call 512-472-1903.

Lyndon Baines Johnson's Library is located on the University of Texas campus, and has 31 million papers from his presidency. Watch a 20-minute multi-media show in the former President's office. For information, call 512-482-5137.

Take a sightseeing ride aboard the paddle-wheeler *Lone Star* from March through November. It leaves from the dock between the Hyatt Regency Hotel and South First Street Bridge on Town Lake. For information, call 512-327-1388.

Arriving pilots can either land at Lakeway Airpark, 17 miles west of Austin, or at Robert Mueller Municipal Airport, three miles northeast of the city. Both have rental cars available.

INFORMATION
McKinney Falls State Park
Route 2, Box 701B
Austin, Texas 78744
512-243-1643

MONAHANS SANDHILLS STATE PARK
48

LOCATION   The park is six miles northeast of Monahans. From I-20, follow Park Road 41 north.

FEATURES   The park features 4,000 acres of Sahara-like sand dunes, some rising 70 feet. These dunes are remnants of a Permian-era sea, located here around 280 million years ago. The sandhills, only partly located in the park, presented a formidable obstacle to the early pioneers and wagon trains.

ACTIVITIES   Tour the interpretive center and museum. Walk through the large "forest" of Harvard oaks, three-foot-tall trees with roots reaching as deep as 90 feet. A two-mile park road circles the dune area. Go sand surfing, and enjoy a picnic.

Camp in the 24-site campground in the dunes. Food service is available. Birders come to spot approximately 80 species of birds.

Arriving pilots can land at Roy Hurd Memorial Airport, one mile southwest of Monahans. It has a courtesy car.

INFORMATION
Monahans Sandhills State Park
Box 1738
Monahans, Texas 79756
915-943-2092

MUSTANG ISLAND STATE PARK
49

LOCATION   The island is 14 miles south of Port Aransas, on Texas 53.

ACTIVITIES   Enjoy great Gulf fishing, with five miles of beach frontage. Fishing tournaments are held during the summer. During the winter, fish for croaker

Monahans Sandhills State Park has 4,000 acres of wind-sculpted sand dunes, and lies in the middle of one of the largest oak forests in the country. The "forest" is not readily apparent because the Havard Oaks in it are all under four feet tall. (courtesy of the Texas Tourist Agency)

and flounder. Camp in the 48-site campground, with water and electrical hookups. Go birding for shore and migratory birds.

Drive a circle tour over the causeway to Padre Island, and north to Mustang Island. Return from Port Aransas by ferry and causeway through Aransas Pass, named for the seaway from the Gulf into Corpus Christi Bay. While crossing the pass, watch for porpoises playing in the water.

Port Aransas is a very popular Gulf vacation spot because of its large number of fishing opportunities. Charter boats are available.

The annual Shrimporee is held in October in Aransas Pass. The festivities begin with the blessing of the fleet, and include a parade, a world-renown shrimp eating contest, an outhouse race, and a concert. For information, call 512-758-3713.

Aransas Wildlife Refuge is near Austwell. It's one of the most famous of the national refuges, serving as a winter home for the whooping crane and 350 other species of birds. From mid-October through mid-April, stop at the observation tower along the road, to watch for whooping cranes. The best viewing times are in the early morning and late evening during spring, fall and winter. Drive along the 16-mile paved loop road to visit various wildlife habitats.

Take a self-guided tour along footpaths through the preserve. Bring along a picnic to enjoy.

Take a 3.5-hour boat tour of the tidal marshes, leaving from the Sea Gun Inn, nine miles north of Rockport, on Texas 35. For information, call 512-729-2341.

Padre Island National Seashore is nearby, and preserves an undeveloped 70 miles of land in the middle of the island. Only a few roads are paved, but you can rent a four-wheel vehicle in Corpus Christi, suitable for driving in the sand.

A national park service pavilion is near the northern boundary of the seashore, with a recreation building, snack bar, beach rentals, information about swimming and camping beaches, and nature trails.

Beachcombers delight in collecting seashells, driftwood, and occasional glass floats from Portugal or the Orient. Federal law prohibits collecting historical artifacts such as flint points, antique coins, or other items over 100 years old. Watch for herons and rare brown pelicans at the southern end of the island.

On the island, enjoy camping, picnicking, play golf, ride horseback, and go hiking the nature trails. Go boating, sailing, wind surfing, scuba diving, and swimming. Go fishing from a charter boat in Laguna Madre for snapper, mackerel, marlin, and sailfish, or fish from the lighted Queen Isabella fishing pier.

Boardsailers arrive here in May for the Winter Park blowout. In August, the Texas International Fishing Tournament features three days of competition. In early December, attend "Christmas by the Sea" festivities, including a lighted boat parade and sandman building contests.

Tour the U.S. Naval Air Station, located on a peninsula at the southeastern edge of Corpus Christi. Tours are available at 1:00 P.M. Thursdays, from the North Gate on Ocean Drive.

In Corpus Christi, celebrate Buccaneer Days in April, the Texas Jazz Festival in mid-July, and Bayfest in mid-September.

Arriving pilots can land at Mustang Beach, two miles southwest of Port Aransas. The Gulf beach is approximately two miles away.

INFORMATION

Mustang Island State Park
P.O. Box 326
Port Aransas Texas 78373
512-749-5246

Padre Island National Seashore
9405 South Padre Island Drive
Corpus Christi, Texas 78418
512-937-2621

PALMETTO STATE PARK
50

LOCATION The park is 10 miles southeast of Luling, and north of Gonzales, on the San Marcos River. From U.S. 183 and F.M. 1856, follow Park Road 11 south for 2.3 miles.

FEATURES The park features a rare, almost tropical botanical garden, including the dwarf palmetto, and many other plants found nowhere else in the Southwest. It's used as a field laboratory by several Texas universities.

ACTIVITIES   Go fishing, tubing, and swimming in the lake and river, and hike the trails. Anglers come to fish a small oxbow lake for bass, crappie, and cat-fish. The park serves as a checkpoint for the 419-mile-long Texas Water Safari held in July.

Pick up a guidebook to take a nature walk along one of three ½-mile long trails through the hardwoods. Camp in the campground, built on the bank of the river. Take a scenic 2-mile drive along Park Road 11.

Birders come here, particularly in the winter, where over 240 species have been spotted.

Drive through Noah's Land Wildlife Park, 17 miles northeast of Gonzales on Texas 304, 5.5 miles north of I-10. The park has 110 species of rare and exotic ani-mals roaming through the grasslands. For information, call 210-540-4654.

Arriving pilots can land at The Carter Memorial Airport, three miles north of Luling. However, it has no rental cars.

INFORMATION
Palmetto State Park
Route 2, Box 66D
Gonzales, Texas 78629
210-672-3266

PALO DURO CANYON STATE PARK
51

LOCATION   The park is on the Prairie Dog Town fork of the Red River. From U.S. 87, go 12 miles east of Canyon on Texas 217. From Amarillo, go south on Ranch Road 1541 and then eight miles east on Texas 217.

FEATURES   Palo Duro is Spanish for "hard wood," referring to the juniper growing in the area. It's Texas' largest state park.

As you drive in, the park road crosses the river 6 times within four miles. The water is generally shallow, but during a heavy rain, check the water level gauges in the river crossings before continuing across.

The canyon is nine miles wide in the park, and the drive is considered one of the most impressive in the state. The canyon's geological features date back over 200 million years. While driving into the canyon, watch for a 75-foot pillar of soft mudstone named "The Lighthouse."

Ancient stone projectile points have been found here, left behind by nomadic Indians who hunted mammoth and other Ice Age animals almost 12,000 years ago.

ACTIVITIES   Enjoy 15 miles of scenic driving, watching for Texas Long-horns. Horseback ride along 20 miles of equestrian trails, and explore 30 miles of hiking trails. Rental horses are available.

Camp in the 116-site campground, with water and electrical hookups, and a dump station. Camping supplies are available at the Goodnight Trading Post.

Tour the museum and ride aboard "The Sad Monkey," a miniature railroad that operates here daily during the summer, and on weekends the remainder of the year.

Summer visitors can watch *Texas*, an outdoor musical presented in the Pioneer Amphitheater, Monday through Saturday, at 8:30 P.M. All seats are reserved, so reservations are required. A barbecue dinner is served nightly before the show. Canyon nights are often cool, so bring along a light jacket. Write "Texas," Box 268, Canyon, Texas 79015, or pick up tickets at the "Texas" Information Office, 2010 4th Avenue in Canyon, or at the theater. For information, call 806-655-2181.

Visit the Panhandle Plains Historical Museum, 2401 4th Avenue, east of U.S. 87 on Texas 217. The museum features five major exhibitions. Walk through the reconstructed pioneer town, and see the T-Anchor Ranch headquarters, one of the Panhandle's oldest buildings. For information, call 806-656-2244.

Buffalo Lake National Wildlife Refuge is 12 miles west of Canyon, and three miles south of Umbarger, on F.M. 168. It provides a winter sanctuary to an estimated one million ducks and geese. Walk its interpretive trail, or drive the 4.5-mile auto interpretive trail.

In Amarillo, attend the world's largest livestock auction, held at the Western Stockyards at 100 Manhattan, Monday and Tuesday, from 9 to 7.

From June 1 through September 15, attend "Cowboy Morning," a Western-style chuckwagon breakfast served on the open range. Reservations are required. Check at the city visitor center, 1000 Polk St.

Drive north 42 miles to visit Cal Farley's Boys' Ranch, and Old Tascosa.

For another scenic drive, go south of Claude to Tule Canyon, where the highway drops into a beautiful gorge with some sheer-faced, knife-edged buttes.

Arriving pilots can land at Garfield Field, six miles northwest of Canyon. However, it has no rental cars.

INFORMATION
Palo Duro Canyon State Park
Route 2, Box 285
Canyon, Texas 79015
806-488-2227

POSSOM KINGDOM
STATE RECREATION AREA
52

LOCATION   The park is 17 miles northeast of Caddo, on the southwestern shore of Possom Kingdom Lake. From U.S. 180, follow Park Road 33. The lake is also 30 miles northwest of Mineral Wells via Texas 337, and is accessible from Breckenridge, Caddo, Graford, and Graham.

FEATURES   Lake Possom Kingdom's 17,700-acre reservoir is surrounded by scenic woodlands.

ACTIVITIES   Stay in one of the cabins, or camp in the 116-site campground, 58 with water and electrical hookups, 39 with water hookups only, and a dump station. Groceries are available.

Observe the Texas Longhorn herd kept in the park. Go pan fishing from the lighted fishing pier, swim in Possom Kingdom Lake, and go boating from the ramp. Boat rentals are available. The clear water attracts snorkelers and scuba divers.

INFORMATION
Possom Kingdom State Recreation Area
Box 36
Caddo, Texas 76029
817-549-1803

RUSK/PALESTINE STATE PARK
53

LOCATION   The park is three miles west of Rusk. From U.S. 69, drive west on U.S. 84 to Park Road 76.

ACTIVITIES   The park is open year-round. Go camping in the campground, with 94 paved sites, all sites with water and electrical hookups, 31 with full hookups, and a dump station. Enjoy fishing for bass in City Park Lake, hiking the nature trails, playing tennis, and boating with a 5 mile per hour limit.

An antique steam engine pulls vintage coaches through the dense East Texas forest from the depot in Rusk State Park, crossing 30 wooden trestles, and traveling 25.5 miles to Palestine, the nation's longest, skinniest state park. Trains leave simultaneously from Rusk and Palestine. They operate weekends, March through late May, daily except Tuesday and Wednesday through Labor Day, and then back to weekends through November. Reservations are advisable at least 3 weeks in advance. In Texas, call 1-800-442-8951, or 903-683-2561.

In Rusk, walk across the 546-foot footbridge, believed to be the nation's longest. It was originally constructed in 1861 for crossing the valley during the rainy season. It's located 2 blocks east of the town square.

Hike the 2.6-mile New Birmingham Trail. It follows the route that served as the major artery in 1880, between New Birmingham and rest of the state. The trail is southeast of Rusk off F.M. 343, from U.S. 69 south.

For a scenic woodland drive, follow U.S. 69 either north and south, or F.M. 347, and F.M. 747, going north from U.S. 84 west. Neither is shown on most state maps.

INFORMATION
Rusk/Palestine State Park
Route 4, Box 431
Rusk, Texas 75785
903-683-5126

SAN JACINTO BATTLEGROUND
STATE HISTORICAL PARK
54

LOCATION   The park is 21 miles east of Houston, on Texas 225, and then three miles north on Texas 134.

FEATURES   The site commemorates the final battle between the Texan and Mexican armies, on April 21, 1836, resulting in Texas gaining its independence. Here, Sam Houston's Texans overwhelmed the superior forces of Mexican General Santa Anna.

ACTIVITIES   Tour the battleship *Texas* moored here, the only survivor of the dreadnought class. For information, call 713-479-2411.

Take an elevator to the top of the 561-foot San Jacinto Monument. At the base of the obelisk, tour the museum depicting the area's history, beginning with Cortez' arrival and continuing through the Civil War. Watch a multi-media presentation of "Texas Forever, The Battle of San Jacinto." The museum and observation deck are open every day from 9:30 to 5:30, but the museum is closed Mondays.

While in Houston, tour the Lyndon B. Johnson Space Center, headquarters of the United States' manned space program. It's 25 miles southeast of downtown Houston, and three miles east of I-45, on NASA Road 1. Take a self-guided tour of the visitor orientation center to see its exhibit of lunar rocks, photos from Mars, and movies of space flights and orbital rendezvous. A limited number of special guided tours may be arranged by reservations made in advance. Call 713-483-4321.

Arriving pilots have their choice of several airports within 15 miles of Houston. However, William P. Hobby Airport is closest to the park, and is eight miles southeast of the city. It has rental cars.

INFORMATION
San Jacinto Battleground State
   Historical Park
3800 Park Road 1836
La Porte, Texas 77571
713-479-2431

San Jacinto Monument
3800 Park Road 1836
La Porte, Texas 77571
713-479-2019

SEA RIM STATE PARK
55

LOCATION   The park is 10 miles west of Sabine Pass, now annexed to Port Arthur, off Texas 87, on the Gulf of Mexico. From US. 69/287, follow Texas 87 south, then go southwest for 20.7 miles to Park Road 69. Continue north another .3-mile.

ACTIVITIES   The park's 15,000 acres are open year-round, except when hurricanes threaten the area. It has 20 campsites with electrical and water hookups, and three miles of primitive beach camping. The Marshlands Unit is accessible only by private boat.

Go water-skiing, swimming from the beach, and fishing. Go boating, rent a canoe, or take an airboat tour. Boating trails provide access to the marsh. Hike the ⅔-mile-long boardwalk nature trail to learn about marsh ecology, stop by the observation blinds, and tour the interpretive center.

Port Arthur is a year-round angler's destination. Purchase a fishing map from the Chamber of Commerce, showing locations for catching over 25 varieties of freshwater and saltwater fish.

Tour Pompeiian Villa, at 1953 Lakeshore Drive. It was built by Isaac Ellwood, the "barbed-wire king." The villa is furnished with objects from the 18th to the 20th centuries. Guided tours are offered Monday through Friday, from 9 to 4. The house is registered on the National Register of Historic Places. For information, call 409-983-5977.

Sabine Pass Battleground State Historical Park is 15 miles south of town on F.M. 3322, off Texas 87. The park marks the site of the Civil War battle of September 8, 1863, when the Union attempted to invade Texas at Sabine Pass, but was defeated. Go boating from the ramp, enjoy a picnic, and watch the ships entering and leaving the Gulf of Mexico.

Pleasure Island is connected to Port Arthur by the M. L. King–Gulfgate Bridge. The lake opens into the Gulf of Mexico, and has a marina, boat ramps, and miles of fishing levees for fishing redfish, drum, trout, and to do some excellent crabbing as well. A golf course is also available.

INFORMATION
Sea Rim State Park
Box 1066
Sabine Pass, Texas 77655
409-971-2559

SEMINOLE CANYON STATE PARK
56

LOCATION   The park is eight miles west of Comstock, on U.S. 90. It's also 20 miles east of Langtry, on U.S. 90.

FEATURES　　The park contains pictographs covering the walls of two large limestone caverns, that date from 10,000 to 2,000 B.C.

ACTIVITIES　　Go on a guided (but strenuous) hiking tour, offered Wednesday through Sunday, to see Fate Bell shelter's rock art. Tour the visitor center to see displays on early man and the area's history.

Camp in the campground, with 31 paved sites, eight with water, 23 with electrical hookups, and a dump station. Hike the nature trails. Take a gentle three-mile walk to an overlook above the Rio Grande River.

In Langtry, tour the Judge Roy Bean Visitor Center, featuring a rustic saloon, courtroom, and billiard hall of the controversial judge. The center preserves the historic site where the judge ruled with his own brand of homespun law and sixshooter justice. He was often referred to as the "Law West of the Pecos River." Listen to the special sound programs. Stroll through the five-acre cactus garden, especially in April, when it's in bloom.

For a scenic overlook, stop by the roadside park on U.S. 90, on the east rim of the canyon, approximately 18 miles east of Langtry. From here, you can get a good idea of the difficulties faced by the early pioneers, who attempted to cross the Pecos River through the canyon bottom without benefit of bridges. Water from Armistad Lake is now about 100 feet deep in the canyon.

INFORMATION
Seminole Canyon State Park
P.O. Box 820
Comstock, Texas 78837
915-292-4464

TYLER STATE PARK
57

LOCATION　　The park is 10 miles north of Tyler via F.M. 14, and two miles west on Park Road 16.

ACTIVITIES　　Camp in the 147-site forested campground, with 39 sites offering full hookups, and 68 with water and electricity. Groceries are available.

Go swimming, boating, canoeing, kayaking, and sailing in Tyler State Park Lake (5 mile per hour limit). Rental recreational boats and fishing boats for bass fishing are available.

Hike the trails, ride minibikes in the special area provided, purchase a snack at the snack bar, and attend a program in the amphitheater.

In Tyler, take your children through the Caldwell Zoo, at 2203 Martin Luther King Drive. Tour Goodman-LeGrand home, located at 624 North Broadway. It was constructed in 1859 by Gallatin Smith, a wealthy young Tyler bachelor and Confederate officer. The museum houses artifacts of antebellum years, 18th-century dental and medical tools, and period furniture. It's open daily from 1 to 5, but closed holidays. For information, call 903-531-1286.

Flower lovers can wander through the municipal rose garden, the nation's largest rose showcase, located on West Front Street. It features 38,000 rose bushes, with almost 500 varieties represented. Roses bloom from May through November. For information, call 903-593-2131.

Brookshire's World of Wildlife Museum, on Southwest Loop 323 at Old Jacksonville Highway, features mounted animal and fish specimens from Africa, North America, and Texas. It also features a grocery store from the early 1900s. The museum is open Monday through Friday, but is closed holidays. For information, call 903-534-3000, extension 3112.

Arriving pilots can land at Tyler Pounds Field, three miles west of Tyler. It has rental cars.

INFORMATION
Tyler State Park
Route 9
Tyler, Texas 75706
903-597-5338

VIRGINIA

Most travelers have seen the state's well-known slogan, "Virginia is for Lovers." For lovers of natural beauty or history, you've come to the right place.

The state was the site of the first permanent settlement in the New World, and was the birthplace of eight American presidents. Both the American Revolution and the Civil War took place on its soil, with more Civil War battles fought here than in any other state.

Virginia's eastern shore, a 70-mile-long peninsula, has 15 major lakes, and over 112 miles of Atlantic Ocean frontage. It is bordered on its other side by the Chesapeake Bay. Eighteen secluded barrier islands provide excellent surf fishing and shelling. Assateague and Chincoteague are home to herds of wild ponies, where visitors flock each summer to attend Pony Penning. It features a round-up of the wild ponies, descended from Japanese sikas, released here in 1923, grand carnivals, and wonderful food.

One of the longest U.S. rails-to-trails bikeways, covering 45 miles, is located in Northern Virginia. Giant limestone caverns are found along the Shenandoah Valley.

Grayson Highlands and Sky Meadows provide access points to 450 miles of the Appalachian Trail, with the longest stretch of the trail running along the west side of the state. In addition, over 200 miles of other hiking trails are available. Mt. Rogers is the state's highest peak, at 5,729 feet.

Virginia maintains 35 state parks. Several historic state parks preserve a sample of the state's historical heritage. These include George Washington's Grist Mill and Sayler's Creek Battlefield.

The parks are open year-round, but are geared to seasonal activities from Memorial Day through Labor Day. Vacation cabins are located in eight parks: Claytor Lake, Douthat, Fairy Stone, Hungry Mother, Seashore, Staunton River, Twin Lakes, and Westmoreland. Camping facilities are available in 19 parks, and also housekeeping cabins, that may be rented on a weekly basis. For camping and cabin reservations, call 804-490-3939. For general state park information, call 804-786-1712.

Freshwater fishing is permitted in many of the state parks, and Virginia state licenses are required. However, tidal saltwater fishing is free, and no licenses or permits are required. For information, contact the Commission of Game and Inland

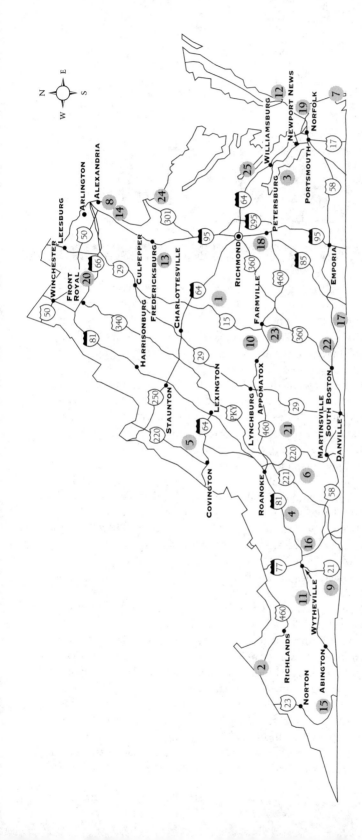

VIRGINIA STATE PARKS

1. Bear Creek Lake State Park
2. Breaks Interstate Park
3. Chippokes Plantation State Park
4. Claytor Lake State Park
5. Douthat State Park
6. Fairy Stone State Park
7. False Cape State Park
8. George Washington's Grist Mill Historical State Park
9. Grayson Highlands State Park
10. Holliday Lake State Park
11. Hungry Mother State Park
12. Kiptopeke State Park
13. Lake Anna State Park
14. Mason Neck State Park
15. Natural Tunnel State Park
16. New River Trail State Park
16. Shot Tower Historical State Park
17. Occoneechee State Park
18. Pocahontas State Park
19. Seashore State Park and Natural Area
20. Sky Meadows State Park
21. Smith Mountain Lake State Park
22. Staunton River State Park
23. Twin Lakes State Park
24. Westmoreland State Park
25. York River State Park

Fisheries at 804-257-1000. Anglers have access to four large lakes, several rivers, and the Chesapeake Bay where they can fish for bass, trout, crappie, and bream.

For leaf-peeping, be sure to drive Skyline Drive, which runs 105 miles through Shenandoah National Park. This drive then connects to the Blue Ridge Parkway for another 217 miles of scenic color. Colors here usually peak the second weekend in October. For details, contact the Virginia Division of Tourism at 1-800-932-5827 or 1-804-786-4484.

BEAR CREEK LAKE STATE PARK
1

LOCATION   Bear Creek State Park is 4.5 miles northwest of the Cumberland, in the heart of Cumberland State Forest, in central Virginia. From U.S. 60, go north on Virginia 622 and then west on Virginia 629.

ACTIVITIES   Go bass fishing, swimming, and boating from the ramp on Bear Creek Lake, with boat rentals available. Enjoy lakeside camping in the 68-site campsite, 10 with water and electrical hookups, and a dump station. Bring a picnic and hike the trails. Snacks are sold at the concession stand. Attend interpretive programs.

INFORMATION
Bear Creek Lake State Park
Route 1, Box 253
Cumberland, Virginia 23040
804-492-4410

BREAKS INTERSTATE PARK
2

LOCATION   Breaks is seven miles east of Breaks, on the border of Virginia and Kentucky. It's eight miles north of Haysi, Virginia, and seven miles east of Elkhorn, Kentucky. From U.S. 460, go west on Virginia 83, and north on Virginia 80.

FEATURES   Breaks Canyon is a five mile-long, 1,600-foot gorge, cut by the Russell Fork of the Big Sandy River. It's the largest canyon east of the Mississippi, and is often called the "Grand Canyon of the South."

ACTIVITIES   Camp in the campground from April through October, with 122 sites offering electrical hookups, and a dumping station. Stay in one of four housekeeping cabins, open year-round, or in the Breaks Motor Lodge. Get a snack at the snack bar, or a meal in Rhododendron Lodge's restaurant, open from April through October.

Hike and bike the trails. Drive the paved road to overlooks along the canyon rim. Go fishing in Laurel Lake, stocked with bass and bluegill. Go swimming in

Breaks Interstate Park contains the largest canyon east of the Mississippi
(courtesy of the Virginia Division of Tourism)

the Olympic-size pool, or rent a paddle boat to go boating. Tour the visitor center and attend interpretive programs, from April through October. Attend the Autumn Gospel Song Festival on Labor Day weekend.

INFORMATION
Breaks Interstate Park
P.O. Box 100
Breaks, Virginia 24607
540-865-4413 or 1-800-982-5122

CHIPPOKES PLANTATION STATE PARK
3

LOCATION   The park is six miles east of Surry on the James River. Access to the park is via Virginia 10.

FEATURES   Chippokes Plantation State Park is located on a working farm which has operated for over 360 years. The plantation was part of America's first permanent English colony, and is registered as a National Historic Landmark. It was named for Chief Choupouke, who befriended the first settlers.

ACTIVITIES The park is open from early April through late October. Stop by the visitor center to watch the slide program, and attend interpretive programs. Tour the antebellum mansion Wednesday through Sunday, from Memorial Day through Labor Day. Stroll through the azalea and dogwood gardens, and tour the Farm and Forestry Museum.

Go biking and hiking on the bicycle/hiking trails, and swim in the pool, overlooking the James River. Enjoy saltwater fishing, and purchase a snack at the snack bar. Attend the annual Pork, Peanut, and Pine Festival.

Take the Jamestown-Scotland Ferry to Jamestown. It runs daily from 5 A.M. to 12:30 A.M. For information, call 804-834-3994. Jamestown was the first permanent English settlement in the New World. Tour the museum to see an engraving of Captain John Smith's original map, plus Native American artifacts dating back to 10,000 B.C. Climb aboard three replicas of the ships that made the first voyage to the New World.

Charles C. Steirly Heron Rookery Natural Area is five miles northeast of Waverly. A registered National Natural Landmark, it preserves one of the state's few remaining rookeries. Contact Chippokes State Park for information.

Berkeley Plantation is 6.5 miles west of Charles City on Virginia 5, and then one mile south. It's on the James River between Richmond and Williamsburg. Benjamin Harrison, son of the builder of Berkeley Plantation, was one of the signers of the Declaration of Independence. William Henry Harrison, our ninth president, and Benjamin Harrison, our 23rd president, had their roots here. *Taps* was composed here in 1862, while Civil War Union Forces camped on the plantation, and the first official Thanksgiving was celebrated here in 1619. Tour the restored mansion and stroll through the boxwood gardens. Stop at the Coach House Tavern for refreshments. For information, call 804-829-6018.

Visit Surry Nuclear Information Center, 10 miles east of Surry. Take Virginia 10 to Virginia 650, then continue north for 10 miles. It's open Monday through Friday from 9 to 4. For information, or to arrange for a demonstration of the see-through reactor, call 804-357-5410.

Visit Williamsburg, Yorktown, and Busch Gardens. See York River State Park for details.

INFORMATION
Chippokes Plantation State Park
Surry, Virginia 23883
804-294-3625

CLAYTOR LAKE STATE PARK
4

LOCATION The park is off I-81, Exit 33, southeast of Dublin. It's also four miles south of Radford on I-81, then two miles north on Virginia 660.

ACTIVITIES   Camp in the 136-site campground, 44 sites with water and electrical hookups, and a dumping station, or stay in one of 12 housekeeping cabins, overlooking the lake. Snacks are available at the snack bar. Go boating from the marina in 21-mile-long Claytor Lake (motor boats permitted). Boat rentals, fuel, and refreshments are available at the marina. Enjoy swimming, water-skiing, and fishing for bass.

Go hiking, and rent a horse to go horseback riding on bridle trails, beside the lake and through the forest. Tour the visitor center in the historic Howe House to see exhibits on early region settlers, and attend interpretive programs. Each summer, attend the arts and crafts festival. In July, attend the annual Pulaski Old Time Bluegrass Fiddlers Convention.

Incoming pilots can land at New River Valley Airport, two miles north of Dublin. It's seven miles from the state park. A courtesy car and van are available.

INFORMATION
Claytor Lake State Park
Dublin, Virginia 24084
540-674-5492

DOUTHAT STATE PARK

5

LOCATION   Douthat is six miles north of Clifton Forge. Take Exit 8 off I-64, onto Virginia 629, and continue north four miles.

FEATURES   Douthat, located in the Allegheny Mountains, is a National Historic Landmark because of the role its design played in the development of parks nationwide.

ACTIVITIES   Camp in the 127-site campground, with a dumping station, and groceries available. Stay in one of 31 housekeeping cabins, or in the small lodge that can accommodate nine visitors. Go swimming and fishing in 50-acre Douthat Lake, that's stocked with trout. Enjoy a meal in the restaurant overlooking the lake, or get a snack from the snack bar. Hike the trails, and go boating from the ramp, with rentals available. Tour the visitor center and attend interpretive programs.

INFORMATION
Douthat State Park
P.O. Box 212
Milboro, Virginia 24460
540-862-7200

FAIRY STONE STATE PARK
6

LOCATION Fairy Stone is eight miles west of Bassett, on Virginia 57. From the Blue Ridge Parkway, take Virginia 8/57/58.

FEATURES The park, nestled in the Blue Ridge Mountains' foothills, is home to the lucky "fairy stones." These small, mysteriously formed stone crosses appear naturally only in this part of the world. The crosses are listed as a National Registered Historic Landmark.

ACTIVITIES The park's lake adjoins Philpott Reservoir. Camp in the 88-site campground, 51 sites with water and electrical hookups, and a dumping station, or stay in one of 24 housekeeping cabins. Go freshwater fishing, swimming, and boating in Fairy Stone Lake, with boat rentals available. Hike the trails, bike along the bicycle trail, and enjoy a picnic. Tour the visitor center and attend interpretive programs. Eat in the restaurant overlooking the lake. Attend the Gospel Music Festival held in May.

Incoming pilots can land at Blue Ridge Airport, eight miles southwest of Martinsville. Rental cars are available.

INFORMATION
Fairy Stone State Park
Route 2, Box 723
Stuart, Virginia 24171
540-930-2424

FALSE CAPE STATE PARK
7

LOCATION The park is southeast of Virginia Beach, five miles south of Sandbridge, on the Atlantic Ocean. It has no vehicular access.

FEATURES The park covers 4,300 acres in a six-mile-long area, and contains maritime forests and dunes that front the Atlantic Ocean.

ACTIVITIES Hikers and bikers can enter the park via four miles of trails through Back Bay National Wildlife Refuge. The refuge is located at 4005 Sandpiper Road. Boaters can navigate Back Bay to dock at either Barbour Hill or False Cape Landing.

No motorized vehicles are allowed on this four-mile stretch of beach. Bring along mountain bikes to cycle through the refuge's three routes: the beach, the east dike, and the west dike. The west dike is the least sandy, while the beach provides the easiest walking at low tide. Bring along plenty of insect repellent, and watch for cottonmouth snakes if you step off the trails.

Stop by Seashore State Park to get park information and camping permits. Enjoy primitive camping on the beach in the nine-site campground. Bring along extra-long tent stakes and a tarp for shade. No water is available, so you'll have to haul your own. As you hike in to your campsite, watch for egrets, herons, ibis, and other waterbirds.

Stroll, bike, run, or skate along the three-mile boardwalk in Virginia Beach, where the Atlantic Ocean meets Chesapeake Bay. Watch summer evening performances by jugglers and musicians. Go windsurfing, jet skiing, parasailing, scuba diving, canoeing, and sailing. Enjoy both freshwater and saltwater fishing. Attend interpretive programs.

The Chesapeake Bay Bridge-Tunnel is the world's largest bridge-tunnel complex, and it links Virginia Beach/Norfolk with Virginia's Eastern Shore. The bridge is 17.6 miles long, and is one of the Seven Wonders of the Modern World. Fish from the 625-foot Sea Gull Fishing Pier for bluefish, trout, flounder, and shark. It's on the first of the bridge's four man-made islands, 3.5 miles from Virginia Beach.

Mackay Island National Wildlife Refuge is south of the park.

The Shamrock Marathon and Sportsfest is held in Virginia Beach each March, and the East Coast Surfing Championship occurs each August at Rudee Inlet. Call 1-800-VA BEACH for information.

Tour the Virginia Marine Science Museum at 717 General Booth Boulevard. Its huge aquarium houses the world's largest collection of Chesapeake Bay fish. Stroll along the outdoor boardwalk, and watch the IMAX presentation. For information, call 804-437-4949 or 804-425-FISH.

You can also tour the Life-Saving Museum of Virginia, at 24th and Oceanfront, to learn about the Coast Guard and the shipwrecks lying off the Virginia coast. For information, call 804-422-1587.

At Fort Story, look for the Cape Henry Memorial, erected to mark the place where the English colonists, who settled here in Jamestown, first stepped ashore. The Cape Henry Lighthouse, circa 1791, is across the street. It was used to guide area ships until 1881, and is open from mid-March through October. For information, call 804-422-9421.

Historic homes to visit include Upper Wolfsnare at 2040 Potters Road, 804-491-3490; Lynnhaven House at 4405 Wishart Road, 804-460-1688; and Francis Land House Historic Site at 3131 Virginia Beach Boulevard, 804-340-1732. The Adam Thoroughgood House, 1636 Paris Road, was completed around 1680, and is one of the country's oldest brick houses. It's closed Mondays. For information, call 804-460-0007.

Incoming pilots can land at Norfolk International Airport, a half-mile northeast of Norfolk. Rental cars are available.

INFORMATION

False Cape State Park
4001 Sandpiper Road
Virginia Beach, Virginia 23456
804-426-7128

Back Bay National Wildlife Refuge
P.O. Box 6286
4005 Sandpiper Road
Virginia Beach, Virginia 23456
804-721-2412

GEORGE WASHINGTON'S GRIST MILL HISTORICAL STATE PARK

8

LOCATION   Take Mount Vernon Highway, Virginia 235. It's a quarter-mile south from U.S. 1, and three miles west of the Mt. Vernon Estate.

FEATURES   George Washington operated this grist mill on Dogue Run for almost 30 years, grinding wheat and corn into flour and meal.

ACTIVITIES   Tour the visitor center, watch the slide show, and attend an interpretive program. Visit the five floors of the rebuilt mill to see period machinery. It's open daily from late May through Labor Day. Admission is charged.

Mount Vernon is on George Washington Parkway in Alexandria. It's America's most visited historic estate. It was the home and burial site of George and Martha Washington, and has over 30 acres of grounds, and a mansion featuring its original paint colors. Walk past its stables, kitchen, and gardens. Some visitors arrive here via a Potomac boat cruise. For information, call 703-780-2000.

Bikers and hikers have access to the 17-mile-long Mount Vernon Trail in the Potomac River Valley, paralleling the George Washington Memorial Parkway. It goes from Mt. Vernon to the Lincoln Memorial in Washington, D.C. Once in Washington, you can access another bike trail leading to the C&O Canal.

INFORMATION
George Washington's Grist Mill Historical State Park
George Washington Memorial Parkway
Mount Vernon, Virginia 22121-0037
703-550-0960 or 703-780-3383

GRAYSON HIGHLANDS STATE PARK

9

LOCATION   Grayson is midway between Independence and Damascus. Take I-81 to Marion, then follow Virginia 16 to Volney, and go west on U.S. 58.

FEATURES   Grayson is located near Virginia's highest point, and provides views of peaks rising 5,000 feet.

ACTIVITIES   Tour the visitor center's display on pioneer life, and attend interpretive programs. Camp in the 73-site campground, with a dumping station, and groceries available. Follow hiking trails to the waterfalls and overlooks, and climb to the summit of Haw Orchard Mountain. Equestrians can ride their own horses on the bridle paths, and camp in the 20-site equestrian camping area, with its own stable area. Enjoy fishing for trout.

Come in September to attend the Grayson Highlands Fall Festival.

Grayson adjoins the Mt. Rogers National Recreation Area, site of Virginia's highest peak, at 5,729 feet. Hike the trails into deep isolated gorges with cliffs, rockfalls, and waterfalls, or climb to the summit of Mt. Rogers. Watch for wildlife from the large knobby "mountain balds." For area information, call 540-783-5196.

INFORMATION
Grayson Highlands State Park
Route 2, Box 141
Mouth of Wilson, Virginia 24363
540-579-7092

HOLLIDAY LAKE STATE PARK
10

LOCATION   The park is between Appomattox and U.S. 60, inside Buckingham-Appomattox State Forest. From Appomattox, go six miles northeast on Virginia 24, then four miles on Virginia 626/629.

ACTIVITIES   Holliday Lake offers freshwater fishing for stocked bass and crappie. Go boating, with sailboat and canoe rentals available, and swimming from the beach. Go camping in the 60-site campground, with a dumping station. Enjoy hiking the trails, including the Lakeshore Nature Trail, and watch for the beavers. Bring along a picnic to eat while overlooking the lake. Snacks are available at the concession stand. Tour the visitor center and attend interpretive programs.

A nearby attraction is the Appomattox Court House National Historic Park where General Robert E. Lee surrendered, thus ending the Civil War. Stop at the visitor center and pick up a map of the village. See some restored and reconstructed buildings including McLean House, Meeks' Store, Clover Hill Tavern, and the courthouse. Hike a five-mile trail, and watch living history demonstrations.

Outside of the village are a few sites associated with the events of the surrender. Lee's headquarters is northeast of the village, on Virginia 24. Grant's headquarters is in the opposite direction, and a small Confederate cemetery is west of the village. A hiking trail and highway connect all these locations.

Incoming pilots can land at Lynchburg Regional/Preston Glenn Field, five miles southwest of Lynchburg. Rental cars are available.

INFORMATION

Holliday Lake State Park
Route 2, Box 622
Appomattox, Virginia 24522
804-248-6308

Appomattox Court House National
  Historical Park
P.O. Box 218
Appomattox, Virginia 24522
804-352-8987

HUNGRY MOTHER STATE PARK
11

LOCATION   The park is three miles northeast of Marion on Virginia 16, off I-81. Take either Exit 16 or 17.

FEATURES   Hungry Mother State Park encompasses a 2,180-acre natural preserve. Molly's Knob, 3,270 feet in height, provides a panoramic view of the park and surrounding countryside. According to legend, Molly Marley collapsed after wandering in the woods for days, after escaping with her child from their Indian captors. The child managed to find a group of houses, but could only say "hungry mother." However, when the search party found Molly, she had died.

ACTIVITIES   Go boating from the ramp in Hungry Mother Lake, with rentals available. Enjoy fishing and swimming from the six-mile-long lake shoreline, situated in the heart of Walker Mountains. Camp in the 32-site campground, all sites with water and electrical hookups, and a dumping station, or stay in one of 20 housekeeping cabins.

Tour the hilltop visitor center and attend interpretive programs. Hike 12 miles of trails. Snacks are sold at the snack bar, or you can purchase a restaurant meal. Horseback rentals are available.

Attend Hungry Mother Arts and Crafts Festival in July.

Arriving pilots can land at Mountain Empire Airport, outside of Marion/Wytheville. Rental cars are available.

INFORMATION
Hungry Mother State Park
Route 5, Box 109
Marion, Virginia 24363
540-783-3422

KIPTOPEKE STATE PARK
12

LOCATION   The park is on Virginia's Eastern shore, three miles north of the Chesapeake Bay Bridge Tunnel on U.S. 13, then west on Virginia 704.

ACTIVITIES   Camp in the 111-site campground, 42 sites with full hookups, and a dumping station. Go boating from the ramp in the ocean, and saltwater fishing from the lighted fishing pier. Hike the trails, bike the bicycle trails, and swim in the guarded swimming area. Attend interpretive programs.

Birders come to observe birds passing along the major migratory flyway. Attend the annual birding festival in early October.

The Chesapeake Bay Bridge-Tunnel is 17.6 miles long. It's considered the world's largest bridge-tunnel complex, and acclaimed as one of the Seven Wonders of the Modern World. Stop at the 625-foot Sea Gull Fishing Pier, 3.5 miles from Virginia Beach, to fish for bluefish, trout, flounder, and shark. For information, call 804-331-2960.

The park is near Fisherman's Island National Wildlife Refuge and Cape Charles Lighthouse.

INFORMATION
Kiptopeke State Park
3540 Kiptopeke Drive
Cape Charles, Virginia 23310
804-331-2267

LAKE ANNA STATE PARK
13

LOCATION   Lake Anna is off I-95, 22 miles southwest of Fredericksburg. From Virginia 208, which runs between U.S. 1 and 522, take Virginia 601 north for 3.2 miles to reach the park entrance.

FEATURES   The park has approximately 8.5 miles of acreage along Lake Anna's shoreline.

ACTIVITIES   Go swimming in the lake, and purchase a snack at the concession stand. Go boating (motor boats permitted), picnicking, and hike eight miles of trails. Tour the visitor center to learn about the area's gold mining, and attend interpretive programs. Go panning for gold, and enjoy freshwater fishing for bass from the lighted fishing pier.

Stop by the Fredericksburg Battlefield Visitor Center, at 1013 Lafayette Blvd. beside historic Sunken Road, and watch its orientation slide program. Tour Mary Washington's House, the last home of George Washington's mother, with its 18th-century furnishings. It's at 1200 Charles Street. For information, call 540-373-1569.

Rising Sun Tavern, circa 1706, is at 1306 Caroline, and was the home of Charles Washington, George's brother. Watch daily living history demonstrations. For information, call 540-371-1494.

Fredericksburg and Spotsylvania National Military Park are divided into seven major units. Stop by the Battlefield Visitor Center on Lafayette Blvd., across from the National Cemetery in Fredericksburg, to begin your self-guided tour of all four battlefields and three historic buildings. The tour includes Chatham Manor, at 120 Chatham Lane, that served as a command post and communications center during the Battle of Fredericksburg. Take a tour of the five-room museum, with living history programs presented summers. Drive the self-guided five-mile auto tour along the Confederate trench line. Hike 4.7-mile Lee Drive trail that begins at Howison Hill, and goes to Prospect Hill.

Drive through the four-mile-long Spotsylvania Court House Battlefield, on Virginia 613, 1.5 miles northwest of Spotsylvania. It was the scene of some of the most intense fighting in the U.S., when the Union and Confederate armies fought to control the shortest route to Richmond. For information, call 804-891-8687.

Stop by Chancellorsville Visitor Center on Virginia 3, 10 miles west of Fredericksburg, site of the Battle of Chancellorsville. Living history programs are presented summers. Take a five-mile self-guided auto tour of the battlefield.

Wilderness Battlefield is on Virginia 20, 1.5 miles west of Virginia 3. Here General Robert E. Lee's army fought Union General Ulysses S. Grant's army. It has a four-mile self-guided auto tour through the battlefield, and a four-mile hiking trail that begins on Virginia 20, a quarter-mile from the exhibit shelter, and ends at the Longstreet marker on Virginia 621.

In Fredericksburg, tour Kenmore and its gardens at 1201 Washington Avenue. The mid-18th-century home was once owned by George Washington's sister. It contains three very elaborately decorated rooms of the period, including one of the "100 Most Beautiful Rooms in America." For information, call 540-373-3381.

Fredericksburg Area Museum and Cultural Center, at 905 Princess Anne Street, has six permanent exhibit galleries. For information, call 540-371-3037.

Incoming pilots can land at Lake Anna Airport at Bumpass. However, no rental cars are available. You can also land at Shannon Airport, two miles south of Fredericksburg, or Louisa County/Freeman Field, two miles southeast of Louisa, and 18 miles from the park. Both airports have rental cars.

INFORMATION

Lake Anna State Park
Off Virginia 208
Spotsylvania, Virginia 22553
540-854-5503

Fredericksburg and Spotslvania
National Military Park
120 Chatham Lane
Fredericksburg, Virginia 22405
540-371-0802

MASON NECK STATE PARK
14

LOCATION   The park is one mile north of Woodbridge on U.S. 1, then 2.5 miles east on Virginia 242.

ACTIVITIES   Hike the trails, tour the visitor center and attend interpretive programs. Birders come to bird watch and to make weekend eagle counts. Launch your cartop boat to go boating, and enjoy saltwater fishing.

Mason Neck National Wildlife Refuge is nearby. In the refuge, you can hike a four-mile trail through wetlands along the edge of the Potomac River. Watch for bald eagles and blue herons. To reach it, take Exit 163 off I-95, to Virginia 1. Go south to Gunston Road, then east to High Point Road and follow signs.

Take a guided tour of Gunston Hall, home of George Mason, author of the Virginia Declaration of Rights in 1776. It's four miles east of Lorton, on Virginia

242. The house features many different styles of woodcarving. Stroll through the formal gardens. Annual events held here include a Kite Festival in March, Historic Virginia Garden Week in April, and an Antique Car Show in September. For information, call 703-550-9220.

INFORMATION
Mason Neck State Park
Lorton, Virginia 22079
703-550-0960 or 703-339-6234

NATURAL TUNNEL STATE PARK
15

LOCATION   Go north from Weber City via U.S. 23, and 1.5 miles east on Virginia 871. It's also two miles north of Clinchport. The park is near Powell Mountain and Jefferson National Forest.

FEATURES   Natural Tunnel was carved through a limestone ridge in the mountains. The 850-foot-long tunnel is as tall as a 10-story building.

ACTIVITIES   Go camping in the 30-site campground, with a dumping station, (open Memorial Day through Labor Day. Bring along a picnic, tour the visitor center, and attend programs in the natural rock amphitheater. The park showcases local and regional productions. Snacks are available. Ride the chair lift, go swimming in the Olympic-size pool (open Memorial Day through Labor Day), and visit the wide chasm between the steep stone walls. Go trout fishing and hike the trails that includes one leading to the summit of Lover's Leap, located on the crater's rim.

Tour Southwest Virginia Museum, on West First Street and Wood Avenue in Big Stone Gap, to learn the history of the culture and industry of the area. Exhibits range from Indian and pioneer artifacts, including a collection of fine china, and a 1,100-pound lump of coal. It's closed March 1 through Memorial Day; from September 2 through January 1; and on Mondays. For information, call 540-523-1322.

Take a guided tour of the June Tolliver House, on Jerome and Clinton Streets. It was the 1890 residence of one of the characters in Trail of the Lonesome Pine. Attend the outdoor musical, Trail of the Lonesome Pine, in the June Tolliver Playhouse, Thursday through Saturday at 8:30 P.M., from mid-June through August. For information, call 540-523-1235.

INFORMATION
Natural Tunnel State Park
Route 3, Box 250
Duffield, Virginia 24227
540-940-2674

NEW RIVER TRAIL STATE PARK

SHOT TOWER HISTORICAL STATE PARK
16

LOCATION   New River Trail State Park has accesses at Ivanhoe, Fries, Galax, Draper, Pulaski, Byllesby Dam, and Shot Tower Historical State Park.

To reach Shot Tower, take Poplar Camp Exit from I-77, and go north on Virginia 52 for two miles, near Wytheville.

FEATURES   Shot Tower was constructed over 150 years ago to manufacture ammunition for the early settlers' firearms. Lead was melted in a kettle at the top of a 75-foot tower. It was then poured through a sieve, and fell through the tower down the 75-foot shaft, where it landed in a kettle of water. It's listed as a National Historic Mechanical Engineering Landmark.

The tower is the headquarters for the New River Trail State Park.

ACTIVITIES   New River Trail is a 57-mile-long linear park that follows an abandoned railroad right-of-way. It parallels the New River for 29 miles. Visitors enjoy hiking, bicycling, and horseback riding. Also enjoy freshwater fishing. Concessions are available.

Tour the visitor center at Shot Tower, and attend interpretive programs. The tower is open Monday through Friday from noon to 5:00, and weekends from 10 to 6, from Memorial Day through Labor Day. Bring along a picnic, and hike the short trail through the grounds to reach the picnic area overlooking the river.

INFORMATION
New River Trail State Park
Shot Tower Historical State Park
Route 1, Box 81 X
Austinville, Virginia 24312
540-699-6778

OCCONEECHEE STATE PARK
17

LOCATION   Occoneechee State Park is in southern Virginia, across the lake from Clarksville. It's on the John H. Kerr Reservoir, also called Buggs Island Lake. From Clarksville, go 1.5 miles east on U.S. 58 to the intersection with U.S. 15.

FEATURES   Buggs Island Lake has 800 miles of shoreline. The park was named for the Occoneechee Indians, who lived here from circa 1250 through the late 1600s.

ACTIVITIES   Camp in the 143-site campground, 40 sites with electrical and water hookups and a dumping station, and convenience store available. Bring along a picnic, and attend programs in the amphitheater. Go freshwater fishing and boating from the ramp in the lake (power boats permitted). Boat rentals are available. Hike the hiking trails.

Arriving pilots can land at Marks Municipal Airport, two miles south of Clarksville, and three miles from the state park. A courtesy car is available upon request. You can also land at Mecklenburg-Brunswick Regional Airport, located four miles southeast of South Hill. Rental cars are available.

INFORMATION
Occoneechee State Park
P.O. Box 818
Clarksville, Virginia 23927-9449
804-374-2210

POCAHONTAS STATE PARK
18

LOCATION   The park is 20 miles from downtown Richmond, and four miles southwest of Chesterfield. Take Exit 6 off I-95, and go west on Virginia 10 to Virginia 655.

ACTIVITIES   Go swimming in the pool. Enjoy catfish fishing and boating in Beaver Lake, with rentals available. Hike around the lake, tour the visitor center, and attend interpretive programs. Camp in the 37-site campground, with a dumping station, or stay in a cabin. Rent a bicycle to bike the bicycle trail. Purchase a snack at the snack bar.

In Chesterfield, take a guided tour of the plantation house, Magnolia Grange, circa 1822. Period furnishings show how prominent families lived during that era. For information, call 804-796-1479.

Chesterfield County Museum on Virginia 10, is in the Courthouse Complex. It has a history of the county from prehistoric times through the 20th century. It's built as a replica of the 1750 Colonial courthouse, where Baron von Steuben drilled Colonial troops. The British, with Benedict Arnold's aid, burned it down in 1781. A jail, circa 1892, is next door. Tours are available. For information, call 804-748-1026.

In Richmond, tour Edgar Allan Poe's Museum at 1914 East Main Street. Built in the 1730s, it's Richmond's oldest house, and one of five houses devoted to Poe's life. It contains the world's largest Poe collection. Behind the stone house is the small Enchanted Garden inspired by two of Poe's poems, *To One in Paradise,* and *To Helen.*

Watch bateau racers on the James River, as they go from Lynchburg to Richmond. Take a self-guided tour of nine National Historic Landmarks in downtown Richmond, including the John Marshall House, the Museum, the White House of the Confederacy, the Valentine Museum, and the 1812 Wickham House.

You can also take a guided walking tour, "200 years of History and Architecture," which leaves from the Valentine Museum on Monday through Saturday, from 10 to noon, April through October (weather permitting). Make reservations by 4 P.M. the day preceding the tour by calling 804-780-0107.

Many annual events occur in Richmond including the James River Wine Festival in May, and an Azalea Festival Parade held in April. For a calendar of events, call 1-800-365-7272.

Richmond National Battle Park Headquarters is in Richmond, at 3215 Broad Street. It was once the largest hospital in operation. Begin your battlefield tour here. For information, call 804-226-1981.

Petersburg National Battlefield, southeast of the park, is located next to the city that endured the longest siege in U.S. history, during the Civil War from 1864–1865. Tour the Siege Museum at 15 West Bank Street, to see exhibits and a film documenting the siege. Hike the seven-mile multi-use trail open to hiking, biking, and horseback riding. You can also hike .75-mile Meade Station Trail, and one-mile Fort Stedman Colquitt's Salient Trail.

Drive along historic Siege Road. Pick up a brochure for the self-guided auto tour of the Union and Confederate lines built around Petersburg. The 16-mile drive begins on Crater Road. For information, call 804-732-3531.

Tour Centre Hill Mansion, with its entrance on Adams and Tabb Streets. This 1823 mansion has been host to three U.S. Presidents. For information, call 804-733-2400. The Trapezium House, circa 1817, is at Market and High Streets in Petersburg, and legends refer to the house as having ghosts. For information, call 804-733-2400.

Appomattox Iron Works Industrial Heritage Park is at 20-28 West Old Street in Petersburg. The one-acre complex has 19th-century buildings and operational antique machinery. For information, call 800-232-IRON.

Incoming pilots can land at Petersburg Municipal Airport, located five miles southwest of Petersburg. You can also land at Byrd International Airport, six miles east of Richmond, or at Chesterfield County Airport, located four miles southwest of Richmond. All three airports have rental cars available.

INFORMATION
Pocahontas State Park
10300 Park Road
Chesterfield, Virginia 23832
804-796-4255

SEASHORE STATE PARK
AND NATURAL AREA
19

LOCATION Seashore State Park is on U.S. 60 at Cape Henry in Virginia Beach, on the Atlantic Ocean. The Seashore State Park Natural Area is between U.S. 60 and two inland saltwater bodies: Broad Bay and Linkhorn Bay.

FEATURES   Much of Seashore State Park consists of the Seashore Natural Area, designated as a National Natural Landmark. Several of the 58 different kinds of oak trees found in Tidewater Virginia grow here.

Virginia Beach is known as the world's longest resort beach, boasting 28 miles of wide, sandy coastline.

ACTIVITIES   Explore over 19 miles of hiking trails and boardwalks winding through the natural area, with lagoons, bogs, large cypress trees, and rare plants. These trails have been designated as National Recreation Trails.

Tour the visitor center from April through October, and attend interpretive programs. Camp in the 240-site campground, with a dumping station, or stay in one of 20 housekeeping cabins.

Go power boating from the ramps, with parking available at the Narrows. Enjoy saltwater fishing, and cycle the bicycle trail, with rentals available. Snacks and groceries are available.

Old Cape Henry Lighthouse is in Fort Story, at Virginia Beach. It was built on top of the tallest dune in Cape Henry to warn ships away from the treacherous shoals. America's oldest government-built lighthouse, circa 1791, is open from mid-March through the end of October.

Upper Wolfsnare, an 18th-century home at 2040 Potters Road, Virginia Beach, is open from June through September, on Wednesday and Thursday. For information, call 804-491-0127.

Take a narrated cruise from Virginia Beach, from Memorial Day through Labor Day.

The Chesapeake Bay Bridge-Tunnel is 17.6 miles long, and is considered the world's largest bridge-tunnel complex. It's acclaimed as one of the Seven Wonders of the Modern World, and links Virginia Beach/Norfolk with Virginia's Eastern Shore. Go fishing for bluefish, trout, flounder, and shark from Sea Gull Fishing Pier, located on the first of the bridge's four man-made islands, 3.5 miles from Virginia Beach.

In Virginia Beach, tour the Adam Thoroughgood house and garden, east of the junction of U.S. 13 and U.S. 60. For information and hours, call 804-460-0007.

Francis Land's House, circa 1732, is at 3131 Virginia Beach Blvd. Costumed guides conduct tours Wednesday through Saturday from 9 to 5, and Sundays from noon to 5. For information, call 804-340-1732.

Tour the Virginia Marine Science Museum, a quarter-mile south of Rudee Bridge, on General Booth Avenue. For hours and information, call 804-425-FISH.

Tour NASA's visitor center off Virginia 134, at the NASA Langley Research Center. It has over 50 space exhibits including Apollo 12's command module. For information, call 804-864-6000.

Tour the Mariners' Museum in Newport News. Take Exit 62A from I-64 onto U.S. 60, to see the Crabtree collection of miniature ships. Included is the *Mora,* the ship sailed by William the Conqueror, as well as Columbus' *Santa Maria* and the *Pinta.* Observe costumed interpreters who bring maritime life alive. Tours are conducted Monday through Friday, at 11 A.M. and 1:30 P.M. Go fishing in the lake, and wander around the grounds to see various artifacts. Watch the movie *Mariner,* to learn about life at sea. For information, call 804-595-0368.

Stop by the Virginia Living Museum, 524 J. Clyde Morris Blvd., between Virginia 143 and U.S. 60, to see its outdoor displays. Stroll the boardwalk to see a bald eagle, otter, and other animals. For information, call 804-595-1900.

In Norfolk, tour Moses Myers House at 323 E. Freemason. Constructed in 1791, it's the only historic house that interprets the traditions of early Jewish immigrants. For information, call 804-627-2737. Special events, festivals, and free outdoor concerts occur in Town Point Park on the Elizabeth River, at 120 West Main. For details, call 804-627-7809.

Take a tall ship cruise from Waterside, in Norfolk. For information, call 804-627-SAIL. Norfolk Botanical Gardens, with its azaleas and rhododendrons that bloom from early spring through late summer, offers guided boat tours along a network of canals winding through the gardens. Tram tours along 12 miles of roadway are also available. Enjoy a snack at the teahouse. For details, call 804-441-5830. In April, attend the annual Azalea Festival.

Learn more about General Douglas MacArthur by visiting the memorial on City Hall Avenue. Watch the film on his life, and tour 11 galleries. For information, call 804-441-2965.

The city of Norfolk is located on one of the world's great natural harbors. The famous battle between the *Monitor* and the *Merrimac* occurred here in 1862.

INFORMATION
Seashore State Park
2500 Shore Drive
Virginia Beach, Virginia 23451
804-481-2131

SKY MEADOWS STATE PARK
20

LOCATION   Sky Meadows is one mile south of Paris, on Virginia 17.

ACTIVITIES   Tour Mount Bleak Mansion to see how an 1850s family lived. Attend nature and history programs in the spring through the fall. Equestrians come to ride the bridle trail. Campers can camp in the 12-site primitive hike-in campground that provides access to the Appalachian Trail. Go freshwater fishing, tour the visitor center and attend interpretive programs.

In the summer, attend Trail of the Lonesome Pine Outdoor Drama in Stone Gap. For information, call 540-523-1235.

INFORMATION
Sky Meadows State Park
Paris, Virginia 24219
540-592-3556

SMITH MOUNTAIN LAKE STATE PARK
21

LOCATION   The park is 26 miles south of Bedford, on the north shore of Smith Mountain Lake. From U.S. 460, take Virginia 122 south to Virginia 608. Then go east to Virginia 626 and head south. You can also take Virginia 43 from U.S. 460, to Virginia 626.

FEATURES   Smith Mountain Lake is the state's second largest body of fresh water. The park has 16 miles of lake frontage.

ACTIVITIES   Go swimming, freshwater fishing for bass, and power boating on Smith Mountain Lake, with boat rentals available. Go primitive camping in one of 50 sites, enjoy miles of hiking trails, tour the visitor center, and attend interpretive programs. Snacks are available at the snack bar.

Special events include Smith Mountain Raritan's Bass Fishing Tournament in March, Aspiring Anglers Junior Fishing Tournament in June, and Roanoke Jaycees Annual Triathlon in July.

In Bedford, tour the museum at 201 E. Main to see Civil War relics and 19th-century clothing. It's open Tuesday through Saturday from 10 to 5. For information, call 540-586-4520.

The Booker T. Washington National Monument is between Bedford and Rocky Mount, on Virginia 122. The monument is the birthplace and early childhood home of the famous black leader and educator. Stop at the National Park's visitor center to watch the orientation film before walking the Plantation Trail. Pick up a trail guide marked with symbols, indicating which buttons to push to hear dramatized readings about life here during the 19th-century. You can also hike the 9.2-mile Dickey Hill Trail. For information, call 540-721-2094.

Incoming pilots can land at Moneta Airport, four miles southeast of Smith Mountain. However, no rental cars are available. You can also land at Smith Mountain Lake Airport, located near the state park.

INFORMATION
Smith Mountain Lake State Park
Route 1, Box 41
Huddleston, Virginia 24104
540-297-6066

STAUNTON RIVER STATE PARK
22

LOCATION   The park is 18 miles east of South Boston. From U.S. 360, follow Virginia 344 for 10 miles. It's also nine miles southeast of Scottsburg. It has a lengthy shoreline along the John H. Kerr Reservoir, also called Buggs Island Lake.

ACTIVITIES   Go boating on Buggs Island Lake, with power boats permitted, and boat rentals available. Go swimming in the pool. Camp in the 66-site campground, with a dump station, or stay in a housekeeping cabin. Groceries and a snack bar are available. Play tennis, hike the trails, tour the visitor center and attend interpretive programs, or enjoy freshwater fishing.

Approximately 10 miles north of the main park is the Staunton River Bridge where, in 1864, a small contingent of old men and boys repelled a large Federal force.

Arriving pilots can land at William M. Tuck Airport, located three miles east of South Boston. Rental cars are available.

Staunton River State Park was the site of the only battle of the Civil War in this area. On June 25, 1864, a small contingent of old men and boys numbering 700, repelled a Federal force of 2,000 (courtesy of the Virginia Division of Tourism)

INFORMATION
Staunton River State Park
Route 2, Box 295
Scottsburg, Virginia 24589
804-572-4623

TWIN LAKES STATE PARK

SAYLER'S CREEK BATTLEFIELD
HISTORICAL STATE PARK
23

LOCATION   The park is in the state's center, three miles southwest of Burkeville, off U.S. 360. Go two miles west on Virginia 621. Twin Lakes is in the Piedmont section of Virginia, in the Prince Edward–Gallion State Forest.

ACTIVITIES   Go swimming, boating, and freshwater fishing in Prince Edward Lake. From Memorial Day through Labor Day, camp in the 33-site campground, with a dump station, or stay in one of the 6 housekeeping cabins. Hike the trails, and get a snack from the snack bar. Attend interpretive programs.

Sayler's Creek Battlefield Historical State Park is east of Farmville on Virginia 617, two miles north of Virginia 307. Here the last major battle of the Civil War in Virginia occurred in 1865. General Lee's troops, retreating from Petersburg, were defeated here, forcing his surrender at Appomattox three days later. Tour this registered National Historic Landmark open year-round.

Arriving pilots can land at Crewe Municipal Airport, one mile east of Crewe, and 15 miles from the state park. Rental cars are available.

INFORMATION
Twin Lakes State Park
Sayler's Creek Historical Battlefield
Green Bay, Virginia 23942
804-392-3435

WESTMORELAND STATE PARK
24

LOCATION   Westmoreland is on Virginia 347, six miles west of Montross, reached via Virginia 3. It's on the northern edge of Northern Neck, a peninsula between the Potomac and Rappahannock Rivers.

FEATURES   The park lies between two of Virginia's most historic shrines. Wakefield, George Washington's Birthplace National Monument, is in Northern Neck, eight miles west of Westmoreland via Virginia 3 and 204. Stratford, the birthplace of General Robert E. Lee, joins Westmoreland off Virginia 3, west of Montross.

ACTIVITIES   Go camping in the 138-site campground, 40 sites with water and electrical hookups, and a dump station. You can also stay in one of 24 housekeeping cabins, or in one of 6 overnight cabins with sleeping rooms only. Equestrians can ride bridle trails, and hikers can explore hiking trails. Go swimming in the Olympic-size swimming pool.

Enjoy power boating from the ramp on the Potomac River, with boat rentals available. Enjoy saltwater fishing. Groceries and snacks are sold in the park, or you can enjoy a meal in the restaurant. Tour the visitor center and attend interpretive programs.

Tour Wakefield, built to represent an 18th-century plantation house, and observe costumed guides demonstrate agricultural techniques used on the Colonial farm. Hike around the grounds, follow the trail by the picnic area, and go fishing. During the summer, attend the Colonial Crafts show, Indian and Black Heritage History days, Gentry Weekend, and Colonial Medicine Days. For information, call 804-224-1732.

Tour the restored manor house at Stratford Hall Plantation, circa 1738. The Hall is once again a working plantation, with crops, cattle, and horses. Purchase ground corn or barley at Stratford Store and enjoy refreshments in the log cabin dining room. Hike the trail to the bluffs of the Potomac River. For information, call 804-493-8038.

Hike the Chesapeake Nature Trail on Virginia 3, west of Lancaster Courthouse. The well-labeled trail identifies some of the trees and wildflowers of the area.

INFORMATION
Westmoreland State Park
Route 1, Box 53-H
Montross, Virginia 22420
804-493-8821

YORK RIVER STATE PARK
25

LOCATION   York River State Park is on the York River, midway between Richmond and Hampton Roads. It's 11 miles north of Williamsburg. From I-64, take Croaker Exit, 54-B. Go north on Virginia 607 for one mile, then right on Virginia 606. Go two more miles to reach the park entrance.

FEATURES   Taskinas Creek and its surrounding marsh are designated as a Chesapeake Bay National Estuarine Research Reserve.

ACTIVITIES   Tour the visitor center, attend an interpretive program or bird walk, go hiking, and bring along a picnic. Enjoy boating on the York River, with power boats permitted, and take a canoe trip on Taskinas Creek, starting from the visitor center. Enjoy both freshwater and saltwater fishing. Equestrians can rent horses to ride the bridle trails, and bicyclists can explore bike trails.

Visit Yorktown Victory Center, on Virginia 238 and Colonial Parkway, to learn the story of the American Revolution. Watch *The Road to Yorktown*. Stroll through the recreated Continental Army camp, 18th-century farm site, and tobacco barn. Watch costumed staff demonstrate Colonial cooking, and medical and military techniques. For information, call 804-253-4838.

Begin your tour of Yorktown Colonial National Historic Park at the visitor center, accessed via I-64, Exits 57 A and B. Yorktown Battlefield is the site of the last major battle of the American Revolution. General Cornwallis surrendered here in 1781, marking the beginning of America's independence, and ending the British dream of a North American empire. A Celebration of Victory is held here every October 19 to commemorate the historic event.

Stop by the Yorktown Battle Visitor Center, at the end of Colonial Parkway, to walk through a full-size replica of the quarter deck of a British warship, see the collection of Revolutionary War artifacts, and watch the film, *Victory at Yorktown*. Pick up a map for a self-guided auto tour past Washington's headquarters, and sites of his encampments and fortifications. En route, you pass Moore House, where negotiations were conducted leading to Cornwallis' surrender. A living history program tells the story of the arguments occurring there in October of 1781.

In Yorktown, many residents live in restored homes, including that of Thomas Nelson, a signer of the Declaration of Independence. Look for cannonballs still lodged in its brick walls. It's open summers. Watch the theatrical presentation, *If These Walls Could Talk*. Performance schedules are posted at the visitor center.

From Yorktown, continue on to tour Jamestown Festival Park, where you can see three ships: *Susan Constant, Godspeed* and *Discovery*. Jamestown National Historical Site is the site of America's first permanent English settlement. Here the British began their dream of a New World empire in 1607. The colony managed to survive until 1699 when, after several seasons of crop failure and disease, a general revolt divided the community, and the government was removed to Williamsburg.

Hike a three- or five-mile nature loop, and tour the reconstructed fort. Stop at the reconstructed glasshouse to watch costumed craftsmen demonstrate the art of glassblowing. You can also see the ruins of the original glasshouse built in 1608. Purchase pottery at the 17th-century Dale House.

The Jamestown Visitor Center and Museum shows an interesting film, and has one of the most extensive collections of 17th-century artifacts in the U.S. Take a conducted tour of the town site, or do your own one-mile self-guided tour. For information, call 804-229-1733.

Bicyclists can cycle along 23-mile Colonial Parkway, that connects Jamestown and Yorktown with historic Williamsburg, forming Virginia's famous historic triangle.

Busch Gardens is a European-theme family entertainment park, open from mid-March through October. It's three miles east of Williamsburg, on U.S. 60. Tour the representative 17th-century European countries, including England, France, Germany, and Italy. Choose from over 100 rides, exhibits, and shows. Tour the Brewery to sample their products. For information, call 804-253-3350.

Tour Carter's Grove, eight miles southeast of Williamsburg, via Scenic Country Road. For information, call 804-229-1000.

Visit Colonial Williamsburg, which was the Revolutionary War capital of Virginia from 1699 to 1780. Stop by the information center to obtain admission tickets to most of the historic homes. Watch *Williamsburg—the Story of a Patriot*.

Tour Bassett Hall and garden, circa 1760, home to the John D. Rockefeller, Jr. family. Reservations are suggested. Call 804-229-1000.

Make a reservation for a carriage or wagon ride at the 1770 Court House, on Market Square. You can also make a reservation for dinner at one of the 18th-century taverns by calling 1-800-229-2141. No reservations are necessary for lunch.

Tour Berkeley Plantation, site of the first official Thanksgiving in 1619 where *Taps* was composed in 1862, while Civil War Union forces were encamped here. It's on Virginia 5, 6.5 miles west of Charles City on the James River.

Shirley Plantation is 9.5 miles west of Charles City, via Virginia 5. The mansion, circa 1723, has a "hanging staircase." Tour the working plantation, designated a National Historic Landmark. For information, call 804-829-5121.

Sherwood Forest Plantation, home of former President John Tyler, is 18 miles west of Williamsburg on Virginia 5, John Tyler Memorial Highway. The mansion, listed on the National Register of Historic Places, is still privately-owned. Stroll the grounds that has 80 varieties of century-old trees, and tour the mansion, the longest frame house in America. For information, call 804-829-5377.

Richmond National Battlefield Park consists of nine units plus the Chimborazo Visitor Center, at 3215 E. Broad Street. The center has a slide program, movie, and self-guiding tour brochure of the battlefields. To make a complete tour of the park, pick up a map of the 100-mile area. The park preserves the sites of two Civil War campaigns: McClellan's Peninsula Campaign of 1862, and Grant's Campaign in 1864. Special living history programs are presented during the summer.

Tour Fort Harrison's visitor center. Self-guided hiking trails are at the Watt House, Fort Harrison, Fort Brady, and Drewry's Bluff.

To learn more about the Civil War, visit the Museum of the Confederacy, located next to the White House of the Confederacy, two blocks north of Broad, at 12th and Clay. Purchase a combination ticket for both the museum, White House, John Marshall House, and Valentine Museum. For information, call 804-649-1861.

Attend musical performances during the Festival of Arts from mid-June through mid-August, in Dogwood Dell Amphitheater. It's next to the carillon in William Byrd Park, at the south end of the Boulevard at Idlewood Avenue. For information, call 804-780-8136.

Pilots can land at Patrick Henry International Airport, Williamsburg-Jamestown Airport, Newport News, Richmond International Airport, Byrd Field, and Norfolk. All airports have rental cars.

INFORMATION
York River State Park
Williamsburg, Virginia 23188
804-566-3036 or 804-564-9057
Colonial National Historical Park
804-898-3400, extension 53

WEST VIRGINIA

Most of the state is located within the Appalachians, the oldest mountain chain on earth, making it a host to a wide variety of plants and wildlife. Spruce Knob, rising 4,861 feet, is its highest point.

West Virginia has 36 state parks and four levels of campgrounds: deluxe with hookups, standard campgrounds generally without hookups, rustic, and primitive. Most campsites are available on a first-come first-served basis, but a few sites can be reserved in Babcock, Beech Fork, Blackwater Falls, Canaan Valley, Holly River, North Bend, Pipestem, and Watoga State Parks. Two state parks offer Rent-A-Camp facilities: Tomlinson Run and Twin Falls. In addition, cabin or lodge reservations may be made by calling the park directly, or 1-800-CALL WVA.

The 270-mile-long Allegheny Trail, including the 75-mile Greenbrier River Trail, connects several state parks. It begins at the Pennsylvania border near Coopers Rock State Park, and passes through Blackwater Falls, Canaan Valley, and Watoga State Parks, to end at Lindside near the Virginia border. For information on other state hiking trails, contact West Virginia Scenic Trails Association at 304-844-5157 or 304-296-5158. Enroll in "Hiking West Virginia" to earn an award for trekking across the state parks.

Monongahela National Forest covers almost 900,000 mountainous acres, and includes the Cranberry Glades Botanical Area, Spruce Knob Lake, Dolly Sods, Otter Creek Wilderness Areas, Hills Creek Falls, the Sinks of Gandy, Seneca Rocks, and the Highland Scenic Highway. To get a copy of *A Comprehensive Hiking Guide to the Monongahela National Forest,* write West Virginia Highlands Conservancy, P.O. Box 306, Charleston, West Virginia 25321.

In the fall, drive Highland Scenic Highway, West Virginia 150. It goes through the southern Monongahela National Forest, from the Cranberry Visitor Center on West Virginia 55, and joins U.S. 219. Another colorful drive is along West Virginia 60, the old Midland Trail. The earliest color changes occur in the southern part of the state where the mountains are highest. Come in late September for these, and in late October to see the largest part of the state at peak color. For information on fall color tours, call 1-800-CALL WVA.

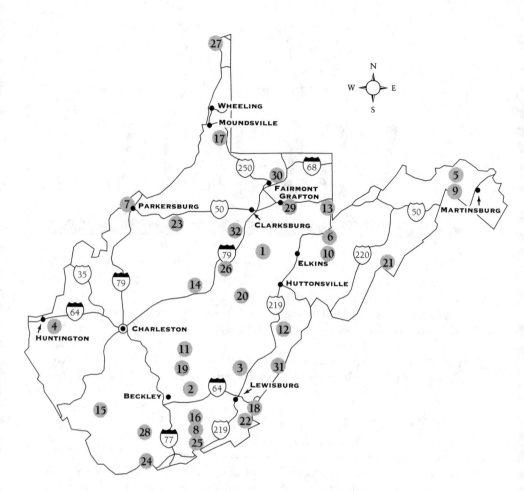

WEST VIRGINIA STATE PARKS

1. Audra State Park
2. Babcock State Park
3. Beartown State Park and Droop Mountain Battlefield State Park
4. Beech Fork State Park
5. Berkeley Springs State Historic Park
6. Blackwater Falls State Park
7. Blennerhassett Island Historical State Park
8. Bluestone State Park
9. Cacapon State Park
10. Canaan Valley State Park
11. Carnifex Ferry Battlefield State Park
12. Cass Scenic Railroad State Historic Park
13. Cathedral State Park
14. Cedar Creek State Park
15. Chief Logan State Park
16. Grandview State Park
16. Little Beaver State Park
17. Grave Creek Mound State Park

18. Greenbrier River Trail State Park and Greenbrier State Forest
19. Hawk's Nest State Park
20. Holly River State Park
21. Lost River State Park
22. Moncove Lake State Park
23. North Bend State Park and North Bend Rail Trail
24. Pinnacle Rock State Park
25. Pipestem Resort State Park
26. Stonewall Jackson State Park
27. Tomlinson Run State Park
28. Twin Falls State Park
29. Tygart Lake State Park
30. Valley Falls State Park and Prickett's Fork State Park
31. Watoga State Park
32. Watters Smith Memorial State Park

Mountain bikers enjoy coming to the national forest to cycle along old logging roads, former narrow-gauge railroad beds, and out of the Slatyfork's Elk River Touring Center. Cyclists have access to 500 miles of marked trails. Easier rides are available along the 75-mile Greenbrier River Trail, but for more challenging riding, tackle some of the single-track trails along 50-mile Gauley Divide/Sharp's Knob Trail near the inn, or the steep 12-mile ride on Sharp's Knob/Lookout Tower loop. Rental bikes are available. For information, call 304-572-3771.

The state has many covered bridges for you to visit, with several close to the state parks.

The New River Gorge National River, geologically one of the world's oldest rivers and often called the "Grand Canyon of the East," is surrounded with 1,000-foot limestone cliffs and narrow, forested river bottoms. Covering 52 miles, the New River Gorge has a reputation for having some of North America's best whitewater. Licensed outfitters provide guides for whitewater adventures along rapids rated class I through VI. Rock climbers have over 20 miles of cliffs for climbing, including over 700 completed routes. The New River is next to four state parks: Babcock, Bluestone, Hawk's Nest, and Pipestem.

The 23-mile Upper New River from Hinton to Thurmond has relatively calm water for canoeing and floating, through Class I and II rapids. If you take the 12-mile run from Thurmond to Fayette Station, you have access to rapids from Class III, IV, and V. Go for a half-day hike while in Fayette Station Road, to reach the ruins of the mountainside mining community of Kaymoor.

Whitewater enthusiasts also tackle the Gauley River, ranked seventh among the world's great whitewater rivers. The river is considered a "technical" river. In a 30-mile stretch, the river falls over 650 feet, with over 100 named major rapids, many rated Class V and VI. Water is released into the river from the Summersville Dam in May and June following spring rains, and again in the fall. Gauley River National Recreation Area is adjacent to Carnifex Ferry Battlefield State Park.

The Cheat River was named for its deceptive appearance. From April through June, it provides the most rapids in the shortest stretch. Rapids are classified from Class III to V+. For a whitewater rafting brochure, call 1-800-CALL WVA.

AUDRA STATE PARK
1

LOCATION   The park is 10 miles west of Belington, on the banks of the Middle Fork River. From Buckhannon and the junction of West Virginia 20 and U.S. 119, go northeast for six miles on U.S. 119 to Volga Road. Continue east for eight miles.

FEATURES   Audra, a Lithuanian word meaning "thunderstorm," was given this name because of its thundering spring runoff.

ACTIVITIES   Go swimming, fishing for catfish, climbing on the mammoth river rocks, or inner tubing from the river beach. Camp beside the river in one of 65 campsites, with a dump station. Pick up a snack from the snack bar, or buy groceries nearby. Go hiking in the forest among the rhododendron thickets, and enjoy a picnic.

In mid to late May, attend West Virginia's Strawberry Festival in Buckhannon, featuring a carnival, band contests, parades, and berry auctions. For information, call 304-472-0936 or 304-472-2095.

Visit 140-foot-long Carrollton covered bridge, the "kissing bridge," which spans the Buckhannon River. Circa 1852, it's the third longest and third oldest covered bridge in West Virginia. It's one mile from U.S. 119, south of Philippi, at the intersection of West Virginia 36 and 11/3. The Union and Confederate soldiers fought their first land battle of the Civil War here in 1861. The first weekend in June, attend the Blue and Grey Reunion Civil War Reenactment in Philippi, that includes concerts, food, and arts and crafts exhibits.

Arriving pilots can land at Buckhannon–Upshur County Airport, two miles east of Buckhannon. It has rental cars.

INFORMATION
Audra State Park
Route 4, Box 564
Buckhannon, West Virginia 26201
304-457-1162

BABCOCK STATE PARK
2

LOCATION   The park is four miles southwest of Clifftop on West Virginia 41, on the slopes of the New River Gorge.

ACTIVITIES   Fish for trout in the mountain stream. Purchase freshly-ground cornmeal, buckwheat, and whole wheat flour from the reconstructed Glade Creek Grist Mill. It was constructed from parts of old mills collected from all over the state. The mill is one of the state's most photographed scenes.

Stay in one of 26 cabins, open from the last weekend in April through the fourth Monday in October, or camp in the 51-site campground, 30 sites with electrical hookups, and a trailer dumping station. Eat a meal in the restaurant, or pick up supplies in the commissary open on weekends in the spring and fall, and daily from Memorial Day through Labor Day. Attend seasonal interpretive programs.

Go boating and trout fishing in Boley Lake. Swim in the pool, hike the extensive trails, and go horseback riding, with rentals available at the park stables from May through October. For information, call 304-438-7116 or 304-438-6205.

During the winter, go cross-country skiing. In mid-April, mountain bicyclists arrive to race in the park's 20K-40K mountain bike race. For information, call 304-574-BIKE or 304-438-3004.

Camp Washington Carver is adjacent to the park, and was built in 1939 as the first 4-H camp for African-Americans. Its Great Chestnut Lodge is the largest log structure of its kind in the U.S. The camp contains West Virginia's Mountain Cultural Center, with a summer schedule of concerts, theater, and exhibits. It includes the Cabaret Dinner Theater series, and an annual Golden Oldies Festival featuring popular performers from the 1950s and 1960s. The popular Appalachian String Band Festival is held in August. For area information, call 304-438-6429 or 304-438-8625.

INFORMATION
Babcock State Park
Route 1, Box 150
Cliftop, West Virginia 25831
304-438-3004

BEARTOWN STATE PARK

DROOP MOUNTAIN BATTLEFIELD STATE PARK

3

LOCATION   Beartown is three miles south of Droop and southwest of Hillsboro, off U.S. 219, in southeastern West Virginia.

Droop Mountain Battlefield State Park is three miles south of Droop, on U.S. 219.

FEATURES   Beartown's name comes from a local legend, claiming that colonies of black bears once inhabited the park's rock formations. The rock is droop sandstone that breaks up into huge blocks, forming deep fissures and sheer cliffs.

ACTIVITIES   Beartown's natural area is open for day-use only. Walk along boardwalks, over the fallen rocks that have formed miniature canyons and valleys, and hike the trails.

Cranberry Glades Botanical Area is north of Beartown. It has four bogs with cranberries, bog rosemary, and deep layers of peat native to the Canadian muskeg 800 miles north of here. Hike the half-mile-long boardwalk that has interpretive signs.

The adjacent 35,600-acre Cranberry Wilderness Area is located within a black bear sanctuary, and has over 70 miles of trails ranging in length from three to 13.5 miles, and has primitive backpacker campsites. Adjoining the wilderness area is the 20,000-acre Cranberry backcountry, laced with hiking trails and abandoned

Glade Creek Grist Mill, Babcock State Park
(photo by David Fattaleh, courtesy of the West Virginia Div. of Tourism & Parks)

roads used by hikers, equestrians, and cross-country skiers. A visitor center in Cranberry Glades has information on all three areas. It's open daily from Memorial Day through Labor Day, and weekends in September and October.

Visit Droop Mountain Battlefield, where the state's largest Civil War engagement occurred on November 6, 1863. Union troops led by General William W. Averell defeated a Confederate army commanded by General John Echols. This was West Virginia's last important site of Southern opposition. Part of the battlefield has been restored and marked. Tour the museum with Civil War artifacts. Hike one of the seven trails to reach scenic overlooks, and climb the observation tower for good views of the Greenbrier Valley. Bring along a picnic.

Take a walking tour of the Lewisburg Historic District, with over 70 buildings dating from the 18th century. It was the scene of a Civil War battle in May, 1862. Guidebooks are available, and skirmish sites are marked with bronze plaques. For information, call 304-645-1000.

Visit Lost World Caverns in Lewisburg, with waterfalls, hex stone formations, and a 1,000-foot long main room. For information, call 304-645-6677.

INFORMATION

Beartown State Park
H.C. 64, Box 189
Hillsboro, West Virginia 24946
304-653-4254

Droop Mountain State Park
Hillsboro, West Virginia 24946
1-800-225-5982

BEECH FORK STATE PARK
4

LOCATION   The park is on the upper end of Beech Fork Lake, 15 miles southeast of Huntington, on West Virginia 152. It's also five miles west of Beech Fork, on West Virginia 64 to West Virginia 10, then continue southeast four miles.

ACTIVITIES   Go bass fishing and boating, from the ramp, on Beech Fork Lake. Camp in the 275-site campground, with a dumping station, and some sites with full hookups. It's open year-round, but without winter water hookups. Purchase supplies from the camp store. Tour the visitor center, attend seasonal programs, hike the trails, and play tennis.

The 3,900-acre park is surrounded by an additional 10,000 acres of public hunting land, where you can do additional hiking.

Take a 12-hour excursion on the Kanawha and Ohio Rivers, aboard the *West Virginia Belle*. It travels between Huntington and South Charleston, from April through October. You can also enjoy shorter cruises. For information, call 304-744-4008.

Attend Charleston's Sternwheeler Regatta's 10-day celebration, held in late August through Labor Day weekend. For information, contact P. A. Denny Sternwheeler at 304-348-0709 or 304-348-6419.

Other major annual events in Charleston include the Martin Luther King celebration in January, the State Jazz Festival in late March, the Vandalia Gathering in the Charleston Cultural Center on Memorial Day weekend, and the West Virginia Black Cultural Festival held at the Cultural Center in October. For information on the Cultural Center, call 304-558-0220.

For a scenic train trip, go to the Heritage Village Huntington Rail Station. When the fall colors are in full swing, take a steam engine ride on the New River Trail, from Huntington to the New River Gorge. For information, call 304-522-6140.

The first weekend in June, attend the Virginia Point Celebration with Appalachian music, hot air balloons, and riverboat rides. In late July, attend Summerfest/Tri-State Fair and Regatta in Huntington, featuring powerboat and jet ski racing, a carnival, and nightly entertainment.

The Kanawha Trace is a 32-mile foot trail that runs from Barboursville, at the confluence of the Mud and Guyandotte Rivers, to Fraziers Bottom, on the Kanawha River. To access the trail, go to Camp Arrowhead near Milton. For information, call 304-523-3408.

In Milton, go for a hot air balloon ride, and attend a performance at the Mountaineer Opry House. Stop by Mud River's 155-year-old covered bridge near Blenko Glass Company. Take the Milton Exit off I-64 on U.S. 60, where it intersects West Virginia 25. In the fall, attend West Virginia's State Pumpkin Festival.

Arriving pilots can land at Robert Newton Field, six miles northeast of Huntington. You can also land at Tri-State Milton J. Ferguson Field, three miles south of Huntington. Both airports have rental cars.

INFORMATION
Beech Fork State Park
Route 2, Box 333
Barboursville, West Virginia 25504
304-522-0303

BERKELEY SPRINGS STATE HISTORIC PARK
5

LOCATION   The park is in the center of Berkeley Springs.

FEATURES   Berkeley Springs has been a health spa since the mid-18th century because of its mineral waters, that maintain a constant temperature of 74.3 degrees.

ACTIVITIES   Enjoy a mineral bath, massage, and heat treatment. Warm mineral baths are available at the 1815 Roman Bath House. Work out in the exercise and fitness room. Enjoy swimming in the pool, open from Memorial Day to Labor Day. On Saturday evenings in July and August, attend free music concerts. On Columbus Day weekend, downtown Berkeley Springs hosts an Apple Butter Festival.

Tour Berkeley Castle, circa 1885, ¼ mile northwest of Berkeley Springs on West Virginia 9W. The Victorian structure features a large stonewalled ballroom, wide carved staircase, and a collection of antiques. For information, call 304-258-3274 or 1-800-544-4540. Take a self-guided tour of the town to see property originally owned by George Washington's family, plus some owned by other early Americans.

The fourth weekend in January, attend Moveable Spa Feast to enjoy great eating and weekend spa specials. For information, call 1-800-447-8797. The third weekend in April, attend Celebrate West Virginia, a festival that highlights the state's wines. For information, call 304-258-9147 or 1-800-447-8797.

Arriving pilots can land at Potomac Airpark, four miles north of Berkeley Springs. However, it has no rental cars.

INFORMATION
Berkeley Springs State Historic Park
121 South Washington Street
Berkeley Springs, West Virginia 25411
304-258-2711

BLACKWATER FALLS STATE PARK
6

LOCATION   The park is two miles southwest of Davis, off West Virginia 32, on Blackwater Falls State Park Road.

ACTIVITIES   Blackwater Falls plunge 63 feet into a 500-foot deep gorge. Several overlooks of the gorge are available. Follow "Gentle Trail," a paved and level path for handicapped visitors, or go down the stairs to reach the foot of the falls. The Falls of Elakala are spanned by a wooden footbridge.

Stay in the 55-room lodge on the edge of the gorge, or in one of 25 deluxe cabins scattered throughout the woods, open year-round. A restaurant overlooking Blackwater Canyon is open year-round. Stay in the 65-site campground, with 30 sites providing electrical hookups, open from April through October. Groceries are available nearby. A snack bar is located in the trading post.

Go horseback riding, with rentals and guided rides available from the park stables, from Memorial Day through Labor Day. Fish for bass, swim in Pendleton Lake, and rent a rowboat or paddleboat to go boating.

Play tennis, and go hiking along several miles of trails. These trails pass through stands of red spruce, black cherry, and rhododendron. Eight-mile Davis Trail connects Blackwater Falls and Canaan Valley State Park, and has good backpacking campsites. The trail intersects Canyon Loop Road for additional backpacking. A 7.9-mile section of the Allegheny Trail makes an inn-to-inn connection between Canaan and Blackwater Falls State Park.

During the spring, wildflowers cover the area. In late May, attend the annual Wildflower Pilgrimage for a weekend of lectures, hikes, and feasts. Golfers can play at Canaan Valley Resort, 10 miles from the park.

Mountain bikers will find miles of single track trails, railroad grades, and dirt roads lacing the forest on the Allegheny Plateau in the Blackwater Falls/Canaan Valley area. A popular ride is along the North Fork of the Blackwater Canyon, where you get scenic views of the waterfalls. It follows an old railroad grade trail from historic Thomas to Hendricks. For the rider seeking more of a challenge, explore Plantation Trail, a nine-mile single track that winds through a spruce, hemlock, and rhododendron forest. A series of mountain bike races are held from April through September.

Go cross-country skiing at the Nordic Learning Center during the winter. Ski rentals, shuttle buses, clinics, and guided tours are available. Rent a toboggan or sled to go down the toboggan run, which is served by a rope tow. Stop for hot chocolate in the warming hut.

Fairfax Stone Historic Monument is nearby, marking the western boundary of land granted to Lord Fairfax by the King of England in the 18th century.

INFORMATION
Blackwater Falls State Park
Drawer 490, Route 29
Davis, West Virginia 26260
304-259-5216: lodge
304-259-5429: cabins

BLENNERHASSETT ISLAND
HISTORICAL STATE PARK
7

LOCATION   Blennerhassett Mansion is on the Ohio River Island at Parkersburg.

FEATURES   Harman Blennerhassett and Aaron Burr were accused of plotting to seize Mexico from Spanish rule, to create a new nation. As a result, federal troops confiscated Blennerhassett's property. Both men were eventually acquitted, but Blennerhassett's fortune was used up in his court battles.

ACTIVITIES   Sternwheelers shuttle visitors from Parkersburg's Point Park to the island, every hour from Tuesday through Friday, and every half-hour on the weekend. For information, call 304-485-3859.

Tour the reconstructed mansion and grounds to see the ancient archeological digs. Take a horse-drawn carriage or wagon ride, or rent a bicycle to tour the island. Mock military encampments help visitors relive many periods from the island's history. Stop by Blennerhassett Island's Craft Village, where artisans demonstrate crafts from the 1798–1806 era.

Tour the Blennerhassett Museum and Welcome Center, at 2nd and Juliana in downtown Parkersburg. It's open year-round, and features personal items belonging to the Blennerhassetts, Civil War relics, and an archeological exhibit. Each June, the drama of Blennerhassett-Burr is recreated in the musical production, *Eden on the River,* presented at Parkersburg's historic Smoot Theater.

While in Parkersburg, tour the first floor of the Tillinghast Cook House, an authentic-middle class Early American home, circa 1825. It's open from March through October. For information, call 304-422-6961.

The first weekend in May, attend "Rendezvous on the River," when muzzleloaders and mountain men gather for an encampment, recreating frontier life on the island.

Fifteen minutes east of Parkersburg, on West Virginia 50, is Mountwood Park. Go fishing, paddleboating, and ride aboard the *R. Buchannan* excursion boat. Take the children to the petting zoo, and go for free rides on the carousel.

North of the park is Henderson Hall Historic District, in Williamstown. A pre–Civil War mansion, circa 1836, it's the focal point of this historic district. For information, call 304-375-2129 or 304-295-4772.

INFORMATION
Blennerhassett Island Historical State Park
P.O. Box 283
Parkersburg, West Virginia 26101
304-428-3000 or 1-800-225-5982

BLUESTONE STATE PARK
8

LOCATION   The park is five miles south of Hinton, on the shore of the Bluestone River. From the intersection of I-64, go south 16 miles on West Virginia 20.

ACTIVITIES   Stay in one of the 25 deluxe cabins, open year-round, or camp in the 87-site campground, with a dumping station, and 22 sites with electrical hookups. Eat in the park restaurant, or purchase groceries nearby.

The park is adjacent to the state's third largest body of water, Bluestone Lake, where you can go bass fishing, water-skiing, and boating from the boat launch. Rental boats are available. Swim in the pool, and attend a summer nature program. Pick up a brochure at the dam office showing the three nature trails that pass through the wilderness.

An adjacent area provides public hunting, equestrian trails, fishing, camping, hiking, and picnicking. Park visitors also have access to Pipestem State Park's facilities, including a 9-hole golf course.

Bluestone Lake hosts many annual water festival activities, including an annual four-day "West Virginia Water Festival," held each August.

Go to a performance in the Eco Theater in Hinton. For information, call 304-466-3497. Take a self-guided walking tour of Hinton's National Historic District, starting from the Summers County visitor center. For information, call 304-466-5420. Attend Railroad Days in October, with two weekends of street fairs and parades. Ride aboard the Collis B. Huntington Historic Railroad's steam excursion trains.

The New River is considered one of West Virginia's best fishing rivers for bass, muskellunge, walleye, catfish, and carp. One of its most popular fishing spots is in the upper section of the river, from Hinton to Meadow Creek.

While in Hinton, tour the visitor center, located on the river on the West Virginia 3 bypass. Watch the slide program, presented daily from Memorial Day weekend through Labor Day. For information, call 304-466-0417.

Stop by the New River Gorge National River Park's visitor center, north of Fayetteville. It's open year-round, and has a boardwalk for viewing the New River Gorge Bridge, the second highest bridge in the U.S., and the longest steel arch in the world. It towers 876 feet above the river's whitewater. Attend outdoor dramas in the Cliffside Amphitheater. For information, call 304-256-6800. The southern park headquarters in Hinton offers interpretive programs.

Fayetteville is the starting point for many whitewater rafting trips down the New and Gauley Rivers. Rafters arrive from April through October. Rafters also go to Hinton to begin rafting the New River.

At Oak Hill in mid-June, attend Whitewater Wednesday, featuring a 16-mile trip down the New River, bluegrass music, and a barbecue. New River Gorge Bridge Day is on the third Saturday in October.

430 State Parks of the South

From Thurmond, take a thrilling jetboat ride upriver for three miles, to get a better look at 20-foot Sandstone Falls, or take a boat tour of the scenic gorge. For information, call 304-469-2525 or 304-465-5551.

INFORMATION
Bluestone State Park
Box 3, Athens Star Route
Hinton, West Virginia 25951
304-466-2805

CACAPON STATE PARK
9

LOCATION   The resort and state park is 10 miles south of Berkeley Springs, on U.S. 522.

ACTIVITIES   Stay in the 50-room lodge, in the 11-room Cacapon Inn, or in one of 30 completely furnished cabins. The inn is closed from the fourth Monday in October, through the first weekend in May. The deluxe cabins and restaurant are open year-round, while the standard cabins are open from the last weekend in April through the fourth Monday in October. Get a snack at the snack bar, or purchase groceries nearby.

Play golf on the 18-hole championship course. For a tee time, call 304-258-1022. Either hike the trails, or rent a horse at the stable, to climb 1,400 feet to reach the summit of Cacapon Mountain. Go fishing, swimming, and boating on the lake, with rowboat and paddleboat rentals available. Attend nature programs, presented year-round. During the winter, go cross-country skiing.

INFORMATION
Cacapon State Park
Route 1, Box 304
Berkeley Springs, West Virginia 25411
304-258-1022: park and lodge
304-258-1442: restaurant

CANAAN VALLEY STATE PARK
10

LOCATION   The park is 10 miles south of Davis, on Virginia 32. It's in the highest U.S. valley east of the Mississippi River.

ACTIVITIES   At 6,000-acre Canaan Valley State Park, stay in one of the 15 deluxe cabins, in the 250-room lodge, or camp in one of 34 campsites with full hookups, and a dump station available. The lodge, cabins, campground, and restaurant are open year-round.

Groceries are available nearby. Since the park is above 3,000 feet, it stays cool during the summer. Ride the chair lift to the top of Weiss Knob.

Play miniature golf, or challenge yourself on the 18-hole championship course. Go swimming in the indoor pool, work out in the fitness center, play tennis on the lighted courts, go trout fishing in the Blackwater River, and hike along miles of trails. A 7.9-mile section of the Allegheny Trail provides an inn-to-inn connection between Canaan Valley and Blackwater Falls State Park.

Attend nature/recreation programs, presented year-round. Rent a horse to go horseback riding, or go for a hay ride in Dry Fork. For reservations, call 304-866-4728.

During the winter go snowshoeing, and cross-country or alpine skiing in the ski resort, located 3,200 feet above sea level. Skiing lessons and rentals are available. Rent a sled or a toboggan to go tobogganing. Rent skates to go ice skating on the skating rink.

Visit nearby Seneca Rocks, a sheer wall that rises 1,000 feet above the floor of the South Branch Valley, at the intersection of West Virginia 33 and 28. Watch seasoned climbers scaling the rock face, or take a back trail to watch the climbers, and to get a good look at the surrounding landscape. Tour the mini-museum and visitor center, at the base of the rocks, to watch an audiovisual presentation and introduction to rock climbing. For information, call 304-567-2827.

You can take climbing lessons at Seneca Rocks Climbing School in Seneca Rocks. For information, call 304-259-5117 or 304-567-2600. Rent a boat to go floating on a branch of the Potomac. For more excitement on the rivers, come during the spring run-off, and try the whitewater.

You can also visit Seneca Caverns, three miles east of U.S. 33 at Riverton, and take a guided tour of its unusual mineral formations, open from April through October. Smoke Hole Caverns, eight miles southwest of Petersburg on West Virginia 28/55, is open year-round, and features the longest ribbon stalactite in the world, plus the second-highest room found in any known cave. For information, call 304-257-4442.

Dolly Suds Wilderness Area covers over 10,200 acres of the Monongahela National Forest, and has a Canadian-like climate. Hikers come to pick wild blueberries in late July, and to hike along 25 miles of trails. Come visit its bogs, beaver ponds, and go camping.

INFORMATION
Canaan Valley State Park
Rt. 1, Box 330
Davis, West Virginia 26260
304-866-4121

CARNIFEX FERRY BATTLEFIELD
STATE PARK
11

LOCATION   The battlefield is 10 miles southwest of Summersville.

FEATURES   Carnifex Ferry was the site of a major Civil War battle, fought to control passage across the Alleghenies. Here the Union forces gained firm control of the Kanawha Valley, on September 10, 1861.

ACTIVITIES   The Patteson House, once located between the Union and Confederate lines, has been restored as an interpretive museum, with local Civil War artifacts. Go hiking to scenic overlooks, take a guided walking tour using a cassette tape, and enjoy a picnic. An annual battle reenactment is offered in September.

Carnifex Ferry is adjacent to the Gauley River National Recreation Area, with a 26-mile stretch of world class whitewater. In fact, it's ranked as number two in the U.S. and 7th in the world, for its whitewater. It's considered to be one of the East's supreme whitewater streams. Summersville Dam, part of the Gauley River National Recreation Area, is the second highest rock-fill dam in the eastern U.S. Whitewater rafters come to the Gauley River in spring and fall. Begin below the Summersville Dam to plunge through its chutes and rapids. The Upper Gauley boasts 60 rapids, and the Lower Gauley has over 35 rapids. Both feature Class V whitewater.

Summersville Lake, 26 miles long, with 82 miles of shoreline, is West Virginia's largest lake. It's considered one of the best diving lakes in the eastern U.S. because of its 40-foot visibility. Besides scuba diving, you can also go sailing, boating, wind surfing, fishing for bass and walleye, and water-skiing.

Take a short horseback ride, or an overnight trip to a wilderness cabin, from Fraly Stables in Summersville. Call 304-872-5151, or 1-800-654-6442.

In late June, attend Summersville's "Music from the Mountains." During the summer, Summersville hosts the Bluegrass Country Music Festival, and an annual Potato Festival in September with street dancing, distance run, and antique car show. In Clay, attend the Golden Delicious Apple Festival held in the fall.

Arriving pilots can land at Summersville Airport, four miles south of Summersville. Rental cars are available.

INFORMATION

Carnifex Ferry Battlefield State Park
Route 2, Box 435
Summersville, West Virginia 26651
304-872-3773

CASS SCENIC RAILROAD
STATE HISTORIC PARK
12

LOCATION   The park is in downtown Cass.

FEATURES   Cass Railroad, circa 1900, is a remnant of the original logging railroad, with an authentic Shay steam locomotive. Cass was founded in 1900 during a lumber boom, to house workers employed by the West Virginia Pulp and Paper Company. The town is one of the best preserved lumber company towns in the U.S.

ACTIVITIES   Watch the slide presentation, *The Cass Showcase*. Take a two-hour trip to Whittaker Station, offered daily at 11:00, 1:00, and 3:00, from Memorial Day weekend through Labor Day, or on weekends only from the first weekend after Labor Day through the last weekend in October.

Overnight in one of the 13 restored lumber employee cottages, open year-round. Hike the trails. Camping, a restaurant, and groceries are available nearby.

You can also take a 22-mile train ride from the old lumber town of Cass through the scenic Allegheny Mountains, to reach the summit of the state's second highest peak, Bald Knob. The 4.5-hour trip is offered from Memorial Day through October, and weekends during October. Special Saturday night dinner trains, running from mid-June through August, include live entertainment and a barbecue. Reservations are suggested. Another ride goes along the scenic Greenbrier River to Durbin. For information, call 304-456-4300.

In mid-May, attend Railfan weekend. Fall color runs are offered the first two weeks in October.

Nearby Seneca State Forest has 10 additional campsites, rustic cabins, trout fishing, hunting, and boating in Seneca Lake, with rentals available. For information, call 304-799-6213.

INFORMATION

Cass Scenic Railroad State Historic Park
Box 107
Cass, West Virginia 24927
304-456-4300

CATHEDRAL STATE PARK
13

LOCATION   The park is north of Aurora, 10 miles from the intersection of West Virginia 72 and 50.

FEATURES   The giant hemlocks are estimated to be 350 years old, and rise up to 90 feet, with 21-foot trunks. The state's largest hemlock is found here.

ACTIVITIES   The forest is listed in the National Registry of Natural History Landmarks. Hike through the centuries-old forest of virgin hemlock and hardwoods, providing you with a glimpse of the primeval forests that once covered much of the eastern U.S.

Cathedral Trail loops through the park, following the fern-bordered Rhine Creek part of the way. You can take side trips off the main trail to see the huge trees, many surrounded by rhododendron.

Bring along a picnic to enjoy in the shelter. Go cross-country skiing in the winter.

INFORMATION
Cathedral State Park
Aurora, West Virginia 26705
304-735-3771

CEDAR CREEK STATE PARK
14

LOCATION   The park is southeast of Glenville. From U.S. 33/119, go southeast four miles on West Virginia 17. It's 25 miles west of I-79.

ACTIVITIES   Camp beside Cedar Creek in one of 35 campsites, with electrical hookups, and a dumping station. Purchase groceries at the camp store. Fish for trout in the fishing ponds in late winter and early spring, and for bass and catfish year-round. Cedar Creek has good muskie fishing during the summer.

Go for a bicycle ride, attend seasonal nature programs, and play tennis and miniature golf. Hike the trails, swim in the pool, go boating with rentals available, and attend seasonal nature/recreational programs. Visit the reconstructed one-room schoolhouse.

On Labor Day weekend, go to Jackson's Mill for its annual Stonewall Jackson Heritage Arts and Crafts Jubilee. It features Appalachian crafts, Civil War reenactments, turkey calling, square dancing, and mountain music. For information, call 304-269-1863.

Stonewall Jackson Lake is south of Weston, and has marinas, camping with hookups, swimming, boating ramps, hiking trails, and over 80 miles of shoreline. Take a cruise aboard the *Stonewall Jackson* Paddlewheeler. Go fishing for bass, crappie, walleye, and muskellunge. Play 18 holes of golf.

In Glenville, attend the West Virginia Folk Festival during the summer, when many musicians converge to "pick, strum, fiddle, dance and sing."

Anglers can fish the Little Kanawha River, well known for its muskie. Fish weighing over 25 pounds have been landed. Additional fishing for bass and crappie is available in Burnsville Lake. Anglers can also fish in Sutton Lake for bass, or in Sutton Dam's tailwaters for trophy muskie and pike.

Bulltown Historic Area has a collection of early homes, barns, and churches dating back to pre-1900. The site also commemorates the Battle of Bulltown, fought during the Civil War. Hike the mile-long interpretive trail, linking remnants of Union trenches. Tour the interpretive center that has artifacts from the battle. For information, call 304-853-8170 or 304-853-2371.

The Walkersville covered bridge crosses the West Fork River. To reach this 39-foot bridge, circa 1903, follow West Virginia 19 south from Walkersville.

Go to Ravenswood in mid-August to attend the annual Ohio River Festival.

INFORMATION
Cedar Creek State Park
Route 1, Box 9
Glenville, West Virginia 26351
304-462-7158

CHIEF LOGAN STATE PARK
15

LOCATION   The park is four miles north of Logan, on West Virginia 10/119.

ACTIVITIES   Open for day-use only, Chief Logan State Park is located in the heart of the state's southern coal fields. Dine in the restaurant. Attend the play, *The Aracoma Story,* a fact-based drama about Shawnee Princess Aracoma, daughter of Indian Chief Cornstalk, and Boling Baker, an English scout. For information, call 304-752-0253.

Go fishing, swimming, play tennis on the lighted courts, hike, and play miniature golf. Visit the old steam locomotive, typical of those used to pull coal cars to market. Work out on the exercise trail. Camp in the 25-site campground, 15 sites with water and electrical hookups. Dine in the park restaurant. In April, come for their annual spring wildflower hike.

INFORMATION
Chief Logan State Park
Logan, West Virginia 25601
304-792-7125

GRANDVIEW STATE PARK

LITTLE BEAVER STATE PARK
16

LOCATION   Grandview State Park is northeast of Beaver. Little Beaver State Park is east of Beaver, on I-64.

FEATURES   In 1994, Grandview State Park became part of the New River Gorge National Park.

ACTIVITIES   Grandview State Park is open for day-use only, where you can attend an outdoor drama in the amphitheater featuring a popular Broadway production, from May through August. For information, call 304-253-8313.

The New River Gorge Bridge, rising 876 feet above the water, is the longest steel arch bridge in the world. Attend Bridge Day the third Saturday in October, when jumpers arrive to "fly" from the bridge. The Canyon Rim Visitor Center, in the New River National Park in Lansing, offers a wonderful view of the New River Gorge and Bridge. Watch the audiovisual program about the 53-mile long river, and enjoy the view from two overlooks, or from the 70-foot-long descending boardwalk. For information, call 304-574-2115.

The park's overlooks provide a beautiful panorama of the New River, that curves to form Horseshoe Bend at the bottom of the gorge. Come in the spring to enjoy a spectacular rhododendron display, and hike the trails. Go cross-country skiing in the winter.

The New River's gorge is called "The Grand Canyon of the East," with rapids ranging from Class I to Class V, that can be rafted, kayaked, or canoed from the spring through the fall.

At Little Beaver State Park, you can go swimming, fishing, and boating on the 18-acre lake, from the dock, with rowboats and paddleboat rentals available. Hike the trails, and camp in the 30-site campground.

Visit Beckley Exhibition Coal Mine National Historic Site, where retired miners conduct underground tours in remodeled mine cars through the mine's 1,500 feet of passageways, dating back to its pre-mechanized days. It's open from the first weekend in April through November 1. For information, call 304-256-1747. In Beckley, tour Wildwood House's museum, and General Alfred Beckley's house. Circa 1836, the house is furnished with period antiques. For information, call 304-252-8216.

Fifteen miles south of Beckley is WinterPlace, one of the most accessible ski resorts in the U.S. For skiing conditions, call 304-787-3221.

Incoming pilots can land at Raleigh County Memorial Airport, three miles east of Beckley. It's five miles from Grandview State Park, and has rental cars.

INFORMATION
Grandview State Park
Route 9
Beaver, West Virginia 25813
304-763-3145

Little Beaver State Park
Route 9, Box 179
Beaver, West Virginia 25813
304-763-2494

GRAVE CREEK MOUND STATE PARK
17

LOCATION   In Moundsville, take 8th Street off West Virginia 2, and continue to Jefferson Street.

FEATURES   Grave Creek Mound State Park contains the largest conical mound in North America, rising 69 feet above its 295-foot base. Originally surrounded by a moat, it was constructed about 2,000 years ago by Indians from the Adena culture. When excavated in 1838, it revealed two burial chambers with ornaments, bone tools, shells, and a small tablet of sandstone with signs, interpreted as a kind of pre-Columbian writing.

ACTIVITIES   Tour the Delf Norona Museum and Culture Center's display of artifacts, including a replica of the Grave Creek tablet, and displays telling about the mound, the Adena Indians, and other cultures that once lived in the vicinity. Food is available in the park, and admission is charged.

INFORMATION
Grave Creek Mound State Park
Moundsville, West Virginia
304-843-1410

GREENBRIER RIVER TRAIL STATE PARK

GREENBRIER STATE FOREST
18

LOCATION   From Lewisburg, take the Greenbrier Hotel Exit off I-64, to U.S. 60 west. Go two miles to the Greenbrier River, turn right and follow signs to reach the trail.

Once part of the Chesapeake and Ohio Railroad, the 76-mile-long trail runs from North Caldwell to Cass, following the Greenbrier River. It passes through many small towns, over 35 bridges, and through two tunnels.

The Greenbrier State Forest is 1.25 miles south of Caldwell, on West Virginia 60/14.

ACTIVITIES   The Greenbrier River is listed in *Canoe* magazine as one of the best places to paddle a canoe in North America. It offers from 30 to 90 miles of spring canoeing and floating. Go hiking, backpacking, mountain bicycling, horseback riding, and fishing along the Greenbrier River Trail.

Go cross-country skiing along the trail during the winter. It passes through Greenbrier and Seneca State Forests, Watoga, Droop Mountain, and Cass Scenic Railroad State Parks.

Greenbrier State Forest has 16 campsites, all with electrical hookups, 12 cabins, a golf course, restaurant, groceries, horseback riding, fishing, and boat rentals available nearby. Go swimming, hike the trails, and attend seasonal nature/recreation programs. In April, take the "Show-Me" hike. A reenactment of the Battle of Dry Creek is presented semi-annually at the end of August.

In White Sulphur Springs you can enjoy hiking, camping, canoeing, fishing, mountain biking, horseback riding, and cave exploring. Play golf at the Valley Country Club. For information on the Monongahela National Forest, stop by the ranger station. Festivals include West Virginia's Dandelion Festival held Memorial Day weekend.

At Caldwell, take West Virginia 219 and West Virginia 63 to Organ Cave, three miles south of Ronceverte. It's seven miles from I-64, Exit 175. Registered as a National Historic Landmark, it's the third largest and oldest commercial cave in the U.S. General Robert E. Lee's men made ammunition here, and 37 wooden hoppers have been preserved. Look for the natural limestone formation that resembles the general. The cave was named for a limestone organ that is almost 40 feet tall, and produces beautiful tones when its pipes are struck with a hammer. For information, call 304-647-5551.

Lost World Caverns are north of Lewisburg, on West Virginia 219, and feature a large main room, with several waterfalls and numerous stalagmites.

Arriving pilots can land at Greenbrier Valley Airport, four miles north of Lewisburg. Rental cars are available.

INFORMATION

Greenbrier River Trail State Park
Star Route 125
Caldwell, West Virginia 24925
304-574-3771

Greenbrier State Forest
HC-30, Box 154
Caldwell, West Virginia 24925-9709
304-536-1944

HAWK'S NEST STATE PARK
19

LOCATION　　The park is on U.S. 60, 1¾ mile west of Ansted.

FEATURES　　Hawk's Nest was named for its lookout point located 585 feet above the New River Gorge, and for the fish hawks that once nested on the rocks. The northwestern end of the New River Gorge National River culminates here. The New River Gorge Bridge is the world's largest steel span bridge, and rises 876 feet above the river. In October, parachutists come to celebrate Bridge Day by jumping off the bridge.

ACTIVITIES　　Tour the rustic museum, with early pioneer and Indian artifacts housed in a 1930s building, open from April through October. Stay in the 31-room lodge built on the edge of the gorge, with a restaurant, open year-round.

Ride aboard the aerial tramway that links the lodge with the marina and boat dock on the lake below. If you arrive in late April, the view from the tram overlooks cloudlike flowers in the silver bell trees, and wild lupine that grow in the canyon. The tram doesn't operate from the end of October through April.

Take a pontoon boat excursion to the New River Gorge Bridge, or rent a paddleboat or rowboat. Attend special events including the Country Roads Festival in September, plus winter dinner theater performances.

Go whitewater rafting in the narrow canyon of the New River, North America's oldest river. Play tennis, go fishing, and hiking.

Drive to the Hawk's Nest Overlook, a quarter-mile west of the tram, to see a broad panorama of the gorge. Nearby you can see the double-truss steel railroad bridge that spans the New River. Hiking trails into the park leave from the overlook.

The Contentment Historical Complex is in Ansted, displaying early period furnishings and cultural items. Colonel George Imboden's house, "Contentment," circa 1830, is ¾ mile northwest of Ansted, on U.S. 60. It's open Sundays by appointment in May, and from June through September. For information, call 304-465-5032 or 304-658-4006.

INFORMATION
Hawk's Nest State Park
Route 60, P.O. Box 857
Ansted, West Virginia 25812
304-658-5196: park
304-658-5212: lodge
304-658-4735: restaurant

HOLLY RIVER STATE PARK
20

LOCATION   The park is two miles north of Hacker Valley, off West Virginia 20.

ACTIVITIES   Laurel Fork of the Holly River offers great trout fishing. Stay in one of nine guest cabins, open from the last weekend in April through the fourth Monday in October, or camp in the 88-site campground, 62 sites with electrical hookups. It's open from April 1 through deer hunting season. Eat in the restaurant, open from the last Saturday in April through-Labor Day, or purchase your own groceries.

Hiking trails wind through the woods of huge hemlocks, beech, and maples to reach secluded waterfalls where you can camp overnight. Climb scenic Potato Knob. Go swimming, fishing for trout, play tennis, ride bikes along miles of paved campground roads, and attend seasonal nature/recreation programs.

INFORMATION
Holly River State Park
P.O. Box 8
Hacker Valley, West Virginia 26222
304-493-6353

LOST RIVER STATE PARK
21

LOCATION   The park is four miles east of Mathias.

FEATURES   The park encompasses 3,712 acres of woodlands, some virgin timber, and the grounds of Lee Sulphur Springs, a 19th-century resort owned by General Robert E. Lee's family. The old cabin was built by Lee's father, General "Light Horse" Harry Lee.

ACTIVITIES   Tour General Lee's restored cabin, open weekends from Memorial Day weekend through Labor Day weekend, and by appointment Monday through Friday. Call the park office from Memorial Day through Labor Day. Big Ridge and White Oak Trails take hikers up to Big Ridge's Cranny Crow for a great overlook of the surrounding highlands of eastern West Virginia.

Stay in one of the 24 cabins, open from the last weekend in March through the second Monday in December. Camp by a picnic shelter, or in the old pioneer farm cabin. Groceries are available, or you can eat in the restaurant. Rent a horse from the park stables to go horseback riding, either all day or overnight, from Memorial Day through Labor Day. Go swimming, play tennis, and attend seasonal nature/recreational programs.

In nearby Moorefield, take a train ride on the 52.4-mile-long shortline railroad through the Potomac Highlands in April, May, September, and October. For information, call 304-538-RAIL.

INFORMATION
Lost River State Park
Route 2, Box 24
Mathias, West Virginia 26812
304-897-5372
304-897-5325: restaurant

MONCOVE LAKE STATE PARK
22

LOCATION   The park is six miles north of Gap Mills, on West Virginia 8.

ACTIVITIES   Camp in the 50-site campground, open from April 1 through deer hunting season. Go swimming, bass fishing, and rent paddle and rowboats to go boating in 144-acre Moncove Lake. Hike the trails, and attend seasonal recreation/nature programs. Moncove Lake Wildlife Management Area is adjacent to the park where you can go hunting for deer and small game.

INFORMATION
Moncove Lake State Park
P.O. Box 224
Gap Mills, West Virginia 24942
304-772-3450

NORTH BEND STATE PARK

NORTH BEND RAIL TRAIL
23

LOCATION   The park is two miles east of Cairo off West Virginia 31, in the valley of the North Fork of the Hughes River.

FEATURES   North Bend Rail Trail, once a main line of the Chessie Railroad, is 61 miles long, and goes from Walker to Wilsonburg, west of Clarksburg. The trail is part of the 5,500-mile American Discovery Trail that is slated to extend from coast to coast.

The 1,405-acre state park's central area is on a bluff at a horseshoe bend in the North Fork of the Hughes River.

ACTIVITIES   The state park, cabins, and restaurant are open year-round. Stay in the 30-room North Bend Lodge, or in one of eight deluxe cabins. You can also camp in one of two riverside campgrounds by the Hughes River, with a total of 80 campsites, 26 with electrical hookups, and a dump station. Fish for bass. Park visitors can play miniature golf or go to the nearby golf course.

Participate in year-round nature and recreational programs. The park has a playground and a nature trail designed for the handicapped. It has information stations in both print and Braille, and also provides outdoor games and equipment for the blind. An annual sports jamboree for the handicapped is held in July.

Go swimming in the pool, play tennis, and hike the trail that skirts the rim of the escarpment. You can also explore other trails through the woodlands to reach the various overlooks and dramatic rock formations. Bicyclists can ride the park roads or along three of the park trails. Hike, bike, or horseback ride on the nearby North Bend Rail Trail. A five-mile section passing through the park is one of its more scenic sections, and has a fine gravel trail running beside the Hughes River.

Go cross-country skiing on the park trails during the winter. In January, attend Winter Wonder Weekend featuring sleigh rides, cross-country ski demonstrations, indoor sports, and fireside games.

INFORMATION
North Bend State Park
P.O. Box 221
Cairo, West Virginia 26337
304-643-2931: park
304-643-4161: restaurant

North Bend Rail Trail
c/o North Bend State Park

PINNACLE ROCK STATE PARK
24

LOCATION   The park is near Bluefield, in the southern part of the state, along U.S. 52.

FEATURES   The park was constructed by the Civilian Conservation Corps, marking the beginning of the Pocahontas Coal Fields.

ACTIVITIES   Open for day use only, enjoy a picnic, fish for stocked trout, and go hiking. A stone staircase leads to the park's namesake and a great panoramic view.

The Bluefield Area Arts and Crafts Center features art exhibits, dinner theater productions, and other performing arts performances.

Take a walking tour of Bramwell's Historic District, known for its Victorian and Tudor mansions once owned by coal barons. For information, call 304-248-7114.

Arriving pilots can land at Bluefield/Princeton's Mercer County Airport, four miles northeast of Bluefield. It has rental cars.

INFORMATION
Pinnacle Rock State Park
Box 342
Bramwell, West Virginia 27415
304-248-8362

PIPESTEM RESORT STATE PARK
25

LOCATION   Pipestem State Park is off I-64 on West Virginia 20, and 14 miles from the Athens Road Exit.

FEATURES   Bluestone Dam closes a 2,048-foot gap between the mountains, and rises 165 feet above the stream bed. The 4,024-acre park overlooks the 1,000-foot Bluestone River Gorge.

Pipestem was named for the hollow-stemmed shrub, Spirea alba, from which Shawnee Indians and early settlers made stems for their pipes. They used a corn-cob or expensive clay to form the pipe's bowl.

ACTIVITIES The resort is located near Bluestone Dam, and features an 18-hole championship golf course, as well as a nine-hole par three course. Enjoy swimming either in the heated indoor or outdoor swimming pools. Go hiking, and play tennis on the lighted tennis courts. Tour the nature center and arboretum. Attend dinner theater performances.

Rent a horse from the park stables to go horseback riding, or arrange for an overnight trail ride along an old Indian trail down Bluestone Gorge, to stay overnight in the 125-year-old cabin.

Anglers enjoy trout fishing in Long Branch Lake, Bluestone River, or in nearby Bluestone Lake. The lake's tailwaters challenge both fishing and canoeing enthusiasts.

Stay in the 113-room lodge on the canyon rim, or in the 30-room Mountain Creek Lodge in Bluestone Gorge, accessible only by tramway. It's closed from November 1 through March 31st, or Easter weekend. McKeever Lodge is open year-round. Eat in the lodge dining room, in Mountain Creek's dining room, or at the Black Bear snack bar. Stay in one of 25 deluxe cabins, open year-round, or camp in one of the 82 campsites, 31 sites with full hookups, 50 with electrical hookups, and a dumping station. The campground is open year-round, and has nine sites with water hookups, available during the winter.

Visit Canyon Rim Center's handicrafts shop and art gallery. Ride the tram that climbs 3,600 feet, and leaves from the visitor center. In May, attend Century Day Bird Count.

In mid-March, attend Appalachian weekend featuring crafts, music, clogging, and storytelling.

During the winter, go sledding and cross-country skiing along marked trails, with ski rentals and instruction available. Rent a toboggan or sled to go sliding down the toboggan hill, equipped with a rope tow.

Nearby Camp Creek State Park is off I-77 and U.S. 19, at the Camp Creek interchange. It has camping facilities in a modern 25-site campground, rustic camping in a 12-site campground, picnicking, game courts, fishing, and hiking. The adjacent state forest has 5,300 acres with campsites, fishing for stocked trout, hunting, and hiking trails.

INFORMATION
Pipestem Resort State Park
Box 150
Pipestem, West Virginia 25979
304-466-1800 or 1-800-CALL-WVA

STONEWALL JACKSON STATE PARK
26

LOCATION The park is south of Roanoke, on I-79.

ACTIVITIES   Stonewall Jackson Lake is the state's second largest, and has a 374-slip marina with boat rentals. Its fishing pier provides handicapped access, where anglers can catch crappie, bluegill, muskie, bass, and walleye. Take a cruise aboard the *Stonewall Jackson* Paddlewheel.

Camp in the 34-unit campground, with full hookups. Work out on the fitness trail and explore the hiking trails. Play 18 holes of golf. Hunting is available in the adjacent wildlife management area.

Arriving pilots can land at Buckhannon–Upshur County Airport, two miles west of Buckhannon. It's 12 miles from the lake and has rental cars.

INFORMATION
Stonewall Jackson State Park
Route 1, Box 0
Roanoke, West Virginia 26423
304-269-0523

TOMLINSON RUN STATE PARK
27

LOCATION   The park is two miles north of New Manchester off West Virginia 8, along Tomlinson Run. It's within a mile of the Ohio River, at the tip of the state's northern peninsula.

ACTIVITIES   Camp in the 54-site campground, 39 sites with electrical hookups, and a dumping station, or stay in one of five Rent-A-Camp sites, available from Memorial Day through Labor Day. Groceries are available nearby.

Anglers can fish in various ponds and in Tomlinson Run Lake for bass, bluegill, and trout. Go swimming in the Olympic-size pool; boating, with rowboat and paddleboat rentals available; play tennis and miniature golf. Hike the park trails.

Bethany, located south of the park, has more historical sites per capita than any other American town. The college's Old Main is listed as a National Landmark. For walking tour information of the historic town, call 304-829-7285. Alexander Campbell's mansion, circa 1793, was the home of the town's founder, and was visited by many famous men, including Calhoun, Clay, Webster, and Garfield. For information, call 304-829-7285.

The Fish Creek covered bridge is southeast of the park, off U.S. 250. It's on West Virginia 20 near Hundred. The bridge, circa 1881, is 36 feet long.

INFORMATION
Tomlinson Run State Park
P.O. Box 97
New Manchester, West Virginia 26056
304-564-4346

TWIN FALLS STATE PARK
28

LOCATION   The resort park is eight miles northeast of Pineville.

FEATURES   Twin Falls was named for the two waterfalls that drop 20 feet.

ACTIVITIES   You can stay in the 20-room guest lodge, or in one of 13 deluxe cabins, and dine in the restaurant. Both the lodge and restaurant are open year-round. Camp in the 50-unit campground, 25 sites with electrical hookups, and a dumping station, or in one of five Rent-A-Camp's fully equipped campsites. Get groceries from the camp store.

Play golf on the 18-hole championship course, and play tennis on the tennis courts. Go swimming in the pool, and bicycling along park roads. Visit the 19th-century Pioneer Farm's living museum.

Hike the scenic trails in the summer, including 1.5-mile Falls Trail,, that takes you to the two waterfalls that drop into a pool encircled by rhododendron. The trail then continues beside Marsh Fork Stream, and climbs above Black Ford Stream to reach Black Fork Falls. Attend year-round nature/recreation programs.

Go cross-country skiing along the trails during the winter.

INFORMATION
Twin Falls State Park
P.O. Box 1023
Mullens, West Virginia 25882
304-294-4000: park
304-294-6069: cabins

TYGART LAKE STATE PARK
29

LOCATION   The park is south of Grafton. From U.S. 119, go south four miles on Tygart Lake's access road.

FEATURES   Tygart Lake Dam is 230 feet high, and is one of the oldest and largest concrete dams east of the Mississippi.

ACTIVITIES   Go boating, hiking, and camp in one of the coves found along the twisting shoreline. Enjoy bass fishing, water-skiing, scuba diving, and swimming in 13-mile-long Tygart Lake. Rent a boat and purchase concessions at the marina.

Park visitors can play golf at the nearby Tygart Lake Golf Course. Attend seasonal nature/recreation programs.

Stay overnight in 20-room Tygart Lake Lodge overlooking the lake. It's closed from November 1 through Easter weekend. Dine in the restaurant, stay in the 40-site campground, 14 sites with electrical hookups, or in one of the 10 deluxe cabins.

The Tygart River has rapids ranging in difficulty from Class I through Class V, and includes Wells Falls, the most runable drop in north-central West Virginia.

History buffs can visit nearby Prickett's Fort State Historic Park. It's two miles west of Fairmont from I-79, Exit 139. Tour the visitor center to learn the history of the Monogahela Valley. The fort has been reconstructed to resemble its 1774 appearance, and has 16 cabins, a meetinghouse, and storehouse located within its compound. Watch authentic demonstrations of pioneer crafts including muzzle loading, cloth weaving, and forging tools at the blacksmith shop.

In Grafton, visit the International Mother's Day Shrine, to see where the celebration had its origin. It's open from April through October.

Visit the Simpson Creek covered bridge, also known as the W. T. Law Bridge. It's near Bridgeport's Exit 121 off I-79, then northwest on West Virginia 24/2.

INFORMATION
Tygart Lake State Park
Route 1, Box 260
Grafton, West Virginia 26354
304-265-3383: park
304-265-2320: lodge
304-265-3100: golf course

VALLEY FALLS STATE PARK

PRICKETT'S FORT STATE PARK
30

LOCATION   Valley Falls State Park is 15 miles south of Fairmont, off West Virginia 310.

Prickett's Fort State Park is two miles west of Fairmont from I-79, Exit 139.

FEATURES   Valley Falls was once the site of the largest Cherokee village in the area. The Indians referred to the area as "Evil Spirit Falls," while later white explorers called it "Hard Around Falls," and later, "Falls of the Big Buddy," or Monongahela.

Originally the site of a lumber and grist mill, you can see grooves where rock was cut for a millrace in 1837. A bridge takes you across the millrace to the remains of the gristmill.

ACTIVITIES   Two waterfalls at Valley Falls drop 12 feet and 18 feet respectively. Bring along a picnic, and go fishing for walleyed pike, channel catfish, and smallmouth bass. Enjoy hiking on 5 trails that cover 13 miles. The 1,145-acre park is popular for whitewater rafting. Expert rafters rate the Tygart among one of the best mountain rivers, and Valley Falls provides Class II and III whitewater trips that stop short of the falls.

At Prickett's Fort State Park, watch the outdoor drama, *Prickett's Fort: An American Frontier Musical,* presented in July. Tour the restored fort, circa 1774, with 16 cabins, meeting hall, storehouse, and demonstrations of pioneer crafts. Go boating from the ramp on the Monongahela River. For information, call 304-363-3030. Seasonal programs feature a militia encampment, an apple butter weekend, and an 18th-century Christmas market. The Job Prickett House, circa 1859, is near the fort, and is filled with family antiques. It's open from mid-April through October.

Walk or bike 2.5 miles from Prickett's Fort State Park to downtown Fairmont, passing through a lighted tunnel.

The second weekend in May, attend Traditional Music Weekend in Fairmont, when dulcimers, fiddles, and banjos perform traditional Appalachian music in Prickett's Fort State Park. On Memorial Day weekend, attend Three Rivers Festival and Regatta with a parade, canoe races, "anything that floats" race, live entertainment, and food. For information, call 304-363-2625.

Go for a cruise aboard the *Gateway* clipper ship. Near Fairmont, visit the 148-foot Barrackville covered bridge, one of the state's oldest, used to carry traffic for over 125 years. It's off U.S. 250, where it intersects West Virginia 32.

Coopers Rock State Forest, the state's largest, is northeast of Prickett's Fort in Bruceton Mills, and 13 miles east of Morgantown off U.S. 48. Fish in either of the two trout streams or in the six-acre trout lake. Camp in the 25-site campground, go rock climbing, biking, boating, and hiking along the northern section of the Allegheny Trail. Snacks are available in the snack bar, located in the trading post. Watch for the remains of the Henry Clay Iron Furnace, circa 1834, used to make iron products. Today you can still see the 30-foot pyramidal stone structure.

During the fall, the forest is known as the "Scarlet Heartland," and provides an excellent overlook of the hills and mountains in four counties, from its 1,200-foot perch above Cheat Lake and Cheat River Gorge. During the winter, enjoy cross-country skiing. Go fishing, hunting, hiking, picnicking, water-skiing, and swimming at Cheat Lake. For information, call 304-594-1561.

In September in Morgantown, attend the Mason-Dixon Festival, featuring a river regatta, cruises, crew races, and musical drama presented along the Monongahela River.

Arriving pilots can land at Fairmont Municipal Airport, three miles south of Fairmont. Rental cars are available.

INFORMATION

Valley Falls State Park
Route 6, Box 2424
Fairmont, West Virginia 26554
304-363-3319

Prickett's Fort State Park
Route 3, Box 486
Point Pleasant, West Virginia 26554
304-363-3030

WATOGA STATE PARK
31

LOCATION   The park is 10 miles south of Huntersville, on West Virginia 21. It's in the Appalachian highlands along the state's eastern border.

FEATURES   Watoga is Cherokee, and means "the river of islands." Beaver Creek, a tributary of the Greenbrier River, forms the park's western boundary. Its shallow meanderings have created many sandbars and islands, giving the park its name.

ACTIVITIES   Watoga is the state's largest state park, and provides easy access to the Greenbrier River. Stay in one of the 33 deluxe cabins, open from the last weekend in March through the second Monday in December, or camp in one of two campgrounds, with a total of 88 campsites. In Beaver Creek, 12 of its 38 sites have electrical hookups. Riverside's campground is beside the Greenbrier River and has 50 sites, 19 with electrical hookups, and dumping stations. Riverside campground remains open from April 1 through deer hunting season. Eat in the restaurant, open from Memorial Day through Labor Day. Groceries are also available.

Go boating on the park's 11-acre lake, with rowboats and paddleboats available for rent. The park is laced with hiking trails, or you can rent a horse from the stable and ride the bridle trails. Go bass fishing, swimming, and play tennis.

Enjoy mountain biking and backpacking in adjacent Monongahela National Forest, with 850 miles of hiking trails and roadways winding through the wooded hills, offering views of some of the East's highest mountain peaks. The Greenbrier River Trail, and part of the 230-mile-long Allegheny Trail, also pass through the park. Visitors can play golf on a nearby course. During the winter, go cross-country skiing.

Nearby attractions include Beartown State Park, where a boardwalk leads through a wild hilltop with house-size rocks and boulders carved into unusual forms by erosion.

Nearby Droop Mountain Battlefield was the site of the largest Civil War engagement in West Virginia, on November 6, 1863, when Union forces defeated a Confederate army and secured the territory assigned to the new state by President Lincoln five months earlier. Part of the battlefield has been restored and marked. Tour the museum with its Civil War artifacts. Hike trails to scenic overlooks and to an observation tower. Attend the battle reenactment in the fall.

Calvin Price Forest's 9,482 acres are adjacent to the park, and offer prime hunting, hiking, fishing, and primitive camping.

Seneca State Forest, north of the park, borders the Greenbrier River, and has seven rustic guest cabins, 10 campsites, boating with rentals available, trout fishing in the lake, and thousands of acres for hiking. It also provides access to the Greenbrier River Trail. For information, call 304-799-6213.

Cass Scenic Railroad State Historic Park in downtown Cass, features a remnant of the original logging railroad. Take a train ride from Memorial Day through October, when the trees display their spectacular fall foliage. For information, call 304-456-4300.

Pearl S. Buck's birthplace, circa 1858, is at Stulting Place in Hillsboro. She was the only American to win both the Pulitzer Prize for fiction, and the Nobel Prize for literature, and is famous for her novels about Chinese life. Regular tours and annual events such as Author's Day, held in August, are featured. The Stulting barn has been restored, and contains an assortment of early farm implements. Pearl Buck's father's homestead, the Sydenstricker house, was relocated here to become part of the historical farm complex. For information, call 304-653-4430.

While in Hillsboro, visit the Locust Creek covered bridge, circa 1870s. It's three miles off U.S. 219 on Locust Road, West Virginia 20, near its intersection with Denmar Road, West Virginia 31.

Greenbank National Radio Astronomy Observatory is on West Virginia 92, near Green Bank. Its gigantic radio telescopes are at the largest research installation, where scientists from all the world come to study interstellar impulses captured by its radio telescopes. One of its telescopes is a 140-equatorially mounted telescope, the largest of its kind in the world. Visitors can take an hour-long narrated bus tour, offered daily on the hour, and watch a 15-minute movie on radio astronomy. It's open Wednesday through Sunday, from mid-June through Labor Day, and weekends only in September and October. For information, call 304-456-2011.

The Botanical Area and Cranberry Mountain Visitor Center is in Mill Point. This unique area encompasses four bogs, and is adjacent to the Cranberry Wilderness Area, with 35,600 acres for visitors to go hiking, bicycling, backpacking, and fishing. For information, call 304-653-4826. From the visitor center, drive the Highland Scenic Highway over West Virginia 150 to north of Edray, on West Virginia 219.

Go to Hills Creek Scenic Area at Mill Point. Follow the forest trail into a narrow gorge with three waterfalls, the tallest dropping 65 feet. For information, call 304-653-4826.

The second weekend in July, Marlinton celebrates Pioneer Days with local music, tours of local historic landmarks, and old-time games.

INFORMATION
Watoga State Park
Star Route 1, Box 140
Marlinton, West Virginia 24954
304-799-4087

WATTERS SMITH MEMORIAL STATE PARK
32

LOCATION   Watters Smith Memorial State Park is south of Clarksburg, between Lost Creek and West Milford.

ACTIVITIES   History buffs enjoy visiting here to take a guided tour through the replica log cabin, circa 1876. Visit 19th-century farm buildings, including a blacksmith's shop, smokehouse, and an interpretive farm museum, open from Memorial Day through Labor Day. Hike the trails, and go swimming in the pool. For information, call 304-745-3081.

Center Point covered bridge is northwest of Watters Smith. Built in 1890, the bridge is 42 feet long, and was restored in 1982. From the Salem exit off U.S. 50, go 12 miles north on West Virginia 23. Fletcher covered bridge is near Wolf Summit. Built in 1891, the 58-foot-long bridge spans Ten Mile Creek. It's north of Maken off U.S. 50, at the intersection of West Virginia 5/29.

Attend an annual Labor Day celebration and West Virginia Italian Heritage Festival in Clarksburg. For festival information, call 304-622-7314.

Fort New Salem is west of Clarksburg, off West Virginia 50 in Salem. The fort offers living interpretations of the frontier period of the Appalachians. Attend an Apple Butter Festival in October, featuring apple butter making, entertainment, and a muzzle loading and shooting contest.

INFORMATION
Watters Smith Memorial State Park
P.O. Box 296
Lost Creek, West Virginia 26385
304-745-3081

Index

Name of Park	CG	FS	HK	CO	VC	WA	PG
Daisy State Park	•	•	•		•	•	27
DeGray Lake Resort State Park	•	•	•	•	•	•	28
Devil's Den State Park	•	•	•	•	•	•	29
Hampson Museum State Park					•		30
Jacksonport State Park	•	•	•			•	30
Jenkins' Ferry Battleground							
State Historical Monument		•				•	31
Lake Catherine State Park	•	•	•	•	•	•	31
Lake Charles State Park	•	•	•	•	•	•	33
Lake Chicot State Park	•	•	•	•	•	•	34
Lake Dardanelle State Park	•	•	•		•	•	34
Lake Fort Smith State Park	•	•	•		•	•	35
Lake Frierson State Park	•	•	•			•	36
Lake Ouachita State Park	•	•	•	•	•	•	37
Lake Poinsett State Park	•	•	•		•	•	38
Logoly State Park	•	•	•		•		38
Louisiana Purchase							
State Historic Monument							38
Mammoth Spring State Park		•	•		•	•	39
Millwood State Park	•	•	•	•	•	•	40
Moro Bay State Park	•	•	•		•	•	40
Mount Nebo State Park	•		•	•	•	•	34
Old Davidsonville State Park	•	•	•		•	•	41
Old Washington Historic State Park				•	•		41
Ozark Folk Center					•	•	42
Petit Jean State Park	•	•	•	•	•	•	43
Pinnacle Mountain State Park		•	•		•	•	44
Prairie Grove Battlefield State Park		•			•		45
Queen Wilhelmina State Park	•		•	•	•		45
Toltec Mounds							
Archeological State Park					•		46
Village Creek State Park	•	•	•		•	•	47
White Oak Lake State Park	•	•	•		•	•	47
Withrow Springs State Park	•	•	•	•	•	•	48
Woolly Hollow State Park	•	•	•	•	•	•	49

FLORIDA

Name of Park	CG	FS	HK	CO	VC	WA	PG
Amelia Island State Recreation Area		•	•			•	93
Anastasia State Park	•	•	•			•	53
Bahia Honda State Park	•	•	•	•		•	55
Big Lagoon State Recreation Area	•	•	•			•	105
Big Talbot Island State Park		•	•			•	93

Name of Park	CG	FS	HK	CO	VC	WA	PG
Bill Baggs Cape Florida State Recreation Area		•	•	•	•	•	56
Blackwater River State Park	•	•	•			•	56
Blue Spring State Park	•	•	•	•	•	•	57
Bulow Creek State Park				•			58
Bulow Plantation Ruins State Historic Park		•	•		•	•	58
Caladesi Island State Park		•	•	•		•	59
Cayo Costa State Park	•	•	•	•		•	59
Chekika State Recreation Area	•	•	•		•	•	61
Collier-Seminole State Park	•	•	•		•	•	63
Crystal River State Archeological Site			•		•		65
Dade Battlefield State Historic Site			•		•		65
Dead Lakes State Recreation Area	•	•	•				66
DeLeon Springs State Recreation Area		•	•	•		•	67
Delnor-Wiggins Pass State Recreation Area		•	•			•	67
Devil's Millhopper State Geological Site			•		•		68
Don Pedro Island State Recreation Area		•	•			•	77
Edward Ball Wakulla Springs State Park			•	•		•	69
Egmont Key State Park		•				•	70
Fakahatchee Strand State Preserve			•				63
Falling Waters State Recreation Area	•	•	•			•	71
Faver-Dykes State Park	•	•	•			•	53
Florida Caverns State Park	•	•	•		•	•	71
Fort Clinch State Park	•	•	•		•	•	72
Fort Cooper State Park		•	•			•	73
Fort Gadsden State Park		•			•		73
Fort Pierce Inlet State Recreation Area		•	•		•	•	73
Fort Zachary Taylor State Historic Site		•			•	•	74
Gainesville-Hawthorne State Trail			•				96
Gamble Plantation State Historic Site							75
Gamble Rogers Memorial State Recreation Area at Flagler Beach	•	•	•			•	76
Gasparilla Island State Recreation Area		•	•		•	•	77
General James A. Van Fleet State Trail		•					78
Grayton Beach State Recreation Area	•	•	•			•	78
Guana River State Park		•	•			•	53
Henderson Beach State Recreation Area		•	•			•	79
Highlands Hammock State Park	•		•	•	•		79
Hillsborough River State Park	•	•	•	•		•	80
Homosassa Springs State Wildlife Park			•	•		•	81
Hontoon Island State Park	•	•	•			•	57

Name of Park	CG	FS	HK	CO	VC	WA	PG
Honeymoon Island State Recreation Area		•				•	59
Hugh Taylor Birch State Recreation Area		•	•	•		•	82
Ichetucknee Springs State Park				•	•	•	83
John D. MacArthur Beach State Park		•	•	•			84
John Pennekamp Coral Reef State Park	•	•	•	•		•	84
John U. Lloyd Beach State Recreation Area		•	•	•		•	82
Jonathan Dickinson State Park	•	•	•	•	•	•	86
Koreshan State Historic Site	•	•	•		•	•	87
Lake Griffin State Recreation Area	•	•	•			•	87
Lake Jackson Mounds State Archeological Site							91
Lake Kissimmee State Park	•	•	•			•	88
Lake Louisa State Park		•				•	89
Lake Manatee State Recreation Area	•	•	•			•	90
Lake Talquin State Park		•	•				91
Little Manatee River State Recreation Area	•	•	•			•	92
Little Talbot Island State Park	•	•	•			•	93
Long Key State Recreation Area	•	•	•			•	94
Maclay State Gardens		•	•		•	•	91
Manatee Springs State Park	•	•	•	•		•	95
Marjorie Kinnan Rawlings State Historic Site							96
Mike Roess Gold Head Branch State Park	•	•	•		•	•	97
Myakka River State Park	•	•	•	•	•	•	98
New Smyrna Sugar Mills Ruins State Historic Park		•				•	100
North Shore State Recreation Area		•				•	100
Ochlockonee River State Park	•	•	•			•	101
O'Leno State Park	•	•	•			•	101
Oleta River State Recreation Area	•	•	•			•	102
Olustee Battlefield State Historic Site							83
Oscar Scherer State Park	•	•	•			•	102
Pahokee State Recreation Area	•	•	•			•	103
Paynes Creek State Historic Site		•	•				104
Paynes Prairie State Preserve	•	•	•		•	•	96
Peacock Springs State Recreation Area						•	104
Perdido Key State Recreation Area		•				•	105
Rainbow Springs State Park	•	•				•	107

Name of Park	CG	FS	HK	CO	VC	WA	PG
Ravine State Gardens			•				107
Rocky Bayou State Park	•	•	•			•	106
San Felasco Hammock State Preserve			•		•		50
Sebastian Inlet State Recreation Area	•	•		•	•	•	110
St. Andrews State Recreation Area	•	•	•	•	•	•	108
St. George Island State Park	•	•	•			•	108
St. Joseph Peninsula State Park	•	•	•	•		•	109
St. Lucie Inlet State Preserve		•				•	86
Stephen Foster State Folk Culture Center					•		111
Suwannee River State Park	•	•	•			•	111
Three Rivers State Recreation Area	•	•	•			•	112
Tomoka State Park	•	•	•	•		•	112
Torreya State Park	•	•	•		•		113
Tosohatchee State Reserve	•	•	•				114
Waccasassa Bay State Preserve/ Cedar Key Scrub State Reserve		•					114
Washington Oaks State Park		•	•				115
Wekiwa Springs State Park	•	•	•	•		•	115
Withlacoochee State Forest	•	•	•			•	65
Withlacoochee State Trail		•					65
Yulee Sugar Mill Ruins State Historic Site							81

GEORGIA

Name of Park	CG	FS	HK	CO	VC	WA	PG
Alexander H. Stephens State Historic Park	•	•	•		•	•	119
Amicalola Falls State Park	•	•	•	•	•	•	119
Black Rock Mountain State Park	•	•	•		•		120
Bobby Brown State Park	•	•	•			•	121
Cloudland Canyon State Park	•		•	•	•		122
Crooked River State Park	•	•	•	•	•	•	123
Elijah Clark State Park	•	•	•	•	•	•	124
F. D. Roosevelt State Park	•	•	•			•	124
Florence Marina State Park	•	•			•	•	125
Fort McAllister State Historic Park					•		127
Fort Mountain State Park	•	•	•	•	•	•	126
Fort Yargo State Park							127
General Coffee State Park	•	•	•			•	128
George T. Bagby State Park	•	•	•	•		•	129
George L. Smith State Park	•	•				•	129
Georgia Veterans State Park	•	•			•	•	130
Gordonia-Altamaha State Park	•	•				•	131

KENTUCKY

Name of Park	CG	FS	HK	CO	VC	WA	PG

LOUISIANA

Name of Park	CG	FS	HK	CO	VC	WA	PG
Bayou Segnette State Park	•	•	•			•	189
Chemin-A-Haut State Park	•	•	•			•	190
Chicot State Park	•	•	•			•	191
Cypremort Point State Park		•				•	191
Fairview Riverside State Park	•	•	•			•	192
Fontainebleau State Park	•	•	•			•	193
Grand Isle State Park	•	•			•	•	193
Lake Bistineau State Park	•	•	•			•	194
Lake Bruin State Park	•	•	•			•	195
Lake Claiborne State Park	•	•	•			•	195
Lake D'Arbonne State Park	•	•	•			•	196
Lake Fausse Pointe State Park	•	•	•	•	•	•	197
North Toledo Bend State Park	•	•	•		•	•	198
St. Bernard State Park	•	•	•			•	198
Sam Houston Jones State Park	•	•	•			•	200

MISSISSIPPI

Name of Park	CG	FS	HK	CO	VC	WA	PG
Buccaneer State Park	•	•	•	•	•	•	204
Clarkco State Park	•	•	•	•	•	•	204
Florewood River Plantation State Park					•		205
George Payne Cossar State Park	•	•	•	•	•	•	206
Golden Memorial State Park		•	•		•	•	207
Great River Road State Park	•	•	•	•	•	•	207
Holmes County State Park	•	•	•	•	•	•	208
Hugh White State Park	•	•	•	•	•	•	208
J. P. Coleman State Park	•	•	•	•	•	•	209
John W. Kyle State Park	•	•	•	•	•	•	209
Lake Lowndes State Park	•	•	•	•	•	•	210
LeFleur's Bluff State Park	•	•	•	•	•	•	211
Legion State Park	•	•	•		•	•	212
Leroy Percy State Park	•	•	•	•	•	•	214
Natchez State Park	•	•	•		•	•	214
Paul B. Johnson State Park	•	•	•	•	•	•	215
Percy Quinn State Park	•	•	•	•	•	•	216
Roosevelt State Park	•	•	•	•	•	•	217
Shepard State Park	•	•	•		•	•	217
Tishomingo State Park	•	•	•	•	•	•	218
Tombigbee State Park	•	•	•	•	•	•	219
Trace State Park	•	•	•			•	220
Wall Doxey State Park	•	•	•	•	•	•	220
Winterville Mounds State Historic Site					•		221

Name of Park	CG	FS	HK	CO	VC	WA	PG

OKLAHOMA

Name of Park	CG	FS	HK	CO	VC	WA	PG
Alabaster Caverns State Park	•	•	•				249
Arrowhead State Park	•	•	•	•		•	250
Beavers Bend State Park	•	•	•	•	•	•	251
Bernice State Park	•	•				•	276
Black Mesa State Park	•	•	•			•	253
Boiling Springs State Park	•	•	•				253
Cherokee Landing State Park	•	•	•	•		•	274
Cherokee State Recreation Area	•	•				•	276
Clayton State Park	•	•				•	254
Feyodi Creek State Park	•	•				•	258
Fort Cobb State Park	•	•				•	255
Foss Reservoir State Park	•	•				•	255
Fountainhead State Park	•	•	•	•	•	•	250
Great Salt Plains State Park	•	•	•			•	256
Greenleaf State Park	•	•	•	•	•	•	257
Heavener Runestone State Park			•		•		263
Heyburn State Park	•	•	•	•		•	257
Honey Creek State Recreation Area	•	•				•	276
Hotchatown State Park	•	•	•			•	251
Keystone State Park	•	•	•	•		•	258
Lake Murray State Park	•	•	•	•	•	•	260
Lake Texoma State Park and Resort	•	•	•	•		•	261
Lake Wister State Park	•	•	•	•	•	•	263
Little Blue State Park	•	•				•	276
Little River State Park	•	•	•	•	•	•	264
Little Sahara State Park	•		•	•			265
Okmulgee Lake State Park	•	•	•			•	265
Osage Hills State Park	•	•	•			•	265
Quartz Mountain State Park	•	•	•	•	•	•	266
Raymond Gary State Park	•	•				•	269
Red Rock Canyon State Park	•	•	•				269
Robbers Cave State Park	•	•	•	•		•	270
Roman Nose State Park and Resort	•	•	•	•	•	•	271
Sallisaw State Park	•	•				•	271
Sequoyah Bay Recreation Area	•					•	272
Sequoyah State Park	•	•	•	•	•	•	272
Spavinaw State Park	•	•				•	276
Spring River Canoe Trail State Park	•	•				•	276
Talimena State Park	•		•				273
Tenkiller State Park	•	•	•	•		•	274
Twin Bridges State Recreation Area	•	•		•		•	276

Name of Park	CG	FS	HK	CO	VC	WA	PG
Upper Spavinaw State Park	•	•				•	276
Wah-Sha-She State Park	•	•	•			•	278
Walnut Creek State Park	•	•				•	258

SOUTH CAROLINA

Name of Park	CG	FS	HK	CO	VC	WA	PG
Aiken State Park	•	•	•			•	281
Andrew Jackson State Park	•	•			•	•	282
Baker Creek State Park	•	•	•			•	292
Barnwell State Park	•	•	•			•	282
Caesar's Head State Park			•	•	•		283
Calhoun Falls State Park	•	•				•	283
Charlestowne Landing State Park			•	•	•		284
Cheraw State Park	•	•	•			•	286
Chester State Park	•	•	•			•	286
Colleton State Park	•	•	•			•	287
Croft State Park	•	•	•			•	287
Devils Fork State Park	•	•	•		•	•	288
Dreher Island State Park	•	•	•			•	289
Edisto Beach State Park	•	•	•			•	289
Givhans Ferry State Park	•	•	•			•	290
Goodale State Park		•	•			•	290
Hamilton Branch State Park	•	•				•	292
Hampton Plantation State Park							291
Hickory Knob State Resort Park	•	•	•	•	•	•	292
Hunting Island State Park	•	•	•		•	•	293
Huntington Beach State Park	•	•	•	•	•	•	294
Jones Gap State Park	•	•	•		•		294
Keowee-Toxaway State Park	•	•	•			•	295
Kings Mountain State Park	•	•	•	•	•	•	296
Lake Greenwood State Park	•	•	•	•		•	296
Lake Hartwell State Park	•	•	•		•	•	298
Lake Warren State Park		•	•		•	•	299
Lake Wateree State Park	•	•	•			•	299
Landsford Canal State Park		•	•		•		300
Lee State Park	•	•	•			•	300
Little Pee Dee State Park	•	•	•			•	301
Lynches River State Park		•	•		•	•	301
Myrtle Beach State Park	•	•	•		•	•	302
Oconee State Park	•	•	•	•	•	•	303
Old Dorchester State Park		•	•				304
Old Santee Canal State Park		•	•		•	•	304
Paris Mountain State Park	•	•	•			•	305
Poinsett State Park	•	•	•	•	•	•	305

About the Author

Vici DeHaan was an elementary schoolteacher in the Boulder Valley Schools for thirty-one years, where she taught grades kindergarten through sixth.

She is the author of ten other books: *Runners' Guide to Boulder County, Bicycling the Front Range, Bicycle Tours of the Colorado Rockies, Hiking Guide to the Boulder Mountain Parks and Plains, Moving through the Ratings from Private Pilot to Professional Pilot, Pilots' Guide to National Parks and Monuments, Pilots' Guide to Historical National Parks and Monuments, State Parks of the West, State Parks of the Midwest,* and *State Parks of the Northeast.*

Vici DeHaan is an avid outdoorsperson who has hiked in the Colorado Rockies all her life. She has run races ranging from the mile through a marathon, and has competed in triathlons and duathlons. She has completed 15 marathons including ones in New York, Honolulu, Los Angeles, Phoenix, and up Pikes Peak. She has held several course records in her age division. In September 1995, she ran her 500th race, a 10K in Leadville.

She has sung in various Boulder choirs for 42 years, and is currently singing with the Rocky Mountain Chorale, the Boulder Chorale, and the Bach Festival Chorus. She also plays handbells at First United Methodist Church.

She holds a private pilot's license and ground instructor's certificate, and has flown all over the United States, Mexico, and Canada in a small plane. She has five children and two grandchildren, and lives in Boulder, Colorado.